The Enduring Legacy

Biblical Dimensions in Modern Literature

The Enduring Legacy

Biblical Dimensions in Modern Literature

EDITED BY
Douglas C. Brown

CHARLES SCRIBNER'S SONS   NEW YORK

Library of Congress Cataloging in Publication Data

Brown, Douglas Charles, 1937–   comp.
   The enduring legacy.

   Bibliography: p.
   1. American literature—20th century.   2. English
literature—20th century.   3. Bible in literature.
I. Title.
PS507.B8   820'.8'038   75-13863
ISBN 0-684-13848-4

Printed in the United States of America.

1 3 5 7 9 11 13 15 17 19 M/P 20 18 16 14 12 10 8 6 4 2

ACKNOWLEDGMENTS

*Grateful acknowledgment is made to the following publishers and authors for
permission to reprint copyrighted material:*

ANDERSON HOUSE for the selection from Act III, Scene 2 of *Journey to Jerusalem* by Maxwell Anderson, copyright 1940 by Maxwell Anderson and renewed
1968 by Gilda Oakleaf Anderson. All rights reserved.

THE ESTATE OF MARY ROSE BRADFORD and the law offices of Landrum, Granet,
Brent, Silberstein & Weiner, Los Angeles, California, for "Little David" from
Ol' Man Adam and His Chillun (1928) by Roark Bradford, published by Harper &
Row, Publishers, Inc.

THE CLARENDON PRESS, Oxford, for "From Everlasting to Everlasting" (editor's
title) from "The Third Century" in *Centuries of Meditation* by Thomas Traherne,
ed. Dobell, 1908.

CHATTO & WINDUS, LTD. See NEW DIRECTIONS PUBLISHING CORPORATION.

COLLINS PUBLISHERS, London. See PANTHEON BOOKS.

CONFRONTATION for "Abraham and Isaac" by Roberta Kalechofsky, reprinted
from the Winter 1970-71 edition of *Confrontation*, a literary journal of Long
Island University.

JOAN DAVES for "I've Been to the Mountain Top" from a speech by Martin
Luther King, Jr., copyright © 1968 by the Estate of Martin Luther King, Jr.

E. P. DUTTON & CO., INC., for "Solomon the King" (editor's title) from *The Life
of Solomon* by Edmund Fleg, translated by Viola Gerard Garvin, copyright 1931,
1957 by E. P. Dutton & Co., Inc.; and for "A Little Paradise Poem" (editor's title),
from Record 11 of *We* by Eugene Zamiatin, translated by Gregory Zilboorg, copyright 1924 by E. P. Dutton & Co., Inc, and renewed 1952 by Gregory Zilboorg.

PAUL ENGLE for "An Old Palestinian Donkey" from his *Poems in Praise* published by Random House, Inc., copyright © 1959 by Paul Engle.

FABER AND FABER, LTD., for Canadian rights to the following: "The Vision of
the Shepherds" from *For the Time Being* by W. H. Auden; "Journey of the
Magi" from *Collected Poems 1909-1962* by T. S. Eliot; "Bar-Room Matins" from
The Collected Poems of Louis MacNeice, ed. E. R. Dodds; and "Moses" from
Collected Poems 1921-1958 by Edwin Muir.

FARRAR, STRAUS & GIROUX, INC., for "Temptation" from *The Best of Simple* by Langston Hughes; for "The Strong Ones" from *A Day of Pleasure* by Isaac Bashevis Singer, copyright © 1963, 1965, 1966, 1969 by Isaac Bashevis Singer; and for "The God of Galaxies" from *Collected and New Poems 1924-1963* by Mark Van Doren, copyright 1952, 1963 by Mark Van Doren.

IRVING FINEMAN for "In the Fields of Boaz" (editor's title) from his novel *Ruth* (Harper & Row, Inc.), copyright 1949 by Irving Fineman.

HARCOURT BRACE JOVANOVICH, INC., for "Journey of the Magi" from *Collected Poems 1909-1962* by T. S. Eliot, copyright 1936 by Harcourt Brace Jovanovich, Inc., and renewed 1963, 1964 by T. S. Eliot; for "The Holy Innocents" from *Lord Weary's Castle* by Robert Lowell, copyright 1946 by Robert Lowell; and for "Eve Speaks," copyright 1917, 1945 by Louis Untermeyer, and "Goliath and David," copyright © 1956 by Louis Untermeyer, both reprinted from his *Long Feud: Selected Poems.*

HARPER & ROW, PUBLISHERS, INC., for "Behold de Rib!" from the conclusion to chapter 8 of *Mules and Men* by Zora Neale Hurston, copyright 1935, 1963 by Zora Neale Hurston; and for "The Mysterious Stranger" (from chapters 2 and 3) from *The Mysterious Stranger and Other Stories* by Mark Twain, copyright 1922 by Mark Twain Company and renewed 1950 by Clara Clemens Samossond.

HOLT, RINEHART AND WINSTON, INC., for "The Emancipator of Your God" (editor's title) from *A Masque of Reason* (lines 47-79), reprinted from *The Poetry of Robert Frost*, ed. Edwin Connery Lathem, copyright 1945 by Robert Frost, copyright © 1969 by Holt, Rinehart and Winston, Inc., and copyright © 1973 by Leslie Frost Ballantine.

HORIZON PRESS, NEW YORK, for "The Face of Adam" (editor's title) from *Our Visit to Niagra* by Paul Goodman, copyright © 1960.

HOUGHTON MIFFLIN COMPANY for "What Adam Said" from *Complete Poetical Works* by Archibald MacLeish, copyright © 1962 by Archibald MacLeish; and for "The Sharing" (editor's title) from chapter 6 of *Earth Abides* by George Stewart, copyright 1949 by George Stewart.

THE MARGOT JOHNSON AGENCY for *Cain* from *The Next Room of the Dream*, copyright © 1962 by Howard Nemerov.

ALFRED A. KNOPF for "The Last Supper" from *Jesus the Son of Man* by Kahlil Gibran, copyright 1928 by Kahlil Gibran, renewed 1956 by Administrators C. T. A. of Kahlil Gibran Estate and Mary G. Gibran; and for "Peter and John" by Elinor Wylie, copyright 1928 by Alfred A. Knopf, Inc., and renewed 1956 by Edwina C. Rubinstein, reprinted from *Collected Poems of Elinor Wylie.*

LITTLE, BROWN AND CO., in association with the ATLANTIC MONTHLY PRESS, for "The Eye of the Soldier" from *The Brides of Solomon and Other Stories* by Geoffrey Household, copyright © 1957 by Geoffrey Household.

MACMILLAN PUBLISHING CO., INC., for "Sisera" by Edwin Arlington Robinson, copyright 1932 by Edwin Arlington Robinson, renewed 1960 by Ruth Nivison and Barbara R. Holt, originally published in *Theatre Arts Monthly.*

WILLIAM MORRIS AGENCY, INC., on behalf of Archibald MacLeish, for selections from his play *J.B.*, reprinted from the edition of the play published by Samuel French, Inc., copyright © 1956, 1957, 1958 by Archibald MacLeish.

ROBERT NATHAN for "The Testing of Jonah" (editor's title) from his novel *Jonah* (Alfred A. Knopf, Inc.), copyright 1925, 1934 by Robert Nathan.

NEW DIRECTIONS PUBLISHING CORPORATION, CHATTO & WINDUS, LTD., AND THE EXECUTORS OF THE ESTATE OF HAROLD OWEN for "At a Calvary Near the Ancre" and "The Parable of the Old Men and the Young" from *Collected Poems* by Wilfred Owen, copyright 1946, 1963 by Chatto & Windus, Ltd.

THE NEW YORK TIMES for portions of "About a Trespass on a Monument" by Archibald MacLeish (New York Times, Dec. 7, 1958), used to preface the selections from *J.B.*, copyright © 1958 by The New York Times Company.

OXFORD UNIVERSITY PRESS, INC., for selections from Act I, Scene 1 from *The Firstborn* by Christopher Fry, copyright 1952 by Christopher Fry; for U.S. rights to "Bar-Room Matins" from *The Collected Poems of Louis MacNeice*, ed. E. R. Dodds, copyright © 1966 by The Estate of Louis MacNeice; and for U.S. rights to "Moses" from *Collected Poems 1921-1958* by Edwin Muir, copyright © 1960 by Willa Muir.

PANTHEON BOOKS, a division of Random House, Inc., and COLLINS PUBLISHERS, London, for "Evil Days" from *Doctor Zhivago* by Boris Pasternak, translated by Bernard Guilbert Guerney, copyright © 1958 by Pantheon Books, Inc.

PENGUIN BOOKS LTD. for "A Boy's Head" from *Selected Poems of Miroslav Holub*, translated by Ian Milner and George Theiner, copyright © 1967 by Miroslav Holub, translation copyright © 1967 by Penguin Books.

A. D. PETERS AND COMPANY, LONDON, for the conclusion to Act I of *Noah* by André Obey, from the Samuel French edition of the play, translated by Arthur Wilmurt. *Noah* was originally published by William Heinemann in 1935.

RANDOM HOUSE, INC., for U.S. rights to "The Vision of the Shepherds" from *For the Time Being* by W. H. Auden, copyright 1944, 1972 by W. H. Auden, reprinted from his *Collected Longer Poems*; for "Go Down, Moses," copyright 1941 by William Faulkner from his *Go Down, Moses*; for "Moses," copyright 1944 by Karl Shapiro from his *Selected Poems*; for "The Recognition of Eve," copyright 1951 by Karl Shapiro from his *Poems for a Jew*; and for "Look, How Beautiful" from *The Beginning and the End and Other Poems* by Robinson Jeffers, copyright © 1963 by Garth Jeffers and Donnan Jeffers.

RUTGERS UNIVERSITY PRESS, New Brunswick, N. J., for "A.D. 2267" from *Of Flesh and Bone* (1967) by John Frederick Nims.

CHARLES SCRIBNER'S SONS for "Calvary" from *The Children of the Night* (1897) by Edwin Arlington Robinson.

SEGAL, RUBINSTEIN, & GORDAN, Los Angeles, Calif., for "Woodstock" by Joni Mitchell, copyright © 1969 by Siquomb Publishing Corporation. All rights reserved.

SIMON & SCHUSTER, INC., for "Prologue to *The Last Temptation of Christ*" and "Voices in the Wilderness" (editor's title) from chapter 10 of *The Last Temptation of Christ* by Nikos Kazantzakis, translated by P. A. Bien, copyright © 1960 by Simon & Schuster, Inc.

THE UNIVERSITY OF NORTH CAROLINA PRESS for "Job" from *Poems 1947-1961* by Elizabeth Sewell, copyright 1962 by Elizabeth Sewell.

THE VIKING PRESS, INC., for "The Creation" from *God's Trombones* by James Weldon Johnson, copyright 1927 by The Viking Press, Inc., and copyright © 1955 by Grace Neil Johnson; for "Only Man" from *The Complete Poems of D. H. Lawrence*, ed. Vivian de Sola Pinto and F. Warren Roberts, copyright © 1964, 1971 by Angelo Ravagli and C. M. Weekely, Executors of the Estate of Frieda Lawrence Ravagli; and for "The Resurrection Is to Life Not to Death" (editor's title) from chapter 10 of *The Rainbow* by D. H. Lawrence, copyright 1915 by D. H. Lawrence and renewed 1943 by Frieda Lawrence.

Preface

AN UNDERSTANDING OF the Bible and the lasting influence it has had throughout the centuries is essential for a full appreciation of much of our history and our culture. In his *Religious History of America* (New York: Harper and Row, 1966), Edwin S. Gaustad has observed:

> The Bible flavored the common man's speech, inspired the artist's brush, determined the poet's imagery, bestowed purpose on a people. This is *the* book. And the American people, more than they know it, are a people of that book.

Today, however, most students of literature have only the vaguest knowledge of the Bible or its contents. Such ignorance makes virtually incomprehensible what some of our greatest poets, novelists, dramatists and painters are saying.

Unfortunately, the Supreme Court's 1963 decision outlawing devotional reading in the public schools made many systems reluctant at first to offer biblical studies of any kind. Justice Tom C. Clark's majority opinion, however, included a recommendation that the Bible still be studied for its "literary and historic qualities." In recent years an increasing number of schools have become aware of the need for such instruction. The growing popularity of elective programs on the secondary level has accelerated this movement toward incorporating biblical studies into the curriculum. Although students have shown great enthusiasm for biblical studies once they have been made available, many schools are still hesitant to offer such courses because of the unavailability of materials in the "Bible as literature" field appropriate for a public school setting. Even more pressing is the virtual lack of any comprehensive collection of literature reflecting biblical influence.

THE ENDURING LEGACY is designed to fill this longstanding need for a collection of biblical literature and modern literature *directly* reflecting biblical themes and allusions. No other anthology to date has drawn together selections from both the Old and New Testaments with such a wealth of poetry, short stories, plays, and songs—more than fifty-five modern selections in all—which depend upon an awareness and understanding of the Bible. Without a study of such modern works, a course in the Bible may suffer from the "ancient history" syndrome—that is, a feeling that the course lacks any relevance to contemporary concerns. A study of the literature included in this collection, however, should convince even the most reluctant reader that the various themes and metaphors embedded in the Bible stories have a contemporaneity that compels the modern author to turn to them again and again, reinterpreting the ancient stories in light of his own experience and in turn using his—and our—own times to shed additional light on the biblical literature serving as its inspiration. Thus, this anthology attempts to accomplish a two-fold purpose: first, to show how a better understanding of modern literature can be brought about by tracing its biblical influences; and second, to discover what insights modern authors can lend to an appreciation of the biblical literature to which they allude.

The biblical and modern selections included in THE ENDURING LEGACY have been arranged into four major units. Within these units, each biblical selection is followed by one to seven modern pieces which reinterpret or in some way draw upon the plot, themes, imagery, and/or language of the biblical selection. In the first unit, for example, passages from Genesis dealing with the Garden of Eden and the Fall of Man are followed by several modern pieces that improvise on the biblical themes in various ways. Joni Mitchell, in her song "Woodstock," insists that we must "get ourselves back to the garden," since the knowledge man received in "the devil's bargain" has only been used to create tools of destruction and dehumanization. The Russian novelist Eugene Zamiatin, on the other hand, depicts a return to Eden as potentially dehumanizing. The brief excerpt from his novel *We* entitled "A Little Paradise Poem" presents a dystopian view of what might happen should a man give up the "freedom without happiness" that Adam and Eve once chose in exchange for the "happiness without freedom" that the novel's totally regulated and automated society claimed to provide.

Each of the four units attempts to suggest important thematic and stylistic relationships among the biblical selections, which, for the most part, are arranged chronologically. The first unit, *Beginnings*, focuses on the primeval stories recounted in the early chapters of Genesis: the Creation, the Garden of Eden, Adam and Eve and the introduction of sin into the world, Cain and Abel and the first murder, and Noah and the Great Deluge. The second unit, *Of Courage and Dreams*, represents some of the major events in the lives of the patriarchs and other legendary figures of the Old Testament whose faith and vision were instrumental in helping the Hebrews carry out the terms of their covenant with the God of Israel. Included are the stories of Abraham and the sacrifice of Isaac; Joseph and his brothers; Moses; Deborah and the Kenite woman Jael, whom she inspired to slay Sisera, leader of the Canaanites, oppressors of the Hebrews for twenty years; and the young shepherd David. The third unit, *The Ways of God and Man*, centers upon the wisdom literature and protest stories of the Old Testament: the Book of Job, which challenged the prevailing view that a man was rewarded or punished on this earth according to how righteous or evil he was; Ecclesiastes, an examination of earthly existence, informed by the notion that "all is vanity"; and the Song of Songs, Ruth, and Jonah, each of which explores various dimensions of love. The final unit, *Greater Love*, turns to the four Gospels of the New Testament and focuses on the various stages of the career of Jesus of Nazareth, whose death stands as a symbol of the "greater love" with which he conducted his messianic mission to make all men free.

Each of these units begins with an introduction that explores the historical and literary background of the biblical pieces, the relationships among them, and the central issues they raise; the second half of each introduction discusses the individual modern selections in light of these themes. Brief headnotes to both the biblical and modern pieces have been provided wherever it was thought necessary to fill in background or establish context. Most of the modern selections and some of the more difficult biblical works are followed by questions designed to provoke thought about the readings. An attempt has been made to avoid obvious questions, in favor of including only those questions which probe the significance of the literature. A special effort was made to suggest connections between the ideas dealt with in the selections and the concerns of those who would be using this anthology. Thus, the themes of freedom, individual dignity, tolerance, and love appear regularly throughout the collection. In addition, a number of paintings, engravings, and other art works—ranging from medieval illuminated manuscript pages to modern paintings—have been included both to illustrate the themes of this book and to stress that the Bible's "enduring legacy" is a multimedia phenomenon.

THE ENDURING LEGACY features a wide range of biblical selections, but no attempt has been made to include all the "most important" portions. Choices have been made on the basis of availability of provocative and accessible modern literature based on biblical allusion and theme. Thus, this anthology should be considered but a sampling both of the literature of the Bible and of the poetry, drama, fiction, and songs reflecting biblical influence. To encourage the reader to pursue both at greater length, a number of bibliographies have been appended, directing the adventurous student to novels, plays, and other literature with biblical aspects, as well as to nonfiction works, records, and films useful in the study of biblical literature.

Finally, a list of the most familiar and oft-used expressions, phrases, and sayings from the Bible has been included. These have often served as a source of titles for literature, art, and music, and many have found their way into our everyday speech. A glance at this list should help to explain why the King James version of the Bible, first published in 1613, has been used throughout, rather than a more modern version. It is this translation which, for more than three-and-a-half centuries, has been the most familiar to English-speaking writers and readers, and thus is the version that has most directly influenced our language and literature.

I would like to express my gratitude to all those who assisted me in completing this project: to my colleagues at Trenton High School in Trenton, Michigan—especially to Eugene Bacon, the dramatics director, who turned me on to many of the drama selections included, and to Thelma Wheeler, our media center specialist, who helped me to locate sources for much of my material; to Ruth Selden, vice president and executive editor of Frederick Ungar Publishing Company, who gave her kind permission to use her cuttings and titles for several stories originally included in her collection entitled *The Ways of God and Men: Great Stories from the Bible in World Literature* (published by Stephen Daye Press, an imprint of Frederick Ungar Publishing Company); and to my wife Charlotte and five children, who had to put up with a part-time husband and father during those nights on end when I would bury myself in my basement workshop.

To my two editors at Charles Scribner's Sons I owe a special debt of gratitude. It was Edward J. Cutler who first encouraged me to pursue the project. And it was Diane Flanel whose editorial counsel helped minimize the effects of my lack of experience in writing and anthologizing, and whose enthusiasm buoyed me up during those days when nothing was going right. Without her patient and steadfast encouragement, this book would probably never have gotten past the "high hopes" stage.

Contents

Unit 2: Of Courage and Dreams 75

Unit 3:   The Ways of God and Man   **183**

Unit 4:   Greater Love   **295**

List of Illustrations

The Enduring Legacy

Biblical Dimensions in Modern Literature

UNIT 1

BEGINNINGS

Ancient of Days (1794) by William Blake. THE PIERPONT MORGAN
LIBRARY, NEW YORK.

ALTHOUGH THE BIBLE is a deeply religious work, its framework is primarily historical. The Old Testament is fundamentally a chronicle of the Jewish nation and its relationship with the God who called it into being to serve His divine will. The portions of Genesis which precede the call of Abraham and the founding of this nation have a more universal focus, however. They are concerned not with the Hebrews as such, but with mankind in general. Here unfold the archetypal accounts of the creation of order out of chaos, the molding of man from dust and of woman from man, the first instances of sin, pain, suffering, and murder, the great Flood, and the earliest convenant between man and God. These accounts cannot, properly speaking, be regarded as history in the way that much of the Old Testament can be understood. Rather, they should be seen as highly imaginative, poetic, and usually symbolic stories formulated to explain the creation of the universe, the origins of man, and the foundations of his personal relationship with the God of Creation. Men of all ages have pondered the questions explored by the writers of these primeval tales: What is the basic nature of God, of man, of good and evil? How was the earth peopled? Did man fall of his own free will or was it fate that determined his actions? Even today these issues, so lyrically and powerfully set forth in biblical times, continue to fire the imaginations of men, resulting in the writing of a great many literary interpretations and retellings of these ancient tales uniquely adapted to our own time.

Genesis opens with a poetic description of the seven successive stages of creation. God calls forth each step through divine fiat, ultimately giving man, created on the sixth day in "His own image," domination over the entire earth. The measured, majestic movement of this "Creation hymn" is achieved by the employment of simple, direct language and by the repetition of key phrases: "And God said, 'Let there be . . .' "; "And it was so"; "And God called . . ."; "And God saw it was good." Many writers have been inspired by the strictly patterned, highly stylized account of Creation. Two examples included in this unit illustrate the special attraction its language and thematic content have held for black authors: "The Creation," one

of the most popular pieces in *God's Trombones,* James Weldon
Johnson's collection of sermons based on the Old Testament, and
"Behold de Rib" by Zora Neale Hurston, also a sermon, which uses
the details of the early chapters of Genesis to comment on woman's
relationship with man. Each of the writers finds the language and
imagery of the Bible wonderfully adaptable to the language of the
black man, and each manages to instill in the ancient themes new and
moving meanings.

Embodied in the early chapters of Genesis are the beginnings of a
pattern that is repeated many times in the narratives of the Old
Testament: the establishment of God's grace, man's disobedience, his
punishment, and his ultimate restoration to grace through God's mercy.
The starting point for this recurrent cycle of sin and redemption is the
Garden of Eden. Many modern writers have seen fit to draw on this
theme, sensing perhaps that something of this same pattern has
continued into their own times. Both the serenity of the Garden and
Adam and Eve's fall from grace have inspired a wide range of literary
adaptations and responses, among them allegories of personal growth
and discovery, celebrations of the innocence and beauty of life in
the Garden, and works of dystopian literature concerned with man's
abuse of knowledge.

Many writers have interpreted man's fall from innocence as being
essential to his discovery of self. The Adam of Archibald MacLeish's
"What Adam Said," for example, dates his life not from the moment
that "God breathed the breath of life into his nostrils," but from that
moment of recognition under the "apple tree" when he first sensed
the mystery and power inherent in his own physical being. Another
frequently heard explanation of the Fall is that man is not content
merely to dwell in innocent bondage to the divine will; by nature he is
driven to know, to discover himself and the world around him, to
create, to become the master of his own destiny. Thus, he accepts the
temptation of knowledge that is offered him. Through the act of eating
the fruit of "the tree of knowledge of good and evil," man was
symbolically rejecting his total dependence upon the divine ordering
of his life, embracing instead the world of experience with all its
temptations and hardships. This is the Original Sin of which Adam
was guilty. In Louis Untermeyer's poem "Eve Speaks," it is Eve who
defends this sin to God, explaining to Him why she consciously
rejected the "peace of Eden" and sought to claim for Adam the
"something more than joy/Beyond perfection" that she felt lay in the
challenges and hardships that awaited them in the world beyond
the Garden.

Many attempts have been made to pinpoint the exact whereabouts
of the Garden of Eden, the original paradise where man was placed in
charge of all Creation, assured of happiness and security so long
as he obeyed the will of his Creator. But the geographical location of
Eden is not nearly as significant as the place it has assumed in the
hearts and dreams of men and women, whose subconscious longing to
return to God's grace and the serene harmony of the Garden has
motivated their efforts and inspired their art throughout the ages.
Writers such as Thomas Traherne, a seventeenth-century religious
poet and essayist, have put this longing into words. In "From
Everlasting to Everlasting," for example, he compares the glorious
and uncorrupted world that Adam knew before the Fall to the world
occupied by a child before it becomes aware of the cares, deceits, and
temptations of the adult world. For Traherne, a man aspiring to enter
the Kingdom of Heaven must somehow unlearn the "dirty devices
of the world" and strive to regain the innocence and purity of thought
and action which his adulthood has robbed him of. Centuries later,
with pollution, nuclear weapons, and a dehumanizing technocracy the
all too apparent results of mankind's use (or abuse) of knowledge,
Joni Mitchell voices a similar desire to return to the bliss of Eden. In
"Woodstock," her anthem to the nation of children who flocked to that
massive musical celebration, Joni Mitchell sets forth a dream in
which she sees bombers "riding shotgun in the sky/Turning into
butterflies." We must renounce "the devil's bargain," she suggests, and
"get ourselves back to the garden." Raging against an adult world
riddled with prejudice and violence, Simple, in Langston Hughes'
short story "Temptation," comically voices a similar need in his desire
to escape the hardships of Harlem and the "rough world" and hold
on to the ways of the Garden: "That apple has turned into an atom
now. . . . If I was Adam I would just stay in Eden in the Garden with
no rent to pay, no landlords to dodge, no time clock to punch. . . ."
As Simple's friend is quick to remind him, he is not Adam, and
he cannot literally return to the Garden to escape the unpleasantries of
his present-day world, but his point is certainly well taken. Underlying
each of these works and many others like them is the understanding
that man's thirst for knowledge inevitably results in the corruption
of his ways and his alienation from the values that were so much
a part of the original paradise. It is impossible to return literally to
the Garden, but it may certainly be desirable to strive to recapture
something of the serenity and sense of well-being of that golden
age of innocence.

Still other writers have been moved to explore the negative aspects

of the "return to the Garden" motif. The utopian visions of such
earlier dreamers as Plato in *The Republic* and Thomas More in *Utopia*
have more recently given way to dystopian nightmares describing
automated Edenic societies in which the new Adams are reduced to
blissful bondage, their lives totally regulated and standardized by
the sophisticated technology of the future. Works such as *We* by
Eugene Zamiatin and the short poem "A.D. 2267" by John Frederick
Nims portray futuristic man in the ultimate stages of dehumanization.
Both strongly suggest that, unbeknownst to man, his efforts to
simulate a modern Eden with his towering knowledge have resulted
in his total alienation from the true spirit of "happiness" and "love"
that reigned in the Garden before the Fall.

With the gaining of knowledge came the first awareness of death.
The first biblical death is also the first murder—Cain's slaying of Abel,
whose offerings God found more acceptable than those of his brother.
It is here that Cain raises the question, "Am I my brother's keeper?"
The implied answer is "yes," and for his failure to realize his obligation
to his fellow man, Cain is made "a fugitive and a vagabond in the
earth." The following questions still plague us, however: Why did
Cain slay his brother? Why did God put a mark on his forehead and
say, "Whosoever slayeth Cain, vengeance shall be taken sevenfold"?
What is the significance of his act beyond that of introducing violence
into the world? Howard Nemerov touches provocatively upon possible
answers to these questions in *Cain*, his poetic rendering of the first
murder, in which the unfortunate son of Adam is portrayed with
unusual sympathy. God touches upon the central theme of the play
when He tells Cain shortly before he decides to murder his brother:

> All things can be done, you must only
> Do what you will. Things are as they are
> Until you decide to change them.

Each man must determine for himself what action he is to take; he
must do so to "be master here"; then he must assume responsibility for
the consequences of that action, for in so doing he discovers the limits
of his own powers.

The violence Cain introduced into the world with the murder of
his brother became rampant during the period in which Noah lived.
The people had grown corrupt, and the "wickedness of man was great
in the earth." God repented that He had made man and vowed to
"destroy man whom I have created from the face of the earth."
Once again, however, a means of redemption is provided for the
faithful—an ark to float above the world-destroying deluge.

In an age of seemingly endless violence, when two global wars have been waged, each promising to be the war that would end all wars, it is not surprising that the story of Noah should be so popular. In his poem "Noah," Herman Hagedorn urges every man to "build your arks, each to his need!" Before a new world can be built, he says, "first there will be rain, there will be night." It hardly seems surprising that the poem appeared in 1940, when the world once again had grown violent; but the poet could not have predicted the destructive rains which were to pour down on Hiroshima, reminding many of the words to the spiritual, "No more water, but fire next time," suggesting the fiery destruction foretold in the Book of Revelation. In the 1950s and 60s when racial tensions flared into city-burning holocausts, the fiery deluge seemed equally imminent. It is this new "age of Noah" that the Reverend Frederick D. Kirkpatrick refers to in his apocalyptic "The Cities Are Burning."

It is, of course, all too easy to dwell on man's abuse of knowledge, the employment of his godlike powers to pollute his environment and to wage war on his fellow man. We must not overlook the fact that it is also his knowledge which gives him vision—vision which enables a Noah to build an ark to provide for his salvation, to hold on to all that is important, and to start out again after great tragedy. It is this use of the story of Noah which Miroslav Holub employs in his poem "A Boy's Head." In it, the poet says, will be a "spaceship," but there is also "Noah's ark,/which shall be first." We may be "caught in the devil's bargain," as Joni Mitchell suggests; but whether the knowledge we obtained in the exchange is used for good or evil depends on us. As Miroslav Holub concludes:

> There is much promise
> in the circumstance
> that so many people have heads.

IN THE BEGINNING GOD
(Genesis)

In the beginning God created the heaven and the earth. And the earth was without form, and void; and darkness was upon the face of the deep. And the Spirit of God moved upon the face of the waters. And God said, "Let there be light": and there was light. And God saw the light, that it was good: and God divided the light from the darkness. And God called the light Day, and the darkness he called Night. And the evening and the morning were the first day.

And God said, "Let there be a firmament in the midst of the waters, and let it divide the waters from the waters." And God made the firmament, and divided the waters which were under the firmament from the waters which were above the firmament: and it was so. And God called the firmament Heaven. And the evening and the morning were the second day.

And God said, "Let the waters under the heaven be gathered together unto one place, and let the dry land appear": and it was so. And God called the dry land Earth; and the gathering together of the waters called he Seas: and God saw that it was good. And God said, "Let the earth bring forth grass, the herb yielding seed, and the fruit tree yielding fruit after his kind, whose seed is in itself, upon the earth": and it was so. And the earth brought forth grass, and herb yielding seed after his kind, and the tree yielding fruit, whose seed was in itself, after his kind: and God saw that it was good. And the evening and the morning were the third day.

And God said, "Let there be lights in the firmament of the heaven to divide the day from the night; and let them be for signs, and for seasons, and for days, and years; and let them be for lights in the firmament of the heaven to give light upon the earth." And it was so. And God made two great lights; the greater light to rule the day, and the lesser light to rule the night: he made the stars also. And God set them in the firmament of the heaven to give light upon the earth, and to rule over the day and over the night, and to divide the light from the darkness: and God saw that it was good. And the evening and the morning were the fourth day.

And God said, "Let the waters bring forth abundantly the moving creature that hath life, and fowl that may fly above the earth in the open firmament of heaven." And God created great whales, and every living creature that moveth, which the waters brought forth abundantly, after their kind, and every winged fowl after his kind: and God saw that it was good. And God blessed them, saying, "Be fruitful, and multiply, and fill the waters in the seas, and let fowl multiply in the earth." And the evening and the morning were the fifth day.

And God said, "Let the earth bring forth the living creature after his kind, cattle, and creeping thing, and beast of the earth after his kind": and it was so. And God made the beast of the earth after his kind, and cattle after their kind, and every thing that creepeth upon the earth after his kind: and God saw that it was good.

And God said, "Let us make man in our image, after our likeness: and let them have dominion over the fish of the sea, and over the fowl of the air, and over the cattle, and over all the earth, and over every creeping thing that creepeth upon the earth." So God created man in his own image, in the image of God created he him; male and female created he them. And God blessed them, and God said unto them, "Be fruitful, and multiply, and replenish the earth, and subdue it: and have dominion over the fish of the sea, and over the fowl of the air, and over every living thing that moveth upon the earth."

And God said, "Behold, I have given you every herb bearing seed, which is upon the face of all the earth, and every tree, in the which is the fruit of a tree yielding seed; to you it shall be for meat. And to every beast of the earth, and to every fowl of the air, and to every thing that creepeth upon the earth, wherein there is life, I have given every green herb for meat." And it was so. And God saw every thing he had made, and, behold, it was very good. And the evening and the morning were the sixth day.

Thus the heavens and the earth were finished, and all the host of them. And on the seventh day God ended his work which he had made; and he rested on the seventh day from all his work which he had made. And God blessed the seventh day, and sanctified it: because that in it he had rested from all his work which God created and made.

[*Genesis 1:1-2:3*]

THE CREATION

(A Sermon)

James Weldon Johnson

And God stepped out on space,
And He looked around and said,
"I'm lonely—
I'll make me a world."

And far as the eye of God could see
Darkness covered everything,
Blacker than a hundred midnights
Down in a cypress swamp.

Then God smiled,
And the light broke,
And the darkness rolled up on one side,
And the light stood shining on the other,
And God said, "That's good!"

Then God reached out and took the light in His hands,
And God rolled the light around in His hands,
Until He made the sun;
And He set that sun a-blazing in the heavens.
And the light that was left from making the sun
God gathered up in a shining ball
And flung against the darkness,
Spangling the night with the moon and the stars.

Then down between
The darkness and the light
He hurled the world:
And God said, "That's good!"

Then God himself stepped down—
And the sun was on His right hand,

And the moon was on His left;
The stars were clustered about His head,
And the earth was under His feet.
And God walked, and where He trod
His footsteps hollowed the valleys out
And bulged the mountains up.

Then He stopped and looked and saw
That the earth was hot and barren.
So God stepped over to the edge of the world
And He spat out the seven seas;
He batted His eyes, and the lightnings flashed;
He clapped His hands, and the thunders rolled;
And the waters above the earth came down,
The cooling waters came down.

Then the green grass sprouted,
And the little red flowers blossomed,
The pine-tree pointed his finger to the sky,
And the oak spread out his arms;
The lakes cuddled down in the hollows of the ground,
And the rivers ran down to the sea;
And God smiled again,
And the rainbow appeared,
And curled itself around His shoulder.

Then God raised His arm and He waved His hand
Over the sea and over the land,
And He said, "Bring forth! Bring forth!"
And quicker than God could drop His hand,
Fishes and fowls
And beasts and birds
Swam the rivers and the seas,
Roamed the forests and the woods,
And split the air with their wings,
And God said, "That's good!"

Then God walked around
And God looked around
On all that He had made.
And He looked at His moon,
And He looked at His little stars;

He looked on His world
With all its living things,
And God said, "I'm lonely still."

Then God sat down
On the side of a hill where He could think;
By a deep, wide river He sat down;
With His head in His hands,
God thought and thought,
Till He thought, "I'll make me a man!"

Up from the bed of the river
God scooped the clay;
And by the bank of the river
He kneeled Him down;
And there the great God Almighty,
Who lit the sun and fixed it in the sky,
Who flung the stars to the most far corner of the night,
Who rounded the earth in the middle of His hand—
This Great God,
Like a mammy bending over her baby,
Kneeled down in the dust
Toiling over a lump of clay
Till He shaped it in His own image;

Then into it He blew the breath of life,
And man became a living soul.
Amen. Amen.

THE FACE OF ADAM
Paul Goodman

This image of the creation of Adam that haunts me is in the picture
of Michelangelo's on the ceiling of the Sistine Chapel in Rome. Yes, it

is that trust-drunken face and its present eyes that I am looking for in the factories and in the fields.

And I have had the thought to arrange Michelangelo's picture as a dramatic tableau for the stage. The stage is divided into two, and stage right (the spectator's left) is at first concealed with a scrim.

Slowly from Left Rear appears the great cart of God and his Angels, moving in an arc toward the center. It is wrapped and blown round by the fluttering cloak of Whirlwind who spoke to Job, noisily agitated by a wind-machine. But the machine quiets down when the Angels begin to speak.

What are the Angels saying, as their cart swings toward the center? For at the decisive moment at which Michelangelo chose to portray

The Creation of Man (1511) by Michelangelo. Sistine Chapel, Rome. ITALIAN GOVERNMENT TRAVEL OFFICE, NEW YORK.

them, their countenances are expressing the most various thoughts, as if they had been thinking or speaking; and there is no doubt that thus the poetic painter meant to tell us *his* different thoughts about the creation of Adam. The fat boy, attentive over God's right shoulder, is wide-eyed, a bit alarmed. The three who are looking over his left shoulder are like three youthful scientists, one wonderstruck with mouth agape, one with his lips grimly intent, and the third, looking straight at it, excitedly curious, with the small smile that we wear for the crucial experiment. But the lovely youth (or is it Eve?) about whose shoulders God's left arm is familiarly flung, and who is clutching at God's forearm for support and almost as if to check him, surely his face is big-eyed with dismay. What does it mean? And lastly, the

chubby child on the right, whom God is touching with a bent forefinger, he is purposely *not* looking on at the scene but seems to be
in a kind of daydream. And besides these, there are faces hidden in
the shadows.

As the cart of God and his Angels approaches the Center of the
stage, God has stretched out his right arm and forefinger, and now as
if by the sweep of his gesture the scrim is opened, disclosing Adam on
the hillside with his extended hand. There is no doubt that at some
instant their fingertips have touched, but already the cart is continuing
in its slow arc toward the exit Left Front, although God, as he goes,
does follow with his eyes his creature.

At the moment of touching, too quick to be noticed, God has thrown
Adam into being, and this is expressed by opening the scrim revealing
him on the hillside. But there is no need for the actor of Adam to imi-
tate the countenance of that moment, nor did the painter paint it,
nor can we guess it; for already it is past, and Michelangelo has painted
us the countenance of Adam at the instant after their fingers have
touched.

This is the trust-drunken face of Adam with boundlessly open eyes,
for his soul is pouring through his eyes looking into God's face that
has not yet vanished. (As it has not yet vanished.) The look of my
Adam is more alive than the solemn look on an animal's face; but it is
more melancholy than the simply serious look of a man absorbed in his
concerns. Adam has on his face the trusting and boundlessly-drinking
look of separation from God, as if to say, "Lo! here now you are for
me—going away, and here I am responding as who can." Not a look
of grief, for God cannot be altogether lost. Nor a look of disappointment, for Adam has not had any expectations. But it is the look toward
God going away, separated from us, just as it is. And after the cart
has made its exit, this look does not change, but it is what the
spectators take home with them, as the curtain falls.

This is the face and the eyes of my Adam, in his portrait by Michelangelo, that is fixed in my soul, and I do not know what to do.—

> Creator of the worlds! O joy
> of speed! and when the powers that lie
>   latent, into being break,
>   I shall not fear the onward wreck
> because I am in love with
> the nature of things unto death,
> and as they loom say, "Lo!"
> Lord favor me, the road I go.

Father! guide and lead me stray
for I stumble forward straight my way
   undeviating, I do not
   notice the pleasant bypaths that
make us this world surprising nor
the precipice that sinks before.
   O give me ground for next a step
   to stagger walking in my sleep.

As I think of my Adam thrown into this world whose resources I have assayed for fifty years of my life, to God I pray for faith, for the conviction that I have ground underfoot for a next step.

THE GARDEN AND THE FALL
(Genesis)

These are the generations of the heavens and of the earth when they were created, in the day that the Lord God made the earth and the heavens, and every plant of the field before it was in the earth, and every herb of the field before it grew: for the Lord God had not caused it to rain upon the earth, and there was not a man to till the ground. But there went up a mist from the earth, and watered the whole face of the ground. And the Lord God formed man of the dust of the ground, and breathed into his nostrils the breath of life; and man became a living soul.

And the Lord God planted a garden eastward in Eden; and there he put the man whom he had formed. And out of the ground made the Lord God to grow every tree that is pleasant to the sight, and good for food; the tree of life also in the midst of the garden, and the tree of knowledge of good and evil. And a river went out of Eden to water the garden; and from thence it was parted, and became into four heads.

And the Lord God took the man, and put him into the garden of Eden to dress it and to keep it. And the Lord God commanded the man, saying, "Of every tree of the garden thou mayest freely eat: but of the tree of the knowledge of good and evil, thou shalt not eat of it: for in the day that thou eatest thereof thou shalt surely die."

And the Lord God said, "It is not good that the man should be alone; I will make him a help meet for him."

And out of the ground the Lord God formed every beast of the field, and every fowl of the air; and brought them unto Adam to see what he would call them: and whatsoever Adam called every living creature, that was the name thereof. And Adam gave names to all cattle, and to the fowl of the air, and to every beast of the field; but for Adam there was not found a help meet for him.

And the Lord God caused a deep sleep to fall upon Adam, and he slept: and he took one of his ribs, and closed up the flesh instead thereof; and the rib, which the Lord God had taken from man, made he a woman, and brought her unto the man.

And Adam said, "This is now bone of my bones, and flesh of my flesh: she shall be called Woman, because she was taken out of Man."

Therefore shall a man leave his father and his mother, and shall cleave unto his wife: and they shall be one flesh. And they were both naked, the man and his wife, and were not ashamed.

Now the serpent was more subtile than any beast of the field which the Lord God had made. And he said unto the woman, "Yea, hath God said, 'Ye shall not eat of every tree of the garden'?"

And the woman said unto the serpent, "We may eat of the fruit of the trees of the garden: but of the fruit of the tree which is in the midst of the garden, God hath said, 'Ye shall not eat of it, neither shall ye touch it, lest ye die.' "

And the serpent said unto the woman, "Ye shall not surely die: for God doth know that in the day ye eat thereof, then your eyes shall be opened, and ye shall be as gods, knowing good and evil."

And when the woman saw that the tree was good for food, and that it was pleasant to the eyes, and a tree to be desired to make one wise, she took of the fruit thereof, and did eat, and gave also unto her husband with her; and he did eat. And the eyes of them both were opened, and they knew that they were naked; and they sewed fig leaves together, and made themselves aprons.

And they heard the voice of the Lord God walking in the garden in the cool of the day: and Adam and his wife hid themselves from the presence of the Lord God amongst the trees of the garden.

And the Lord God called unto Adam, and said unto him, "Where art thou?"

And he said, "I heard thy voice in the garden, and I was afraid, because I was naked; and I hid myself."

And he said, "Who told thee that thou wast naked? Hast thou eaten of the tree, whereof I commanded thee that thou shouldest not eat?"

And the man said, "The woman whom thou gavest to be with me, she gave me of the tree, and I did eat."

And the Lord God said unto the woman, "What is this that thou hast done?"

And the woman said, "The serpent beguiled me, and I did eat."

And the Lord God said unto the serpent, "Because thou hast done this, thou art cursed above all cattle, and above every beast of the field; upon thy belly shalt thou go, and dust shalt thou eat all the days of thy life: and I will put enmity between thee and the woman, and between thy seed and her seed; it shall bruise thy head, and thou shalt bruise his heel."

Unto the woman he said, "I will greatly multiply thy sorrow and thy conception; in sorrow thou shalt bring forth children; and thy desire shall be to thy husband, and he shall rule over thee."

And unto Adam he said, "Because thou hast hearkened unto the voice of thy wife, and hast eaten of the tree, of which I commanded thee, saying, 'Thou shalt not eat of it': Cursed is the ground for thy sake; in sorrow shalt thou eat of it all the days of thy life; thorns also and thistles shall it bring forth to thee; and thou shalt eat the herb of the field; in the sweat of thy face shalt thou eat bread, till thou return unto the ground; for out of it wast thou taken: for dust thou art, and unto dust shalt thou return."

And Adam called his wife's name Eve, because she was the mother of all living. Unto Adam also and to his wife did the Lord God make coats of skins, and clothed them.

And the Lord God said, "Behold, the man is become as one of us, to know good and evil: and now, lest he put forth his hand, and take also of the tree of life, and eat, and live for ever—": therefore the Lord God sent him forth from the garden of Eden, to till the ground from whence he was taken. So he drove out the man; and he placed at the east of the garden of Eden cherubim, and a flaming sword which turned every way, to keep the way of the tree of life.

[*Genesis 2:4–10; 2:15–3:24*]

BEHOLD DE RIB!

Zora Neale Hurston

It wasn't black dark, but night was peeping around the corner. The quarters were getting alive. Woofing, threats and brags up and down the line.

Three figures in the dusk-dark detached themselves from the railroad track and came walking into the quarters. A tall black grim-faced man with a rusty black reticule, followed by two women.

Everybody thought he was a bootlegger and yelled orders to him to that effect. He paid no attention, but set down his bag slowly, opened it still slower and took out a dog-eared Bible and opened it. The crowd quieted down. They knew he was a travelling preacher, a "stump-knocker" in the language of the "job."

Some fell silent to listen. Others sucked their teeth and either went back into their houses or went on to the jook.

When he had a reasonable amount of attention he nodded to the woman at his left and she raised "Death comes a Creepin'" and the crowd helped out. At the end the preacher began:

> You all done been over in Pentecost (got to feeling spiritual by singing) and now we going to talk about de woman that was taken from man. I take my text from Genesis two and twenty-one (Gen. 2:21):

Behold de Rib!
Now, my beloved,
Behold means to look and see.
Look at dis woman God done made,
But first thing, ah hah!
Ah wants you to gaze upon God's previous works.
Almighty and arisen God, hah!
Peace-giving and prayer-hearing God,
High-riding and strong armded God
Walking acrost his globe creation, hah!
Wid de blue elements for a helmet
And a wall of fire round his feet
He wakes de sun every morning from his fiery bed
Wid de breath of his smile
And commands de moon wid his eyes.
And Oh—
Wid de eye of Faith
I can see him
Standing out on de eaves of ether
Breathing clouds from out his nostrils,
Blowing storms from 'tween his lips
I can see!!
Him seize de mighty axe of his proving power
And smite the stubborn-standing space,
And laid it wide open in a mighty gash—
Making a place to hold de world
I can see him—
Molding de world out of thought and power
And whirling it out on its eternal track,
Ah hah, my strong armded God!

He set de blood red eye of de sun in de sky
And told it,
Wait, wait! Wait there till Shiloh come
I can see!
Him mold de mighty mountains
And melting de skies into seas.
Oh, Behold, and look and see! hah
We see in de beginning
He made de bestes every one after its kind,
De birds that fly de trackless air,
De fishes dat swim de mighty deep—
Male and fee-male, hah!
Then he took of de dust of de earth
And made man in his own image.
And man was alone,
Even de lion had a mate
So God shook his head
And a thousand million diamonds
Flew out from his glittering crown
And studded de evening sky and made de stars.
So God put Adam into a deep sleep
And took out a bone, ah hah!
And it is said that it was a rib.
Behold de rib!
A bone out of a man's side.
He put de man to sleep and made wo-man,
And men and women been sleeping together ever since.
Behold de rib!
Brothers, if God
Had taken dat bone out of man's head
He would have meant for a woman to rule, hah
If he had taken a bone out of his foot,
He would have meant for us to dominize and rule.
He could have made her out of back-bone
And then she would have been behind us.
But, no, God Amighty, he took de bone out of his side
So dat places de woman beside us;
Hah! God knowed his own mind.
Behold de rib!
And now I leave dis thought wid you,
Let us all go marchin' up to de gates of Glory.
Tramp! tramp! tramp!

In step wid de host dat John saw.
Male and female like God made us
Side by side.
Oh, behold de rib!
And less all set down in Glory together
Right round his glorified throne
And praise his name forever.
        Amen.

At the end of the sermon the woman on the preacher's left raised, "Been a Listenin' All de Night Long," and the preacher descended from his fiery cloud and lifted the collection in his hat. The singers switched to, "You Can't Hide, Sinners, You Can't Hide." The sparse contribution taken, the trio drifted back into the darkness of the railroad, walking towards Kissimmee.

THE RECOGNITION OF EVE

Karl Shapiro

Whatever it was she had so fiercely fought
Had fled back to the sky, but still she lay
With arms outspread, awaiting its assault,
Staring up through the branches of the tree,
The fig tree. Then she drew a shuddering breath
And turned her head instinctively his way.
She had fought birth as dying men fight death.

Her sigh awakened him. He turned and saw
A body swollen, as though formed of fruits,
White as the flesh of fishes, soft and raw.
He hoped she was another of the brutes
So he crawled over and looked into her eyes,
The human wells that pool all absolutes.
It was like looking into double skies.

And when she spoke the first word (it was *thou*)
He was terror-stricken, but she raised her hand
And touched his wound where it was fading now,
For he must feel the place to understand.
Then he recalled the longing that had torn
His side, and while he watched it whitely mend,
He felt it stab him suddenly like a thorn.

He thought the woman had hurt him. Was it she
Or the same sickness seeking to return;
Or was there any difference, the pain set free
And she who seized him now as hard as iron?
Her fingers bit his body. She looked old
And involuted, like the newly-born.
He let her hurt him till she loosed her hold.

Then she forgot him and she wearily stood
And went in search of water through the grove.
Adam could see her wandering through the wood,
Studying her footsteps as her body wove
In light and out of light. She found a pool
And there he followed shyly to observe.
She was already turning beautiful.

Why do you think Eve "fought birth as dying men fight death"?
What is the significance of her "eyes"? Why must Adam "feel the place
to understand"? What connection does he make between the "longing
that had torn/His side" and the pain he now feels when Eve touches
his wound? How does your knowledge of what follows this moment of
recognition and discovery in the biblical story help you appreciate
the way the poet recreates Adam's bewildered thoughts as to whether
it was Eve or his prior "sickness'" that was the cause of his pain?
At what other moment will Eve again cause him pain? Discuss how
Adam first reacts to Eve. How does his understanding of her grow over
the course of the poem?

EVE SPEAKS

Louis Untermeyer

Pause, God, and ponder, ere Thou judgest me.
Though it be Doomsday, and the trampling winds
Rush blindly through the stark and cowering skies,
Bearing Thy fearful mandate like a sword,
I do not tremble. I am unafraid
Though the red flame of wrath lick up the worlds,
And dizzy stars fall in a golden rain;
Though, in an agonizing fear of life,
The summoned spirits, torn from gentle graves,
Whirl at Thy feet or fly before Thy frown,
Like leaves that run before a scornful breeze,
I do not fly. My soul is unafraid.
Years have swept over me and in the wash
Of foaming centuries have been forgot;
Yet still my soul remembers Paradise,
That perfect echo of Thy gentler mood.
Wrapped in a drowsy luxury we lived,
Beauty our food and idleness our pillow.
Day after day, we walked beneath Thy smile;
And, as we wandered through the glittering hours,
Our souls unfolding with the friendly earth,
Eden grew richer to our ardent eyes.
With every step, a clump of trees, a star,
An undiscovered flower, a hill, a cry,
A new, wild sunset or a wilder bird
Entered our lives and grew a part of us.
Lord, there was naught but happiness—and yet,
Though Adam gloried in the world's content,
And sunned himself in rich complacency,
The thought that there was something more than joy,
Beyond perfection, greater than singing peace
And tranquil happiness, vexed all my hours.
Here in a garden, without taint or care,

We played like children, we who were not children.
Swaddled with ease, lulled with Thy softest dreams,
We lived in perfect calm, who were not perfect.
Eden was made for angels, not for Man.

Often the thought of this would come to me
When Adam's songs seemed empty of all mirth,
When he grew moody, and the reckless fire
Leaped in his eyes and died; or when I saw
Him lying at my side—his brawny arms
Knotted with strength; his bosom deep and broad;
His hands tight-clenched, his mouth firm, even in sleep.
Here was a body made for mighty building,
Here was a brain designed to dream and mould—
To waste such energy on such a life!
I could not think it. Seeing him, I knew
Man made for Eden only, not for more,
Was made in vain. I claimed my Adam, God;
Claimed him for fiercer things and lustier worlds,
Immoderate measures, insolent desires;
Claimed him for great and strengthening defeats.
He was but one of many things to Thee—
A cunning lump of clay, a speaking clod—
One of a universe of miracles.
Each day a fresh creation was to Thee;
Thou hadst infinity to shape and guard—
I only Adam.

Lying awake one night beneath the Tree,
I heard him sighing in a fitful sleep.
A cold, disdainful moon mocked my unrest;
A night-bird circled out beyond the wood.
Never did Eden seem so much a prison.
Past the great gates I glimpsed the unknown world,
Lying unfettered in majestic night.
I saw the broadening stream hold out its arms;
The proud hills called me, and the teasing lure
Of things unheard, unguessed at caught my soul.
Adam was made for this—and this for him.
The peace of Eden grew intolerable.
Better the long uncertainty of toil,
The granite scorn of the experienced world,

And failure upon failure; better these
Than this enforced and rotting indolence.
Adam should know his godhood; he should feel
The weariness of work, and pride of it;
The agony of creation, and its reward.
His hands should rear the dream, his sinews think;
And in a rush of power his strength should rise
And rend, and tame, and wrest its secret from
The sweating, energetic earth,
Until his rude and stumbling soul could grasp
Conquering and unconquerable joys.
So should his purpose work among the stars;
Face, without fear, contemptuous centuries;
Meet the astonished heavens with a laugh,
And answer God with God's own words and deeds.
One thing alone would give all this to him,
One thing would cleave the sealed and stubborn rocks,
Harness the winds, yoke the unbridled seas:
Knowledge, the force and shaper of the world.

And so I knew that we should eat, and learn.

Pause, God, and ponder, ere Thou judgest me.

What is the "something more than joy,/Beyond perfection" that
vexes Eve? Why does she say that "Eden was made for angels, not for
Man"? What qualities does she perceive in Adam that lead her
ultimately to reject Eden? What are the "fiercer things and lustier
worlds" for which she has claimed Adam?

How had Eden become "so much a prison" to her? Explain what Eve
prefers to the "peace of Eden." What does she hope Adam will
accomplish by confronting the "granite scorn of the experienced
world"? What "one thing" will "give all this" to Adam? Do you find
her argument convincing, or would you prefer Eden? In what respect
is Eve's monologue an explanation of why she tempted Adam to sin?

WHAT ADAM SAID

Archibald MacLeish

My life began
Not when I was moulded man
But when beneath the apple tree
I saw what none but I could see:
Adam flesh and Adam bone
And Adam by himself alone.

That day he sees
His own two hands, those mysteries—
His flesh, his bone and yet not his—
That day man knows himself, and is.

ONLY MAN

D. H. Lawrence

Only man can fall from God
Only man.

No animal, no beast nor creeping thing
no cobra nor hyena nor scorpion nor hideous white ant
can slip entirely through the fingers of the hands of god
into the abyss of self-knowledge,
knowledge of the self-apart-from-god.

For the knowledge of the self-apart-from-God
is an abyss down which the soul can slip
writhing and twisting in all the revolutions
of the unfinished plunge
of self-awareness, now apart from God, falling
fathomless, fathomless, self-consciousness wriggling
writhing deeper and deeper in all the minutiae of self-knowledge,
    downward, exhaustive,
yet never, never coming to the bottom, for there is no bottom;
zigzagging down like the fizzle from a finished rocket
the frizzling falling fire that cannot go out, dropping wearily,
neither can it reach the depth
for the depth is bottomless,
so it wriggles its way even further down, further down
at last in sheer horror of not being able to leave off
knowing itself, knowing itself apart from God, falling.

   How does man differ significantly from animals? In what ways does
Lawrence use imagery and word repetition to dramatize the effect
of the "fall"? Why are words like "wriggling" and "writhing"
particularly suitable here? Compare the concept of "self-knowledge"
in "What Adam Said" to that in "Only Man." What feelings are you
left with after reading each of the poems?

TEMPTATION

Langston Hughes

"When the Lord said, 'Let there be light,' and there was light, what I
want to know is where was us colored people?"

   "What do you mean, 'Where were we colored people?' " I said.

   "We must *not* of been there," said Simple, "because we are still
dark. Either He did not include me or else I were not there."

"The Lord was not referring to people when He said, 'Let there be light.' He was referring to the elements, the atmosphere, the air."

"He must have included some people," said Simple, "because white people are light, in fact, *white*, whilst I am dark. How come? I say, we were not there."

"Then where do you think we were?"

"Late as usual," said Simple, "old C. P. Time. We must have been down the road a piece and did not get back on time."

"There was no C. P. Time in those days," I said. "In fact, no people were created—so there couldn't be any Colored People's Time. The Lord God had not yet breathed the breath of life into anyone."

"No?" said Simple.

"No," said I, "because it wasn't until Genesis 2 and 7 that God 'formed man of the dust of the earth and breathed into his nostrils the breath of life and man became a living soul.' His name was Adam. Then He took one of Adam's ribs and made a woman."

"Then trouble began," said Simple. "Thank God, they was both white."

"How do you know Adam and Eve were white?" I said.

"When I was a kid I seen them on the Sunday school cards," said Simple. "Ever since I been seeing a Sunday school card, they was white. That is why I want to know where was us Negroes when the Lord said, 'Let there be light'?

"Oh, man, you have a color complex so bad you want to trace it back to the Bible."

"No, I don't. I just want to know how come Adam and Eve was white. If they had started out black, this world might not be in the fix it is today. Eve might not of paid that serpent no attention. I never did know a Negro yet that liked a snake."

"That snake is a symbol," I said, "a symbol of temptation and sin. And that symbol would be the same, no matter what the race."

"I am not talking about no symbol," said Simple. "I am talking about the day when Eve took that apple and Adam et. From then on the human race has been in trouble. There ain't a colored woman living what would take no apple from a snake—and she better not give no snake-apples to her husband!"

"Adam and Eve are symbols, too," I said.

"You are simple yourself," said Simple. "But I just wish we colored folks had been somewhere around at the start. I do not know where we was when Eden was a garden, but we sure didn't get in on none of the crops. If we had, we would not be so poor today. White folks started out ahead and they are still ahead. Look at me!"

Adam and Eve (1528) by Lucas Cranach the Elder. COURTESY OF THE DETROIT INSTITUTE OF ARTS.

"I am looking," I said.

"Made in the image of God," said Simple, "but I never did see anybody like me on a Sunday school card."

"Probably nobody looked like you in Biblical days," I said. "The American Negro did not exist in B.C. You're a product of Caucasia and Africa, Harlem and Dixie. You've been conditioned entirely by our environment, our modern times."

"Times have been hard," said Simple, "but still I am a child of God."

"In the cosmic sense, we are all children of God."

"I have been baptized," said Simple, "also annointed with oil. When I were a child I come through at the mourners' bench. I was converted. I have listened to Daddy Grace and et with Father Divine, moaned with Elder Lawson and prayed with Adam Powell. Also I have been to the Episcopalians with Joyce. But if a snake were to come up to me and offer me an apple, I would say, 'Varmint, be on your way! No fruit today! Bud, you got the wrong stud now, so get along somehow, be off down the road because you're lower than a toad!' Then that serpent would respect me as a wise man—and this world would not be where it is—all on account of an apple. That apple has turned into an atom now."

"To hear you talk, if you had been in the Garden of Eden, the world would still be a Paradise," I said. "Man would not have fallen into sin."

"Not *this* man," said Simple. "I would have stayed in that garden making grape wine, singing like Crosby, and feeling fine. I would not be scuffling out in this rough world, neither would I be in Harlem. If I was Adam I would just stay in Eden in that Garden with no rent to pay, no landladies to dodge, no time clock to punch—and my picture on a Sunday school card. I'd be a *real gone guy* even if I didn't have but one name—Adam—and no initials."

"You would be *real gone* all right. But you were not there. So, my dear fellow, I trust you will not let your rather late arrival on our contemporary stage distort your perspective."

"No," said Simple.

Why does Simple assume that Adam and Eve were white? What effect do you suspect such experiences have in shaping his image of himself? What does he mean when he says, "That apple has turned into an atom now"? Why does Simple say he would have stayed in Eden? Do you see any disadvantages to such an existence?

FROM EVERLASTING TO EVERLASTING

Thomas Traherne

Certainly Adam in Paradise had not more sweet and curious apprehensions of the world than I when I was a child.

All appeared new and strange at first, inexpressibly rare and delightful and beautiful. I was a little stranger which at my entrance into the world was saluted and surrounded with innumerable joys. My knowledge was divine; I knew by intuition those things which since my apostasy I collected again by the highest reason. My very ignorance was advantageous. I seemed as one brought into the estate of innocence. All things were spotless and pure and glorious; yea, and infinitely mine and joyful and precious. I knew not that there were any sins, or complaints, or laws. I dreamed not of poverties, contentions, or vices. All tears and quarrels were hidden from my eyes. Everything was at rest, free and immortal. I knew nothing of sickness or death or exaction. In the absence of these I was entertained like an angel with the works of God in their splendor and glory; I saw all in the peace of Eden; heaven and earth did sing my Creator's praises, and could not make more melody to Adam than to me. All Time was Eternity, and a perpetual Sabbath. Is it not strange that an infant should be heir of the whole world, and see those mysteries which the books of the learned never unfold?

The corn was orient and immortal wheat which never should be reaped nor was ever sown. I thought it had stood from everlasting to everlasting. The dust and stones of the street were as precious as gold: the gates were at first the end of the world. The green trees when I saw them first through one of the gates transported and ravished me; their sweetness and unusual beauty made my heart to leap, and almost mad with ecstasy, they were such strange and wonderful things. The men! O what venerable and reverend creatures did the aged seem! Immortal cherubims! And young men glittering and sparkling angels, and maids strange seraphic pieces of life and beauty! Boys and girls tumbling in the street were moving jewels: I knew not that they were born or should die. But all things abided eternally as they were in their proper places. Eternity was manifest in the light of the day, and something infinite behind everything appeared, which talked with my expectation and moved my desire. The City seemed to stand in Eden or to be built in Heaven. The streets were mine, the temple was mine, the people were mine, their clothes and gold and silver were mine, as much as their sparkling eyes, fair skins, and ruddy faces. The skies were mine, and so were the sun and moon and stars, and all the world was mine; and I the only spectator and enjoyer of it. I knew no churlish proprieties; nor bounds, nor divisions; but all proprieties and divisions were mine, all treasures and the possessors of them. So that with much ado I was corrupted, and made to learn the dirty devices of this world, which now I unlearn, and become, as it were, a little child again that I may enter into the Kingdom of God.

Why does the speaker say that as a child his "very ignorance was advantageous"? Why would "boys and girls tumbling in the street" seem as "moving jewels"? How does the attitude of a child toward "property" differ from that of an adult? Explain in what sense the speaker became "corrupted." Discuss the essay in relation to Christ's teaching that "Except ye be converted, and become as little children, ye shall not enter into the kingdom of heaven" (Matthew 18:3).

WOODSTOCK

Joni Mitchell

I came upon a child of God,
He was walking along the road,
And I asked him, "Where are you going?"
This he told me: I'm going on down to Yasgurs' Farm,
Gonna join in a rock and roll band,
I'm gonna camp out on the land
And try an' get my soul free.

We are stardust, we are golden,
And we got to get ourselves back to the garden.

Then can I walk beside you?
I have come here to lose the smog,
And I feel to be a cog in something twining.
Maybe it is just the time of year,
Or maybe it's the time of man,
I don't know who I am,
But life is for learning.

We are stardust, we are golden,
And we got to get ourselves back to the garden.

By the time we got to Woodstock
We were half a million strong,
And everywhere was song and celebration,
And I dreamed I saw the bombers
Riding shotgun in the sky
Turning into butterflies
Above our nation.

We are stardust, billion-year-old carbon,
Caught in the devil's bargain,
And we got to get ourselves back to the garden.

What significance does Joni Mitchell attach to the massive . . celebration in music at Woodstock? Reread the biblical passages in which the serpent tempts Eve. What is the "devil's bargain" that we are "caught in"? How is this related to the "bombers riding shotgun in the sky"? How does the image of the "bombers" turning into "butterflies" reinforce the "message" of the song?

To what extent should government participate in the creation of a new Eden for its citizens? What besides bombers would we have to sacrifice in order to "get ourselves back to the garden"? Do you feel the gains in Edenic bliss would compensate for such losses or not?

A LITTLE PARADISE POEM

Eugene Zamiatin

*We tells the story of the minutely organized United State, where all
the citizens are not individuals but only he-Numbers and she-Numbers
existing in identical glass apartments, their every action regulated by
the "Table of Hours." It is a community dedicated to the proposition
that freedom and happiness are incompatible: most citizens believe
their freedom to be more than a fair exchange for a high level of
material happiness.*

*Zamiatin devised this prophetic novel into forty "records" narrated
by citizen D-503. The following selection is taken from "Record
Eleven," in which State Poet R-13 explains the rationale behind the
development of the completely regulated (and mathematically based)
United State. The* Integral *to which the poet refers below is a
spaceship still under construction, the mission of which will be to
"subjugate to the grateful yoke of reason the unknown beings who live
on other planets, and who are perhaps still in the primitive stage
of freedom."*

"I am writing something for your *Integral.* Yes . . . I am!" He was
himself again: bubbling, sprinkling lips, words splashing like a fountain.

"You see, it is the ancient legend of paradise. That legend referred
to us of today, did it not? Yes. Only think of it a moment! There were
two in paradise and the choice was offered to them: happiness without
freedom, or freedom without happiness. No other choice. They, fools
that they were, chose freedom. Naturally, for centuries afterward they
longed for fetters, for the fetters of yore. This was the meaning of
their world weariness, *Weltschmerz.* For centuries! And only we found
a way to regain happiness. . . . No, listen, follow me! The ancient god
and we, side by side at the same table! Yes, we helped god to defeat
the devil definitely and finally. It was he, the devil, who led people to
transgression, to taste pernicious freedom—he, the cunning serpent.
And we came along, planted a boot on his head, and . . . squash! Done
with him! Paradise again! We returned to the simple-mindedness and

innocence of Adam and Eve. No more meddling with good and evil and all that; everything is simple again, heavenly, childishly simple! The Well-Doer, the Machine, the Cube, the giant Gas Bell, the Guardians—all these are good. All this is magnificent, beautiful, noble, lofty, crystalline, pure. For all this preserves our non-freedom, that is, our happiness. In our place, those ancients would indulge in discussions, deliberations, etc. They would break their heads trying to make out what was moral or immoral. But we . . . Well, in short, these are the highlights of my little paradise poem. What do you think of it?

Why does the poet R-13 argue that Adam and Eve were "fools" for choosing freedom? How much freedom are *you* willing to exchange for the "guaranteed happiness" of a carefully regulated society? What has man become in this new, automated society? In what sense is this a satire of the "back to Eden" theme reflected in works such as "Woodstock"?

A.D. 2267

John Frederick Nims

Once on the gritty moon (burnt earth hung far
In the black, rhinestone sky—lopsided star),
Two gadgets, with great fishbowls for a head,
Feet clubbed, hips loaded, shoulders bent. She said,
"Fantasies haunt me. A green garden. Two
Lovers aglow in flesh. The pools so blue!"
He whirrs with masculine pity, "Can't forget
Old superstitions? The earth-legend yet?"

What does the poet suggest man has evolved into by the year 2267? Do you think such a development is *literally* possible? In what respects is it *figuratively* probable? What sense of loss does the poet convey through the "haunting fantasies" of the she-gadget? What possible reason for such a loss is implied in the "masculine pity" displayed by the other gadget?

THE FIRST MURDER
(Genesis)

And Adam knew Eve his wife; and she conceived, and bore Cain, and said, "I have gotten a man from the Lord." And she again bore his brother Abel. And Abel was a keeper of sheep, but Cain was a tiller of the ground. And in process of time it came to pass that Cain brought of the fruit of the ground an offering unto the Lord. And Abel, he also brought of the firstlings of his flock and of the fat thereof. And the Lord had respect unto Abel and to his offering: but unto Cain and to his offering he had not respect. And Cain was very wroth, and his countenance fell.

And the Lord said unto Cain. "Why art thou wroth? And why is thy countenance fallen? If thou doest well, shalt thou not be accepted? And if thou doest not well, sin lieth at the door. And unto thee shall be his desire, and thou shalt rule over him."

And Cain talked with Abel his brother: and it came to pass, when they were in the field, that Cain rose up against Abel his brother, and slew him.

And the Lord said unto Cain, "Where is Abel thy brother?"

And he said, "I know not: am I my brother's keeper?"

And the Lord said, "What hast thou done? The voice of thy brother's blood crieth unto me from the ground. And now art thou cursed from the earth, which hath opened her mouth to receive thy brother's blood from thy hand. When thou tillest the ground, it shall not henceforth yield unto thee her strength; a fugitive and a vagabond shalt thou be in the earth."

And Cain said unto the Lord, "My punishment is greater than I can bear. Behold, thou hast driven me out this day from the face of the earth; and from thy face shall I be hid; and I shall be a fugitive and a vagabond in the earth; and it shall come to pass that every one that findeth me shall slay me."

And the Lord said unto him, "Therefore whosoever slayeth Cain, vengeance shall be taken on him sevenfold." And the Lord set a mark upon Cain, lest any finding him should kill him. And Cain went out from the presence of the Lord, and dwelt in the land of Nod, on the east of Eden.

[Genesis 4:1–16]

The biblical account of Cain's slaying of Abel does not clearly define *why* Cain was so angry with his brother. What do you suspect his motive was? When God asked Cain where his brother Abel was, Cain replied, "Am I my brother's keeper?" Why has this reply become so famous? We often refer to a person who is in constant trouble with the law as having "the mark of Cain." Why is this a misreading of the Cain story? What is the significance of this mark?

CAIN

Howard Nemerov

A field at the edge of a forest. Two altars, or fireplaces anyhow, one blackened and smoking, the other clean stone. To the second altar, enter Cain carrying vegetables.

CAIN:
> The corn is coming along,
> Tomatoes ripening up nicely, in a week
> There should be melons. The apples
> Are still green, but, then, after what happened
> It might be as well if apples were not mentioned.
> There is a good deal I don't understand
> About that story, often as I've heard it told.
> Mother doesn't like to discuss it, of course,
> And I suspect that Adam my father
> Is not entirely clear himself as to what happened,
> Though he wears a very wise expression.   (*Enter Abel.*)

ABEL:
> Well! My sacrifices accepted for the day, I see.
> And nothing more to be done for the moment.
> Not bad. But you, brother,
> I don't see any flames at your offering.
> It's blood and meat the Lord likes,
> Charred on the outside, red and juicy inside;

There's something unmanly about vegetables,
I always say. That's probably your trouble.

CAIN:

Go on, amuse yourself at my expense,
I guess you have the right, for certainly
God favors your offerings of meat,
And leaves my vegetables alone. He leaves
The flowers too, that I bring
Because they are lovely, a something extra
To ornament the altar, and do Him honor
—These lilies that are blooming now.

ABEL *(laughing)*:

You can't imagine the mighty God of All
Eating a lily! What God wants
Is strength. Strong men want strong meat.

CAIN:

If He made All, He made the lilies too.
And He can't be like a man.

ABEL:

I'm not arguing, I'm telling you,
It's simply a matter of fact.
The Lord has put His blessing on blood and meat.
Therefore He prefers me before you,
And I prosper greatly, and sit on the hillside
Watching my flocks, while you
Sweat in your vegetable patch.

CAIN:

You have to kill those poor little lambs.

ABEL:

Well, it's a man's work anyhow.

CAIN:

It's horrible. I've heard them bleat
Before you cut the throat, and I've seen
The fear dumb in their eyes. What must it be like,
I wonder, to die?

ABEL:

We can't tell, till one of us does.
I expect you'll be the first.

CAIN:

Me? Why me?

ABEL:

It's perfectly simple. Death is a punishment.
In dying we are punished for our sin.

CAIN:

Our sin? I haven't sinned. What have I done?

ABEL:

We have all sinned, and all will die.
But God's not respecting your offerings
Is a sign that you will be the first.

CAIN:

You sound rather pleased about it.

ABEL:

Do you suppose I want to be the first?
No, I am essentially a conservative person.
And I can see, looking at my lambs,
That dying's a grim business. I'm in no hurry.
It's only fit that you go first—you were born first.
Vegetarian!

CAIN:

I don't understand. What have I done
That was wrong, or you that was right?
Father and Mother began the fault,
I know the story as well as you do.

ABEL:

You don't accept life as it is, that's your trouble.
Things are the way they are, that's all.
They've been that way from the beginning.

CAIN:

Which isn't so very long ago.

ABEL:

And they will always be as they are.
Accept it, Cain. Face up to reality.

CAIN:

That's easy for a winner to say. *(Enter Adam and Eve.)*

CAIN and ABEL:

Father! Mother! *(They bow their heads.)*

ADAM:

That's right, respect. It's a proper respect
As from the children to the parents
That keeps the world going round. It's a fine day,
And life is what you make it, isn't that so?
And both boys working hard, yes, that's right.
"In the sweat of thy face shalt thou eat thy bread"
Is what He said to me, but it's not so bad
When the children sweat for the father's bread.

(He picks a tomato from Cain's altar and eats it.)

CAIN:

Father, that is my offering to the Lord.

ADAM:

Don't worry, I won't eat it all. Anyhow,
The Lord seems to prefer the flesh and fat
That Abel provides. I must say
That I agree. I'm eating this
Only to stave off hunger till mealtime.
Abel, I smell roast lamb. Good!

ABEL:

Yes, the Lord God has received the essence,
And we may eat whatever is left over.

CAIN:

It seems to me that everything is left except the smoke.

ABEL:

Don't talk of what you don't understand.

ADAM:

It is obvious, Cain, that you don't know
The first principle of sacrifice. It is
The divine effluvium of the beast that rises
To God in heaven, and does Him honor.
A spiritual essence Himself, He feeds on spirit.
The grosser parts are the leftovers of His meal,
Which we may eat, if we do so with humble hearts.

EVE:

Why doesn't He eat the divine effluvium
Of Cain's vegetables?

ABEL:

Whoever heard
Of burning vegetables? Our God
Is an eater of meat, meat, meat.

ADAM:

Mother, don't mix in the relations of man with God.
Remember what happened last time. *(There is a silence.)*

EVE:

It wasn't my fault. It was only a mistake.

ADAM:

A mistake to end all mistakes.

EVE:

You listened to me, wise as you are.

ADAM:

It proves the wisdom of my not doing so again.
He for God alone, and she for God in him;

Remember that, and there won't be any trouble.

CAIN:

    Sir, what really did happen last time,
    I mean in the Garden?

ABEL:

    What's past is past. Cain still believes
    There's something that he doesn't understand,
    Or that you haven't told us, which would make
    Some difference to his situation.

EVE *(to Cain):*

    My poor boy, my poor, dear boy, I too
    Go over it and over it in my mind, I too,
    Though what I did is said to be so dreadful,
    Feel that the Lord's way with me
    Was very arbitrary, to say the least.

ADAM:

    Woman, enough. You'll make us more trouble.

ABEL:

    And as for Cain, he should have the tact
    Not to pursue a subject which so evidently
    Causes his mother pain.

                      (to Cain) Also, our food is ready.
    You may do as you please about that slop of yours,
    But *this family* is going to eat.

(Cain sits to one side, the rest to the other. Cain starts eating a tomato.)

ADAM:

    Not, however, before properly rendering thanks
    To the Most High. Cain, have the decency
    To control your appetite until Abel
    Has sanctified our meal with prayer. Abel.

ABEL:

    Permit us, O Lord, this tender beast
    Slain in Thy Holy Name, Amen. *(All eat.)*

ADAM:

    Mm, good.

CAIN:

    Won't you let me have some? It smells good,
    And I would give you all this fruit.

ADAM:

    Dear boy, don't let us go all over this again.

It's not that we don't care for you personally,
But we simply cannot afford to offend the Lord.
If He does not respect your offering, Cain,
It would be presumptuous in us to do so.
If He means to separate you by this sign,
We must not disobey.

ABEL:

To each according to his labor, you know.

CAIN:

But I haven't done anything wrong—
As far as I'm aware, that is.

ADAM:

As far as you're aware, or we. Who knows
The hidden meaning of God's mysteries?
By the sign you are set off, and that's enough.

ABEL:

I'd set him further off. Suppose that God
In His displeasure should strike Cain
With fire from Heaven? I know that God
Can do whatever He will, but still
If we sit this close there might just be an accident.

CAIN *(moving a bit further away)*:

I don't want to be a danger to you, you all
Seem to understand things so much better than I do.
But what have I done wrong? Answer me that.

ADAM:

Ah, as to that, you would have to ask Him. *(He points upward.)*

CAIN:

Did He really speak to you, Himself—then?

ADAM:

He did indeed, yes. Your father has spoken with God.

CAIN:

What does He look like?

ADAM:

Oh, you don't really see Him, you know,
He doesn't have a form. There was a Voice.

EVE *(covering her ears)*:

Don't. Don't remind me. That Voice!

ADAM:

Mother, have more respect. We are talking
Of divine things. Besides, who was responsible
For His talking to us in that voice,

And saying what He said? Remember that,
Consider your sin, be quiet.

ABEL:

Cain thinks, because he is a gardener,
That he would have been at home in a Garden.
It's illogical, Cain, to suppose
The Garden of the Lord would be anything like yours.

CAIN:

Illogical, yes. Yet if I reason it out,
It does appear that God did once favor gardens,
Since, after all, He put our parents there.
And if I ask myself why He has turned against
Garden and gardener, I will have to answer
That what our parents did while they were there
Was the thing that changed His mind.

ADAM:

I will not have blasphemy, Cain,
And particularly not while we are at meat.
As for disrespect for your father,
I will not have that at any time. After all,
Your mother went through much suffering
To bring you into the world, while I
Labored to give you food and all good things.
For you to reward us with ingratitude
Proves, to my mind, a hidden fault in you,
And sufficiently explains why the All-Wise
Does not respect your offerings as Abel's;
Some wickedness, my boy, which is bringing you to sin.

EVE:

But truly, father, it was our fault.
It was my fault first, then it was yours.

ADAM:

We may have made an error of judgment.
Does Cain suppose he could have done better?
We tried our best to give you boys
A decent life and bring you up to be honest,
Industrious, pleasing in the sight of the Lord.
As a matter of fact, I am convinced
It was a piece of luck to have got out of that garden.
It was no place to bring up children in.
You would have had everything provided for you,
No need to learn the manly virtues,

The dignity of toil, the courage of independence.
No, Cain, hard work never hurt anybody.
What happened to us was the will of God,
Which shows He did not mean us to sit around
On our behinds in a garden all our lives,
But to get out in the world and become
The masters of it.

ABEL:

                 Inventors of the knife,
The wheel, the bow.

ADAM:

Sometimes I could bless that serpent!

EVE:

Stop! What dreadful things you are saying.
Shame, labor, and the pains of birth
The woman knows. Those are the fruits
That grew on the forbidden tree, and I,
The first to sin, was the first to know them.
I shall be the first to know death also.

ADAM:

Mother, don't excite yourself. What's done is done.
As for death, no need to talk of that, I hope,
For many years.

ABEL:

The little lambs are peaceful after death,
Mother. There's only a moment of fright,
And then it's over.

CAIN:

But there's that moment, that small moment.
A man might do anything, if he thought enough
How there's no way out but through that moment.
He might become wild, and run away,
Knowing there was nowhere to run, he might . . .

ABEL:

Might what?

CAIN:

Kill.

ABEL:

He might leave off babbling in that manner,
And remember he is a man, if not a very good one.

CAIN:

But if a man, even if not a very good one,

Is turned away by his God, what does he do?
Where does he go? What could he do
Worse than what is already done to him?
For there is God on the one hand,
And all the world on the other, and this man
Between them. Why should he care,
Seeing he cannot save himself?

ADAM:

These are dangerous thoughts, Cain.
That man might better think
Wherein he has offended.

(The sky darkens. Thunder is heard, and lightning seen.)

ABEL:

Aha! he's done it now, with his talk.
Did you think He would not have heard?
Did you consider the rest of us?

CAIN:

I only meant to ask.

ABEL:

You are being answered. *(He points to the sky.)*

ADAM:

I am afraid, Cain, that Abel is right.
I have faced up to God one time in my life,
It was enough. The coming storm
You brought down on yourself, and you must face
The consequences. I am sorry for you.
Eve, come. Come, Abel. We shall seek shelter elsewhere.

(They leave, and Cain stands alone. Lightning flashes, sounds of thunder, then a stillness.)

CAIN:

Ah, they are right. I am going to die,
And I deserve to die. As Abel said,
There is no argument, the uneasy fear
I feel in my stomach tells me I am wrong,
Am guilty of everything, everything,
Though I cannot say what it is. Lord!
Lord God! Master! I am a wicked man,
The thoughts of my heart are wicked

And I don't know why. Punish me, Lord,
Punish me, but do not let me die. *(Cain kneels.)*
THE VOICE OF GOD in the silence:
Cain.
Cain.
Cain.
CAIN:
Here I am.
GOD:
What do you want?
CAIN:
I want to know.
GOD:
Ask.
CAIN:
Why do You respect my brother's offerings and not mine?
GOD:
That is not the question you want to ask.
CAIN:
Why do You prefer Abel to me?
GOD:
That again is not it. You must ask to the end. *(A long silence.)*
CAIN:
Why are things as they are?
GOD:
I will debate it with you. Do you know
That things are as they are?
CAIN:
But—but they *are*, they just *are*. Besides,
My father says they are.
GOD:
Cain, I am your father.
CAIN:
Sir, as you say.
GOD:
Do you want things to be other than as they are?
CAIN:
I want my offering to be acceptable, Sir.
I want my offering to be preferred over Abel's.
I want to be respected even as he is now.
GOD:
Why do you trouble yourself about it, then?

The thing is easy. If you do well,
Will you not be accepted? And if you do not do well,
Look, sin lies at the door.

CAIN:

Sir, I do not understand.

GOD:

Cain, Cain, I am trying to tell you.
All things can be done, you must only
Do what you will. Things are as they are
Until you decide to change them,
But do not be surprised if afterward
Things are as they are again. What is to stop you
From ruling over Abel?

CAIN *(again, after a silence)*:

I do not know. *(Thunder.)*
I do not know. I said I do not know.
He is not there and I am alone.

(The sky clears, the light grows stronger.)

And this is Abel's knife, which he left here
In his hurry to escape the storm he hoped would slay me.
And that storm was God.
And this is the knife which cuts the throats
Of acceptable sacrifices. *(Enter Abel.)*

ABEL:

You're still alive. Surely the ways of the Lord
Are past understanding. Have you seen my knife?

CAIN *(still kneeling)*:

I have it here.

ABEL:

Throw it to me then. I'm still uneasy
About coming close to you.

CAIN:

I have spoken with God, Abel. If you want your knife,
Come over here and have it. God said things,
Abel, such as I never heard from you. He told me
About the will. Do what you will, He said.
And more than that, He said: You must
Do what you will. Abel, do you understand
That saying?

ABEL *(approaching):*
  The knife, I want the knife.
CAIN:
  Here, then. *(He rises, stabbing Abel, who falls.)*
  My sacrifices shall be acceptable.
ABEL:
  My God, what have you done? *(He dies.)*
CAIN *(standing over him):*
  I have done what I willed. I have changed
  The way things are, and the first man's death is done.
  It was not much, I have seen some of his lambs
  Die harder.
GOD *(speaking casually, conversationally, without thunder):*
  Do you find it good, what you've done? Or bad?
CAIN *(as though talking to himself):*
  Good? Bad? It was my will that I did.
  I do not know anything of good or bad.
GOD:
  Do you find that you have changed
  Things as they are?
CAIN *(staring at Abel):*
  There is this difference, certainly.
  And I have changed inside myself. I see now
  That a man may be the master here.
GOD:
  Like that man on the ground?
CAIN:
  A man. Myself.
GOD:
  How peaceful he is, lying there.
CAIN:
  That's true, I feel uneasy, myself.
  Abel, what have you to say to me now?
  Well, speak up.
GOD:
  He will not speak.
CAIN:
  He is very quiet now, considering
  How much he used to talk. How lonely
  Everything has become! Mother! Father! *(He shouts.)*

The Death of Abel (c. 1860) by Gustave Doré. THE NEW YORK PUBLIC LIBRARY PICTURE COLLECTION.

GOD:
  They will do to you as you have done to him.
CAIN:
  Then I must run away.
GOD:
  Where will you run?
CAIN:
  Anywhere, to be alone.
  There are no other people.
GOD:
  You're wrong about that. Everywhere
  Men are beginning, and everywhere they believe
  Themselves to be alone, and everywhere
  They are making the discovery of the conditions
  Under which they are as they are. One of these
  Discoveries has just been made, by you.
  You will be alone, but alone among many,
  Alone in every crowd.
CAIN:
  Seeing me set apart, they will kill me.
GOD:
  They would. But I have set my sign
  Upon your forehead, that recognizing you,
  Men will be afeared. Shunning you, scorning you,
  Blaming you, they may not kill you.
CAIN *(kneeling):*
  Lord God! You spoke, and I did not know.
GOD:
  I send you away, Cain. You are one
  Of my holy ones, discoverer of limits,
  Your name is the name of one of the ways,
  And you must bear it. You must bear
  The everlasting fear no one can stop,
  The everlasting life you do not want,
  The smell of blood forever on your hand.
  You are the discoverer of power, and you
  Shall be honored among men that curse you,
  And honored even in the moment of the curse.
  From your discovery shall proceed
  Great cities of men, and well defended,
  And these men, your descendants, shall make
  Weapons of war, and instruments of music,

Being drawn thereto by the nature of power;
But they will not be happy, and they will not know
Peace or any release from fear.

CAIN:

May I not die?

GOD:

Because of My sign, only you
May destroy yourself. And because of your fear,
You won't. For you have found
An idea of Me somewhat dangerous to consider,
And mankind will, I believe, honor your name
As one who has faced things as they are,
And changed them, and found them still the same.

CAIN:

If I were sorry, would you raise Abel up?

GOD:

No.

CAIN:

Then I am not sorry. Because You have saved me
From everything but the necessity of being me,
I say it is Your fault. None of this need have happened.
And even my mother's temptation by the serpent in the Garden
Would not have happened but for You; I see now,
Having chosen myself, what her choice must have been.

GOD:

Cain, I will tell you a secret.

CAIN:

I am listening.

GOD:

I was the serpent in the Garden.

CAIN:

I can believe that, but nobody else will.
I see it so well, that You are the master of the will
That works two ways at once, whose action
Is its own punishment, the cause
That is its own result. It will be pain to me
To reject You, but I do it, in Your own world,
Where everything that is will speak of You,
And I will be deaf.

GOD:

You do not reject Me. You cannot.

CAIN:

I do not expect it to be easy.

(after a silence)
I said: I do not expect it to be easy.
But He is gone, I feel His absence.
As, after the storm's black accent,
The light grows wide and distant again,
So He is gone. Of all He said to me,
Only one thing remains. I send you away,
He said: Cain, I send you away.
But where is *Away?* Is it where Abel is,
My brother, as lonely and still as that?

(Enter Adam and Eve; Cain turns away his face.)

ADAM *(at a distance):*
Was it the thunder, Abel, the lightning?

(Coming closer, he sees that Abel is on the ground.)

It can't be. There has been a mistake.
EVE:
Abel, my son, my lamb.

(She runs to the corpse and throws herself down.)

ADAM:
Monster! Unnatural child! Did you do this?
Lord God, let it not go unpunished,
Let it be swiftly visited.
CAIN *(still turned away):*
Suppose it was God that struck Abel down?
Cannot the Lord do as He will do?
ADAM:
Liar! I will never believe it, never.
CAIN:
Well, then, it was a lie. I did it.
But had it been the other way, and I
The brother lying there, would you not have said,
As I have heard you say so many times,
What the Lord does is well done?
ADAM:
Vicious boy! Have you not done enough?
Would you go on to stand against your father?
EVE:
Leave off, leave off. One son and the other son,

All that I had, all that I cared to have,
One son and the other son, and from the beginning
This was the end I carried, the end we lay together
Taking our pleasure for, is now accomplished.

CAIN:

I stand, it seems, alone. Neither against
Nor for father or mother or anything.

ADAM:

If the Lord God will not punish, I must.

EVE:

Leave off, leave off. All that we had
Is halved, and you would destroy the other half?
Abel my son and Cain my son. Old man,
It is your seed that from the beginning
Was set at odds. You ate the fruit
Of the tree of knowledge as well as I,
And sickened of it as well as I, and swelled with lust
As I swelled with the fruit of lust,
And have you yet no knowledge?

ADAM:

Woman, be quiet. This is not woman's work.

EVE:

Oh, fool, what else if not woman's work?
The fruit of the curse has ripened till it fell,
Can you refuse to swallow it? But you will swallow it,
I tell you, stone and all, one son and the other son.

ADAM:

Cain, I am an old man, but it comes to me
That I must do to you as you did to your brother.

EVE:

Fooled in the Garden, and fooled out of it!

CAIN (*turning his face to Adam, who falls back*):

Sir, you will do nothing. I am young and strong,
And I have the knife—but no, that's not it,
I do not want to stand against you, but I must.

ADAM:

There is a sign, a wound, there on your brow
Between the eyes. Cain, I am afraid of you
There is a terror written on your face.

CAIN:

And I am afraid of you. That is my fear
You see written upon me, that your fear answers to.

I am forbidden to be sorry for what I did,
Forbidden to pity you, forbidden to kiss
My mother's tears, and everywhere
In everything forbiden. I feel myself filled
With this enormous power that I do not want,
This force that tells me I am to go,
To go on, always to go on, to go away
And see you both, and this place, never again.

EVE:

My son, my only one, you won't go away?
I'll face the fear I see upon your face,
And you'll comfort me for what you did to me.

ADAM:

And stay me in my age? Cain, I accept it,
Though I shall never understand it, this
That you have done, this final thing
In a world where nothing seemed to end,
Is somehow the Lord God's doing. I fear you,
My son, but I will learn to still my fear,
If you will stay.

CAIN:

No. I would change things if I could.
I tried to change things once, and the change
Is as you see; we cannot change things back,
Which may be the only change worth having,
So the future must be full of fear, which I
Would spare you. If this is riddling talk,
Let it go by; or, to speak plainly,
I am afraid my fear would make me kill you
If I stayed here.

EVE:

This is the end
That we began with. Why should we not
Curse God and die?

ADAM:

Woman, be careful.

EVE:

I have been careful, full of care.
My son, my darling, why not kill us both?
It would be only what we did to you;
And that was only what was done to us.

CAIN:

    Mother, Mother, I must not hear you.
    You and I, we understand things alike,
    And that is curse enough, maybe. But he
    May have his own curse, which we
    Don't understand, that is, to go on,
    Into the darkness, into the light,
    Having the courage not to know
    That what I do to him is what he does to me,
    And both of us compelled, or maybe
    It is a blessing, the blindness of too much light
    That comes from staring at the sun.
                           Father,
    I'd bless you if I could, but I suspect
    That God believes in you.
    And now farewell,
    If that is possible; try not to remember me.

(Cain goes. The scene begins to darken.)

ADAM:

    Old woman, we are alone again, and the night
    Beginning to come down. Do you remember
    The first night outside the Garden?

EVE:

    We slept in the cold sparkle of the angel's sword,
    Having cried ourselves asleep.

ADAM:

    If we went back, do you think, and stood
    At the gate, and said plainly, kill us
    Or take us back, do you think . . . ?

EVE:

    No.

ADAM:

    You're right, we couldn't any more go back
    Than you could be my rib again, in my first sleep.
    The water in the rivers running out of Eden,
    Where must that water be now, do you think?

EVE:

    It must be elsewhere, somewhere in the world;
    And yet I know those rivers glitter with water still.

Abel my son and my son Cain, all that we had is gone.
Old as we are, we come to the beginning again.

ADAM:

Doing as we would, and doing as we must. . . .
The darkness is so lonely, lonelier now
Than on the first night, even, out of Eden.
Having what we've had, and knowing what we know. . . .

EVE:

What have we had, and what do we know?
The years are flickering as a dream, in which
Our sons are grown and gone away. Husband,
Take courage, come to my arms, husband and lord.
It is the beginning of everything.

ADAM:

Must we take the terrible night into ourselves
And make the morning of it? Again?
Old woman, girl, bride of the first sleep,
In pleasure and in bitterness all ways
I love you till it come death or daylight.

How does Nemerov generate sympathy for Cain? Discuss Nemerov's characterizations of Cain, Abel, Adam, and Eve. What do we learn about each of these characters in the family's discussion of the Garden of Eden? Why does Adam feel that it "was a piece of luck to have got out of that garden"? What is the question that God feels Cain wants to ask? What conclusion does Cain come to? What reasons does Cain have for killing Abel? What does God mean when he says that He "was the serpent in the Garden"? In a sense, this is a play of discovery, of Cain's "quest." What does he discover about his world and about himself? What is the significance of Adam's final lines?

BAR-ROOM MATINS

Louis MacNeice

Popcorn peanuts clams and gum:
We whose Kingdom has not come
Have mouth like men but still are dumb

Who only deal with Here and Now
As circumstances may allow:
The sponsored programme tells us how.

And yet the preachers tell the pews
What man misuses God can use:
Give us this day our daily news

That we may hear behind the brain
And through the sullen heat's migraine
The atavistic voice of Cain:

'Who entitled you to spy
From your easy heaven? Am I
My brother's keeper? Let him die.'

And God in words we soon forget
Answers through the radio set:
'The curse is on his forehead yet.'

Mass destruction, mass disease:
We thank thee, Lord, upon our knees
That we were born in times like these

When with doom tumbling from the sky
Each of us has an alibi
For doing nothing—Let him die.

Let him die, his death will be
A drop of water in the sea,
A journalist's commodity.

Pretzels crackers chips and beer:
Death is something that we fear
But it titillates the ear.

Anchovy almond ice and gin:
All shall die though none can win;
Let the Untergang begin—

Die the soldiers, die the Jews,
And all the breadless homeless queues.
Give us this day our daily news.

Why is the "atavistic voice of Cain" so appropriate to the situation satirized in this poem? What is the modern answer to Cain's famous question, "Am I my brother's keeper?"? What purpose does death serve for those offering up their "bar-room matins"? What specifically is MacNeice satirizing in this poem?

THE DELUGE

(Genesis)

And it came to pass, when men began to multiply on the face of the earth, and daughters were born unto them, that the sons of God saw the daughters of men that they were fair; and they took them wives of all which they chose. And the Lord said, "My spirit shall not always strive with man, for that he also is flesh: yet his days shall be a hundred and twenty years."

There were giants in the earth in those days; and also after that, when the sons of God came in unto the daughters of men, and they bore children to them, the same became mighty men which were of old, men of renown.

And God saw that the wickedness of man was great in the earth, and that every imagination of the thoughts of his heart was only evil continually. And it repented the Lord that he had made man on the earth, and it grieved him at his heart. And the Lord said, "I will destroy man whom I have created from the face of the earth; both man, and beast, and the creeping thing, and the fowls of the air; for it repenteth me that I have made them."

But Noah found grace in the eyes of the Lord. Noah was a just man and perfect in his generations, and Noah walked with God. And Noah begot three sons, Shem, Ham, and Japheth.

And God said unto Noah, "The end of all flesh is come before me; for the earth is filled with violence through them; and, behold, I will destroy them with the earth. Make thee an ark of gopher wood; rooms shalt thou make in the ark, and shalt pitch it within and without with pitch. And this is the fashion which thou shalt make it of: the length of the ark shall be three hundred cubits, the breadth of it fifty cubits, and the height of it thirty cubits. A window shalt thou make to the ark, and in a cubit shalt thou finish it above; and the door of the ark shalt thou set in the side thereof; with lower, second, and third stories shalt thou make it.

"And, behold, I, even I, do bring a flood of waters upon the earth, to destroy all flesh, wherein is the breath of life, from under heaven; and every thing that is in the earth shall die. But with thee will I establish my covenant; and thou shalt come into the ark, thou, and thy sons, and thy wife, and thy sons' wives with thee. And of every living thing of all flesh, two of every sort shalt thou bring into the ark, to keep them alive with thee; they shall be male and female. Of fowls after their kind, and of cattle after their kind, of every creeping thing of the earth after his kind, two of every sort shall come unto thee, to keep them alive. And take thou unto thee of all food that is eaten, and thou shalt gather it to thee; and it shall be for food for thee, and for them."

Thus did Noah; according to all that God commanded him, so did he.

And Noah went in, and his sons, and his wife, and his sons' wives with him, into the ark, because of the waters of the flood. Of clean beasts, and of beasts that are not clean, and of fowls, and of every thing that creepeth upon the earth, there went in two and two unto Noah into the ark, the male and the female, as God had commanded Noah. And it came to pass after seven days that the waters of the flood were upon the earth. In the six hundredth year of Noah's life, in the second month, the seventeenth day of the month, the same day were all the fountains of the great deep broken up, and the windows of heaven were opened. And the rain was upon the earth forty days and forty nights.

And the waters prevailed, and were increased greatly upon the earth; and the ark went upon the face of the waters. And the waters prevailed exceedingly upon the earth; and all the high hills, that were under the whole heaven, were covered. Fifteen cubits upward did the waters prevail; and the mountains were covered. And all flesh died that moved upon the earth, both of fowl, and of cattle, and of beast, and of every creeping thing that creepeth upon the earth, and every man. All in whose nostrils was the breath of life, of all that was in the dry land, died.

And God remembered Noah, and every living thing, and all the cattle that was with him in the ark: and God made a wind to pass over the earth, and the waters assuaged. The fountains also of the deep and the windows of heaven were stopped, and the rain from heaven was restrained; and the waters returned from off the earth continually: and after the end of the hundred and fifty days the waters were abated. And the ark rested in the seventh month, on the seventeenth day of the month, upon the mountains of Ararat. And the waters decreased continually until the tenth month: in the tenth month, on the first day of the month, were the tops of the mountains seen.

And it came to pass at the end of forty days that Noah opened the window of the ark which he had made: and he sent forth a raven, which went forth to and fro, until the waters were dried up from off the earth. Also he sent forth a dove from him, to see if the waters were abated from off the face of the ground; but the dove found no rest for the sole of her foot, and she returned unto him into the ark, for the waters were on the face of the whole earth: then he put forth his hand, and took her, and pulled her in unto him into the ark. And he stayed yet other seven days; and again he sent forth the dove out of the ark; and the dove came in to him in the evening; and, lo, in her mouth was an olive leaf plucked off: so Noah knew that the waters were abated from off the earth. And he stayed yet other seven days, and sent forth the dove, which returned not again unto him any more.

And it came to pass in the six hundredth and first year, in the first month, the first day of the month, the waters were dried up from off the earth: and Noah removed the covering of the ark, and looked, and, behold, the face of the ground was dry. And in the second month, on the seven and twentieth day of the month, was the earth dried.

And God spoke unto Noah, saying, "Go forth of the ark, thou, and thy wife, and thy sons, and thy sons' wives with thee. Bring forth with thee every living thing that is with thee, of all flesh, both of fowl, and of cattle, and of every creeping thing that creepeth upon the earth; that they may breed abundantly in the earth, and be fruitful, and multiply upon the earth."

And Noah went forth, and his sons, and his wife, and his sons' wives with him. Every beast, every creeping thing, and every fowl, and whatsoever creepeth upon the earth, after their kinds, went forth out of the ark.

And Noah builded an altar unto the Lord; and took of every clean heart, "I will not again curse the ground any more for man's sake; for altar.

And the Lord smelled a sweet savour; and the Lord said in his heart, "I will not gain curse the ground any more for man's sake; for the imagination of man's heart is evil from his youth; neither will I again smite any more every thing living, as I have done. While the earth remaineth, seedtime and harvest, and cold and heat, and summer and winter, and day and night shall not cease."

And God blessed Noah and his sons, and said unto them, "Be fruitful, and multiply, and replenish the earth. And the fear of you and the dread of you shall be upon every beast of the earth, and upon every fowl of the air, upon all that moveth upon the earth, and upon all the fishes of the sea; into your hand are they delivered. Every moving thing that liveth shall be meat for you; even as the green herb have I given you all things. But flesh with the life thereof, which is the blood thereof, shall ye not eat. And surely your blood of your lives will I require; at the hand of every beast will I require it, and at the hand of man; at the hand of every man's brother will I require the life of man. Whoso sheddeth man's blood, by man shall his blood be shed: for in the image of God made he man."

And God spoke unto Noah, and to his sons with him, saying, "And I, behold, I establish my covenant with you, and with your seed after you; and with every living creature that is with you, of the fowl, of the cattle, and of every beast of the earth with you; from all that go out of the ark, to every beast of the earth. And I will establish my covenant with you; neither shall all flesh be cut off any more by the waters of a flood; neither shall there any more be a flood to destroy the earth."

And God said, "This is the token of the covenant which I make between me and you and every living creature that is with you, for perpetual generations: I do set my bow in the cloud, and it shall be for a token of a covenant between me and the earth. And it shall come to pass, when I bring a cloud over the earth, that the bow shall be seen in the cloud: and I will remember my covenant, which is between me and you and every living creature of all flesh; and the waters shall no more become a flood to destroy all flesh. And the bow shall be in the cloud; and I will look upon it, that I may remember the everlasting covenant between God and every living creature of all flesh that is upon the earth."

And God said unto Noah, "This is the token of the covenant, which I have established between me and all flesh that is upon the earth."

[*Genesis 6:1–8, 9b–10, 12–22; 7:7–12, 18–22; 8:1–9:17*]

NOAH

(from Act I)

André Obey

HAM. (*To* NOAH) Now, are you going to explain?
NOAH. (*His voice vibrating*) Yes!

ALL. Ah!

NOAH. I'll tell you everything. It's a great secret, a terrible secret. It has weighed on my tongue and on my heart for months—for a year — I had no right to unburden myself to you. But today—

JAPHET. Sshh!

NOAH. Eh?

JAPHET. *(In a low voice)* Someone's hiding right over there.

ALL. Where?

JAPHET. Sshh! There. *(He points off* L.*)* In the bushes. *(Something WHISTLES over the stage.)*

THE THREE BOYS. An arrow!

NOAH. Women to the rear! (MAMA *and the* GIRLS *retreat toward the ark. Another WHISTLING.)*

THE THREE BOYS. Another!

NOAH. To the ship! (ALL *move forward the ramp.)*

(A SHOUT offstage. Then A MAN, *a sort of hunter, with a savage face, runs in from the* L., *stops short in the* C. *of the stage, plants himself firmly, and points a spear at* NOAH.*)*

THE MAN. *Stop!—Stop—Stop! (To the* GIRLS, *who are moving up ramp)* Well, you floozies, are you deaf? One move and I nail the old gent to the wall of his house.

JAPHET. *(Trying to drag his* BROTHERS*)* Get him!

MAMA. Don't budge!

MAN. Watch out, you little rooster!

NOAH. Quiet, Japhet, quiet. He'd hit you.

MAN. I sure will.

MAMA *and the* YOUNGSTERS. Bandit!

NOAH. Silence. *(Mutterings from the* YOUNGSTERS.*)* Now, that's enough! *(To the* MAN*)* Put your spear down; you'll tire yourself out. What do you want?

MAN. I seen you. I seen you. You sorcerer. Talking to the animals. Swiping a cow from Mardocheus. Playing with the bears and the lions and tigers, not to mention the elephants. I seen you. The whole village is going to know. I'll tell them. Sorcerer! Sorcerer!

THE THREE BOYS. Stop it!

MAN. You weren't in on it. All you have to do is shut up. What's more, the animals are in there. *(He points to the ark)* They've been scampering up here in droves. That's where they are—in there! (MAMA *and the* YOUNGSTERS *laugh. The* MAN *rushes to the ark and beats on it with his fist. ROARING from the animals.)*

MAMA *and* YOUNGSTERS. *(Frightened)* Oh!

MAN. Hahaha! Who's laughing now? Ah, he's all very sweet and gentle but he does plenty of tricks when you ain't lookin'! He's bad. He's jealous. He never could make anything with his hands. He's a menace to the whole country.

MAMA. Be quiet!

MAN. You know what? This drought that's been frying us for three months, that nobody's never seen nothing like before, that'll knock us all dead with our mouths open this winter—that's him. He done it! He's the one!

NOAH. Aren't you a little bit out of your mind?

MAN. You done it! There! We all got together! We took a vote. And we all voted alike—unanimous—that it's all your fault.

NOAH. Oh, but—

MAN. Get this: I'm on what you call a mission. The head man says to me, "watch that old guy. He acts stupid but he knows all the tricks. Everything that's happened to us—he started them."

MAMA. Oh, Noah, if they think that, that's terrible!

NOAH. Ssshh! Ssshh!

MAN. You look in the air like this— *(He imitates* NOAH *praying)* And right away it gets hotter, all the time hotter. I was watching you. I seen you doing your mugging. *(He imitates* NOAH*)* I was lying on the ground, and it's hot like a grate.

THE YOUNGSTERS. *(In a low voice)* Oh!

MAN. All right, now you got to pay for it. Yeah, you got to come with me. But I don't need all of you. The head'll do. *(He leaps toward* NOAH. MAMA *and the* GIRLS *scream. The* BOYS *line up in front of* NOAH.*)*

NOAH. Sssh. *(He steps in front of them* ALL *and smiles)* What a beast! *(A pause)* The drought— *(He half turns toward his family)* He hoped it would open their eyes; that they'd say to themselves, "It isn't possible. It's a judgment from Heaven." I told them that myself. I sang it in every key. They laughed in my face. They spit on me. They threw stones at me.

MAMA *and* YOUNGSTERS. Yes.

NOAH. Didn't I tell them enough?

MAMA *and* YOUNGSTERS. Oh, yes.

NOAH. I really told them often enough?

MAMA *and the* YOUNGSTERS. Oh, yes, yes, yes.

NOAH. *(Turning toward the* MAN*)* What a beast! To think they're all like you! Lazy! Lying! Wanton! Thieving! *(*MAN *sneers.)* And on top of that, sneering and drunk like that one!

MAN. *(Blowing a berry, probably)* Aw, you old fool. You old ass.

NOAH *(Walking up to him)* Tell me, my good fellow, can you swim?

MAN. What?

NOAH. I asked if you could swim.

MAN. What's it to you?

NOAH. Come now, yes or no. Can you swim?

MAN. Sure.

NOAH. Can you swim a long time?

MAN. Absolutely!

NOAH. You'll have to swim a long time—a terribly long time. So long that it might be better if you couldn't swim at all. Then it would be over sooner.

MAN. Over?

NOAH. That's it; finished.

MAN. What's going to be finished?

NOAH. Everything! You! Your relatives! Your friends! The town! All the towns! This forest! All the trees and the animals, and the men—all in the water! Under the water! With your sins like stones around your necks.

MAN. *(Bending double)* Hahahahaha!

NOAH. *(Bending double too)* Hahahahahahaha!

MAN. Hahahahahaha!

NOAH. It's going to rain. Rain! More than that, it's going to—ah—rain! *(The* MAN, *the* YOUNGSTERS *and* MAMA *raise their eyes to the sky.)*

MAN. Hahahahaha!

HAM. *(To* SHEM, *under his breath)* Has Father got a fever? The sky was never so clear.

NOAH. A rain such as there's never been before. A drenching, a bath, a waterfall! A storm of water! A fury of water! Tempests will scream endlessly through the air. A great wind will yell night and day over the world, like an immense black curtain ripped by lightning. Fish will play in the trees. On the mountain tops, instead of flocks of eagles there will be schools of sharks. And the drowned with their arms outstretched will roll over and over, down and down and down. He told me so.

MAN. Who?

NOAH. God.

MAN. Who's that?

NOAH. God.

MAN. Oh, yeah?

NOAH. *(Louder)* God.

MAN. Sure, sure.

NOAH. *(Very loud)* Blessed God! (MAMA *and* YOUNGSTERS *drop to their knees.)*

MAN. Hahahaha! *(He stutters with glee)* God! Blessed God!—Dear, good, kind— *(He stops short. His hands go to his forehead. The* LIGHT *dims.)*

NOAH. Hah! Did you feel that, my boy? You felt the first drop. *(Savagely)* Right on your head, between the eyes, like an arrow. A perfect shot. (MAMA *and* YOUNGSTERS *rise, trembling.)*

MAN. Oh, you think so? Well, it was a sparrow.

NOAH. And that? *(The* MAN's *hand goes to the back of his neck.)* I suppose that was a nightingale? And that? *(The* MAN's *hand covers his eyes.)* A robin, maybe? *(The* MAN *stretches out his hands and quickly draws them in again.)* And those. A brace of pigeons?

MAMA *and* YOUNGSTERS. Oh!

NOAH. Dance, my good man, dance! *(And the* MAN *dances as if he were trying to avoid a cloud of arrows.)* Fire, O Lord! Pierce this vile target through and through with all Your might!

MAMA *and* YOUNGSTERS. *(Every hand extended)* It's raining, raining raining! *(Pantomime of* YOUNGSTERS *seeking the rain with every gesture around the* MAN, *whose every gesture dodges the rain. The* LIGHT *is growing dim.)*

NOAH. Strike those evil eyes. That prying nose. Those ears. Nail up that lewd mouth whose thread of insults You cut off as with a sword. Pierce the hands which were never raised to You. The feet that strayed. The glutton's belly. O God, split that wicked heart. Fire, fire, King of Archers!

MAN. *(Sinks down, still warding off the rain with both hands)* Help! Help! It's burning— *(The* LIGHT *grows dimmer.)*

MAMA. *(Her hands stretched to the rain)* It's cool like an evening breeze.

THE YOUNGSTERS. *(Their hands outstretched)* Like an evening breeze.

MAMA. Like the blue of heaven.

THE YOUNGSTERS. Like the blue of heaven.

MAMA. Like the laughter of angels.

THE YOUNGSTERS. The laughter of angels.

MAN. *(On his knees)* Help! Help! Help! Help! (THUNDER *rolls.)*

NOAH. We're off! Into the Ark, my good crew! Heavy weather tonight! Go into our home. Into the bark of God! You first, Mama. Ada! Sella! Norma! Shem! Ham! Japhet! And sing, my children, all together! *(A clap of* THUNDER.*)*

(The CHORUS *is singing in unison.* NOAH *goes up last. The storm*

rages. It is completely dark. The ANIMALS *timidly peer out of hatch-ways.)*

MAN. Help me! Help me! Help me! *(The* SINGING *spreads through the ark.)*

CURTAIN

This brief excerpt from Obey's full-length play illustrates the extent to which a dramatist is able to create convincing characterizations as opposed to the brief character sketches found in many biblical accounts. What effect do Obey's characterizations of Noah and the Man have on the reader? In general, what might an author hope to accomplish by recreating and elaborating on a famous biblical tale? Nemerov's *Cain* is also a dramatic reinterpretation of a Genesis story. What differences in tone and mood do you detect between the two works? What are the differences in the way each author draws on the familiar biblical material? Consider these differences in light of what you think is the underlying message or purpose of each play.

===

NOAH

Herman Hagedorn

It's going to rain," said Noah. His friend laughed.
    "You're always saying it's going to rain," he said.
"The earth is brick and dust and you talk of a raft.
    You're getting old. There's something loose in your head."

"It's going to rain," said Noah, with bleak eyes
    That saw nothing, not even a friend's disdain.
"It's going to rain, and the rivers are going to rise,
    I don't know when. But it's going, it's going to rain."

"You're drunk," said his friend. "I was, but I'm sober now."
   "You're cracked." "I was, but I seem to have mended my brain.
The times were all wheels and dust, but now, somehow,
   There are no more wheels and the dust is calling the rain.

"It's going to rain. The clouds will come over the peak
   And the dust will run like an antelope over the plain,
And the dark will cover the sun and the wind will speak,
   And drop and drop like thunder will come the rain.

"And the rain will fall and fall, and the waters rise
   And smother the house and the harvest and leave no trace,
And dissolve the mountains themselves before your eyes
   And inch up your body at last and cover your face.

"It's going to rain. The clouds will come over the peak
   But it can't be long; the wind has an angry note.
And I'm out to cut some lumber and call my men
   In from the fields to lay me a keel for a boat."

"You are a fool, Noah." "I was a fool.
   I do not feel wise now; only somehow sane.
I have walked alone and gone to the Voice to school
   And I am building a boat against the rain."

"I shan't go build a boat. What if it rains?
   There has been rain before. The waters rose.
The waters fell, the good sun shone again.
   The worst nor'easter has a crimson close."

"There will be sunrise after many days,
   But not for those who build themselves no ark.
The fields will sparkle and the peaks will blaze,
   But not the eyes of drowned men in the dark.

"There will be sunrise and a world to make
   New with remembered lore, and fires to light
From old fires loved and tended for hope's sake;
   But first there will be rain, there will be night.

Noah Building the Ark (c. 1510–11) by Raphael. Loggia of the Vatican, Rome.
ALINARI-ART REFERENCE BUREAU.

> "Get lumber and build your arks, each to his need!
>   Unchain the plough. You will not harvest grain.
> It's going to rain," cried Noah. "Won't anyone heed?
>   Build you an ark! I tell you, it's going to rain."

Is this merely a retelling of part of the biblical story? Does knowing
that the poem was written around 1940 suggest a particular historical
focus? In this light, what does the poet mean when he urges
everyone to "build your arks, each to his need"? What "ark" might
you "build" in time of crisis?

DIDN'T IT RAIN

(A Spiritual)

Chorus

> Now, didn't it rain, chillun,
> God's gonna destroy this world with water,
> Now didn't it rain, my Lord,
> Now didn't it rain, rain, rain.

Well, it rained forty days and it rained forty nights,
There wasn't no land nowhere in sight,
God sent a raven to carry the news,
He histe his wings and away he flew.

Chorus

Well, it rained forty days and forty nights without stoppin',
Noah was glad when the rain stopped a-droppin'.
God sent Noah a rainbow sign,
Says, "No more water, but fire next time."

Chorus

They knocked at the window and they knocked at the door,
They cried, "O Noah, please take me on board."
Noah cried, "You're full of sin,
The Lord's got the key and you can't get in."

Chorus

THE CITIES ARE BURNING*

Reverend Frederick D. Kirkpatrick

Lord, you know these cities are burning
All over the U.S.A. Yes—
    These cities are burning now
    All over the U.S.A.
    Yes, you know if these white folks don't settle pretty soon
    We all goin' to wake up in Judgment Day.
You know, God told Noah about it—
'Bout a rainbow sign
There'll be no more water
But there'll be fire the next time.
    The Bible's fulfillin' now
    All over the U.S.A.
    Yes, you know if these white folks don't settle up soon—the
        U.S.A.—
    We all goin' to wake up in Judgment Day.
      Yeah!
You know, the first was in Los Angeles
In a section they call Watts
Then Newark, New Jersey, New York, and eighty more cities
All began to rock.
    Those cities are burning
    All over the U.S.A.
    Yes, you know if these white folks don't settle up soon
    We all goin' to wake up in Judgment Day.
You know Our Father which art in Heaven
White man owed me a hundred dollars
And he didn't give me but seven
Hallowed be Thy Name, Thy Kingdom come
Hadn't taken that seven
You know I wouldn't have gotten none.
    That's why these cities are burning

All over the U.S.A.
The only solution I see to this whole thing
Is non-violence through Martin Luther King.

This apocalyptic vision might be more suitable placed with the final book of the Bible, Revelation, to which the spiritual "Didn't It Rain" points: "God sent Noah a rainbow sign, Says no more water, but fire next time." What is the "fire" Reverend Kirkpatrick is warning us about? In what ways is the cause of this destruction similar to that of Noah's time? What kind of "ark" do you suspect Reverend Kirkpatrick would recommend we "build" to save the world from such destruction?

A BOY'S HEAD

Miroslav Holub

In it there is a spaceship
and a project
for doing away with piano lessons.

And there is
Noah's ark,
which shall be first.

And there is
an entirely new bird,
an entirely new hare,
an entirely new bumblebee.

There is a river
that flows upward.

There is a multiplication table.

There is anti-matter.

And it just cannot be trimmed.

I believe
that only what cannot be trimmed
is a head.

There is much promise
in the circumstance
that so many people have heads.

What makes Noah's ark an appropriate symbol for the poet to place "first" in a boy's head? Why is it so important that a head "cannot be trimmed"? What "promise" is there in the fact that "so many people have heads"? In what sense does the poem present a "beginning"? In what respect might it be appropriate as an introduction to the following unit, *Of Courage and Dreams?*

UNIT 2

OF COURAGE AND DREAMS

The Youthful David (1448) by Andrea del Castagno. NATIONAL GALLERY OF ART, WASHINGTON, D. C.: WIDENER COLLECTION.

UNIT 2

OF COURAGE AND DREAMS

According to the Old Testament, the God of Israel was the God of destiny, one who directed human events to achieve an ultimate purpose or set design of history. His will was to be carried out through a contractual arrangement with the Israelites in which both He and His "chosen people" had rights and responsibilities. The Israelites were to worship God, obey His commandments, and live righteously; God was to make of them a "great nation." He would provide for the righteous man, give him victory over his enemies, even forgive him if he transgressed, provided he came with a penitent heart. Man's willingness to trust in a God who would adhere to the terms of a covenant was a new concept at the time it first arose. Babylonians, for example, felt themselves at the mercy of a capricious and arbitrary god. "What is good in one's sight is evil for a god," they bewailed in their wisdom literature. "What is bad in one's own mind is good for a god."

The great historical narratives of the Old Testament take place primarily during the second millennium B.C., a period which was spanned by the founding and growth of the Hebrew nation under the patriarchs Abraham, Isaac, and Jacob and by the consolidation of the nation's greatness under the Israelite kings David and his son Solomon. Throughout this thousand-year period, it was the consummate courage, vision, and faith of leaders such as Abraham, Isaac, Joseph, Moses, Deborah, and David that managed to keep the people united in the face of severe hardships and suffering and to inspire them to uphold the terms of the covenant. The biblical selections in this unit represent some of the highlights of the careers of these leaders; an attempt has been made to focus in on the repeated emphasis placed by the biblical authors on the courage and dreams of these men and women as they led their people in the name of their God.

The events recounted in these legendary narratives can be viewed loosely as a continuous cycle in which the covenant between God and His chosen people is perpetually being made, broken, and renewed. In a sense, the series of events can be viewed as the continuation of that same cycle of sin and redemption that began with the Fall in the opening chapters of Genesis.

The covenant was first established between God and Abram (later renamed Abraham, or "father of nations"), a simple herdsman called by God nearly four thousand years ago to be the founder and first leader of the Hebrews:

> Now the Lord said to Abram: "Get thee out of thy country, and from thy kindred, and from thy father's house, unto a land that I will show thee: and I will make of thee a great nation, and I will bless thee, and curse him that curseth thee: and in thee shall all families of the earth be blessed."
>
> [Genesis 12:1–3]

God tests the strength of Abraham's obedience to the covenant when He commands the Hebrew to take Isaac, the son of his old age, up to the mountain top to offer him as a sacrifice. Abraham obeys God's command unflinchingly. To reward his loyalty and faith, an angel of the Lord stops the sacrifice before it can be carried out and relates to Abraham the words of the Lord in which His side of the covenant is reaffirmed—that through Isaac, Abraham was to become the "father of nations."

The remainder of Genesis is devoted to Isaac's son Jacob, through whom the covenant is reaffirmed, and to the early flourishing of the Hebrew nation, which saw the gradual spreading of the tribes into Egypt under the leadership of the twelve sons of Jacob (renamed Israel, or "one who struggled with God"). The most famous of these sons were Joseph, whose courage and faith and ability to interpret dreams enabled him to rise to second-in-command in Egypt and to become the instrument of salvation for the brothers who had betrayed him.

The next great leader of the Hebrews to emerge is Moses, whose story is recounted in the books of Exodus, Leviticus, Numbers, and Deuteronomy. Here again the cycle established in Genesis is repeated: the covenant is reestablished, frequently broken, only to be renewed once more. During the gap of about three hundred years that occurs between the end of Genesis and the beginning of Exodus, a period during which the covenant is seemingly lost sight of and forgotten, the Hebrews fall under the bondage of the Egyptians. Moses, a Hebrew who had been raised by Egyptian royalty, is confronted by a voice speaking out of a burning bush which reaffirms the covenant between Yahweh, the God of Israel, and His chosen people. Moses is persuaded that he is the one to deliver the Hebrews from their bondage and to lead them into the Promised Land. As proof of His power and concern, the God of Israel inflicts upon the Egyptians a series of ten plagues, the last of which results in the death of the Egyptian firstborn at the hands of the angel of death passing over the land.

Moses' subsequent leading of the Israelites out of bondage and their miraculous deliverance at the Red Sea may be considered the central event of the Old Testament, probably as significant for the Jews as Jesus' resurrection is for Christians. Molding these former Hebrew slaves into a powerful new nation was to be no simple task, however. Whenever the going became difficult, the Israelites would complain that they were better off as slaves back in Egypt.

Despite their constant fears and murmurings, the covenant was ultimately formalized in the giving of the law to Moses on Mount Sinai. Nevertheless the people continued to violate the terms of the agreement, falling into idol worship, constant complaint, and even open rebellion. Only Moses' determined mediation for the Israelites, during which he reminded God of His covenantal obligation to His chosen people, spared the faithless Israelites from being consumed by the wrath of their God. When finally the people did reach Canaan, the "promised land," Moses was not with them, for in a moment of weakness he had wavered in his faith, and God barred him from entering Canaan. He died on Mount Pisgah shortly before the people left the wilderness, having been granted only a glimpse of the land flowing with "milk and honey."

After Moses' death Joshua assumed the leadership of the Israelites and brought them into the Promised Land. Once again the people fell into idolatry, forgetting the demands of the covenant, for which faithlessness God delivered them into the hands of spoilers to punish them, as is told in the Book of Judges. Several times God responded to their groanings and words of repentance and raised up judges to deliver them from their enemies. One of the most colorful of these was Deborah, under whose leadership the Israelites rose up to defeat the Canaanites who had oppressed them for twenty years. Her efforts were aided by Jael, one of the unsung heroines of the Old Testament, a young woman whose courage and visionary sense of mission in the service of Deborah and God enabled her to slay Sisera, the Canaanite leader who had fled to her tent for sanctuary.

Gideon, Jephthah, and Samson were among the judges to follow Deborah's inspired leadership of the Hebrews, but the people began to grow impatient with their situation (primarily that of a loose confederation of twelve tribes bound together by little more than their faith in one God). They demanded a king of Samuel, whose sons had grown corrupt as judges over them. Samuel annointed Saul as king, but the latter's lack of obedience to God's will soon led to his banishment from God's grace. David, a young shepherd boy, was secretly annointed to succeed him—the same David who shortly thereafter revealed the magnitude of his courage and faith by single-handedly defeating the Philistine giant Goliath. After David became king, Israel grew to unprecedented greatness and became the most powerful empire in the Near East.

Jerusalem, which David selected as the capital of Israel, was built up into a splendid city under the rule of David's son Solomon (treated more fully in Unit 3), whose wealth and wisdom gave him greater power than any other ruler of the time. It was during his reign, however, that Israel's fortunes became most threatened, as Solomon allowed his love of luxury and of pagan women to turn his mind from the ways of the Lord, leading to the ultimate division and Babylonian captivity of the once great kingdom.

Writers today have drawn widely on the legends set forth in these biblical tales of courage and dreams. By elaborating upon the bare essentials of plot, theme, and characterizations so typical of biblical narrative style, they have created poems, stories, and dramas filled with psychological depth and insight that, while sometimes purposefully deviating from the thrust of the original story, are often highly relevant to the concerns of our own time and place. For example, unlike the Abraham of Genesis whose thoughts and feelings are not made accessible to the reader, the Abraham of Roberta Kalechofsky's short story "Abraham and Isaac" is depicted as having serious doubts about his mission; the Isaac of the story battles desperately to fight off his would-be sacrificer, his silent submission in the biblical version transmitted into a bloodcurdling scream as Abraham prepares to lunge at him with his knife. The doubts and terrors experienced by both characters in the modern story are never totally resolved, and Abraham's faith in the goodness of his Lord is far from reaffirmed— an ending that we cannot help but relate to the "crisis of belief" that prevails in modern times.

This device of using a biblical story to convey a very contemporary message is effectively illustrated in Wilfred Owen's "The Parable of the Old Men and the Young," which uses the story of the sacrifice of Isaac to express the poet's anger at mankind's slaughter of its young in international warfare. Here the poet completely reverses the original story to make his point. Abraham is changed from a simple shepherd who listens to the angel and spares his son into an arrogant militarist whose pride catapults his nation into a war and who sacrifices not only his son but other men's as well on the altar of his ego: ignoring the angel's insistence that he "sacrifice the Ram of Pride instead," Owen's Abraham chooses to slay "his son/And half the seed of Europe one by one." Modern minstrel Leonard Cohen makes similar use of this theme in his song "The Story of Isaac," where he points out that those "who build these altars now/To sacrifice these children" are not acting on God's command but on the basis of personal ambition. Similarly, turning to the legend of David and Goliath to convey his negative feelings about war, Louis Untermeyer also reverses the biblical story, making the young warrior refuse to kill. In "Goliath and David" he depicts a compassionate David who views the giant he is about to slay not as an enemy, but as a fellow human being who needs only the outstretched hand of comradeship to appease his rage. David's dream becomes one of brotherhood as he lays down his sling and rises up with Goliath to "play," putting aside the madness of international warfare.

Freedom is another contemporary issue that has been studied by appealing to Old Testament narratives in modern literature. The patriarchal stories of courage and faith have been especially inspiring to the common man held in bondage by an oppressive system. Black American slaves in particular have found in the story of Moses and the Israelites an expression of their own longing for freedom. The slaves sang spirituals about Moses while working in the fields and worshiping in their churches. While direct protest by the slaves might have led to brutal suppression by their masters, little notice was taken of the "happy chillun" singing of Moses and their God. The most famous of these spirituals is undoubtedly "Go Down, Moses," in which the Israelite leader is urged to go "Way down in Egypt land" and "Tell O' Pharaoh,/Let my people go." Those who were black and downtrodden knew who "Pharaoh" was, and they looked forward to the day when they would be delivered from bondage, their "Pharaoh and his host . . . lost" in the waters of the Red Sea.

Although slavery as an American institution was abolished over a century ago, many black Americans found themselves in bondage to modern Pharaohs well into the twentieth century. William Faulkner, in his short story "Go Down, Moses," in fact, seems to be suggesting that Pharaoh represents the whole system of economic and social injustice which results in a young black man running afoul of the law and being executed. "Roth Edmonds sold my Benjamin," chants the young man's grandmother. "Sold him in Egypt. Pharaoh got him—." It is liberation from just such oppression that Dr. Martin Luther King, Jr., prominent leader of the Civil Rights movement of the late 1950s and 60s, spoke of when he promised, on the night before his assassination in Memphis, that "we as a people will get to the promised land."

To the cry for black freedom in recent years has been added the demand for the liberation of women, especially from the oppressive stereotyping of the submissive role women have traditionally played in society. Little is said in the Old Testament concerning the role of women as a group in the development of the Hebrew nation. A few individuals, such as Deborah, Jael, Esther, Ruth, and Judith, have risen among the masses, however, and are counted among the ranks of the great leaders and folk heroes of the Hebrews. Deborah, represented in this unit, emerges from the pages of the Book of Judges as a splendid figure of great courage and vision. Less well-known but no less courageous is Jael, the non-Hebrew woman who lures Sisera, leader of the Canaanite army defeated by the forces of Deborah and Barak, into her tent and coolly dispatches him by driving a nail through his head. Edwin Arlington Robinson strikes a subtle blow for women's liberation in "Sisera," his poetic recreation of the story. Jael is portrayed as a woman possessed with a vision of glory and enraptured by her courageous act of liberation performed in the service of Deborah and the Hebrews whom she loves. Barak is bewildered by her act, however, although it marks the fulfillment of Deborah's earlier prophecy to him—that Sisera would be delivered "into the hand of a woman." To Barak, Jael has not acted as a woman should. His orientation and masculine pride make it impossible for him to comprehend a woman who finds fulfillment in such a deed, a deed which surely would have been hailed as the crowning glory of any man's life.

In a world filled with prejudice, war, and political tyranny, writers today continue to draw inspiration from the legendary men and women of the Old Testament who refused to give up no matter how insurmountable the odds facing them appeared. Many are strongly aware that there is still a vital need for dreamers with the courage to carry out their convictions and to show men and women the way to cast off the bonds of racism, violence, and oppression so they are better able to seek out the promised land of freedom and individual fulfillment.

THE SACRIFICE OF ISAAC
(Genesis)

When God called Abram and made "an everlasting covenant" with
him, He renamed him Abraham, or "father of many nations." Since
Sarah, his aged wife, seemed unable to bear Abraham any children, she
urged him to have a child by her Egyptian handmaid Hagar, who
bore him a son, Ishmael. Afterwards, Sarah regretted her hastiness and
persuaded Abraham to drive Hagar and Ishmael away. In the
meantime, God made it possible for Sarah to bear Abraham a son,
whom they named Isaac. It was through Isaac that God reaffirmed his
promise to "establish an everlasting covenant, and with his seed
after him."
Abraham is residing in a grove in Beersheba when God calls to
him once again.

And it came to pass that God did tempt Abraham, and said unto him,
"Abraham": and he said, "Behold, here I am."

And he said, "Take now thy son, thine only son Isaac, whom thou
lovest, and get thee into the land of Moriah; and offer him there for a
burnt offering upon one of the mountains which I will tell thee of."

And Abraham rose up early in the morning, and saddled his ass, and
took two of his young men with him, and Isaac his son, and cleft the
wood for the burnt offering, and rose up, and went unto the place of
which God had told him. Then on the third day Abraham lifted up his
eyes, and saw the place afar off. And Abraham said unto his young
men, "Abide ye here with the ass; and I and the lad will go yonder
and worship, and come again to you."

And Abraham took the wood of the burnt offering, and laid it upon
Isaac his son; and he took the fire in his hand, and a knife; and they
went both of them together. And Isaac spoke unto Abraham his father,
and said, "My father": and he said, "Here am I, my son." And he said,
"Behold the fire and the wood: but where is the lamb for a burnt
offering?" And Abraham said, "My son, God will provide himself a
lamb for a burnt offering": so they went both of them together.

And they came to the place which God had told him of; and
Abraham built an altar there, and laid the wood in order, and bound

Isaac his son, and laid him on the altar upon the wood. And Abraham stretched forth his hand, and took the knife to slay his son.

And the angel of the Lord called unto him out of heaven, and said, "Abraham, Abraham": and he said, "Here am I."

And he said, "Lay not thine hand upon the lad, neither do thou any thing unto him: for now I know that thou fearest God, seeing thou hast not withheld thy son, thine only son from me."

And Abraham lifted up his eyes, and looked, and beheld behind him a ram caught in a thicket by his horns: and Abraham went and took the ram, and offered him up for a burnt offering in the stead of his son. And Abraham called the name of that place Jehovah-jireh: as it is said to this day, "In the mount of the Lord it shall be seen."

And the angel of the Lord called unto Abraham out of heaven the second time, and said, " 'By myself have I sworn,' saith the Lord, 'for because thou hast done this thing, and hast not withheld thy son, thine only son, that in blessing I will bless thee, and in multiplying I will multiply thy seed as the stars of the heaven, and as the sand which is upon the seashore; and thy seed shall possess the gate of his enemies; and in thy seed shall all the nations of the earth be blessed; because thou hast obeyed my voice.' "

So Abraham returned unto his young men, and they rose up and went together to Beersheba; and Abraham dwelt at Beersheba.

[Genesis 22:1–19]

Why did God "tempt" Abraham? What significance is added to the event by Abraham's knowledge of God's promise that through Isaac he would be the father of many nations?

How much of the character's thoughts are given in this biblical story? Why do you suppose this is so? What thoughts and feelings might the father and son be experiencing during the journey and while at the altar? Do you suspect that Abraham's and Isaac's reactions might differ from those of a father and son today? If so, in what respect?

ABRAHAM AND ISAAC

Roberta Kalechofsky

Inside the tent it was dark and everyone slept. Even Isaac slept. Isaac.

How dreadful is this suffering, Abraham thought. He said this to himself not for pity's sake, but to clarify the obstacles to his will-power, for his suffering was a contender whose strength awed him. Isaac, it breathed in the dark, Isaac, my son.

The preparations for the journey were finished. The servants had collected the provisions and had put them near the door to the tent. Sheep had been milked after sundown and the milk was stored in water bottles and buried in the cool sand. It was expected that the day would be hot. Reports had already come in that many of the out-lying streams and wells were dry. They could not depend upon finding water until they reached higher ground. It behooved them to leave early and to travel fast.

Abraham woke with a start, thinking he heard a footfall outside the tent, animal or man disarraying the provisions. He rose from his mat and went to the doorway where he felt with his hands the tidily wrapped bundles. Everything was in place, but he was no longer tired. He opened the flap to the tent and looked out. There was a vein of light across the horizon, but except for that everything was dark. Dawn was only a suggestion.

In the distance beyond the tents he heard the muffled movement of the flock. They were restless to find grass, for everything was drying. A lamb bleat complainfully. Its voice barely had volume, sounding sur-priseful, sustaining itself with mournful fragility on a note of terror. Its mother moved in closely. There was a scuffling of sounds, then the young cry rose again, harsh with fear. The lamb was hungry and the comfort of its mother was useless. Abraham heard her own offended cry.

He peered out toward the flock. Their fretfulness was contagious. He felt it himself, an irritable apprehension. The herd moved like a wave and its cries were carried off to his distant right. There was silence then, and in the silence he heard his own cries, the creaking of an old and straining willpower. When he turned back into his tent to get ready, his teeth were chattering.

The dew was still heavy as they mounted their asses. No one was in favor of the journey. The herdsmen grumbled that it would delay the flocks for seven days, and Sarah bristled because Abraham insisted that Isaac go too.

"God will protect," he mumbled stiffly and Sarah threw her hands up.

As they mounted their asses she looked at him with entreaty, annoyance and worry. She stood in the tentway, the morning air blowing her grey hair in a frowsy circle, and eyed him with the settled irritation of a wife married half a century to a stubborn man. He would not look back at her. But as the asses started to move, he felt her eyes linger on him and on Isaac. In the final half second Abraham wavered on her behalf. He knew when he returned he would be parted from her forever.

Isaac followed promptly, as it behooved him, though he too felt that the journey was impractical in view of the season, but no judgment passed his lips. He was not of an age to take a critical stand against his father. Next year, he told himself. Already he was allowed to go on such a journey, and for the past year Abraham had been giving him instruction in the details of the camp, for he had meant him to be prepared to take command when he died. Isaac was conscious of his position. He rode beside Abraham and chatted about things, about the servants, about a new tent, with an edge of equality in his voice.

Abraham rode in silence.

At first the asses left tracks in the bedewed sand, but soon the sun rose, the sand dried and the tracks were covered up. The heat was far from its height, but already Abraham felt irritated by it. The glare hurt his eyes and from time to time there were soft explosions of heatlight against his retina. Isaac heard the low gossip of the servants behind him. Occasionally he heard Eliezer whistle a tune and he joined him. A dune rose up and disappeared. The sand turned white and powdery. The sun climbed high over their right shoulders. For almost half a day Abraham rode without talking. By midday the monotony of the desert was crushing, and Isaac resented Abraham's silence.

When the sun passed overhead Eliezer drew in his breath. Ishmael coughed, a low grumble. Isaac looked back at them and shrugged his shoulders, but Abraham seemed unaware. "Can we not stop now?" Isaac said. He wiped his forehead with his hand to emphasize his discomfort.

Abraham turned to him as if his presence surprised him. Isaac felt that he had been presumptuous. "I am tired," he said peevishly. Abraham saw that the sun had passed overhead. He was annoyed with himself for his distractedness and stopped his ass abruptly. Isaac turned and smiled to Eliezer and Ishmael and they smiled back with gratitude.

They sat down in the shadow of the asses and unwrapped the breadloaves, the figcakes and the cheese. All drank milk that day, to consume it before it soured. When they had finished eating Abraham motioned that they mount again. Isaac saw that Eliezer and Ishmael were irritated. He looked down at his toes. "The servants are tired," he said in a low voice. Abraham wrinkled his brow. He looked at Isaac in perplexity as if he heard a new note in his voice, but he nodded agreement that they nap.

Eliezer and Ishmael immediately lay down and covered their heads with their robes. Isaac stood uncertainly and played with the ear of his ass. Abraham watched him. The air was milky, filled with a fine dust which irritated his eyes. He felt them watery and his gaze was unsteady, but he fixed them on Isaac.

"What concerns you for my servants?" he said.

Isaac reddened. He shifted his feet and leaned in towards his ass's head. He felt that Abraham should understand that it behooved him to keep favor with the servants when one day he would have to rule them. He looked across the neck of the ass and said, "Ought not the son of Abraham show concern for his father's servants?"

Abraham felt the future brush him with a feeling of already nonexistence, a foretaste of ghostliness. He looked away too, at the sun, at the sand, at his knees crossed on the ground. "I am still here," he said.

Isaac pressed his lips. He avoided looking at his father and stroked the sloping nose of the ass. "Chi, chi," he murmured to the animal. He dug his hand into a pouch and brought out a bell which he tinkled in front of the animal. "Chi," he shouted, trying to arouse him.

Abraham stretched himself out and covered his face with his robe. He felt discomfort with his son because he had violated his discipline. But underneath his robe his suffering leaped to his side and whispered, But thou art Isaac, doomed. Remorsefully Abraham wished he could undo the reprimand, undo himself as father to this child. Falling asleep he heard Isaac screaming at his ass like a man chieftain. The sounds dunned his sleep like small shocks of life which would not let him shut off the world and rest.

When they took up their journey in the afternoon the sun was low on their left. The air was swollen with heat which struck the back of their throats and burned the lids of their eyes. On their right was a dune that stretched for a distance. They bent eastward until the dune was on their left, then in single file they rode along the margin of shadow that it cast. They did not reach the mountains that night and settled on an oasis which they found by chance. They ate their evening meal in silence, for Abraham's manner made them feel strained. Isaac was disappointed that the trip was dull.

The sun crept down the palm trees and disappeared. With few words to each other Eliezer and Ishmael laid down and went to sleep. Isaac stayed up. He waited for his father to talk to him, but Abraham only sat crosslegged and stared out to where the sun had incomprehensibly disappeared, swallowing one day with it. "Good-night," Isaac coughed gently. Abraham turned around. "Isaac?" he said.

He went to him and Isaac hoped for words of reconciliation. But Abraham only bent down to him and pressed his boy's shoulders, indicating that he lay down and sleep.

He laid himself down too, but he could not bear that Isaac was unhappy. He thought of his irritability during the day with panic. The situation was more than his emotions could deal with and they grew abnormal all by themselves. Two more days, he thought, relieved and griefstricken, falling into sleep.

But, again, he woke with a start at an unfamiliar sound. Within seconds he registered its source. Isaac had risen and was stealing towards the edge of the oasis. Abraham watched him. Isaac crept between the palm trees; the moonlight slanted down his legs. The branches moved. The morning breeze blew, though it was still dark.

Abraham had not risen during moonlight for many years and the thick yellowness startled him with forgotten sensuality. One by one his senses strained to catch it as he watched Isaac, barelegged, make his way to the edge of the oasis. His nostrils dilated with the cold night air. He had forgotten how the earth cools itself, enjoying its chilly body in sumptuous darkness. The breeze blew through his robe. It touched his neck and chest with sensation and the full tide of remembering broke upon him as if the breeze tore aside his aging skin and exposed the youth who had lived in Ur, wrapped in stars and wind. Isaac passed through the edge of the oasis. He walked on to the sand and looked up into the moon, momentously. The world hung in luxury like a jewel waiting for its inheritor. Isaac was immobile, lost in an ancient rapture. Abraham watched him and his body quivered with homesickness for his own youth. He felt himself weeping through his body for its loss, for the loss and waste of it all to the loser.

"Isaac," he said to himself and for a moment he thought his body had broken apart.

"Isaac," he groaned.

Eliezer stirred. "He is there," he called out. Then dumbfoundedly he saw that Abraham saw him perfectly. He grumbled to himself that it was too early to rise, but being up he woke Ishmael.

They started out while it was yet dark. Abraham rode first and Isaac straddled between his father and the servants. Sometimes he hung back to hear their gossip and sometimes he pushed away from them. Half a day they advanced towards the sun. The ground became firmer. The sand did not shift so freely and the footfalls of the asses could be heard. The animals now left tracks in the sand. They were coming to the end of the desert.

By midafternoon they passed out from the monotony of the sand into the mountains.

They climbed only for a short time before they camped inside a cave. Eliezer uncorked the wine bottles and passed them around. Abraham sat apart, against the trunk of a tree, and Isaac ate with the servants. Sulkily Isaac regarded Abraham's separateness.

"He was ever thus," Eliezer said, noting the boy's uneasiness.

"Nay. It is because I intervened for you yesterday," Isaac said.

Eliezer shrugged his shoulders as if to say that was an issue for which there was no remedy.

As soon as they had finished eating Abraham gave the order to continue. Eliezer and Ishmael started forth grudgingly. The asses now had to be led and the party wound its way in single file. The trail was narrow, often hanging over steep canyons that swung greyly beneath them. The rocks were whitened and chalky. A white powder floated everywhere. They came to a dried stream where the waterbed was ribbed with cracks and lizards. Eliezer looked at it with troubled eyes, with a shade of dismal and self righteous confirmation. "Pass it over," Abraham said in the mechanical voice of a father distracting his child from nonsense.

Eliezer pursed his lips and they crossed the stream in silence. Isaac's heart fluttered.

"What ails thee?" Abraham asked him sharply and Isaac was caught by his incisive perceptiveness. "I am tired of journeying," he mumbled under his breath.

Abraham's eyes flickered. He was sorry he had spoken harshly. He said in a softer voice, "Eliezer and Ishmael are good servants. They are right that the drought is bad. We will lose many sheep by this delay."

Isaac was embarrassed. But he said, "Then why do you contend with them?"

"Because," Abraham said in a metallic voice, "they do not have my errand to do."

"Could it not have waited until after the removal?" Isaac asked boldly.

Abraham's eyes flickered again. The time is unpropitious, he had said himself to God.

Now, God answered.

A month, Abraham had pleaded, stay me a month to move my flocks.

Now.

Isaac saw the shade of a surreptitious struggle pass over Abraham's face. He paused. Then prodded by the intelligence of the thing, he asked again, "Could it not have waited?"

"No," Abraham said with a ring of dismissal.

This night Abraham slept too, overcome with strain. His agony found a partial release in the thought that there was only one day left. They had gone too far now to return and he felt that the next day might carry him on its own tide. He had only to endure. But the day did not pass that way. They woke facing a malignant sun. Before them stretched the plains, as level and as hot as the desert, where every blade of grass cracked beneath their feet. Abraham felt the skin on his face dry perceptibly. His hair and eyebrows grew stiff. They rode for hours and there was not the slightest diminution of heat. It blistered the top of his head through his robe. The power of the sun seemed like a betrayal, and all day as they rode his heart knocked violently and there was no thought he could bring to bear upon himself which would calm him.

When they came to a stretch of land that was covered with dwarfed trees and dense bushes, he let them nap. He himself lay down on his back. Isaac lay on his stomach close by him, his head on his arms, his legs parted and bent at the knees. Abraham stared at the sky until his eyes watered and burned, then with a groan he sat up. The blue sky stretched illimitably. Underneath, the ground was dense with life, and next to him the three slept soundly. Only he sat in a hollow of loneliness, his head thrust above the high grass, compacted of agonies that revolved slowly in him like a kaleidoscope, first showing one pattern of pain, and then another. He looked at Isaac sleeping next to him and felt unbearable loneliness. If Isaac could wake and comfort him! Somebody should, he thought with a bitterness that brought tears to his eyes. He was startled by his weakness. I am indeed old, he thought, and suddenly it seemed to him that he was the victim, doomed to suffer before, to suffer at the deed, and to suffer after. Doomed to weep and weep and weep for Isaac, while Isaac slept and dreamed of tomorrow. Of what? Of his coming leadership, of how he would govern servants and lead the camp. I am still here, Abraham said aloud. He blinked his eyes. But this is Isaac, he thought. What had happened to the remorseless sanctity that surrounded him. This is Isaac, he screamed in his heart as if the statement could restore the mere boy undressed of complexity. This is Isaac, he gasped to himself, and with a push of all his energies he reclaimed the original idea. "Up! Up!" he shouted at the others before confirmation could break down again.

They rose and looked at him with confusion. Eliezer blinked at the sky. Abraham thought he smiled ironically. He brushed the thought away, breathless at his weakness, and mounted his ass. "Up! Up!" he shouted and started down the trail across the plains before the others were even mounted.

They went through a forest. Abraham could hear Isaac whistling in the distance behind him. He nudged his ass on as fast as the animal could go, and he came out of the forest much before the others. The sun was setting, but its descent was blocked out by the mountains in front of him. The top of the mountain in the east was levelled to a rocky plateau from which two craggy promontories plunged southward and on top of this plateau, although it was last to view in the fusion of sunset and night, was a huge cropping of rock: dense, broad, level, mute, momentous, recipient of the sacrifices of centuries: ancient, absolute stone.

Abraham veered course easterly and by nightfall they were at the base of the mountain, in the shadow of the plateau. He saw it above him like a thing he had never seen, although he had stared into it for three days.

Eliezer, Ishmael and Isaac were in a comfortable mood now that half the journey was over. They ate their evening meal with relish. They drank wine and Ishmael sang to them. Isaac hummed in the background. Abraham listened to them desperately, for distraction's sake. But soon they went to sleep, Isaac too, still humming to himself, and Abraham was left with the mountain hovering above his head. All night he held Isaac's head in his arm and tried to sleep, but his eyes never closed. He heard Ishmael wake in the morning, then Eliezer and Isaac. They called to him to rise and eat, but he had no appetite. The day had dawned. They ate. He made his preparations.

When they were finished eating he unloaded the wood from the ass and strapped it to Isaac's back. "Abide here with the asses," he said to Eliezer and Ishmael. "I and the lad will go yonder to worship." He raised his eyes surreptitiously to the plateau above him. Then he put his knife in the girdle of his robe, made a torch and indicated to Isaac to follow him up the mountain.

But Isaac stopped him. "Where is the lamb for the burnt offering?" he said, looking about him. "Here is the wood and the fire and the knife, but where is the lamb?"

Abraham's cheeks were pouchy and grey. His eyes were swollen. "God will provide the lamb for the offering," he said, and his voice struck the air like frozen mist. Peremptorily he turned his back and started to climb up. Isaac was bewildered and hesitated. Then he followed his father.

The morning was bright. They took a trail that led between the two promontories, the only trail they could discover. Isaac climbed vigorously. The cool air struck the back of his throat. Abraham walked with his back bent; he kept well ahead of Isaac and all Isaac could see of him was the smoky trail of his torch. Though Isaac climbed rapidly he could not catch up with him and Abraham did not stop to wait for him. Once Isaac turned and far below saw Eliezer and Ishmael throwing a rock to each other. Then the trail bent and they were lost to sight and Isaac was alone in the mountains.

Finally they reached the plateau. Abraham motioned to Isaac to put down the wood. Then he planted his torch in the ground so that his hands would be free. He turned to Isaac, and Isaac waited. Abraham's eyes were puffy, embedded in rings of sunburn. Water floated on his lower rims and he gazed at Isaac through a mist. Suddenly Isaac knew his father's age. "Are you not well?" he said with alarm.

But Abraham did not respond. He turned and walked to the edge of a thicket and stared into it.

"Are you never to forgive me?" Isaac said under his breath.

Abraham did not hear him. He stood at the edge of the thicket and stared into it. Isaac guessed that he meant to wait for the appearance of a lamb. Irritably he reckoned that if they depended on chance they might wait all day. He sat down on a rock and sulkily picked up some pebbles and played with them. The sun was directly overhead. The flies buzzed in the silence. Isaac sighed restlessly. The perspiration flowed on his forehead and the flies buzzed around it. Yet the silence was vast. It seemed to flow from the sun, it penetrated the earth, it swelled with the heat, it spread over the rock and the mountain, it saturated the air and hung on Isaac's shoulders. He struck at the flies. He looked all about him and felt the loneliness of the place. Immensity existed. It was all about him and he was a contradictory element in it. His loneliness frightened him. He felt that his father should see his discomfort and was bewildered that he did not. He wanted to cry and felt dismally that he was too old for that. The silence crushed him until he felt inessential. He had wanted to come and now he could not leave. The silence drew its net tighter and, voiceless, told him that he would never forget this day. Some childish pride in being alive passed out of his life forever. He gave up waiting and dozed.

But, then, suddenly, Abraham was before him and he heard his father's voice calling him. "Isaac," Abraham called, like all the times he had come to waken him in the morning. But there was something terrible in the voice and Isaac struggled sluggishly against it. There was something terrible in his name, and something terrible in his father saying it as if it was not he who was saying it but some dreadful suffering that said it for him, and there was an illimitable sadness in the sound. A world of dread yawned before him in the dark, and fearing to be caught in a vision of life that was unendurable Isaac opened his eyes and was caught.

"Isaac," Abraham said and his hand was upon his shoulder, the knife was at his throat.

Isaac sprang to his feet. "Where is the lamb?" he squeaked.

"Isaac," Abraham whispered hoarsely.

"Where is the lamb?" Isaac cried out.

"You are the lamb," Abraham screamed.

Isaac blinked his eyes. He took a step backwards and fell against the rock. Abraham saw his terror. "God wills it," he cried.

Isaac stared blankly as if he were feeble-minded. His mind dropped into emptiness. His brains shifted round and round with hysterical haste to make sense of this thing. The pattern of his offense arose, the pattern of himself as an offending being. He fixed his eyes on his father. "God?" he said. He turned his head and looked at Abraham out of the side of his eyes, shamefaced and confused.

Abraham's heart fluttered. "Isaac," he screamed as if he were clutching a dying child. The sweat ran on his face. "I will pay for your death with my own," he said breathlessly. But Isaac looked at him blankly, sidewise, uncomprehendingly. He looked at him with uncanny and desperate intelligence. "How will I know?" he said.

Abraham put down his arm and trembled. "Art thou Isaac?" he cried.

Isaac sobbed. His chin dropped on his chest. It was unbearable to answer him, unbearable to look at him, unbearable to accept reproach, unjust to be innocent. All he could do was cry and he heard the sound in his ears, full of animal terror.

An afternoon wind stirred the grass near the rock. It passed over him and his heart stopped. It passed over him again with a terrible sweetness. Cries tore his chest. He opened his eyes and the blueness of the air tore him with love and terror. "Yes, I am Isaac," he screamed and jumped on his father. Abraham staggered under the impact of the young body, carrying Isaac with him like a leech. His nose was buried in his cheek and he felt that he was being smothered. He strained his arms against Isaac's hold until he thought his muscles would break. Astonishment broke upon him. A corner of his mind made a violent estimate of their relative skills and strength. He made one effort after another to free himself until the efforts mounted like waves carrying him to an undesignated spot and he felt himself lifted into a realm of speculation beyond the one that had brought him to the mountain.

With a final effort he pushed Isaac from him. He reared back his head and gasped at the air. "My God," he screamed, "do not struggle with me," and before Isaac could move again he threw him against the rock and held him. With desperation he tore aside the wrappings of throat and sought to plunge his hands on the mere child that was covered beneath them. But Isaac screamed and something eluded him. The wide pale sky stretched with simplicity. And then mingled in Isaac's screams, louder than the commotion of their breaths, he heard a rustle in the thicket behind him. He turned to look and in that moment Isaac threw his father from him and ran into the woods. The ram, frightened by the intruder, ran out into the open.

Abraham's legs crumpled willessly like dry leaves in a wind. He fell to his knees. Understanding upon understanding crashed upon his ears. The sky opened up forever, beyond and beyond and beyond. "Thou art the Lord," he cried, and fell prone upon the ground and wept.

The ram, close by, looked at him curiously. Isaac stayed hidden behind a clump of bushes and stared at him. His breath was short and the taste of terror was still in it. His face was red and his ears rang and burned.

When Abraham recovered himself and stood up, he looked about him; but Isaac did not move.

"Isaac," he called out, "help me prepare the ram."

Isaac hesitated. Abraham heard him breathing in the thicket.

"Isaac," he said softly, but with familiar authority. "Help me prepare the ram."

Isaac looked behind him through the thicket, but it was dense and he could discover no trail on that side. The sun was dangerous.

Already the grass in the clearing was parched. Behind him the bushes closed in darkness. Isaac hesitated a little longer, then he cautiously crept out.

"Isaac," Abraham called to him, "come see how the Lord has saved us." He called to him in such a voice that Isaac felt aged.

Abraham caught the ram with a quivering tenderness and held him in his arms. He brought the ram over for Isaac to look at it. Isaac looked into his small, agitated face and felt a terror for everything that existed. Abraham carried the ram to the rock and swiftly bent over him. Isaac turned his back and when he heard the last wild squeak his head fell forward.

When the sacrifice was over they started down the mountain. The sun was low. Isaac walked behind his father, keeping a measured distance. Once he slipped and Abraham turned to help him, but Isaac shied a step backward. Abraham looked at him with curiosity. But it was not then that he knew. The sun fell behind the highest peak and the mountain stood out in blackness. Isaac waited until his father should be well ahead of him again. Abraham descended. Then not hearing Isaac's step he paused and looked back. Isaac sat on his haunches and watched him. Abraham could not see his face well in the twilight. He peered, but he could not make it out. Isaac faded into the dark of the mountain. Abraham turned and thought he saw his suffering stand up before him again. The dusk gathered together and whispered. Abraham's heart started to knock, as if he had it all to look forward to. He could not see the trail in front of him. He turned again.

"Isaac," he called.

There was no answer for a moment. Then out of the darkness he heard a tremulous, "Yea?"

But Abraham did not know what to say to that. Again he turned and went down and again he heard Isaac's steps far behind him, and in that measured tread he heard the infinite perplexity of everything that ever was.

It was already dark when Eliezer and Ishmael spotted them on a steep, rocky descent. They had to climb backwards over some sharp rocks and in the misty distance, as they groped and bent and let themselves down on their hands and knees, they looked like two desperate figures, goats or peasants, suspicious of their footing.

How does the overall theme of the story differ from that of its biblical counterpart? What effect does the omission of the heavenly voices, both at the beginning and near the end, have in this altered version? Why does Abraham sense "the infinite perplexity of everything that ever was" as he and Isaac descend the mountain? With what impressions are you left at the end of the story? In what ways does the story challenge the concept of faith as we normally think it was practiced in biblical times? In what sense might it be considered a comment on the "crisis of faith" in our own age?

A comparison of this story with the biblical tale will help you see some of the differences between modern and biblical story-telling. In each case consider the characters who appear in the story and to what extent each is developed. Which story reveals the inner thoughts of the characters? What effect does this have on the story? What do all the details describing the landscape and weather add to the modern story? What other differences of style and technique do you notice? What are some of the purposes that can be served by developing a biblical tale into a much longer story? What objections might be raised?

THE PARABLE OF THE OLD MEN AND THE YOUNG

Wilfred Owen

So Abram rose, and clave the wood, and went,
And took the fire with him, and a knife.
And as they journeyed both of them together,
Isaac the first-born spake and said, My Father,
Behold the preparations, fire and iron,
But where the lamb for this burnt-offering?
Then Abram bound the youth with belts and straps,
And builded parapets and trenches there,
And stretched forth the knife to slay his son.
When lo! an angel called him out of heaven,
Saying, Lay not thy hand upon the lad,
Neither do anything to him. Behold,
A ram, caught in a thicket by its horns;
Offer the Ram of Pride instead of him.

But the old man would not so, but slew his son—
And half the seed of Europe, one by one.

———————

What particular words and phrases in this retelling of the Isaac story help prepare you for the dramatic alteration of the biblical tale in the final lines? How does the knowledge that Wilfred Owen was killed in action during World War I affect your reading of the poem?

═══════════════════════════════

THE STORY OF ISAAC*

Leonard Cohen

The door it opened slowly
   My father he came in,
   I was nine years old
And he stood so tall above me,
   Blue eyes they were shining
   And his voice was very cold.
Said "I've had a vision
   And you know I'm strong and holy,
   I must do what I've been told."
So he started up the mountain,
I was running, he was walking
   And his ax was made of gold.

The trees they got much smaller,
   The lake a lady's mirror,
   We stopped to drink some wine.
Then he threw the bottle over,
   Broke a minute later
   And he put his hand on mine.
Thought I saw an eagle

The Sacrifice of Isaac (1455). From *The Four Gospels*, Armenian illuminated manuscript. THE WALTERS ART GALLERY, BALTIMORE, MD.

But it might have been a vulture,
   I never could decide.
Then my father built an altar,
He looked once behind his shoulder,
   He knew I would not hide.

You who build these altars now
   To sacrifice these children,
   You must not do it any more.
A scheme is not a vision
   And you never have been tempted
   By a demon or a god.
You who stand above them now,
   Your hatchets blunt and bloody,
   You were not there before
When I lay upon a mountain
And my father's hand was trembling
   With the beauty of the word.

And if you call me brother now
   Forgive me if I inquire
   Just according to whose plan?
When it all comes down to dust
   I will kill you if I must
   I will help you if I can.
When it all comes down to dust
   I will help you if I must
   I will kill you if I can.
And mercy on our uniform
Man of peace or man of war—
   The peacock spreads his fan.

   The first two stanzas are an imaginative reconstruction of Isaac's thoughts and feelings as his father led him to be sacrificed. What poetic details do you find especially effective in these stanzas? In the third stanza the speaker abandons his narrative and suddenly switches his focus to the present. Describe this change of focus. What do you notice about the imagery in this stanza? How does the present differ from the past? Who are the ones that "build these altars now"? Who are the "Isaacs"? Why does the speaker first say "I will kill you if I must" and then "I will kill you if I can"? What has brought about this alteration of values? What similarities do you see between this song and "The Parable of the Old Men and the Young"?

JOSEPH AND HIS BROTHERS
(Genesis)

The story of Joseph and his eleven brothers is one of the most popular
—and longest—in the Old Testament. Joseph's father was Jacob, son
of Isaac, whose wives, Rachel and Leah, and their handmaidens bore
him twelve sons, who were to become heads of the twelve tribes of
Israel. Favored over all the others were Jacob's sons by Rachel,
Joseph and Benjamin. The jealousy and hatred which developed
toward Joseph as a result of this favoritism and the amazing career
upon which his jealous brothers unwittingly launched him are revealed
in the following pages.

Joseph, being seventeen years old, was feeding the flock with his
brethren. Now Jacob loved Joseph more than all his children, because
he was the son of his old age: and he made him a coat of many colors.
And when his brethren saw that their father loved him more than all
his brethren, they hated him, and could not speak peaceably unto him.

And Joseph dreamed a dream, and he told it his brethren: and
they hated him yet the more. And he said unto them, "Hear, I pray
you, this dream which I have dreamed: for, behold, we were binding
sheaves in the field, and, lo, my sheaf arose, and also stood upright;
and, behold, your sheaves stood round about, and made obeisance to
my sheaf."

And his brethren said to him, "Shalt thou indeed reign over us? Or
shalt thou indeed have dominion over us?"

And they hated him yet the more for his dreams, and for his words.

And he dreamed yet another dream, and told it his brethren, and
said, "Behold, I have dreamed a dream more; and, behold, the sun and
the moon and the eleven stars made obeisance to me."

And he told it to his father, and to his brethren: and his father
rebuked him, and said unto him, "What is this dream that thou hast
dreamed? Shall I and thy mother and thy brethren indeed come to
bow down ourselves to thee to the earth?"

And his brethren envied him; but his father observed the saying.
And his brethren went to feed their father's flock in Shechem.

And Joseph went after his brethren, and found them in Dothan. And when they saw him afar off, even before he came near unto them, they conspired against him to slay him. And they said one to another, "Behold, this dreamer cometh. Come now therefore, and let us slay him, and cast him into some pit, and we will say, 'Some evil beast hath devoured him': and we shall see what will become of his dreams."

And Reuben heard it, and he delivered him out of their hands; and said, "Let us not kill him." And Reuben said unto them, "Shed no blood, but cast him into this pit that is in the wilderness, and lay no hand upon him"; that he might rid him out of their hands, to deliver him to his father again.

And it came to pass, when Joseph was come unto his brethren, that they stripped Joseph out of his coat, his coat of many colors that was on him; and they took him, and cast him into a pit; and the pit was empty, there was no water in it. And they sat down to eat bread: and they lifted up their eyes and looked, and, behold, a company of Ishmaelites came from Gilead with their camels bearing spicery and balm and myrrh, going to carry it down to Egypt.

And Judah said unto his brethren, "What profit is it if we slay our brother, and conceal his blood? Come and let us sell him to the Ishmaelites, and let not our hand be upon him; for he is our brother and our flesh."

And his brethren were content. Then there passed by Midianites merchantmen; and they drew and lifted up Joseph out of the pit, and sold Joseph to the Ishmaelites for twenty pieces of silver: and they brought Joseph into Egypt.

And they took Joseph's coat, and killed a kid of the goats, and dipped the coat in the blood; and they rent the coat of many colors, and they brought it to their father; and said, "This have we found: know now whether it be thy son's coat or no."

And he knew it, and said, "It is my son's coat; an evil beast hath devoured him; Joseph is without doubt rent in pieces."

And Jacob rent his clothes, and put sackcloth upon his loins, and mourned for his son many days. And all his sons and all his daughters rose up to comfort him; but he refused to be comforted; and he said, "For I will go down into the grave unto my son mourning." Thus his father wept for him.

And Joseph was brought down to Egypt; and Potiphar, an officer of Pharaoh, captain of the guard, an Egyptian, bought him of the hands of the Ishmaelites, which had brought him down thither. And the Lord was with Joseph, and he was a prosperous man; and he was in the house of his master the Egyptian. And his master saw that the Lord was with him, and that the Lord made all that he did to prosper in his hand. And Joseph found grace in his sight, and he served him: and he made him overseer over his house, and all that he had he put into his hand.

And it came to pass from the time that he had made him overseer in his house, and over all that he had, that the Lord blessed the Egyptian's house for Joseph's sake; and the blessing of the Lord was upon all that he had in the house, and in the field. And he left all that he had in Joseph's hand; and he knew not aught he had, save the bread which he did eat. And Joseph was a goodly person, and well favored.

And it came to pass after these things, that his master's wife cast her eyes upon Joseph; and she said, "Lie with me."

But he refused, and said unto his master's wife, "Behold, my master wotteth not what is with me in the house, and he hath committed all that he hath to my hand. There is none greater in this house than I; neither hath he kept back any thing from me but thee, because thou art his wife: how then can I do this great wickedness, and sin against God?"

And it came to pass, as she spoke to Joseph day by day, that he hearkened not unto her, to lie by her, or to be with her.

And it came to pass about this time, that Joseph went into the house to do his business; and there was none of the men of the house there within. And she caught him by his garment, saying, "Lie with me": and he left his garment in her hand, and fled, and got him out.

And it came to pass, when she saw that he had left his garment in her hand, and was fled forth, that she called unto the men of her house, and spoke unto them, saying. "See, he hath brought in a Hebrew unto us to mock us; he came in unto me to lie with me, and I cried with a loud voice, and it came to pass, when he heard that I lifted up my voice and cried, that he left his garment with me, and fled, and got him out."

And she laid up his garment by her, until his lord came home. And she spoke unto him according to these words, saying, "The Hebrew servant, which thou hast brought unto us, came in unto me to mock me; and it came to pass, as I lifted up my voice and cried, that he left his garment with me, and fled out."

And it came to pass, when his master heard the words of his wife, which she spoke unto him, saying, "After this manner did thy servant to me"; that his wrath was kindled. And Joseph's master took him, and put him into the prison, a place where the king's prisoners were bound: and he was there in the prison.

[But the Lord watches over Joseph and has mercy on him. Joseph finds favor in the eyes of the prison keeper and is put in charge of all prisoners. Shortly afterwards, he interprets the dreams of two prisoners, Pharaoh's chief baker and chief butler. As he rightly foretells, the baker is put to death in three days; the butler is released and returns to Pharaoh's service. Two years pass. Pharaoh, troubled by a series of strange dreams, beckons his magicians and wise men to interpret them. When they fail, the butler tells Pharaoh of his experience with Joseph, and the ruler summons him from jail.]

Then Pharaoh sent and called Joseph, and they brought him hastily out of the dungeon: and he shaved himself, and changed his raiment, and came in unto Pharaoh. And Pharaoh said unto Joseph: "I have dreamed a dream, and there is none that can interpret it: and I have heard say of thee that thou canst understand a dream to interpret it."

And Joseph answered Pharaoh, saying, "It is not in me: God shall give Pharaoh an answer of peace."

And Pharaoh said unto Joseph, "In my dream, behold, I stood upon the bank of the river. And, behold, there came up out of the river seven kine, fatfleshed and well favored; and they fed in a meadow. And, behold, seven other kine came up after them, poor and very ill favored and leanfleshed, such as I never saw in all the land of Egypt for badness. And the lean and the ill favored kine did eat up the first seven fat kine; and when they had eaten them up, it could not be known that they had eaten them; but they were still ill favored, as at the beginning. So I awoke. And I saw in my dream, and, behold, seven ears came up in one stalk, full and good. And, behold, seven ears withered, thin, and blasted with the east wind, sprung up after them. And the thin ears devoured the seven good ears: and I told this unto the magicians; but there was none that could declare it to me."

And Joseph said unto Pharaoh, "The dream of Pharaoh is one. God hath showed Pharaoh what he is about to do. The seven good kine are seven years; and the seven good ears are seven years: the dream is one. And the seven thin and ill favored kine that came up after them are seven years; and the seven empty ears blasted with the east wind shall be seven years of famine. This is the thing which I have spoken unto Pharaoh: what God is about to do he showeth unto Pharaoh. Behold, there come seven years of great plenty throughout all the land of Egypt: and there shall arise after them seven years of famine; and all the plenty shall be forgotten in the land of Egypt; and the famine shall consume the land. And the plenty shall not be known in the land by reason of that famine following; for it shall be very grievous.

"And for that the dream was doubled unto Pharaoh twice; it is because the thing is established by God, and God will shortly bring it to pass. Now therefore let Pharaoh look out a man discreet and wise, and set him over the land of Egypt. Let Pharaoh do this, and let him appoint officers over the land, and take up the fifth part of the land of Egypt in the seven plenteous years. And let them gather all the food of those good years that come, and lay up corn under the hand of Pharaoh, and let them keep food in the cities. And that food shall be for store to the land against the seven years of famine, which shall be in the land of Egypt; that the land perish not through the famine."

And the thing was good in the eyes of Pharaoh, and in the eyes of all his servants. And Pharaoh said unto his servants, "Can we find such a one as this is, a man in whom the Spirit of God is?"

And Pharaoh said unto Joseph, "Forasmuch as God hath showed thee all this, there is none so discreet and wise as thou art. Thou shalt be over my house, and according unto thy word shall all my people be ruled: only in the throne will I be greater than thou." And Pharaoh said unto Joseph, "See, I have set thee over all the land of Egypt."

And Pharaoh took off his ring from his hand, and put it upon Joseph's hand, and arrayed him in vestures of fine linen, and put a gold chain about his neck; and he made him to ride in the second chariot which he had; and they cried before him, "Bow the knee": and he made him ruler over all the land of Egypt.

And Pharaoh said unto Joseph, "I am Pharaoh, and without thee shall no man lift his hand or foot in all the land of Egypt." And Pharaoh called Joseph's name Zaphnath-paaneah; and he gave him to wife Asenath the daughter of Poti-pherah priest of On. And Joseph went out over all the land of Egypt.

And Joseph was thirty years old when he stood before Pharaoh king of Egypt. And Joseph went out from the presence of Pharaoh, and went throughout all the land of Egypt. And in the seven plenteous years the earth brought forth by handfuls. And he gathered up all the food of the seven years, which were in the land of Egypt, and laid up the food in the cities: the food of the field, which was round about every city, laid he up in the same.

*[When the seven years of famine begin, Egypt is prepared. The food
soon runs out, and Joseph opens the storehouses and begins to sell
corn both to the Egyptians and to men from other lands that have been
struck by the famine. Jacob learns of the Egyptian surpluses and sends
his sons, except for Benjamin, the youngest, to buy corn. The brothers
approach Joseph to make their purchases, but do not recognize
him. To test them, Joseph accuses them of being spies and insists that
he will not sell them anything until they return to their father's
house and fetch the youngest brother; Simeon, meanwhile, is to be
held a hostage. The brothers convince Jacob to let them take Benjamin
and they return to Egypt. After further testing, Joseph is convinced
they have become changed men, and he prepares to reveal himself
to them.]*

Then Joseph could not refrain himself before all them that stood by
him; and he cried, "Cause every man to go out from me." And there
stood no man with him, while Joseph made himself known unto his
brethren. And he wept aloud: and the Egyptians and the house of
Pharaoh heard.

And Joseph said unto his brethren, "I am Joseph; doth my father
yet live?"

And his brethren could not answer him; for they were troubled at
his presence.

And Joseph said unto his brethren, "Come near to me, I pray you."
And they came near.

And he said, "I am Joseph your brother, whom ye sold into Egypt.
Now therefore be not grieved, nor angry with yourselves, that ye sold
me hither: for God did send me before you to preserve life. For
these two years hath the famine been in the land: and yet there are
five years, in the which there shall neither be earing nor harvest. And
God sent me before you to preserve you a posterity in the earth, and
to save your lives by a great deliverance. So now it was not you that
sent me hither, but God: and he hath made me a father to Pharaoh,
and lord of all his house, and a ruler throughout all the land of Egypt.

"Haste ye, and go up to my father, and say unto him, 'Thus saith
thy son Joseph, "God hath made me lord of all Egypt: come down unto
me, tarry not: and thou shalt dwell in the land of Goshen, and thou
shalt be near unto me, thou, and thy children, and thy children's
children, and thy flocks, and thy herds, and all thou hast: and there
will I nourish thee; for yet there are five years of famine; lest thou,
and thy household, and all that thou hast, come to poverty."' And,

behold, your eyes see, and the eyes of my brother Benjamin, that it is my mouth that speaketh unto you. And ye shall tell my father of all my glory in Egypt, and of all that ye have seen; and ye shall haste and bring down my father hither."

And he fell upon his brother Benjamin's neck, and wept; and Benjamin wept upon his neck. Moreover he kissed all his brethren, and wept upon them: and after that his brethren talked with him.

[*Genesis 37: 2b, 3–28; 31–35; 39:1–20; 41:14–48; 45:1–15*]

THE STRONG ONES

Isaac Bashevis Singer

Cheder, too often described as a place where innocent children suffered at the hands of a sloppy, ill-tempered teacher, was not quite that. What was wrong with society was wrong with cheder.

There was one boy with constantly clenched fists who kept looking for a chance to hit someone. Assistant bullies and sycophants surrounded him.

Another boy, for whom it was not practical to use violence, acted the little saint, smiling at everyone, doing favors, and all with an expression that implied immeasurable love. But in his quiet way he schemed to acquire things, to taste something wonderful for nothing. Pious though he was, he showed friendship for the bully while feigning sympathy for his victims. When his friend the bully decided to give someone a bloody nose, the little saint would run to the victim with a handkerchief while gently admonishing the bully, "You shouldn't have done that. . . ."

There was another boy who was interested only in business, trading a button for a nail, a bit of putty for a pencil, a candy for a roll. He was always losing out on bargains, but in the end he got the best of everyone. Half the cheder was indebted to him, since he lent money on interest. He and the bully had an arrangement whereby anyone who reneged had his hat snatched off.

Then there was the liar who boasted that his family was rich and famous and that Warsaw's elite visited his home. Promising us dates, figs, St. John's bread, and oranges from theoretical weddings and circumcisions, and a projected summer vacation, he demanded advance presents from all of us.

Then there was the victim. One day the bully drew blood from him and the next day he gave the bully a present. Smiling with sly submissiveness, the victim indicated another boy who needed a beating.

From my seat in cheder I saw everything, and even though the bully had punched me, I presented him with neither smiles nor gifts. I called him an Esau and predicted that his hereafter would be spent on a bed of nails. He hit me again for that, but I didn't weaken. I would have nothing to do with the bully, the priggish saint, the moneylender, or the liar, nor would I pay them any compliments.

I wasn't making out too well. Most of the cheder boys had grown hostile, informing against me to the teacher and the tutor. If they caught me in the street, they said, they'd break my leg. I recognized the danger. After all, I was too small to take on the entire cheder.

The trip to cheder each morning was agonizing, but I couldn't complain to my parents—they had their own troubles. Besides, they'd probably say, "That's what you get for being different from everyone else. . . ."

There was nothing to do but wait it out. Even the devil had to weary. God, if He supported truth and justice, must inevitably side with me.

The day came when it seemed to me impossible to go on. Even the teacher, in that hellish atmosphere, opposed me, though I knew my Pentateuch. The rebbetzin made malicious remarks about me. It was as if I were excommunicated.

Then, one day, everything changed. The bully miscalculated the strength of a new boy, who just happened to hit back. Then the teacher hurled himself at the bully, who already had a lump on his head. He was dragged to the whipping bench, his pants were pulled down, and he was whipped before all of us. Like Haman, he was punished. When he tried to resume his reign of terror, he was repulsed in favor of the victor.

The moneylender also met his downfall. The father of one boy who had paid out too much interest appeared at cheder to complain. A search of the moneylender's pockets proved so fruitful that he too was whipped.

The saint's hypocrisy was recognized at last, despite his whispered secrets and his flatteries.

Then, as if in response to my prayers, the boys began speaking to me once more. The flatterers and the traders offered me good will and bargains—I don't know why. I might even have formed a group of my own, but I wasn't inclined that way. There was only one boy whose friendship I wanted, and he was the one I chose. Mendel was a fine, decent person without social ambitions. We studied from the same Pentateuch and walked with our arms about each other. Others, jealous, intrigued against us, but our friendship remained constant. We were like David and Jonathan. . . .

Even after I left cheder, our friendship persisted. I had attended several cheders, and from each one I retained a friend. Occasionally, in the evenings, we would meet near the markets and walk along the sidewalk, talking, making plans. My friends' names were Mendel Besser, Mottel Horowitz, Abraham something-or-other, Boruch-Dovid, and others. More or less their leader, I would tell them things my older brother had told my mother. There was a great feeling of trust among us, until one day I had the impression that they resented me. They grumbled about my bossiness; I had to be demoted a little. They were preparing a revolution and I saw it in their faces. And even though I asked how I had offended them, they behaved like Joseph's brothers and could not answer in a friendly way. They couldn't even look at me directly. What was it they envied? My dreams . . . I could actually hear them say as I approached them, "Behold this dreamer cometh . . . Let us slay him and cast him in some pit . . . Let us sell him to the Ishmaelites . . . ."

It is painful to be among one's brothers when they are jealous. They had been good to me, they praised me, and then they were mean. All at once they grew angry. Turning away as I approached, they whispered . . . .

Friendships with me are not casual; I cannot make new friends easily. I wondered if I had sinned against them, or deceived them. But, if so, why hadn't they told me what was wrong?

I could not recollect having harmed them in any way, nor had I said anything against them. And if someone had slandered me, why should my friends believe it? After all, they were devoted to me.

There was nothing to do but wait it out. My kind has to become accustomed to loneliness. And when one is alone there is nothing to do but study. I became a diligent scholar. I would spend whole days in the Radzymin study house and then pore over religious works at home. Purchasing and renting books from peddlers, I read constantly. It was summertime and the days were long. Reading a story of three brothers, I imagined that I could write too, and began to cover both sides of a sheet. "Once there was a king who had three sons. One was wise, one foolish, and one merry . . . ." But somehow the story didn't jell.

On another paper I began to draw freakish humans and fantastic beasts. But this too wearied me, and going out to the balcony, I looked down at the street. Only I was alone. Other boys were running, playing, and talking together. I'll go mad, I thought—there was too much happening in my head all the time. Shouldn't I jump from the balcony? Or spit down on the janitor's cap?

That evening, at the Radzymin study house, a boy approached me, acting as a go-between. He spoke tactfully, suggesting that my friends were eager for an understanding but, since I was the minority, it was up to me to make the first move. In short, he suggested that I submit a plea for a truce.

I was infuriated. "It wasn't I who started this," I said. "Why should I be the one to make up?"

"You'll regret it," he warned.

"Leave!" I commanded.

He left angrily. His job as a trucemaker had been spoiled. But he knew I meant what I said.

Now that they had sent an intermediary, I knew my friends were remorseful. But I would never give in to them.

I grew accustomed to being alone and the days no longer seemed interminable. I studied, wrote, read stories. My brother had brought home a two-volume book called *Crime and Punishment*. Although I didn't really understand it, it fascinated me. Secluded in the bedroom, I read for hours. A student who had killed a crone suffered, starved, and reasoned profoundly. Coming before the prosecutor, he was questioned. . . . It was something like a storybook, but different. Strange and lofty, it reminded me of the Cabala. Who were the authors of books like this, and who could understand them? Now and then a passage was illuminated for me, I understood an episode and became enthralled by the beauty of a new insight.

I was in another world. I forgot about my friends.

At evening services in the Radzymin study house, I was unaware of the men among whom I stood. My mind was wandering, when suddenly the intermediary approached.

"Nothing you have to say can interest me," I said.

"Here's a note," he told me.

It was like a scene from a novel. My friends wrote that they missed me. "We wander about in a daze . . . ." I still remember what they said. Despite this great triumph, I was so immersed in my book that it scarcely seemed important any more that they wanted to make amends. I went out to the courtyard, and there they were. It reminded me of Joseph and his brothers. They had come to Joseph to buy grain, but why had my friends come to me?

Nevertheless, they did come, ashamed and somehow afraid—Simon, Levi, Judah. . . . Since I had not become Egypt's ruler, they were not required to bow down to the earth. I had nothing to sell but new dreams.

We talked together late and I spoke of my book. "This is no storybook, this is literature . . . ." I said. I created for them a fantastic mélange of incidents and my own thoughts, and infected them with my excitement. Hours passed. They begged me to forgive them, confessed that they had been wrong and never would be angry with me again . . . .

They kept their word.

Only time separated us. The rest was accomplished by the German murderers.

How do you explain the fact that the narrator, at first an outsider, eventually becomes a leader among the boys? What led to their becoming angry with him? How does he react to their rejection? What leads the boys to seek him out again? Discuss how Singer uses the Joseph story to develop his theme. What other biblical allusions do you recognize? What is the impact of the final statement?

LET MY PEOPLE GO
(Exodus)

Out of the Bulrushes

And the children of Israel were fruitful, and increased abundantly, and multiplied, and waxed exceedingly mighty; and the land was filled with them.

Now there arose up a new king over Egypt, which knew not Joseph. And he said unto his people, "Behold, the people of the children of Israel are more and mightier than we: come on, let us deal wisely with them; lest they multiply, and it come to pass that, when there falleth out any war, they join also unto our enemies, and fight against us, and so get them up out of the land."

Therefore they did set over them taskmasters to afflict them with their burdens. And they built for Pharaoh treasure cities, Pithom and Raamses. But the more they afflicted them, the more they multiplied and grew. And they were grieved because of the children of Israel. And the Egyptians made the children of Israel to serve with rigor: and they made their lives bitter with hard bondage, in mortar, and in brick, and in all manner of service in the field: all their service, wherein they made them serve, was with rigor.

And the king of Egypt spoke to the Hebrew midwives, of which the name of the one was Shiphrah, and the name of the other Puah: and he said, "When ye do the office of a midwife to the Hebrew women, and see them upon the stools, if it be a son, then ye shall kill him; but if it be a daughter, then she shall live." But the midwives feared God, and did not as the king of Egypt commanded them, but saved the men children alive.

And the king of Egypt called for the midwives, and said unto them, "Why have ye done this thing, and have saved the men children alive?"

And the midwives said unto Pharaoh, "Because the Hebrew women are not as the Egyptian women; for they are lively, and are delivered ere the midwives come in unto them." Therefore God dealt well with the midwives: and the people multiplied, and waxed very mighty. And it came to pass, because the midwives feared God, that he made them houses.

And Pharaoh charged all his people, saying, "Every son that is born ye shall cast into the river, and every daughter ye shall save alive."

And there went a man of the house of Levi, and took to wife a daughter of Levi. And the woman conceived, and bore a son; and when she saw him that he was a goodly child, she hid him three months. And when she could not longer hide him, she took for him an ark of bulrushes, and daubed it with slime and with pitch, and put the child therein; and she laid it in the flags by the river's brink. And his sister stood afar off, to wit what would be done to him.

And the daughter of Pharaoh came down to wash herself at the river; and her maidens walked along by the river's side: and when she saw the ark among the flags, she sent her maid to fetch it. And when she had opened it, she saw the child: and, behold, the babe wept. And she had compassion on him, and said, "This is one of the Hebrews' children."

Then said his sister to Pharaoh's daughter, "Shall I go and call to thee a nurse of the Hebrew women, that she may nurse the child for thee?"

The Finding of Moses (17th c.) by Laurent de La Hyre. COURTESY OF THE DETROIT INSTITUTE OF ARTS.

And Pharaoh's daughter said to her, "Go."

And the maid went and called the child's mother. And Pharaoh's daughter said unto her, "Take this child away, and nurse it for me, and I will give thee thy wages." And the woman took the child, and nursed it.

And the child grew, and she brought him unto Pharaoh's daughter, and he became her son. And she called his name Moses: and she said, "Because I drew him out of the water."

And it came to pass in those days, when Moses was grown, that he went out unto his brethren, and looked on their burdens: and he spied an Egyptian smiting an Hebrew, one of his brethren. And he looked this way and that way, and when he saw that there was no man, he slew the Egyptian, and hid him in the sand. And when he went out the second day, behold, two men of the Hebrews strove together: and he said to him that did the wrong, "Wherefore smitest thou thy fellow?"

And he said, "Who made thee a prince and a judge over us? Intendest thou to kill me, as thou killedst the Egyptian?"

And Moses feared, and said, "Surely this thing is known."

Now when Pharaoh heard this thing, he sought to slay Moses. But Moses fled from the face of Pharaoh, and dwelt in the land of Midian: and he sat down by a well.

Now the priest of Midian had seven daughters: and they came and drew water, and filled the troughs to water their father's flock. And the shepherds came and drove them away: but Moses stood up and helped them, and watered their flock.

And when they came to Reuel their father, he said, "How is it that ye are come so soon today?"

And they said, "An Egyptian delivered us out of the hand of the shepherds, and also drew water enough for us, and watered the flock."

And he said unto his daughters, "And where is he? Why is it that ye have left the man? Call him, that he may eat bread."

And Moses was content to dwell with the man: and he gave Moses Zipporah his daughter. And she bare him a son, and he called his name Gershom: for he said, "I have been a stranger in a strange land."

[*Exodus 1:7–2:22*]

The Burning Bush

And it came to pass in process of time that the king of Egypt died: and the children of Israel sighed by reason of the bondage, and they cried, and their cry came up unto God by reason of the bondage. And

God heard their groaning, and God remembered his covenant with Abraham, with Isaac, and with Jacob. And God looked upon the children of Israel, and God had respect unto them.

Now Moses kept the flock of Jethro his father-in-law, the priest of Midian: and he led the flock to the backside of the desert, and came to the mountain of God, even to Horeb. And the angel of the Lord appeared unto him in a flame of fire out of the midst of a bush: and he looked, and, behold, the bush burned with fire, and the bush was not consumed. And Moses said, "I will now turn aside, and see this great sight, why the bush is not burnt."

And when the Lord saw that he turned aside to see, God called unto him out of the midst of the bush, and said, "Moses, Moses."

And he said, "Here am I."

And he said, "Draw not nigh hither: put off thy shoes from off thy feet, for the place whereon thou standest is holy ground." Moreover he said, "I am the God of thy father, the God of Abraham, the God of Isaac, and the God of Jacob." And Moses hid his face; for he was afraid to look upon God.

And the Lord said, "I have surely seen the affliction of my people which are in Egypt, and have heard their cry by reason of their taskmasters; for I know their sorrows; and I am come down to deliver them out of the hand of the Egyptians, and to bring them up out of that land unto a good land and a large, unto a land flowing with milk and honey. Come now therefore, and I will send thee unto Pharaoh, that thou mayest bring forth my people the children of Israel out of Egypt."

And Moses said unto God, "Who am I, that I should go unto Pharaoh, and that I should bring forth the children of Israel out of Egypt?"

And he said, "Certainly I will be with thee; and this shall be a token unto thee, that I have sent thee: when thou hast brought forth the people out of Egypt, ye shall serve God upon this mountain."

And Moses said unto God, "Behold, when I come unto the children of Israel, and shall say unto them, 'The God of your fathers hath sent me unto you'; and they shall say to me, 'What is his name?' what shall I say unto them?"

And God said unto Moses, "I AM THAT I AM"; and he said, "Thus shalt thou say unto the children of Israel, I AM hath sent me unto you." And God said moreover unto Moses, "Thus shalt thou say unto the children of Israel, 'The Lord God of your fathers, the God of Abraham, the God of Isaac, and the God of Jacob, hath sent me unto you: this is my name for ever, and this is my memorial unto all generations.' "

And Moses said unto the Lord, "O my Lord, I am not eloquent, neither heretofore, nor since thou hast spoken unto thy servant: but I am slow of speech, and of a slow tongue."

And the Lord said unto him, "Who hath made man's mouth? Or who maketh the dumb, or deaf, or the seeing, or the blind? Have not I the Lord? Now therefore go, and I will be with thy mouth, and teach thee what thou shalt say."

And he said, "O my Lord, send, I pray thee, by the hand of him whom thou wilt send."

And the anger of the Lord was kindled against Moses, and he said, "Is not Aaron the Levite thy brother? I know that he can speak well. And also, behold, he cometh forth to meet thee: and when he seeth thee, he will be glad in his heart. And thou shalt speak unto him, and put words in his mouth: and I will be with thy mouth, and with his mouth, and will teach you what ye shall do. And he shall be thy spokesman unto the people: and he shall be, even he shall be to thee instead of a mouth, and thou shalt be to him instead of God. And thou shalt take this rod in thine hand, wherewith thou shalt do signs."

[*Exodus 2:23–3:8a, 10–15; 4:10–17*]

Before Pharaoh

And the Lord said to Aaron, "Go into the wilderness to meet Moses." And he went, and met him in the mount of God, and kissed him. And Moses told Aaron all the words of the Lord who had sent him, and all the signs which he had commanded him.

And Moses and Aaron went and gathered together all the elders of the children of Israel: and Aaron spake all the words which the Lord had spoken unto Moses and did the signs in sight of the people. And the people believed: and when they heard that the Lord had visited the children of Israel, and that he had looked upon their affliction, then they bowed their heads and worshiped.

And afterward Moses and Aaron went in, and told Pharaoh, "Thus saith the Lord God of Israel, 'Let my people go, that they may hold a feast unto me in the wilderness.' "

And Pharaoh said, "Who is the Lord, that I should obey his voice to let Israel go? I know not the Lord, neither will I let Israel go."

And they said, "The God of the Hebrews hath met with us: let us go, we pray thee, three days' journey into the desert, and sacrifice unto the Lord our God; lest he fall upon us with pestilence, or with the sword."

And the king of Egypt said unto them, "Wherefore do ye, Moses and Aaron, let the people from their works? Get you unto your burdens."

And Pharaoh commanded the same day the taskmasters of the people, and their officers, saying, "Ye shall no more give the people straw to make brick, as heretofore: let them go and gather straw for themselves. And the tale of the bricks, which they did make heretofore, ye shall lay upon them; ye shall not diminish aught thereof: for they be idle; therefore they cry, saying, 'Let us go and sacrifice to our God.' Let there more work be laid upon the men, that they may labor therein; and let them not regard vain words."

[*Exodus 4:27–5:4, 6–9*]

The Covenant Reaffirmed

And Moses returned unto the Lord, and said, "Lord, wherefore hast thou so evil entreated this people? Why is it that thou hast sent me? For since I came to Pharaoh to speak in thy name, he hath done evil to this people; neither hast thou delivered thy people at all."

Then the Lord said unto Moses, "Now shalt thou see what I shall do to Pharaoh: for with a strong hand shall he let them go, and with a strong hand shall he drive them out of his land."

And God spake unto Moses, and said unto him, "I am the Lord: and I appeared unto Abraham, unto Isaac, and unto Jacob, by the name of God Almighty; but by my name Jehovah was I not known to them. And I have also established my covenant with them, to give them the land of Canaan, the land of their pilgrimage, wherein they were strangers. And I have also heard the groaning of the children of Israel, whom the Egyptians keep in bondage; and I have remembered my covenant.

"Wherefore say unto the children of Israel, 'I am the Lord, and I will bring you out from under the burdens of the Egyptians, and I will rid you of their bondage, and I will redeem you with a stretched out arm, and with great judgments. And I will take you to me for a people, and I will be to you a God: and ye shall know that I am the Lord your God, which bringeth you out from under the burdens of the Egyptians. And I will bring you in unto the land, concerning the which I did swear to give it to Abraham, to Isaac, and to Jacob; and I will give it to you for a heritage: I am the Lord.'"

And Moses spake so unto the children of Israel: but they hearkened not unto Moses for anguish of spirit, and for cruel bondage.

And the Lord spake unto Moses, saying, "Go in, speak unto Pharaoh king of Egypt, that he let the children of Israel go out of this land."

And Moses spake before the Lord, saying, "Behold, the children of Israel have not hearkened unto me; how then shall Pharaoh hear me, who am of uncircumcised lips?"

And the Lord spake unto Moses and unto Aaron and gave them a charge unto the children of Israel, and unto Pharaoh king of Egypt, to bring the children of Israel out of the land of Egypt.

[Exodus 5:22–6:13]

The Ten Plagues

And the Lord said unto Moses, "See, I have made thee a god to Pharaoh: and Aaron thy brother shall be thy prophet. Thou shalt speak all that I command thee: and Aaron thy brother shall speak unto Pharaoh, that he send the children of Israel out of his land. And I will harden Pharaoh's heart, and multiply my signs and my wonders in the land of Egypt. But Pharaoh shall not hearken unto you, that I may lay my hand upon Egypt, and bring forth mine armies, and my people the children of Israel, out of the land of Egypt by great judgments. And the Egyptians shall know that I am the Lord, when I stretch forth mine hand upon Egypt, and bring out the children of Israel from among them."

And the Lord spoke unto Moses and unto Aaron, saying, "When Pharaoh shall speak unto you, saying, 'Show a miracle for you,' then thou shalt say unto Aaron, 'Take thy rod, and cast it before Pharaoh,' and it shall become a serpent."

And Moses and Aaron went in unto Pharaoh, and they did so as the Lord had commanded: and Aaron cast down his rod before Pharaoh, and before his servants, and it became a serpent. Then Pharaoh also called the wise men and the sorcerers: now the magicians of Egypt, they also did in like manner with their enchantments. For they cast down every man his rod, and they became serpents: but Aaron's rod swallowed up their rods. And he hardened Pharaoh's heart, that he hearkened not unto them, as the Lord had said.

[At the command of the Lord, Moses and Aaron continue to entreat Pharaoh for the release of their people. To punish Pharaoh for his obstinacy and to prove to the Egyptian ruler the supremacy of the Lord's power over that of his magicians, the Lord empowers Moses

*and Aaron to inflict a different plague on the Egyptians after each of
Pharaoh's refusals. First the rivers are turned to blood; then frogs
come forth in great abundance; next lice swarm over the land, then
flies; all the cattle fall ill and die; boils break out on man and beast;
thunder and hail bring destruction on the land; then a swarm of
locusts arrive, followed by darkness covering the land for three days.
But still Pharaoh's heart remained hardened. Following God's
instructions, Moses prepares his people for the final plague to be
inflicted on the Egyptians—the death of the firstborn—after which, as
God assured him, they will surely be allowed out of the land.]*

Then Moses called for all the elders of Israel, and said unto them,
"Draw out and take you a lamb according to your families, and kill
the passover. And ye shall take a bunch of hyssop, and dip it in the
blood that is in the basin, and strike the lintel and the two side posts
with the blood that is in the basin; and none of you shall go out at
the door of his house until the morning. For the Lord will pass through
to smite the Egyptians; and when he seeth the blood upon the lintel,
and on the two side posts, the Lord will pass over the door, and will
not suffer the destroyer to come in unto your houses to smite you. And
ye shall observe this thing for an ordinance to thee and to thy sons
for ever. And it shall come to pass, when ye be come to the land
which the Lord will give you, according as he hath promised, that ye
shall keep this service. And it shall come to pass, when your children
shall say unto you, 'What mean ye by this service?' that ye shall say,
'It is the sacrifice of the Lord's passover, who passed over the houses
of the children of Israel in Egypt, when he smote the Egyptians, and
delivered our houses.'"

And the people bowed the head and worshiped. And the children
of Israel went away, and did as the Lord had commanded Moses and
Aaron, so did they.

And it came to pass that at midnight the Lord smote all the first-
born in the land of Egypt, from the firstborn of Pharaoh that sat on
his throne unto the firstborn of the captive that was in the dungeon;
and all the firstborn of cattle. And Pharaoh rose up in the night, he,
and all his servants, and all the Egyptians; and there was a great cry
in Egypt; for there was not a house where there was not one dead.

And he called for Moses and Aaron by night, and said, "Rise up,
and get you forth from among my people, both ye and the children of
Israel; and go, serve the Lord, as ye have said. Also take your flocks
and your herds, as ye have said, and be gone; and bless me also."

And the Egyptians were urgent upon the people, that they might send them out of the land in haste; for they said, "We be all dead men."

And the people took their dough before it was leavened, their kneadingtroughs being bound up in their clothes upon their shoulders. And the children of Israel did according to the word of Moses; and they borrowed of the Egyptians jewels of silver, and jewels of gold, and raiment: and the Lord gave the people favor in the sight of the Egyptians, so that they lent unto them such things as they required; and they spoiled the Egyptians.

[*Exodus 7:1–5, 8–13; 12:21–36*]

Deliverance

And the children of Israel journeyed from Raamses to Succoth, about six hundred thousand on foot that were men, beside children.

And the Lord went before them by day in a pillar of a cloud, to lead them the way; and by night in a pillar of fire, to give them light; to go by day and night; he took not away the pillar of the cloud by day, nor the pillar of fire by night, from before the people.

And it was told the king of Egypt that the people fled: and the heart of Pharaoh and of his servants was turned against the people, and they said, "Why have we done this, that we have let Israel go from serving us?"

And he made ready his chariot, and took his people with him: and he took six hundred chosen chariots, and all the chariots of Egypt, and captains over every one of them. And the Lord hardened the heart of Pharaoh king of Egypt, and he pursued after the children of Israel.

And when Pharaoh drew nigh, the children of Israel lifted up their eyes, and, behold, the Egyptians marched after them; and they were sore afraid: and the children of Israel cried out unto the Lord. And they said unto Moses, "Because there were no graves in Egypt, hast thou taken us away to die in the wilderness? Wherefore hast thou dealt thus with us, to carry us forth out of Egypt? Is not this the word that we did tell thee in Egypt, saying, 'Let us alone, that we may serve the Egyptians'? For it had been better for us to serve the Egyptians, than that we should die in the wilderness."

And Moses said unto the people, "Fear ye not, stand still, and see the salvation of the Lord, which he will show to you today: for the Egyptians whom ye have seen today, ye shall see them again no more for ever. The Lord shall fight for you, and ye shall hold your peace."

And the Lord said unto Moses, "Wherefore criest thou unto me? Speak unto the children of Israel, that they go forward: but lift thou up thy rod, and stretch out thine hand over the sea, and divide it: and the children of Israel shall go on dry ground through the midst of the sea. And I, behold, I will harden the hearts of the Egyptians, and they shall follow them: and I will get me honor upon Pharaoh, and upon all his host, upon his chariots, and upon his horsemen. And the Egyptians shall know that I am the Lord, when I have gotten me honor upon Pharaoh, upon his chariots, and upon his horsemen."

And the angel of God, which went before the camp of Israel, removed and went behind them; and the pillar of the cloud went from before their face, and stood behind them: and it came between the camp of the Egyptians and the camp of Israel; and it was a cloud and darkness to them, but it gave light by night to these: so that the one came not near the other all the night.

And Moses stretched out his hand over the sea; and the Lord caused the sea to go back by a strong east wind all that night, and made the sea dry land, and the waters were divided. And the children of Israel went into the midst of the sea upon the dry ground: and the waters were a wall unto them on their right hand, and on their left.

And the Egyptians pursued, and went in after them to the midst of the sea, even all Pharaoh's horses, his chariots, and his horsemen. And the Lord said unto Moses, "Stretch out thine hand over the sea, that the waters may come again upon the Egyptians, upon their chariots, and upon their horsemen."

And Moses stretched forth his hand over the sea, and the sea returned to his strength when the morning appeared; and the Egyptians fled against it; and the Lord overthrew the Egyptians in the midst of the sea. And the waters returned, and covered the chariots, and the horsemen, and all the host of Pharaoh that came into the sea after them; there remained not so much as one of them.

But the children of Israel walked upon dry land in the midst of the sea; and the waters were a wall unto them on their right hand, and on their left. Thus the Lord saved Israel that day out of the hand of the Egyptians; and Israel saw the Egyptians dead upon the sea shore. And Israel saw that great work which the Lord did upon the Egyptians: and the people feared the Lord, and believed the Lord, and his servant Moses.

Then sang Moses and the children of Israel this song unto the Lord, saying:

"I will sing unto the Lord for he hath triumphed gloriously:
The horse and his rider hath he thrown into the sea.
The Lord is my strength and song,
And he is become my salvation:
He is my God, and I will prepare him a habitation;
My father's God, and I will exalt him.

"Thou in thy mercy hast led forth the people which thou hast
    redeemed:
Thou hast guided them in thy strength unto thy holy habitation.

"Thou shalt bring them in, and plant them in the mountain of
    thine inheritance,
In the place, O Lord, which thou hast made for thee to dwell in;
In the sanctuary, O Lord, which thy hands have established.
The Lord shall reign for ever and ever."

[*Exodus 12:37; 13:21–22; 14:5–8a, 10–23, 26; 15:1–2, 11, 17–18*]

Why did the King of Egypt order the death of all newborn male
Israelites? What connection do you see between the nature of Moses'
upbringing and his becoming the leader of the Israelites? Why
was Moses forced to become "a stranger in a strange land"? What
does this incident show you about the royally-raised Moses?

Why do you suspect Pharaoh refused to allow the Israelites to go
to the wilderness to hold a three-day feast unto their Lord? How
do the Israelites react to their increased burdens? At what other
times do they show a similar wavering of courage and faith? How do
you account for their constant reluctance to strike out on their own?

In what ways did the Lord of Israel mock the power of Pharaoh,
who claimed that he was a god?

THE FIRSTBORN
(from Act I, Scene I)

Christopher Fry

In this powerful dramatic recreation, Christopher Fry probes the nature of the conflict between Moses and Pharaoh, and the extent to which their lives are bound together. Moses, who has been raised in Pharaoh's court, is seen as a "soldier of genius" who has fallen into disfavor with Pharaoh after killing an Egyptian he saw beating an Israelite. The action of the play begins ten years later. Seti, the Pharaoh, has called Moses back from exile in order that he might once again become a leader in the Egyptian military. In the brief scene that follows, Seti—attended by his sister Anath, the princess who raised Moses as a child, and his son Ramases—is confronted by Moses and Aaron.

 Enter RAMASES, *followed by* MOSES *and* AARON.

SETI:

 I am tempted to call this a visitation and not
 A visit. What words can I find to fit
 So ghostly a homecoming?

RAMASES *(to* ANATH*):*

        Who is this man?

SETI:

 Understand you are welcome. Whatever uncertainty
 You have can go. We welcome you. Look who is here.

ANATH:

 He has seen me. We have looked at one another.

SETI:

 We'll absolve ourselves of the ten years. Who is this?

MOSES:

 My brother.

SETI:

     I had not heard you had a brother.

ANATH:

 A brother, a sister—and a mother. All the three.

SETI:

    Our lives at their most coincidental bring the gods
    Very near. I told my sister we must have you back.
    And so we must, and so Egypt must; and it seems
    That we have. You are come promptly at the word, Moses.

MOSES:

    This is not why I came.

SETI:

                    You would scarcely foresee it.

MOSES:

    I am not who you think. I am a stranger.

SETI:

    Not by a vein or a hair. The past is forgotten.
    You are a prince of Egypt.

MOSES:

               The prince of Egypt
    Died the day he fled.

SETI:

             What do you mean?

MOSES:

    That prince of Egypt died. I am the Hebrew
    Smitten out of the shadow of that prince,
    Vomited out of his dry lips, the cry
    Whipped off the sanded tongue of that prince of Egypt.

SETI:

    What has this long discomfort done for you,
    My friend? It has made you bitter.

MOSES:

                     Make no mistake;
    I have done very well for myself. I haven't come to beg.
    Why was it you decided to ask me to come back?

SETI:

    Isn't it time we laid the crippling ghost
    That haunts us? You evidently thought so too
    To come so far.

MOSES:

            You've a better reason than that.

SETI:

    Why should you want reasons when you have come
    On your own initiative? Why are you here?
    I am asking you candidly. Why did you come?

MOSES:

> My blood heard my blood weeping
> Far off like the swimming of fear under the sea,
> The sobbing at night below the garden. I heard
> My blood weeping. It is here it wept and weeps.
> It was from here I heard coming this drum of despair,
> The hidden bullfrog of my brothers' grief:
> Under your shoes, under your smile, and under
> The foundations of your tomb. From Egypt.

ANATH:

> What was it, Seti, that lay down and died?

SETI:

> Why are you here?

MOSES:

> > To be close to this
> That up to now has only made me uneasy,
> As though a threat of evil whispered beyond
> Control under the wind. I could be
> Uneasy and still eat in Midian.
> I could be Pharaoh in Midian, but in Egypt
> I knew I should be Moses.

SETI:

> > Still you haven't
> Answered my question. Come, what do you want?

MOSES:

> First, that you should know what you are doing.

SETI:

> Take care, Moses.

ANATH:

> > And secondly?

MOSES:

> > What can I hope
> From that until he has understood the first?

SETI:

> What is this mood you have come in which is so ready
> To abuse a decent welcome? There is something shipwreck
> About you that will not do for peaceful places.
> Steady yourself if we're to understand one another.
> I am the Pharaoh, Moses, not the young uncle
> Of the Heliopolis classroom, nor your messroom brother.
> Well, go on.

MOSES:

           A man has more to be
Than a Pharaoh. He must dare to outgrow the security
Of partial blindness. I'm not speaking now
To your crown; I'm speaking to your merciless mischief.

SETI:

You have coarsened during your exile. What you say
Hasn't even the virtue of clarity. If you wish
To consider my offer of reinstatement, go
And consider. I can be patient. Egypt can do
Her work on you like a generous woman, given
Her time. *(He glances at* ANATH.*)*
           Midian will wash off in the Nile.
Go on, go on, I shall not remember this morning.

MOSES:

I think you will. My brother has lived these days
In amongst Israel, while I was sleeping.
He knows both the truth and the injury better than I can.
He has had refuge, this last year, close to your border.
He was hunted out for his friendship to flesh and blood,
And so he has lain with his ear against the door
Hearing pain but unable to come to it.
He stands here with me now so that what shall be said
Shall be truthfully said and what you shall hear
Will have earned hearing because the teller lived it.

AARON:

Twelve hundred thousand Israelites are under
Your dominion. Of these two hundred and twenty thousand
Only, are men. The rest are in the proportion
Of four hundred and fifty thousand women
And five hundred and thirty thousand children.

SETI:

I have my census-takers.

AARON:

               So perhaps
Has Death got his; but I think he has not referred
His undertakings to your dynastic understanding.
Here I have his estimate: between April and July
Sixty-one deaths suffered in old age
But an old age of forced labour, their backs bent twice,
Under the weight of years and under the mule-whip.

Also thirty-eight deaths of healthy men
Who made some show of reluctance or momentary
Impatience.

MOSES:

That was a good cure. They are now
Patient for all eternity.

AARON:

Also the deaths
Of seven pregnant women, forced to dig
Until they had become their own gravediggers.
Also the deaths of nineteen children, twelve
Unofficial crucifixions . . .

SETI:

This is intolerable
Singsong! Am I to compose the epitaphs
For every individual grave of this trying summer?
I have my figures. I do not need yours.

MOSES:

Twelve hundred thousand. These are the men
I have come to find. They are the wound in my mind.
They show me myself covered in blood: and you
Are there, staring back at yourself from that mortal
Mirror, twelve hundred thousand times yourself,
Which, like a dog with its own reflection,
You don't recognize. No recollection?
Not of this child, elect in its private maze?
Not of this boy rashly making manhood
Out of a clumsy alteration? Is this some other
Form of life than yours? What; is nothing like?
The girls dandling to-morrow, the young men
Trying to justify to-day, old men
Sitting by monuments of memory—
All these licking their fingers of experience
To turn the page.—No! I am mistaken.
They are only pestilence-carriers and tomb makers.
But the worst pestilence they carry is the cruelty
Of Pharaoh. That is what I have come to show you.

SETI:

Very well; you have introduced yourself;
I have understood you. Is it not a pity
That you had taken up this attitude
Before you were aware of mine? I can see
How, knowing, as you must, your own capabilities,

You would fill those listless hours of your exile
With dreams of action. Action is what I have for you.
But there's a whiff of anarchy about you.
You cannot hope that I should like it. A generalship—
The confidence of Egypt—these do not look well
On an agitator. Something has to go.—
I have put men to a purpose who otherwise
Would have had not the least meaning.

MOSES:

Aaron,
What am I doing fitting one word against another
To see them melt as soon as they touch this man?
Not the least meaning, except the meaning
Of the breath in your lungs, the mystery of existing
At all. What have we approached or conceived
When we have conquered and built a world? Even
Though civilisation became perfect? What then?
We have only put a crown on the skeleton.
It is the individual man
In his individual freedom who can mature
With his warm spirit the unripe world.
What would you make of man? If you diminish him
To a count of labouring limbs, you also will dwindle
And be an unmeaning body, decomposing
Imperceptibly under heavy ornaments.
They are your likeness, these men, even to nightmares.
I have business with Egypt, one more victory for her,
A better one than Ethiopia:
That she should come to see her own shame
And discover justice for my people.

Anath asks her brother, "What was it, Seti, that lay down and died?"
Who does Moses say has "died the day he fled"? What does he
mean? Who has emerged in his place? Explain "My blood heard my
blood weeping." What is the purpose of Aaron's catalogue of atrocities?
In what respect does Seti misunderstand Moses' "dream of action"?
How does he plan to "cure" Moses of his misguided zeal? Summarize
Moses' final speech and discuss his vision of "individual freedom."
In what sense is Moses' observation that "A man has more to be than
a Pharaoh" an earlier statement of this. Cite other lines that reflect
this theme.

GO DOWN, MOSES
(A Spiritual)

When Israel was in Egypt land,
   Let my people go;
Oppressed so hard they could not stand,
   Let my people go.

    Chorus

    Go down, Moses,
      Way down in Egypt land,
    Tell ol' Pharaoh,
      Let my people go.

Thus spoke the Lord, bold Moses said,
   Let my people go;
If not, I'll smite your first-born dead,
   Let my people go.

    Chorus

No more shall they in bondage toil,
   Let my people go;
Let them come out with Egypt's spoil,
   Let my people go.

    Chorus

The Lord told Moses what to do,
   Let my people go;
To lead his people right on through,
   Let my people go.

    Chorus

'Twas on a dark and dismal night,
   Let my people go;

When Moses led the Israelites,
  Let my people go.

  Chorus

Oh Moses, clouds will cleave the way,
  Let my people go;
A fire by night, a shade by day,
  Let my people go.

  Chorus

When Israel reached the water side,
  Let my people go;
Commanded God, "It shall divide,"
  Let my people go.

  Chorus

"Come Moses, you will not get lost,"
  Let my people go;
"Stretch out your rod and come across,"
  Let my people go.

  Chorus

When they had reached the other shore,
  Let my people go;
They sang a song of triumph o'er,
  Let my people go.

  Chorus

Now Pharaoh said he'd go across,
  Let my people go;
But Pharaoh and his host were lost,
  Let my people go.

  Chorus

Oh take your shoes from off your feet,
  Let my people go;

> And walk into the golden street,
>   Let my people go.
>
> *Chorus*

GO DOWN, MOSES

William Faulkner

1.

The face was black, smooth, impenetrable; the eyes had seen too much. The negroid hair had been treated so that it covered the skull like a cap, in a single neat-ridged sweep, with the appearance of having been lacquered, the part trimmed out with a razor, so that the head resembled a bronze head, imperishable and enduring. He wore one of those sports costumes called ensembles in the men's shop advertisements, shirt and trousers matching and cut from the same fawn-colored flannel, and they had cost too much and were draped too much, with too many pleats; and he half lay on the steel cot in the steel cubicle just outside which an armed guard had stood for twenty hours now, smoking cigarettes and answering in a voice which was anything under the sun but a southern voice or even a negro voice, the questions of the spectacled young white man sitting with a broad census-taker's portfolio on the steel stool opposite:

"Samuel Worsham Beauchamp. Twenty-six. Born in the country near Jefferson, Mississippi. No family. No ——"

"Wait." The census-taker wrote rapidly. "That's not the name you were sen—lived under in Chicago."

The other snapped the ash from the cigarette. "No. It was another guy killed the cop."

"All right. Occupation ——"

"Getting rich too fast.

——none." The census-taker wrote rapidly. "Parents."

"Sure. Two. I don't remember them. My grandmother raised me."

"What's her name? Is she still living?"

"I dont know. Mollie Worsham Beauchamp. If she is, she's on Carothers Edmonds' farm seventeen miles from Jefferson, Mississippi. That all?"

The census-taker closed the portfolio and stood up. He was a year or two younger than the other. "If they dont know who you are here, how will they know—how do you expect to get home?"

The other snapped the ash from the cigarette, lying on the steel cot in the fine Hollywood clothes and a pair of shoes better than the census-taker would ever own. "What will that matter to me?" he said.

So the census-taker departed; the guard locked the steel door again. And the other lay on the steel cot smoking until after a while they came and slit the expensive trousers and shaved the expensive coiffure and led him out of the cell.

2.

On that same hot, bright July morning the same hot bright wind which shook the mulberry leaves just outside Gavin Stevens' window blew into the office too, contriving a semblance of coolness from what was merely motion. It fluttered among the county-attorney business on the desk and blew in the wild shock of prematurely white hair of the man who sat behind it—a thin, intelligent, unstable face, a rumpled linen suit from whose lapel a Phi Beta Kappa key dangled on a watch chain—Gavin Stevens, Phi Beta Kappa, Harvard, Ph.D., Heidelberg, whose office was his hobby, although it made his living for him, and whose serious vocation was a twenty-two-year-old unfinished translation of the Old Testament back into classic Greek. Only his caller seemed impervious to it, though by appearance she should have owned in that breeze no more of weight and solidity than the intact ash of a scrap of burned paper—a little old negro woman with a shrunken, incredibly old face beneath a white headcloth and a black straw hat which would have fitted a child.

"Beauchamp?" Stevens said. "You live on Mr Carothers Edmonds' place."

"I done left," she said. "I come to find my boy." Then, sitting in the hard chair opposite him and without moving, she began to chant. "Roth Edmonds sold my Benjamin. Sold him in Egypt. Pharaoh got him ——"

"Wait," Stevens said. "Wait, Aunty." Because memory, recollection, was about to mesh and click. "If you dont know where your grandson is, how do you know he's in trouble? Do you mean that Mr Edmonds has refused to help you find him?"

"It was Roth Edmonds sold him," she said. "Sold him in Egypt. I dont know whar he is. I just knows Pharaoh got him. And you the Law. I wants to find my boy."

"All right," Stevens said. "I'll try to find him. If you're not going back home, where will you stay in town? It may take some time, if you dont know where he went and you haven't heard from him in five years."

"I be staying with Hamp Worsham. He my brother."

"All right," Stevens said. He was not surprised. He had known Hamp Worsham all his life, though he had never seen the old Negress before. But even if he had, he still would not have been surprised. They were like that. You could know two of them for years; they might even have worked for you for years, bearing different names. Then suddenly you learn by pure chance that they are brothers or sisters.

He sat in the hot motion which was not breeze and listened to her toiling slowly down the steep outside stairs, remembering the grand-son. The papers of that business had passed across his desk before going to the District Attorney five or six years ago—Butch Beauchamp, as the youth had been known during the single year he had spent in and out of the city jail: the old Negress' daughter's child, orphaned of his mother at birth and deserted by his father, whom the grand-mother had taken and raised, or tried to. Because at nineteen he had quit the country and come to town and spent a year in and out of jail for gambling and fighting, to come at last under serious indictment for breaking and entering a store.

Caught red-handed, whereupon he had struck with a piece of iron pipe at the officer who surprised him and then lay on the ground where the officer had felled him with a pistol-butt, cursing through his broken mouth, his teeth fixed into something like furious laughter through the blood. Then two nights later he broke out of jail and was seen no more—a youth not yet twenty-one, with something in him from the father who begot and deserted him and who was now in the State Penitentiary for manslaughter—some seed not only violent but dangerous and bad.

And that's who I am to find, save, Stevens thought. Because he did not for one moment doubt the old Negress' instinct. If she had also been able to divine where the boy was and what his trouble was, he would not have been surprised, and it was only later that he thought to be surprised at how quickly he did find where the boy was and what was wrong.

His first thought was to telephone Carothers Edmonds, on whose farm the old Negress' husband had been a tenant for years. But then, according to her, Edmonds had already refused to have anything to do with it. Then he sat perfectly still while the hot wind blew in his wild white mane. Now he comprehended what the old Negress had meant. He remembered now that it was Edmonds who had actually sent the boy to Jefferson in the first place: he had caught the boy breaking into his commissary store and had ordered him off the place and had forbidden him ever to return. *And not the sheriff, the police,* he thought. *Something broader, quicker in scope. . . .* He rose and took his old fine worn panama and descended the outside stairs and crossed the empty square in the hot suspension of noon's beginning, to the office of the county newspaper. The editor was in—an older man but with hair less white than Stevens', in a black string tie and an old-fashioned boiled shirt and tremendously fat.

"An old nigger woman named Mollie Beauchamp," Stevens said. "She and her husband live on the Edmonds place. It's her grandson. You remember him—Butch Beauchamp, about five or six years ago, who spent a year in town, mostly in jail, until they finally caught him breaking into Rouncewell's store one night? Well, he's in worse trouble than that now. I dont doubt her at all. I just hope, for her sake as well as that of the great public whom I represent, that his present trouble is very bad and maybe final too ——"

"Wait," the editor said. He didn't even need to leave his desk. He took the press association flimsy from its spike and handed it to Stevens. It was datelined from Joliet, Illinois, this morning:

> *Mississippi negro, on eve of execution for murder of Chicago policeman, exposes alias by completing census questionnaire. Samuel Worsham Beauchamp ——*

Five minutes later Stevens was crossing again the empty square in which noon's hot suspension was that much nearer. He had thought that he was going home to his boarding house for the noon meal, but he found that he was not. '*Besides, I didn't lock my office door,*' he thought. Only, how under the sun she could have got to town from those seventeen miles. She may even have walked. "So it seems I didn't mean what I said I hoped," he said aloud, mounting the outside stairs again, out of the hazy and now windless sunglare, and entered his office. He stopped. Then he said,

"Good morning, Miss Worsham."

She was quite old too—thin, erect, with a neat, old-time piling of white hair beneath a faded hat of thirty years ago, in rusty black, with a frayed umbrella faded now until it was green instead of black.

He had known her too all his life. She lived alone in the decaying house her father had left her, where she gave lessons in china-painting and, with the help of Hamp Worsham, descendant of one of her father's slaves, and his wife, raised chickens and vegetables for market.

"I came about Mollie," she said. "Mollie Beauchamp. She said that you ——"

He told her while she watched him, erect on the hard chair where the old Negress had sat, the rusty umbrella leaning against her knee. On her lap, beneath her folded hands, lay an old-fashioned beaded reticule almost as big as a suitcase. "He is to be executed tonight."

"Can nothing be done? Mollie's and Hamp's parents belonged to my grandfather. Mollie and I were born in the same month. We grew up together as sisters would."

"I telephoned," Stevens said. "I talked to the Warden at Joliet, and to the District Attorney in Chicago. He had a fair trial, a good lawyer—of that sort. He had money. He was in a business called numbers, that people like him make money in." She watched him, erect and motionless. "He is a murderer, Miss Worsham. He shot that policeman in the back. A bad son of a bad father. He admitted, confessed it afterward."

"I know," she said. Then he realised that she was not looking at him, not seeing him at least. "It's terrible."

"So is murder terrible," Stevens said. "It's better this way." Then she was looking at him again.

"I wasn't thinking of him. I was thinking of Mollie. She mustn't know."

"Yes," Stevens said. "I have already talked with Mr Wilmoth at the paper. He has agreed not to print anything. I will telephone the Memphis paper, but it's probably too late for that. . . . If we could just persuade her to go on back home this afternoon, before the Memphis paper . . . Out there, where the only white person she ever sees is Mr Edmonds, and I will telephone him; and even if the other darkies should hear about it, I'm sure they wouldn't. And then maybe in about two or three months I could go out there and tell her he is dead and buried somewhere in the North. . . ." This time she was watching him with such an expression that he ceased talking; she sat there, erect on the hard chair, watching him until he had ceased.

"She will want to take him back home with her," she said.

"Him?" Stevens said. "The body?" She watched him. The expression was neither shocked nor disapproving. It merely embodied some old, timeless, female affinity for blood and grief. Stevens thought: *She has*

*walked to town in this heat. Unless Hamp brought her in the buggy
he peddles eggs and vegetables from.*

"He is the only child of her oldest daughter, her own dead first child.
He must come home."

"He must come home," Stevens said as quietly. "I'll attend to it at
once. I'll telephone at once."

"You are kind." For the first time she stirred, moved. He watched
her hands draw the reticule toward her, clasping it. "I will defray the
expenses. Can you give me some idea ——?"

He looked her straight in the face. He told the lie without batting
an eye, quickly and easily. "Ten or twelve dollars will cover it. They
will furnish a box and there will be only the transportation."

"A box?" Again she was looking at him with that expression curious
and detached, as though he were a child. "He is her grandson, Mr
Stevens. When she took him to raise, she gave him my father's name—
Samuel Worsham. Not just a box, Mr Stevens. I understand that can
be done by paying so much a month."

"Not just a box," Stevens said. He said it in exactly the same tone in
which he had said He must come home. "Mr Edmonds will want to
help, I know. And I understand that old Luke Beauchamp has some
money in the bank. And if you will permit me ——"

"That will not be necessary," she said. He watched her open the
reticule; he watched her count onto the desk twenty-five dollars in
frayed bills and coins ranging down to nickels and dimes and pennies.
"That will take care of the immediate expenses. I will tell her—You are
sure there is no hope?"

"I am sure. He will die tonight."

"I will tell her this afternoon that he is dead then."

"Would you like for me to tell her?"

"I will tell her," she said.

"Would you like for me to come out and see her, then, talk to her?"

"It would be kind of you." Then she was gone, erect, her feet crisp
and light, almost brisk, on the stairs, ceasing. He telephoned again,
to the Illinois warden, then to an undertaker in Joliet. Then once
more he crossed the hot, empty square. He had only to wait a short
while for the editor to return from dinner.

"We're bringing him home," he said. "Miss Worsham and you and
me and some others. It will cost ——"

"Wait," the editor said. "What others?"

"I dont know yet. It will cost about two hundred. I'm not counting
the telephones; I'll take care of them myself. I'll get something out of

Carothers Edmonds the first time I catch him; I dont know how much, but something. And maybe fifty around the square. But the rest of it is you and me, because she insisted on leaving twenty-five with me, which is just twice what I tried to persuade her it would cost and just exactly four times what she can afford to pay ——"

"Wait," the editor said. "Wait."

"And he will come in on Number Four the day after tomorrow and we will meet it, Miss Worsham and his grandmother, the old nigger, in my car and you and me in yours. Miss Worsham and the old woman will take him back home, back where he was born. Or where the old woman raised him. Or where she tried to. And the hearse out there will be fifteen more, not counting the flowers ——"

"Flowers?" the editor cried.

"Flowers," Stevens said. "Call the whole thing two hundred and twenty-five. And it will probably be mostly you and me. All right?"

"No it aint all right," the editor said. "But it dont look like I can help myself. By Jupiter," he said, "even if I could help myself, the novelty will be almost worth it. It will be the first time in my life I ever paid money for copy I had already promised before hand I wont print."

"Have already promised before hand you will not print," Stevens said. And during the remainder of that hot and now windless afternoon, while officials from the city hall, and justices of the peace and bailiffs come fifteen and twenty miles from the ends of the county, mounted the stairs to the empty office and called his name and cooled their heels a while and then went away and returned and sat again, fuming, Stevens passed from store to store and office to office about the square—merchant and clerk, proprietor and employee, doctor dentist lawyer and barber—with his set and rapid speech: "It's to bring a dead nigger home. It's for Miss Worsham. Never mind about a paper to sign: just give me a dollar. Or a half a dollar then. Or a quarter then."

And that night after supper he walked through the breathless and star-filled darkness to Miss Worsham's house on the edge of town and knocked on the paintless front door. Hamp Worsham admitted him— an old man, belly bloated from the vegetables on which he and his wife and Miss Worsham all three mostly lived, with blurred old eyes and a fringe of white hair about the head and face of a Roman general.

"She expecting you," he said. "She say to kindly step up to the chamber."

"Is that where Aunt Mollie is?" Stevens said.

"We all dar," Worsham said.

So Stevens crossed the lamplit hall (he knew that the entire house

was still lighted with oil lamps and there was no running water in it)
and preceded the Negro up the clean, paintless stairs beside the faded
wallpaper, and followed the old Negro along the hall and into the
clean, spare bedroom with its unmistakable faint odor of old maidens.
They were all there, as Worsham had said—his wife, a tremendous
light-colored woman in a bright turban leaning in the door, Miss
Worsham erect again on a hard straight chair, the old Negress sitting
in the only rocking chair beside the hearth on which even tonight a
few ashes smoldered faintly.

She held a reed-stemmed clay pipe but she was not smoking it, the
ash dead and white in the stained bowl; and actually looking at her
for the first time, Stevens thought: *Good Lord, she's not as big as a
ten-year-old child.* Then he sat too, so that the four of them—himself,
Miss Worsham, the old Negress and her brother—made a circle about
the brick hearth on which the ancient symbol of human coherence and
solidarity smoldered.

"He'll be home the day after tomorrow, Aunt Mollie," he said. The
old Negress didn't even look at him; she never had looked at him.

"He dead," she said. "Pharaoh got him."

"Oh yes, Lord," Worsham said. "Pharaoh got him."

"Done sold my Benjamin," the old Negress said. "Sold him in Egypt."
She began to sway faintly back and forth in the chair.

"Oh yes, Lord," Worsham said.

"Hush," Miss Worsham said. "Hush, Hamp."

"I telephoned Mr Edmonds," Stevens said. "He will have everything
ready when you get there."

"Roth Edmonds sold him," the old Negress said. She swayed back
and forth in the chair. "Sold my Benjamin."

"Hush," Miss Worsham said. "Hush, Mollie. Hush now."

"No," Stevens said. "No he didn't, Aunt Mollie. It wasn't Mr
Edmonds. Mr Edmonds didn't—" *But she cant hear me,* he thought.
She was not even looking at him. She never had looked at him.

"Sold my Benjamin," she said. "Sold him in Egypt."

"Sold him in Egypt," Worsham said.

"Roth Edmonds sold my Benjamin."

"Sold him to Pharaoh."

"Sold him to Pharaoh and now he dead."

"I'd better go," Stevens said. He rose quickly. Miss Worsham rose
too, but he did not wait for her to precede him. He went down the
hall fast, almost running; he did not even know whether she was following him or not. *Soon I will be outside,* he thought. *Then there will
be air, space, breath.* Then he could hear her behind him—the crisp,

light, brisk yet unhurried feet as he had heard them descending the stairs from his office, and beyond them the voices:

"Sold my Benjamin. Sold him in Egypt."

"Sold him in Egypt. Oh yes, Lord."

He descended the stairs, almost running. It was not far now; now he could smell and feel it: the breathing and simple dark, and now he could manner himself to pause and wait, turning at the door, watching Miss Worsham as she followed him to the door—the high, white, erect old-time head approaching through the old-time lamplight. Now he could hear the third voice, which would be that of Hamp's wife—a true constant soprano which ran without words beneath the strophe and antistrophe of the brother and sister:

"Sold him in Egypt and now he dead."

"Oh yes, Lord. Sold him in Egypt."

"Sold him in Egypt."

"And now he dead."

"Sold him to Pharaoh."

"And now he dead."

"I'm sorry," Stevens said. "I ask you to forgive me. I should have known. I shouldn't have come."

"It's all right," Miss Worsham said. "It's our grief."

And on the next bright hot day but one the hearse and the two cars were waiting when the southbound train came in. There were more than a dozen cars, but it was not until the train came in that Stevens and the editor began to notice the number of people, Negroes and whites both. Then, with the idle white men and youths and small boys and probably half a hundred Negroes, men and women too, watching quietly, the Negro undertaker's men lifted the gray-and-silver casket from the train and carried it to the hearse and snatched the wreaths and floral symbols of man's ultimate and inevitable end briskly out and slid the casket in and flung the flowers back and clapped-to the door.

Then, with Miss Worsham and the old Negress in Stevens' car with the driver he had hired and himself and the editor in the editor's, they followed the hearse as it swung into the long hill up from the station, going fast in a whining low gear until it reached the crest, going pretty fast still but with an unctuous, an almost bishoplike purr until it slowed into the square, crossing it, circling the Confederate monument and the courthouse while the merchants and clerks and barbers and professional men who had given Stevens the dollars and half-dollars and quarters and the ones who had not, watched quietly from doors and upstairs windows, swinging then into the street which at the edge of town would become the country road leading to the destination seventeen miles away, already picking up speed again and followed still by the two cars containing the four people—the high-headed erect white woman, the old Negress, the designated paladin of justice and truth and right, the Heidelberg Ph.D.—in formal component complement to the Negro murderer's catafalque: the slain wolf.

When they reached the edge of town the hearse was going quite fast. Now they flashed past the metal sign which said Jefferson. Corporate Limit. and the pavement vanished, slanting away into another long hill, becoming gravel. Stevens reached over and cut the switch, so that the editor's car coasted, slowing as he began to brake it, the hearse and the other car drawing rapidly away now as though in flight, the light and unrained summer dust spurting from beneath the fleeing wheels; soon they were gone. The editor turned his car clumsily, grinding the gears, sawing and filling until it was back in the road facing town again. Then he sat for a moment, his foot on the clutch.

"Do you know what she asked me this morning, back there at the station?" he said.

"Probably not," Stevens said.

"She said, 'Is you gonter put hit in de paper?' "

"What?"

"That's what I said," the editor said. "And she said it again: 'Is you gonter put hit in de paper? I wants hit all in de paper. All of hit.' And I wanted to say, 'If I should happen to know how he really died, do you want that in too?' And by Jupiter, if I had and if she had known what we know even, I believe she would have said yes. But I didn't say it. I just said, 'Why, you couldn't read it, Aunty.' And she said, 'Miss Belle will show me whar to look and I can look at hit. You put hit in de paper. All of hit.' "

"Oh," Stevens said. *Yes,* he thought. *It doesn't matter to her now. Since it had to be and she couldn't stop it, and now that it's all over and done and finished, she doesn't care how he died. She just wanted him home, but she wanted him to come home right. She wanted that casket and those flowers and the hearse and she wanted to ride through town behind it in a car.* "Come on," he said. "Let's go back to town. I haven't seen my desk in two days."

What does Molly Beauchamp want Stevens to do? What is the significance of this act? Why do you think Stevens goes out of his way to fulfill the request of "an old nigger woman"? Why does he go to

Miss Worsham's? What makes him flee so apologetically and
desperately? Why does Molly insist on having the editor print "all of
hit" in the paper? What has Stevens finally accomplished?

The biblical allusions operate much more loosely here than in many
of the other pieces in this book. The action is not carefully modeled
on a particular bible story as in the case of Nemerov's "Cain" or
Fry's "The Firstborn." Yet, Faulkner's use of a biblical title and of
occasional direct and indirect biblical references strongly suggests that
he wanted his readers to view the story in the context of these
allusions. What light does the Joseph story shed on Molly Beauchamp's
referring to her dead grandson as "my Benjamin"? Why does she
think it was Mr Edmonds who "sold him in Egypt"? Consider Stevens'
attempt to console Molly: "It wasn't Mr Edmonds. Mr Edmonds
didn't—". Who or what *did*? Who or what is "Pharaoh" in the story?
During the funeral procession Faulkner refers to the dead Negro as
"the slain wolf." Consider this in light of Genesis 49:27, wherein
Jacob, in blessing his son Benjamin, refers to him as "a ravenous wolf,
in the morning devouring the prey, and at even dividing the spoils."

Explain the extent to which "Go Down, Moses" is an appropriate
title for this story. What does your knowledge of the Joseph and Moses
stories and of the spiritual for which it is named contribute to your
understanding of the work?

TOWARD THE PROMISED LAND
(Exodus, Numbers, and Deuteronomy)

*After their miraculous escape from Egypt, the Israelites began their
journey toward the Promised Land. Their way was not to be an easy
one, however.*

*The account of the people's travails, of Moses' face-to-face
encounters with God, and of his gallant efforts to quell the doubts,
fears, and rebelliousness of the Israelites is recounted in the books of
Exodus, Leviticus, Numbers, and Deuteronomy, encompassing a full
one-sixth of the Old Testament. The selections that follow—"Manna
from Heaven," "The Tablets of Stone," "The Golden Calf," "The
Murmurings of the People," "The Disobedience of Moses," and "The
Death of Moses"—represent some of the highlights of this moving story.*

Manna from Heaven

So Moses brought Israel from the Red Sea, and they went out into
the wilderness of Shur; and they went three days in the wilderness,
and found no water. And when they came to Marah, they could not
drink of the waters of Marah, for they were bitter: therefore the name
of it was called Marah. And the people murmured against Moses, saying, "What shall we drink?"

And he cried unto the Lord; and the Lord showed him a tree, which
when he had cast into the waters, the waters were made sweet: there
he made for them a statute and an ordinance, and there he proved
them, and said, "If thou wilt diligently hearken to the voice of the
Lord thy God, and wilt do that which is right in his sight, and wilt
give ear to his commandments, and keep all his statutes, I will put
none of these diseases upon thee, which I have brought upon the
Egyptians: for I am the Lord that healeth thee."

And they came to Elim, where were twelve wells of water, and
threescore and ten palm trees; and they encamped there by the waters.

And they took their journey from Elim, and all the congregation of
the children of Israel came unto the wilderness of Sin, which is

between Elim and Sinai, on the fifteenth day of the second month, after their departing out of the land of Egypt. And the whole congregation of the children of Israel murmured against Moses and Aaron in the wilderness: and the children of Israel said unto them, "Would to God we had died by the hand of the Lord in the land of Egypt, when we sat by the fleshpots, and when we did eat bread to the full: for ye have brought us forth into this wilderness, to kill this whole assembly with hunger."

Then said the Lord unto Moses, "Behold, I will rain bread from heaven for you; and the people shall go out and gather a certain rate every day, that I may prove them, whether they will walk in my law, or no. And it shall come to pass, that on the sixth day they shall prepare that which they bring in; and it shall be twice as much as they shall gather daily."

And Moses and Aaron said unto all the children of Israel, "At even, then ye shall know that the Lord hath brought you out from the land of Egypt: and in the morning, then ye shall see the glory of the Lord; for that he heareth your murmurings against the Lord: and what are we that ye murmur against us?"

And Moses said, "This shall be, when the Lord shall give you in the evening flesh to eat, and in the morning bread to the full; for that the Lord heareth your murmurings which ye murmur against him: for what are we? Your murmurings are not against us, but against the Lord."

And Moses spake unto Aaron, "Say unto all the congregation of the children of Israel, 'Come near before the Lord: for he hath heard your murmurings.'"

And it came to pass, as Aaron spake unto the whole congregation of the children of Israel, that they looked toward the wilderness, and, behold, the glory of the Lord appeared in the cloud.

And the Lord spake unto Moses, saying, "I have heard the murmurings of the children of Israel: speak unto them, saying, 'At even ye shall eat flesh, and in the morning ye shall be filled with bread; and ye shall know that I am the Lord your God.'"

And it came to pass, that at even the quails came up, and covered the camp: and in the morning the dew lay round about the host. And when the dew that lay was gone up, behold, upon the face of the wilderness there lay a small round thing, as small as the hoar frost on the ground. And when the children of Israel saw it, they said one to another, "It is manna": for they wist not what it was.

And Moses said unto them, "This is the bread which the Lord hath given you to eat. This is the thing which the Lord hath commanded, 'Gather of it every man according to his eating, an omer for every man, according to the number of your persons; take ye every man for them which are in his tents.'"

And the children of Israel did so.

[Exodus 15:22–16:17]

The Tablets of Stone

In the third month, when the children of Israel were gone forth out of the land of Egypt, the same day came they into the wilderness of Sinai. For they were departed from Rephidim, and were come to the desert of Sinai, and had pitched in the wilderness; and there Israel camped before the mount.

And Moses went up unto God, and the Lord called unto him out of the mountain, saying, "Thus shalt thou say to the house of Jacob, and tell the children of Israel: 'Ye have seen what I did unto the Egyptians, and how I bore you on eagles' wings, and brought you unto myself. Now therefore, if ye will obey my voice indeed, and keep my covenant, then ye shall be a peculiar treasure unto me above all people: for all the earth is mine. And ye shall be unto me a kingdom of priests, and a holy nation.' These are the words which thou shalt speak unto the children of Israel."

And the Lord said unto Moses, "Go unto the people, and sanctify them today and tomorrow, and let them wash their clothes, and be ready against the third day: for the third day the Lord will come down in the sight of all the people upon Mount Sinai."

And it came to pass on the third day in the morning, that there were thunders and lightnings, and a thick cloud upon the mount, and the voice of the trumpet exceedingly loud; so that all the people that was in the camp trembled. And Moses brought forth the people out of the camp to meet with God; and they stood at the nether part of the mount. And Mount Sinai was altogether on a smoke, because the Lord descended upon it in fire; and the smoke thereof ascended as the smoke of a furnace, and the whole mount quaked greatly. And when the voice of the trumpet sounded long, and waxed louder and louder, Moses spake, and God answered him by a voice. And the Lord came down upon Mount Sinai, on the top of the mount: and the Lord called Moses up to the top of the mount; and Moses went up.

And God spake all these words, saying, "I am the Lord thy God, which have brought thee out of the land of Egypt, out of the house of bondage.

"Thou shalt have no other gods before me.

"Thou shalt not make unto thee any graven image, or any likeness of any thing that is in heaven above, or that is in the earth beneath, or that is in the water under the earth: thou shalt not bow down thyself to them, nor serve them: for I the Lord thy God am a jealous God, visiting the iniquity of the fathers upon the children unto the third and fourth generation of them that hate me; and showing mercy unto thousands of them that love me, and keep my commandments.

"Thou shalt not take the name of the Lord thy God in vain; for the Lord will not hold him guiltless that taketh his name in vain.

"Remember the sabbath day, to keep it holy. Six days shalt thou labor, and do all thy work: but the seventh day is the sabbath of the Lord thy God: in it thou shalt not do any work, thou, nor thy son, nor thy daughter, thy manservant, nor thy maidservant, nor thy cattle, nor thy stranger that is within thy gates: for in six days the Lord made heaven and earth, the sea, and all that in them is, and rested the seventh day: wherefore the Lord blessed the sabbath day, and hallowed it.

"Honor thy father and thy mother: that thy days may be long upon the land which the Lord thy God giveth thee.

"Thou shalt not kill.

"Thou shalt not commit adultery.

"Thou shalt not steal.

"Thou shalt not bear false witness against thy neighbor.

"Thou shalt not covet thy neighbor's house, thou shalt not covet thy neighbor's wife, nor his manservant, nor his maidservant, nor his ox, nor his ass, nor any thing that is thy neighbor's."

And he gave unto Moses, when he had made an end of communing with him upon Mount Sinai, two tables of testimony, tables of stone, written with the finger of God.

[*Exodus 19:1–6, 10–11, 16–20; 20:1–17; 31:18*]

The Golden Calf

And when the people saw that Moses delayed to come down out of the mount, the people gathered themselves together unto Aaron, and said unto him, "Up, make us gods, which shall go before us; for as for this Moses, the man that brought us up out of the land of Egypt, we wot not what is become of him."

And Aaron said unto them, "Break off the golden earrings, which are in the ears of your wives, of your sons, and of your daughters, and bring them unto me."

And all the people broke off the golden earrings which were in their ears, and brought them unto Aaron. And he received them at their hand, and fashioned it with a graving tool, after he had made it a molten calf: and they said, "These be thy gods, O Israel, which brought thee up out of the land of Egypt."

And when Aaron saw it, he built an altar before it; and Aaron made proclamation, and said, "Tomorrow is a feast to the Lord."

And they rose up early on the morrow, and offered burnt offerings, and brought peace offerings; and the people sat down to eat and to drink, and rose up to play.

And the Lord said unto Moses, "Go, get thee down, for thy people, which thou broughtest out of the land of Egypt, have corrupted themselves. They have turned aside quickly out of the way which I commanded them: they have made them a molten calf, and have worshipped it, and have sacrificed thereunto, and said, 'These be thy gods, O Israel, which have brought thee up out of the land of Egypt.'"

And the Lord said unto Moses, "I have seen this people, and, behold, it is a stiffnecked people: now therefore let me alone, that my wrath may wax hot against them, and that I may consume them: and I will make of thee a great nation."

And Moses besought the Lord his God, and said, "Lord, why doth thy wrath wax hot against thy people, which thou hast brought forth out of the land of Egypt with great power, and with a mighty hand? Wherefore should the Egyptians speak, and say, 'For mischief did he bring them out, to slay them in the mountains, and to consume them from the face of the earth'? Turn from thy fierce wrath, and repent of this evil against thy people. Remember Abraham, Isaac, and Israel, thy servants, to whom thou sworest by thine own self, and saidst unto them, 'I will multiply your seed as the stars of heaven, and all this land that I have spoken of will I give unto your seed, and they shall inherit it for ever.'"

And the Lord repented of the evil which he thought to do unto his people.

And Moses turned, and went down from the mount, and the two tables of the testimony were in his hand: the tables were written on both their sides; on the one side and on the other were they written. And the tables were the work of God, and the writing was the writing of God, graven upon the tables.

And when Joshua heard the noise of the people as they shouted, he said unto Moses, "There is a noise of war in the camp."

And he said, "It is not the voice of them that shout for mastery, neither is it the voice of them that cry for being overcome: but the noise of them that sing do I hear."

And it came to pass, as soon as he came nigh unto the camp, that he saw the calf, and the dancing: and Moses' anger waxed hot, and he cast the tables out of his hands, and broke them beneath the mount. And he took the calf which they had made, and burnt it in the fire, and ground it to powder, and strewed it upon the water, and made the children of Israel drink of it.

And when Moses saw that the people were naked (for Aaron had made them naked unto their shame among their enemies), then Moses stood in the gate of the camp, and said, "Who is on the Lord's side? Let him come unto me." And all the sons of Levi gathered themselves together unto him.

And he said unto them, "Thus saith the Lord God of Israel, 'Put every man his sword by his side, and go in and out from gate to gate throughout the camp, and slay every man his brother, and every man his companion, and every man his neighbor.'" And the children of Levi did according to the word of Moses: and there fell of the people that day about three thousand men.

And it came to pass on the morrow that Moses said unto the people, "Ye have sinned a great sin: and now I will go up unto the Lord; peradventure I shall make an atonement for your sin."

And Moses returned unto the Lord, and said, "Oh, this people have sinned a great sin, and have made them gods of gold. Yet now, if thou wilt forgive their sin—; and if not, blot me, I pray thee, out of thy book which thou hast written."

And the Lord said unto Moses, "Whosoever hath sinned against me, him will I blot out of my book. Therefore now go, lead the people unto the place of which I have spoken unto thee: behold, mine Angel shall go before thee: nevertheless in the day when I visit I will visit their sin upon them."

And the Lord plagued the people, because they made the calf, which Aaron made.

[After this the Lord continues to be angry with his "stiffnecked people"; but the Israelites go into mourning and look to Moses to intercede for them. Once again Moses ascends Mount Sinai and comes

*face to face with his God, who rewrites the word of the law on two
new tables of stone and delivers them to Moses, commanding that he
present them anew to his people. "And when Aaron and all the children
of Israel saw Moses, behold, the skin of his face shone."]*

[Exodus 32:1–20, 25–35]

The Murmurings of the People

And the Lord spake unto Moses, saying, "Send thou men, that they
may search the land of Canaan, which I give unto the children of
Israel: of every tribe of their fathers shall ye send a man, every one
a ruler among them." And Moses sent them to spy out the land of
Canaan.

And they returned from searching of the land after forty days. And
they brought up an evil report of the land which they had searched
unto the children of Israel, saying, "The land, through which we have
gone to search it, is a land that cateth up the inhabitants thereof;
and all the people that we saw in it are men of a great stature. And
there we saw the giants, the sons of Anak, which come of the giants:
and we were in our own sight as grasshoppers, and so we were in
their sight."

And all the congregation lifted up their voice, and cried; and the
people wept that night. And all the children of Israel murmured against
Moses and against Aaron: and the whole congregation said unto
them. "Would God that we had died in the land of Egypt! Or would
God we had died in this wilderness! And wherefore hath the Lord
brought us unto this land, to fall by the sword, that our wives and our
children should be a prey? Were it not better for us to return into
Egypt?"

And they said one to another, "Let us make a captain, and let us
return into Egypt." Then Moses and Aaron fell on their faces before
all the assembly of the congregation of the children of Israel.

And Joshua the son of Nun, and Caleb the son of Jephunneh, which
were of them that searched the land, rent their clothes: and they spake
unto all the company of the children of Israel, saying, "The land,
which we passed through to search it, is an exceeding good land. If
the Lord delight in us, then he will bring us into this land, and give
it us; a land which floweth with milk and honey. Only rebel not ye
against the Lord, neither fear ye the people of the land; for they are
bread for us: their defense is departed from them, and the Lord is
with us: fear them not."

But all the congregation bade stone them with stones. And the glory of the Lord appeared in the tabernacle of the congregation before all the children of Israel.

And the Lord said unto Moses, "How long will this people provoke me? And how long will it be ere they believe me, for all the signs which I have showed them? I will smite them with the pestilence, and disinherit them, and will make of thee a greater nation and mightier than they."

And Moses said unto the Lord, "Then the Egyptians shall hear it (for thou broughtest up this people in thy might from among them); and they will tell it to the inhabitants of this land: for they have heard that thou Lord art among this people, that thou Lord art seen face to face, and that thy cloud standeth over them, and that thou goest before them, by day time in a pillar of a cloud, and in a pillar of fire by night. Now if thou shalt kill all this people as one man, then the nations which have heard the fame of thee will speak, saying, 'Because the Lord was not able to bring this people into the land which he sware unto them, therefore he hath slain them in the wilderness.' And now, I beseech thee, let the power of my Lord be great, according as thou hast spoken, saying, 'The Lord is longsuffering, and of great mercy, forgiving iniquity and transgression, and by no means clearing the guilty, visiting the iniquity of the fathers upon the children unto the third and fourth generation.' Pardon, I beseech thee, the iniquity of this people according unto the greatness of thy mercy, and as thou hast forgiven this people, from Egypt even until now."

And the Lord said, "I have pardoned according to thy word: but as truly as I live, all the earth shall be filled with the glory of the Lord. Because all those men which have seen my glory, and my miracles, which I did in Egypt and in the wilderness, and have tempted me now these ten times, and have not hearkened to my voice; surely they shall not see the land which I sware unto their fathers, neither shall any of them that provoked me see it.

"How long shall I bear with this evil congregation, which murmur against me? I have heard the murmurings of the children of Israel, which they murmur against me. Say unto them, 'As truly as I live,' saith the Lord, 'as ye have spoken in mine ears, so will I do to you: your carcases shall fall in this wilderness; and all that were numbered of you, according to your whole number, from twenty years old and upward, which have murmured against me, doubtless ye shall not come into the land, concerning which I sware to make you dwell therein, save Caleb the son of Jephunneh, and Joshua the son of Nun. But your little ones, which ye said should be a prey, them will I bring in, and they shall know the land which ye have despised. But as for you, your carcases, they shall fall in this wilderness. And your children shall wander in the wilderness forty years, and bear your whoredoms, until your carcases be wasted in the wilderness. After the number of the days in which ye searched the land, even forty days, each day for a year, shall ye bear your iniquities, even forty years, and ye shall know my breach of promise.' I the Lord have said, 'I will surely do it unto all this evil congregation, that are gathered together against me: in this wilderness they shall be consumed, and there they shall die.' "

[*Numbers 13:1–2, 17, 25, 32–33; 14:1–23, 27–35*]

The Disobedience of Moses

Then came the children of Israel, even the whole congregation, into the desert of Zin in the first month: and the people abode in Kadesh; and Miriam died there, and was buried there. And there was no water for the congregation: and they gathered themselves together against Moses and against Aaron.

And the people chode with Moses, and spake, saying, "Would God that we had died when our brethren died before the Lord! And why have ye brought up the congregation of the Lord into this wilderness, that we and our cattle should die there? And wherefore have ye made us to come up out of Egypt, to bring us in unto this evil place? It is no place of seed, or of figs, or of vines, or of pomegranates; neither is there any water to drink."

And Moses and Aaron went from the presence of the assembly unto the door of the tabernacle of the congregation, and they fell upon their faces: and the glory of the Lord appeared unto them.

And the Lord spake unto Moses, saying, "Take the rod, and gather thou the assembly together, thou, and Aaron thy brother, and speak ye unto the rock before their eyes; and it shall give forth his water, and thou shalt bring forth to them water out of the rock: so thou shalt give the congregation and their beasts drink."

And Moses took the rod from before the Lord, as he commanded him. And Moses and Aaron gathered the congregation together before the rock, and he said unto them, "Hear now, ye rebels; must we fetch you water out of this rock?"

And Moses lifted up his hand, and with his rod he smote the rock twice: and the water came out abundantly, and the congregation drank, and their beasts also.

And the Lord spake unto Moses and Aaron, "Because ye believed me not, to sanctify me in the eyes of the children of Israel, therefore ye shall not bring this congregation into the land which I have given them."

[*Numbers 20:1–12*]

The Death of Moses

And Moses went up from the plains of Moab unto the mountain of Nebo, to the top of Pisgah, that is over against Jericho: and the Lord showed him all the land of Gilead, unto Dan, and all Naphtali, and the land of Ephraim, and Manasseh, and all the land of Judah, unto the utmost sea, and the south, and the plain of the valley of Jericho, the city of palm trees, unto Zoar.

And the Lord said unto him, "This is the land which I swore unto Abraham, unto Isaac, and unto Jacob, saying, 'I will give it unto thy seed': I have caused thee to see it with thine eyes, but thou shalt not go over thither."

So Moses the servant of the Lord died there in the land of Moab, according to the word of the Lord. And he buried him in a valley in the land of Moab, over against Beth-peor: but no man knoweth of his sepulchre unto this day.

And Moses was a hundred and twenty years old when he died: his eye was not dim, nor his natural force abated. And the children of Israel wept for Moses in the plains of Moab thirty days: so the days of weeping and mourning for Moses were ended.

And Joshua the son of Nun was full of the spirit of wisdom; for Moses had laid his hands upon him: and the children of Israel hearkened unto him, and did as the Lord commanded Moses.

And there arose not a prophet since in Israel like unto Moses, whom the Lord knew face to face, in all the signs and the wonders, which the Lord sent him to do in the land of Egypt to Pharaoh, and to all his servants, and to all his land, and in all that mighty hand, and in all the great terror which Moses showed in the sight of all Israel.

[*Deuteronomy 34:1–12*]

Under what circumstances do the Israelites "murmur" (complain)? What do these former slaves seemingly prefer? How do you account for this preference considering the hardness of their lot back in Egypt? What provisions does God make for their welfare?

After the scouts return from the land of Canaan, reporting the presence of giants, what do the people plan to do? What does God propose to do in light of the Israelites' disobedience? What arguments does Moses set forth to dissuade God from so doing? What is their punishment instead? Who are exempted?

When Moses is first approached by God with the idea of becoming the leader of the Hebrews, he shows a weakness that later leads to his act of disobedience in the wilderness. What is this weakness? How does God show his mercy toward Moses?

I'VE BEEN TO THE MOUNTAIN TOP

Dr. Martin Luther King, Jr.

The following passage is taken from the speech made by Dr. Martin Luther King, Jr., in Memphis, Tennessee, on April 3, 1968, the day before his assassination.

"And then I got into Memphis. And some began to say the threats—or talk about the threats that were out. Or what would happen to me from some of our sick white brothers.

"Well, I don't know what will happen now. We've got some difficult days ahead. But it really doesn't matter with me now. Because I've been to the mountain top. I won't mind.

"Like anybody, I would like to live a long life. Longevity has its place. But I'm not concerned about that now. I just want to do God's will.

"And He's allowed me to go up to the mountain. And I've looked over, and *I've seen the promised land.*

"I may not get there with you, but I want you to know tonight that we as a people will get to the promised land.

"I'm so happy tonight. I'm not worried about anything. I'm not fearing any man. Mine eyes have seen the glory of the coming of the Lord."

In what ways does Dr. King use biblical allusions to reinforce his message? To what extent is the parallel between his activities and those of Moses appropriate? What is the "promised land" to which he refers? How does the knowledge that King was assassinated the very next day affect your reading of the speech?

MOSES

Karl Shapiro

By reason of despair we set forth behind you
And followed the pillar of fire like a doubt,
To hold to belief wanted a sign,
Called the miracle of the staff and the plagues
Natural phenomena.

We questioned the expediency of the march,
Gossiped about you. What was escape
To the fear of going forward and Pharaoh's wheels?
When the chariots mired and the army flooded
Our cry of horror was one with theirs.

You always went alone, a little ahead,
Prophecy disturbed you, you were not a fanatic.
The women said you were meek, the men
Regarded you as a typical leader.
You and your black wife might have been foreigners.

We even discussed your parentage; were you really a Jew?
We remembered how Joseph had made himself a prince,
All of us shared in the recognition, sense of propriety,
Devotion to his brothers and Israel.

We hated you daily. Our children died. The water spilled.
It was as if you were trying to lose us one by one.
Our wandering seemed the wandering of your mind,

The cloud believed we were tireless,
We expressed our contempt and our boredom openly.

At last you ascended the rock; at last returned.
Your anger that day was probably His.
When we saw you come down from the mountain, your
    skin alight
And the stones of our law flashing,
We fled like animals and the dancers scattered.

We watched where you overturned the calf on the fire,
We hid when you broke the tablets on the rock,
We wept when we drank the mixture of gold and water.
We had hoped you were lost or had left us.
This was the day of our greatest defilement.

You were simple of heart; you were sorry for Miriam,
You reasoned with Aaron, who was your enemy.
However often you cheered us with songs and prayers
We cursed you again. The serpents bit us,
And mouth to mouth you entreated the Lord for our sake.

At the end of it all we gave you the gift of death.
Invasion and generalship were spared you.
The hand of our direction, resignedly you fell,
And while officers prepared for the river crossing
The One God blessed you and covered you with earth.

Though you were mortal and once committed murder
You assumed the burden of the covenant,
Spoke for the world and for our understanding.
Converse with God made you a thinker,
Taught us all early justice, made us a race.

_____

Considering their doubts and fears, why do the people follow Moses?
What makes them so doubtful? Why do they actually *hate* Moses?
What did Aaron do which justifies his being called Moses' "enemy"?
What is it, according to the final lines, that makes Moses such an
admirable leader?

Moses Breaks the Tablets with the Commandments (early 16th c.) by Domenico Beccafumi. Duomo, Pisa. SCALA, NEW YORK/FLORENCE.

MOSES

Edwin Muir

He left us there, went up to Pisgah hill,
And saw the holiday land, the sabbath land,
The mild prophetic beasts, millennial herds,
The sacred lintel, over-arching tree,
The vineyards glittering on the southern slopes,
And in the midst the shining vein of water,
The river turning, turning toward its home.
Promised to us. The dream rose in his nostrils
With homely smell of wine and corn and cattle,
Byre, barn and stall, sweat-sacrificed smell of peace.
He saw the tribes arrayed beside the river,
White robes and sabbath stillness, still light falling
On dark heads whitened by the desert wave,
The Sabbath of Sabbaths come and Canaan their home.
All this he saw in dreaming. But we who dream
Such common dreams and see so little saw
The battle for this land, the massacres,
The vineyards drenched in aboriginal blood,
The settlement, unsatisfactory order,
The petty wars and neighboring jealousies
And local troubles. But we did not see,
We did not see and Moses did not see,
The great disaster, exile, diaspora,
The holy bread of the land crumbled and broken
In Babylon, Caesarea, Alexandria
As on a splendid dish, or gnawed as offal.
Nor did we see, beyond, the ghetto rising,
Toledo, Cracow, Vienna, Budapest,
Nor, had we seen, would we have known our people
In the wild disguises of fantastic time,
Packed in dense cities, wandering countless roads,
And not a road in the world to lead them home.
How could we have seen such things? How could we have seen

That plot of ground pledged by the God of Moses
Trampled by sequent tribes, seized and forgotten
As a child seizes and forgets a toy,
Strange languages, strange gods and customs borne
Over it and away with the light migrations,
Stirring each century ancestral dust.
All this was settled while we stood by Jordan
That first great day, could not be otherwise.
Moses saw that day only; we did not see it;
But now it stands becalmed in time for ever:
White robes and sabbath peace, the snow-white emblem.

This poem presents a dramatic contrast between dream and reality, a contrast between what Moses envisioned and what those who followed experienced. Describe Moses' dream. Who are the "we" referred to throughout? What did they and Moses both not see? What is meant by the "wild disguises of fantastic time"? Where is "home"? How has the passing of time changed the speaker's understanding of Moses' vision on "that first great day"? Why is it important that a people have a "snow-white emblem" in spite of the fact that, no matter how hard they struggle, their dreams may never fully be realized?

THE LATEST DECALOGUE

Arthur Hugh Clough

Thou shalt have one God only; who
Would be at the expense of two?
No graven images may be
Worshipped, except the currency:
Swear not at all; for for thy curse
Thine enemy is none the worse:
At church on Sunday to attend

Will serve to keep the world thy friend:
Honour thy parents; that is, all
From whom advancement may befall:
Thou shalt not kill; but need'st not strive
Officiously to keep alive:
Do not adultery commit;
Advantage rarely comes of it:
Thou shalt not steal; an empty feat,
When it's so lucrative to cheat:
Bear not false witness; let the lie
Have time on its own wings to fly:
Thou shalt not covet; but tradition
Approves all forms of competition.

The sum of all is, thou shalt love,
If any body, God above:
At any rate shall never labour
More than thyself to love thy neighbour.

Deborah (1896) by E. A. Abbey. THE NEW YORK PUBLIC LIBRARY PICTURE COLLECTION.

INTO THE HAND OF A WOMAN: THE STORY OF DEBORAH
(Judges)

*After Moses' death, Joshua led the Israelites into the Promised Land.
Beginning with his sacking of the city of Jericho, he launched a
campaign that resulted in the conquest and division of much of
Canaan. The victory was not a permanent one, however. After
Joshua's death, the Israelites "did evil in the sight of the Lord," as
they had done in the desert, and returned to worshiping false gods
such as Baal. Again God was angered by the "stiff-necked people,"
and to punish them He several times "delivered them into the hands of
spoilers who spoiled them." Each time, when the Israelites cried
out to Him for help, He responded and "raised up judges" to deliver
them. One of the greatest of these was Deborah, whose courage and
prophetic vision inspired Barak and the Israelite army to conquer the
northern Canaanites, who had cruelly subjected them for twenty years.
Following is the story of her victory—one which would not have
been complete without the heroism of another Israelite woman, Jael,
who in the service of Deborah and of God, slayed Sisera, the leader
of the fallen Canaanite army who had escaped Barak's forces.*

And the children of Israel again did evil in the sight of the Lord, when
Ehud was dead. And the Lord sold them into the hand of Jabin king
of Canaan, that reigned in Hazor; the captain of whose host was
Sisera, which dwelt in Harosheth of the Gentiles. And the children
of Israel cried unto the Lord: for he had nine hundred chariots of
iron; and twenty years he mightily oppressed the children of Israel.

And Deborah, a prophetess, the wife of Lapidoth, she judged Israel
at that time. And she dwelt under the palm tree of Deborah between
Ramah and Bethel in Mount Ephraim; and the children of Israel
came up to her for judgment.

And she sent and called Barak the son of Abinoam out of Kedesh-
naphtali, and said unto him, "Hath not the Lord God of Israel commanded, saying, 'Go and draw toward Mount Tabor, and take with
thee ten thousand men of the children of Naphtali and of the children

of Zebulun. And I will draw unto thee to the river Kishon Sisera, the captain of Jabin's army, with his chariots and his multitude; and I will deliver him into thine hand'?"

And Barak said unto her, "If thou wilt go with me, then I will go: but if thou wilt not go with me, then I will not go."

And she said, "I will surely go with thee: notwithstanding the journey that thou takest shall not be for thine honor; for the Lord shall sell Sisera into the hand of a woman."

And Deborah arose, and went with Barak to Kedesh. And Barak called Zebulun and Naphtali to Kedesh; and he went up with ten thousand men at his feet: and Deborah went up with him.

Now Heber the Kenite, which was of the children of Hobab the father-in-law of Moses, had severed himself from the Kenites, and pitched his tent unto the plain of Zaanaim, which is by Kedesh.

And they showed Sisera that Barak the son of Abinoam was gone up to Mount Tabor. And Sisera gathered together all his chariots, even nine hundred chariots of iron, and all the people that were with him, from Harosheth of the Gentiles unto the river of Kishon.

And Deborah said unto Barak, "Up; for this is the day in which the Lord hath delivered Sisera into thine hand: is not the Lord gone out before thee?"

So Barak went down from Mount Tabor, and ten thousand men after him. And the Lord discomfited Sisera, and all his chariots, and all his host, with the edge of the sword before Barak; so that Sisera lighted down off his chariot, and fled away on his feet. But Barak pursued after the chariots, and after the host, unto Harosheth of the Gentiles: and all the host of Sisera fell upon the edge of the sword; and there was not a man left. Howbeit Sisera fled away on his feet to the tent of Jael the wife of Heber the Kenite: for there was peace between Jabin the king of Hazor and the house of Heber the Kenite.

And Jael went out to meet Sisera, and said unto him, "Turn in, my lord, turn in to me; fear not."

And when he had turned in unto her into the tent, she covered him with a mantle. And he said unto her, "Give me, I pray thee, a little water to drink; for I am thirsty."

And she opened a bottle of milk, and gave him drink, and covered him. Again he said unto her, "Stand in the door of the tent, and it shall be, when any man doth come and inquire of thee, and say, 'Is there any man here?' that thou shalt say, 'No.'"

Then Jael Heber's wife took a nail of the tent, and took a hammer in her hand, and went softly unto him, and smote the nail into his temples, and fastened it into the ground; for he was fast asleep and weary. So he died.

And, behold, as Barak pursued Sisera, Jael came out to meet him, and said unto him, "Come, and I will show thee the man whom thou seekest."

And when he came into her tent, behold, Sisera lay dead, and the nail was in his temples.

So God subdued on that day Jabin the king of Canaan before the children of Israel. And the hand of the children of Israel prospered, and prevailed against Jabin the king of Canaan, until they had destroyed Jabin king of Canaan.

Then sang Deborah and Barak the son of Abinoam on that day, saying,

> "Praise ye the Lord for the avenging of Israel,
> When the people willingly offered themselves.
> Hear, O ye kings; give ear, O ye princes;
> I, even I, will sing unto the Lord;
> I will sing praise to the Lord God of Israel.

> "Blessed above women shall Jael
> The wife of Heber the Kenite be;
> Blessed shall she be above women in the tent.
> He asked water, and she gave him milk;
> She brought forth butter in a lordly dish.
> She put her hand to the nail,
> And her right hand to the workmen's hammer;
> And with the hammer she smote Sisera,
> She smote off his head,
> When she had pierced and stricken through his temples.
> At her feet he bowed, he fell, he lay down:
> At her feet he bowed, he fell:
> Where he bowed, there he fell down dead.

> "So let all thine enemies perish, O Lord:
> But let them that love him be as the sun
> When he goeth forth in his might."

[*Judges 4:1–5:3, 24–27, 31*]

SISERA

Edwin Arlington Robinson

From Taanach to Harosheth, by the river,
Barak had driven Sisera and his thousands
Till there were only a last few of them
Alive to feel, while there was time to feel,
Jehovah's hand and Israel's together,
Smiting invincibly. A slave of Canaan
For twenty years, now Israel was a slave
No more; and by the waters of Megiddo,
King Jabin's army was a picture drawn
Of men who slept. Sisera felt the dead
Behind him, and he knew the sound of death
Pursuing him—a sound that sang no hope
Or mercy for the few that were alive
Of Israel's enemy, and the last alive
That were to sleep that day, and for so long
As to be loved and trumpeted no more
By time and man than all who are forgotten.

Sisera, soon to see himself alone
Among the slain, or soon as one of them
To see not even himself left of his host,
Suddenly from his chariot, to rough ground,
Leapt as an animal from a flying cage
That plunged and rocked and staggered might have leapt,
Blindly, to wild escape and a short freedom.
Prone for a moment on hard earth he lay,
Bruised and amazed to find himself unbroken,
And with a quicker leap was up again,
And running—running as he believed no manner
Of man had run before—to the one place
He knew that might receive him yet and save him.
Heber the Kenite had no world to lose
Or win with either side, and was not fighting.
He was in Canaan frequently, moreover,

King Jabin's guest and friend; and his wife Jael
Was Jabin's adoration and desire,
And Sisera's despair. She frightened men
With her security, and she maddened them
With dark hot beauty that was more than woman's,
And yet all woman—or, as Jabin said
To Heber, enviously, perhaps all women
In one. If Sisera's fear remembered now
That there was more of Israelite in Jael
Than Canaanite or Kenite, he was running
Too fast and furiously and ruinously
For memories to be following him so far
As to the tents of Heber, where he prayed
For Jael and sanctuary. Her smile would save
A captain, as her frown would blast a king,
If she but willed it so. Sisera's feet
Flew as he thought of that, and his thought flew
Before him like a promise that he followed,
And followed flying. For an insane hour
He flew, and for another, and for a third,
And then fell helpless at the feet of Jael,
Who smiled at him unseen—which was as well
For Sisera; for her smile would save no captains,
Or none today.

        "If this comes out of Canaan
For me to save, then Israel must be free,"
She thought; and a thought slowly filled her heart
With music that she felt inflaming her
Deliriously with Deborah's word fulfilled.
Again she smiled, and went for cloths and water
To wash his heated face and his closed eyes,
Which, having seen her and been sure of her,
Saw nothing else until he felt the touch
Of her cool fingers and of her warm breath,
Incredible and together. His eyes opened
And found hers over them, shining at him
With a protection in them that he feared
Was too much like a mother's.

        "Speak," she said,
"And tell me who has fallen in this battle,

And who fares well. We Kenites are peace-lovers,
Not mixed with either camp—yet we must know.
Tell me, and sleep."

                    "Yes, if you let me drink,"
He whispered, "I will tell you. Let me drink,
Or let me die. Let me die here with you,
If I must die. Not many of us are left
To die. This day is Israel's. Let me drink,
Or let me die. Let me die here with . . ."

                                        "No,"
She said, and smiled at him mysteriously.
"We are alive; and while we live—who knows?"
He reached with a blind hand for one of hers,
And held it while she said, "No, you must drink,"
And smiled: "Is there in Israel or in Canaan
A bowl of sleep like this for one so weary
As you? I have seen weariness before,
But never a man so made of weariness
That he shall not be flesh and bone again
Till sleep has made him so. Is it not cool
And healing as you feel it on your tongue,
And in your throat, and through you everywhere—
Like life itself? It is the milk of life
That you are drinking. It will make you leap
Like a new lion when you are awake.
Yes, when you are awake. Now, now, my friend,
Now is your time to sleep."

                    "Before I sleep,
Hear this," he said: "There will come after me
Some ravening fiend of Israel to destroy me.
They will have nothing left of us alive.
For twenty years they have worn Canaan's yoke,
And always, in their dreams have known Jehovah,
Still watching them. They have believed in him;
And their belief will be the end of me—
Unless you say to them no man of Canaan
Has crossed your sight this day. If I say this
Asleep, or still awake, I am not here.
No man was here . . . No man . . ."

                                   "No, Sisera,"
She said with lips that moved without a sound,
"No man was here that will depart from here,
Except as weary meat for scavengers.
Was that what you were saying? It must have been,
For that was what I heard." She waited, crouching,
And watched him with exalted eyes of triumph
That were not any longer woman's eyes,
But fixed and fierce and unimagined fires
Of death alive in beauty and burning it.
"No, Sisera; when they come, if they do come,
No man will be awaiting them. No man
Is here today who has not seen his last
Of Israel, and feared all there is for him
To fear of Israel. You are asleep
As only trust and weariness together
Makes a man sleep; and you will not feel this."
She laid an eager finger on his temple,
And pressed it, satisfied. Still watching him,
She moved away; and searching among shadows,
Found all she sought. "No, Sisera," she said,
Crooning above his face like a mad mother,
"There is no fear of Israel, or of earth,
Or of men living on earth, or things not men,
That you need fear today, or more tomorrow.
When they come here for you and say to me,
'Where is he?' I shall say, 'He is not here.
All that is here is yours. Take it away.'
See, Sisera! See what I have found for you.
Here is a nail as long as a man's life—
And sharp as death; and here is a brave hammer.
I found them there in the dark, where I remembered
Seeing them once. We had all best remember
Things we have seen, for soon or late we need them.
So, Sisera!"

                        Slowly she drew away
The pillow she had lent his head to lie on,
And left his head lying sidewise on the floor.
Still crouching, she surveyed him, saying softly,
"So this is Canaan, who for twenty years
Believed that he was more than Israel!

Who is he now? What is he, Sisera?
You will not answer; for where Canaan sleeps
This day and night, there will be sleep indeed.
I can see thousands of you lying quiet;
And one will be one more."

                        The nail, sure-driven,
Transfixed a silent head that would not move
When she would see its face. And with him there,
What was a face? She had seen Sisera's face
Before; and it was no more Sisera now
Than were his fingers or his feet, she thought.
A face was not a man; and a man dead
Was less, or so it looked, than was a nail.
And she had driven the nail to make him dead,
For Deborah to celebrate, and for Barak
To see, and for all Israel to see.
Her life within her body was like fire—
A fire that healed in her the wrongs and sorrows
Of Israel sold in Canaan to a king
Who made a sport of his malignity,
And Sisera's; and now Sisera was dead.
All Israel would be told in a few hours
That Sisera was dead. And Deborah then
Would say to Barak: "The Lord's will be done!
Jael has killed Sisera—sing!—sing to the Lord!"

Still crouching over him, and watching him
Like an avenging image, she could hear
The coming sound of horses, and soon with it,
Confirming it, a murmur of men talking.
"Barak!" she told her heart; and her heart said,
"Barak!" And Jael arose in her rejoicing.
Outside she saw them, Barak and his men,
Who had known where to come. With arms aloft,
And eyes afire with triumph and thanksgiving,
She stood awaiting Barak. "Yes, he is here,"
She said; "and he is yours for no more seeking.
He will not fly away from you again."

"Hardly, if he is here," said Barak, halting.
He smiled at her with battle-heated eyes,

And met the fire of hers with admiration,
Mingled with weariness and victory,
And with a searching wonder. Then a spasm
Of silent laughter shook him and his voice:
"If he is here, you must have promised him
More than a man may give to make him stop.
We might have seized him, if necessity
Had said we must, and we might have him now
To count with his lost thousands; but we knew
That Heber's tent would hold him, if such running
As his might last until you took him in.
At first, and for some time, we only watched him;
And all the horses watched him. Never since man
Was born to run has there been such a running
As this of Sisera's here today in Canaan.
Children who are unborn will emulate it;
And aged men will rise up out of chairs,
Remembering Sisera, and sit down again.
There's not a curse's worth of Canaan left,
Nor more than Sisera left of Jabin's army;
And Sisera's only safety is between
Jehovah and a woman—which is good,
If Jael is the Lord's woman. Well, where is he?"

Jael, who had partly heard him, turned and said,
"Follow me, Barak. I will show him to you.
And you, having seen how quiet and safe he is,
Will praise me. I shall have praise of Israel,
And of Jehovah shall have praise and glory,
For this that I have done. Since I remember,
I have heard voices of high prophecy,
Telling me to fulfil myself with patience
And readiness against an untold hour.
Now is the hour. The chosen of the Lord
Are told, if they will hear; and when the Lord
Has need of them they serve him—as they must.
My way to serve him was magnificent,
And will be praised for ever . . . See him, Barak!
Tell Deborah what you saw. Tell Deborah
That he is dead! Tell her that he is dead!
Tell her that everything that she foretold
Has come to pass. Tell her that he is dead!"

Barak, abrupt in battle, and in slaughter
Not subtle, till now had always made of war
A man's work, and of death attending it
An item necessary for a total.
So long as he should live, and live to fight
For Israel and for glory of the Lord,
Others would cease to live if they opposed him;
For that was the Lord's way, and Israel's way.
But this was not. He stared at Sisera's head,
Where the nail was, and slowly shook his own
Before he spoke: "I am not sure of this,"
He said, and looked at her uncertainly,
As if to ask for the first time, perhaps—
Whose hand held death for him. She who did this
Might one day flout her fealty to Jehovah
And lust for Baal. She might do anything.
So Barak only scowled and said to Jael,
"I am not sure of this. How was this done—
If he was not asleep?"

                                    "He was asleep,"
Jael said; and her eyes measured him with scorn
For one so artless and inquisitive;
"The Lord put him to sleep, and gave me strength
Of more than one small woman to destroy him.
So there he is. Tell Israel to rejoice.
Tell Deborah to rejoice. Tell Deborah
Where you saw Sisera dead, and bring her here
That she may see him. It was she who said
That Sisera was to die—and he is dead.
What is one man, or one man's way of dying,
So long as Israel has no more of him!"

Taut and erect she stood, and her possession
Bewildered Barak and astonished him
Into an awkward silence. All he did
Was to look down at Sisera, and once more
At Jael, not sure that he was looking at her.
At last he sighed, and made as if to throw
His hands away, having no use for them;
And having sighed again, he said to Jael,
"A world that holds so much for men to know

Must have been long in making. The Lord pondered
More than six days, I think, to make a woman.
The book of woman that has troubled man
So long in learning is all folly now.
I shall go home tonight and make another.
The wisest man alive, wherever he is,
Is not so wise that he has never wondered
What women do when they are left together,
Or left alone." He stood with folded arms
And with shut jaws, gazing at Sisera's head,
And at the driven nail piercing his head.
Scowling and thoughtful, he considered them
In silence, and then said, after some time,
"The tiger's wife, we're told. . . . I've all to learn.
Is this what women do?"

        "Tell Deborah,"
Jael answered, as if answering a voice
Farther away than Barak's, "that I killed him.
Tell Deborah, who foretold it, that a woman,
A woman filled with God, killed Sisera
For love of Israel, and that you have seen him,
As he is now, with no more harm in him.
Tell Deborah this right hand of mine was God's
That hammered in the nail—while Sisera slept.
Tell her my hand was God's that held the nail—
While Sisera slept. Say Jael and God together
Made Sisera what you see. Sing to the Lord,
Barak! And say to Deborah, 'Jael says,
Sing to the Lord!' For now there shall be peace
In Israel, and a sound of women singing—
A sound of children singing, and men singing—
All singing to the Lord! There is no king
In Canaan who is king of Israel now!
This day is ended—and there is no King
In Israel but the Lord! Sing to the Lord!
Let Israel see the dark of a day fading,
And sing!—praising a day that has an end.
Let Israel see the light of a day breaking,
And sing!—hailing a day that has a dawn.
Sing to the King of Israel her Thanksgiving!
Sing to the King of Glory! Sing to the Lord!"

Why does Sisera flee to Jael's tent? To what does Jael refer when she speaks of "Deborah's word fulfilled"? Explain how "a man dead" is "less, or so it looked, than was a nail." What suspicions does Barak harbor concerning how Jael lured Sisera into her "trap"? Why does the fact that a woman committed the act so bewilder him? Study Jael's final speech. Why does she say she killed Sisera? Why does she seem to revel in the fact that a woman performed the deed in the service of a woman judge? Do you think her speech shows that she views the event primarily as a woman's victory, or does she see some greater significance to her deed? Reread the end of the biblical story and discuss Deborah's response to Jael's heroism.

DAVID AND GOLIATH

(1 Samuel)

David was the first great king of Israel, although Saul was the first to sit on the Hebrew throne. During his reign he led the Israelites in many important battles, eventually establishing Israel as the major power in the Near East. He is most often remembered, however, for his courage as a young shepherd boy who challenged the Philistine giant Goliath with nothing more than his faith in God and five smooth stones.

But the Spirit of the Lord departed from Saul, and an evil spirit from the Lord troubled him. And Saul's servants said unto him, "Behold now, an evil spirit from God troubleth thee. Let our lord now command thy servants, which are before thee, to seek out a man, who is a cunning player on a harp: and it shall come to pass, when the evil spirit from God is upon thee, that he shall play with his hand, and thou shalt be well."

And Saul said unto his servants, "Provide me now a man that can play well, and bring him to me."

Then answered one of the servants, and said, "Behold, I have seen a son of Jesse the Bethlehemite, that is cunning in playing, and a mighty valiant man, and a man of war, and prudent in matters, and a comely person, and the Lord is with him."

Wherefore Saul sent messengers unto Jesse, and said, "Send me David thy son, which is with the sheep."

And Jesse took an ass laden with bread, and a bottle of wine, and a kid, and sent them by David his son unto Saul. And David came to Saul, and stood before him: and he loved him greatly; and he became his armorbearer. And Saul sent to Jesse, saying, "Let David, I pray thee, stand before me; for he hath found favor in my sight."

And it came to pass, when the evil spirit from God was upon Saul, that David took a harp, and played with his hand: so Saul was refreshed, and was well, and the evil spirit departed from him.

Now the Philistines gathered together their armies to battle, and were gathered together at Shochoh, which belongeth to Judah, and pitched between Shochoh and Azekah, in Ephesdammim. And Saul and the men of Israel were gathered together, and pitched by the valley of Elah, and set the battle in array against the Philistines. And the Philistines stood on a mountain on the one side, and Israel stood on a mountain on the other side: and there was a valley between them.

And there went out a champion out of the camp of the Philistines, named Goliath, of Gath, whose height was six cubits and a span. And he had a helmet of brass upon his head, and he was armed with a coat of mail; and the weight of the coat was five thousand shekels of brass. And he had greaves of brass upon his legs, and a target of brass between his shoulders. And the staff of his spear was like a weaver's beam; and his spear's head weighed six hundred shekels of iron: and one bearing a shield went before him.

And he stood and cried unto the armies of Israel, and said unto them, "Why are ye come out to set your battle in array? Am not I a Philistine, and ye servants to Saul? Choose you a man for you, and let him come down to me. If he be able to fight with me, and to kill me, then will we be your servants: but if I prevail against him, and kill him, then shall ye be our servants, and serve us." And the Philistine said, "I defy the armies of Israel this day; give me a man, that we may fight together."

When Saul and all Israel heard those words of the Philistine, they were dismayed, and greatly afraid.

[David in the meantime has left Saul and returned to his father's home in Bethlehem to tend his sheep. During the course of the battle between the Israelites and the Philistines, Jesse sends him back to the valley of Elah to deliver provisions to his three older brothers who are engaged in Saul's forces. On his return to the camp he learns of Goliath's challenge and the Israelites' fear. After a heated argument with his eldest brother, who thinks he has come only to watch the battle and get into mischief, the youth goes directly to Saul to offer his services.]

And David said to Saul, "Let no man's heart fail because of him; thy servant will go and fight with this Philistine."

And Saul said to David. "Thou art not able to go against this Philistine to fight with him; for thou art but a youth, and he a man of war from his youth."

And David said unto Saul, "Thy servant kept his father's sheep, and there came a lion, and a bear, and took a lamb out of the flock; and I went out after him, and smote him, and delivered it out of his mouth:

and when he arose against me, I caught him by his beard, and smote him, and slew him. Thy servant slew both the lion and the bear: and this uncircumcised Philistine shall be as one of them, seeing he hath defied the armies of the living God."

David said moreover, "The Lord that delivered me out of the paw of the lion, and out of the paw of the bear, he will deliver me out of the hand of this Philistine."

And Saul said unto David, "Go, and the Lord be with thee."

And Saul armed David with his armor, and he put a helmet of brass upon his head; also he armed him with a coat of mail. And David girded his sword upon his armor, and he assayed to go; for he had not proved it.

And David said unto Saul, "I cannot go with these; for I have not proved them." And David put them off him. And he took his staff in his hand, and chose him five smooth stones out of the brook, and put them in a shepherd's bag which he had, even in a scrip; and his sling was in his hand: and he drew near to the Philistine.

And the Philistine came on and drew near unto David: and the man that bore the shield went before him. And when the Philistine looked about, and saw David, he disdained him: for he was but a youth, and ruddy, and of a fair countenance. And the Philistine said unto David, "Am I a dog, that thou comest to me with staves?"

And the Philistine cursed David by his gods. And the Philistine said to David, "Come to me, and I will give thy flesh unto the fowls of the air, and to the beasts of the field."

Then said David to the Philistine, "Thou comest to me with a sword, and with a spear, and with a shield: but I come to thee in the name of the Lord of hosts, the God of the armies of Israel, whom thou hast defied. This day will the Lord deliver thee into mine hand; and I will smite thee, and take thine head from thee; and I will give the carcases of the host of the Philistines this day unto the fowls of the air, and to the wild beasts of the earth; that all the earth may know that there is a God in Israel. And all this assembly shall know that the Lord saveth not with sword and spear: for the battle is the Lord's, and he will give you into our hands."

And it came to pass, when the Philistine arose, and came and drew nigh to meet David, that David hastened, and ran toward the army to meet the Philistine. And David put his hand in his bag, and took thence a stone, and slung it, and smote the Philistine in his forehead, that the stone sunk into his forehead; and he fell upon his face to the earth.

So David prevailed over the Philistine with a sling and with a stone, and smote the Philistine, and slew him; but there was no sword in the hand of David. Therefore David ran, and stood upon the Philistine, and took his sword, and drew it out of the sheath thereof, and slew him, and cut off his head therewith. And when the Philistines saw their champion was dead, they fled.

And the men of Israel and of Judah arose, and shouted, and pursued the Philistines. And the wounded of the Philistines fell down by the way to Shaaraim, even unto Gath, and unto Ekron. And the children of Israel returned from chasing after the Philistines, and they spoiled their tents.

And David took the head of the Philistine, and brought it to Jerusalem; but he put his armor in his tent.

[1 Samuel 16:14–17:11, 32–54]

What proof does David have that the Lord is with him? Why does he reject the armor Saul offers him? What does David take with which to slay the giant Goliath? What effect does David's slaying of the Philistine leader have on the enemy? On the Israelites?

LITTLE DAVID

Roark Bradford

Well, de Hebrews whupped de Philistines and de Philistines whupped de Hebrews. But neither side wouldn't stay whupped. So finally de Lawd sort of got tired stayin' round to he'p out de Hebrews all de time, so he app'inted a man name King Saul to be king er de Hebrews.

"King Saul," say de Lawd, "you take and lead my people while I go back and 'tend to my angels a little."

Ole King Saul was a purty good king when hit come to fightin', but when hit come to jest plain ev'yday kingin', ole Saul wa'n't so much. But as long as he whupped de Philistines de people hung wid him, and sort of put up wid him for de rest er de time. So Saul started to think he was purty good all de way round.

"What a king needs," say ole King Saul, "is a heap er music round de camp." So he sont out and got a little boy name Little David to come and play on his harp round de camp.

Little David was one er deseyar boys which could do mighty nigh anything and could do hit good. But when hit come right down to hit, he could make up songs and sing 'em better'n he could do anything else. He always was makin' up a song and playin' hit on his harp and singin'. Even while he was out herdin' his daddy's sheep he'd take and put his harp in his pocket and set out on de hillside and sing:

"Ef I could I sholy would,
I wanter stand on de rocks whar Moses stood.
Little David, play on yo' harp, hallelu! hallelu!
Little David, play on yo' harp, hallelu!"

So while he was singin' a big bear come and stole a sheep and he had to git up and run de bear down to git de sheep back. Den he went on back and sung some mo':

"Old Joshua was de son of Nun,
And he never quit fightin' to de fightin' was done.
Little David, play on yo' harp, hallelu! hallelu!
Little David, play on yo' harp, hallelu!"

So 'bout dat time yar come a line and stole another sheep, so Little David had to git up and run him down.

"Dis ain't gittin' nowheres," he say. "I'm gittin' sick and tired er runnin' deseyar thievin' varmints down ev'y time they steals a sheep. I bet I'm gonter fix me somethin' which'll do my runnin' for me." So he tuck and cut de tongue outer his shoe and got two strings and make him a sling-shot. So he set down and started singin' again:

"Old Joshua stood on de top er de hill,
And he looked at de sun and de sun stood still.
Little David, play on yo' harp, hallelu! hallelu!
Little David, play on yo' harp, hallelu!"

So 'bout dat time a wolf come up and steal hisse'f a sheep. But David didn't git up and run after him. He jest got a rock and put hit in de sling-shot and slung hit round his head about twice, and ker-blip! de wolf thought de lightnin' had done struck him!

Saul and David (1896) by Emil Nolde. GERMAN INFORMATION CENTER, NEW YORK.

So when ole King Saul sont for Little David, Little David not only tuck 'long his harp, but he tuck 'long his sling-shot, too. So one day he was settin' out in front of ole King Saul's tent, playin' and singin' away, to all at once hit started to git dark and de yearth started to tremble and de ground started to shake.

"What dat, ole King Saul?" say Little David.

"Dat's old Goliar," say old King Saul.

"Who he?" say David.

"De he-coon er de Philistines," say King Saul.

"What do he want?" say David.

"Trouble," say ole King Saul.

"Well, you de king, ain't you?" say Little David. "Can't you ease his worries 'long dat line?"

"Who, me?" say Saul. "I'm a married man. Cou'se I ain't skeered of him, but still and at de same time I got a wife and a family dependin' on me for s'port. So I don't see no reason how come I should git out and git hurted by no gi'nt."

"He's a gi'nt?" say Little David.

"Twenty foot tall," say King Saul.

"What else is he?" say David.

"Jest wait to he gits out in de clearin' and starts makin' his say-so," say King Saul.

So 'bout dat time ole Goliar stepped out in de clearin' and commenced makin' his say-so.

"I'm a cross betwixt a wild cat and de yaller ianders," he say. "I'm sired by Trouble and dammed by Sudden Death. I drinks nothin' but stump water and a rattlesnake bit me and died. I breathes out forked lightnin' and I spits out thunder. When I laughs de skies pop open, and when I groans hit rolls up like a ball er yarn. I kills my friends and I makes hamburgers outer my enemies. Tornadoes and harrycanes follow me round like pet dogs, and lines and tigers is my playmates. I'm bad. I'm mean. I'm vicious, and jest natchally can't help it. When I gits sick hit takes nothin' less'n a Hebrew man's meat to cyore me. And I feel a buck auger comin' on. So look out! I'm reekin' wid meanness and I'm huntin' trouble."

"Sounds hard, don't he?" say Little David.

"Sounds?" say ole King Saul. "Son, dat big scound'el is hard!"

"Is you skeered of him?" say Little David.

"Naw, I ain't skeered of him," say ole King Saul, " 'cause I got sense enough to keep outn his way."

"I ain't skeered of him," say Little David.

"You kin run purty fast, kin you?" say Saul.

"Naw, I ain't de runnin' kind," say Little David. "I'm jest goin' up yonder and whup dat scound'el befo' supper time."

"You gonter which?" say ole King Saul.

"I'm gonter whup him," say Little David, "or else he gonter whup me."

"Well," say ole King Saul, "be keerful and don't meet up wid de ole Fool Killer on yo' way over, 'cause efn de Fool Killer meet up wid you, he gonter beat ole Goliar to you."

Little David didn't said a word. He jest tuck his harp in one hand and his sling-shot in de yuther, and he went off singin':

> "When I gits to heaven I'm gonter be like Job.
> I'm gonter wawk all around in my long, white robe.
> Little David, play on yo' harp, hallelu! hallelu!
> Little David, play on yo' harp, hallelu!"

So when ole Goliar seed Little David he say, "What you doin' over yar on my side, little ole Hebrew boy?"

"I thought I yared somebody say you was lookin' for trouble," say Little David.

"Don't play wid me, little boy," say Goliar. "I'm in a bad humor and I ain't kilt me no Hebrew since yistiddy. Trot 'long back home befo' I gits mad and spatters you up ag'in' de side er de yearth."

"You don't want to fight wid me?" say Little David. "I yared 'bout deseyar boys wid de big say-so, and f'm what I yars, hit's all say-so and no do-so."

Well, dat made old Goliar good and hot, so he arch up his back and squnch down his shoulders and start stiff-laiggin' round and roarin' and bellowin'. "I'm comin', so jest watch out for me," he say. "I'm dealin' death and destruction right yar and now." And he dance stiff-laigged round Little David, jest groanin' and gruntin' like hit's hurtin' him powerful bad to hold hisse'f back to he gits done wid his dancin' and tawkin'.

"I'm comin', 'cause I can't hold myse'f back no longer," say ole Goliar and he started twarg Little David.

So Little David jest drap a rock into his sling-shot and slung hit round his head, and ker-blop! he tuck ole Goliar right between de eyes and ole Goliar never knowed what hit him.

So 'bout dat time de Lawd stepped out f'm behind a bush and say: "Well, dat settles hit, Little David. You gonter be king over my people."

"Aw, Lawd," say Little David, "ole King Saul is de king."

"You mean he was de king," say de Lawd. "I been holdin' on to him 'cause he makes out like he kin fight. But you not on'y kin sing, but you kin outfight him, too, and ev'ybody knows ole King Saul can't sing. So hit's jest like I say, son. You de king, and no argyment wid me 'bout hit."

'Well, thanky, Lawd," say Little David. So he picks up his harp and wawked on back to camp, singin':

> "Little David was a shepherd's boy,
> And he killed ole Goliar and he hollered wid joy.
> Little David, play on yo' harp, hallelu! hallelu!
> Little David, play on yo' harp, hallelu"

How does this black folk retelling of the story of David make him more "real"? Why do you think Saul is made out to be such a coward? What other reason is given for the Lord's preferring David to Saul as king of Israel? The italicized passages that appear throughout the story are from a spiritual entitled "Little David." What effect does the author achieve by writing his own "Little David" around the words of the spiritual?

GOLIATH AND DAVID

Louis Untermeyer

Goliath

See the dazzled stripling stand,
Naked as an empty hand.
And here am I, a clanking mass
Blotting out the yellow grass
With a body only sent
For the world's astonishment:
Arms as great as monstrous boughs

Where no bird would dare to house,
Fingers like some poisonous growth
Even jungle-beasts must loathe,
And a goggling head awry
Like a black moon in the sky.
Here I wait, uneagerly,
For the child that faces me,
Frightened by my length of limb—
And the clean, young grace of him
Unaware that cheek and brow
Taste their last of sunlight now.
Oh, that it were I, not he!
Oh, that God would take from me
This power only schooled in harm
And send it through that puny arm
With such a fire that it might well
Break through this hugely rotting shell.
But there will be no miracle.
There is no help. Young David, fly!
I am destruction's demon, aye,
Too sick to live, too strong to die.

David

And there he looms, no more defiant
Than any hill. So that's the giant!
That is the thing that should alarm me
More than the sight of hell's own army
Commanded by its master devil.
But this—why, this is nothing evil.
Its eyes are cow's eyes; it looks civil;
A thing that only babes could fear.
Yet I—what am I doing here?
What part have I, the least of shepherds,
Among these hungry spears and scabbards?
What! Have I tended sheep and cattle
Only to lead the wolves to battle?
Am I possessed of howling demons
That I should seek the blood of humans?
God, take this madness out of me.
Give me my pastures, let me be—

Far from this clash of words and weapons—
Where nothing cries and little happens,
Save when a star leaps from the heavens
Or a new rush of song enlivens
The heart that beats in balanced measures,
Unshaken by more passionate seizures.
See, I will fling this silly pebble
Away from me to end my trouble
And pluck harp-strings again till they
Charm every darker thought away.
Come, old Goliath, come and play!

Why is the order of names reversed here? How does the poet depict Goliath? Why does Goliath wish God to send his power "through that puny arm" of David's? What does he mean that he is "Too sick to live, too strong to die"?

How does David's view of the giant differ from that of his biblical counterpart? What message is the poet attempting to communicate through this twist? How does the poet draw on David's skill as a harpist to make this point?

UNIT 3

THE WAYS OF GOD AND MAN

Job and the Comforters (1825) by William Blake. THE TATE GALLERY, LONDON.

T HE BIBLE is a collection of many different types of literature. Besides historical narrative and chronicle, one can find legend, fable, parable, proverb, short story, drama, poetry, and philosophy. In this unit the emphasis is on the philosophic, poetic, and protest writings of the Old Testament. Selections from five biblical books have been included: Job, Ecclesiastes, Song of Songs, Ruth, and Jonah. These works, like those in the first unit, come to grips with issues that have confronted mankind throughout the ages, posing questions concerning the nature of God and His will for man, of justice and injustice, of man's relationship with his fellow man and with God. Here, too, particularly in the Song of Songs, Ruth, and Jonah, the nature of love is examined: of love between a man and a woman, between members of a family, between people of one nation and another, and between God and all nations. If there is any answer that emerges from these philosophic and lyrical probings of the ways of God and men, it is that love somehow makes all the cares and burdens of this world seem more bearable and even worthwhile.

On the surface at least, our world of computers, mass production, overpopulation, and pollution seems a far cry from that of the Old Testament writers, whose subjects herded sheep, traveled by camel or donkey, and gleaned in the fields. Nevertheless, man himself has changed little, if at all. He still exhibits sorrow and even despair when struck by personal misfortune. In a world where events seem to happen arbitrarily and beyond his control, he is still often driven to wonder what life is all about and whether his existence has any particular meaning. He still struggles with racial, national, and religious prejudices, while feeling somehow that the conflicts between races, nations, and religions are inconsistent with the belief in one God in whose image all mankind was created. No simple answers are provided by the biblical writings in this unit, but the issues that they raise and the ways in which they deal with them are indeed worthy of consideration.

One of the characteristics which most distinguished the relationship between the Hebrews and their God from that between other peoples and their gods was the covenantal agreement that provided for a rational means of dealing with the Lord. Nevertheless, tragedy— whether national or personal—undoubtedly struck the Hebrews many times, even when their devotion to God and their trust in Him seemed to be complete. How were the people to react to such misfortune, given the special assurances of the covenant? In more general terms, how can a person find meaning in his actions and experiences unless there exists a relationship between what he does and what happens to him as a result? The Book of Job addresses itself to just this question. Job is a godly man who is inflicted with extreme misfortune as the result of Satan's challenge to God that were He to strip Job of all his good fortune he would surely curse God: his servants are killed, all his belongings carried away, his children slain, and his skin broken out in boils from head to foot. Although he seriously calls the purpose of his existence into question, Job refuses to curse God or lose faith in his creator. The central issue in Job's drama is his questioning the *reason* behind his misfortunes: why should he, a blameless and righteous man, be treated so harshly by his God? He demands that God answer him directly on this account. His friends, the "comforters," try to justify God's way to Job by accusing him of being a vile sinner: God would surely not inflict such misfortune upon a truly innocent man; nor would He sit by indifferently if someone else were to so inflict him; thus Job must have done *something* to deserve such treatment. Job remains steadfast, however, insisting that he has done nothing. Finally, God himself appears abruptly as the Voice out of the whirlwind to proclaim that He is not accountable to Job and that Job cannot comprehend the inscrutable ways of God. The splendid catalog of wonders the Voice depicts has a powerful effect upon Job, who is awed by the magnificence of God's creation, and he humbles himself before the incomprehensible will of his Lord. In the end Job still has no answers as to *why* he has suffered so. He understands, however, that there is a God, and it is the assurance of the grandeur of the creation that enables him to accept and rise above his suffering with confidence that there is meaning and purpose in life.

The Book of Job challenged many of the prevailing beliefs of its time. One of these was that a man is rewarded with good for his righteousness and with evil for iniquity. Shall a man serve God merely because he fears retribution if he fails to do so, or does God merit our worship regardless of what happens to us? Are human beings nothing more than guinea pigs in a Skinnerian game of reward and punishment? Is there any alternative to believing that those who suffer are not really innocent, but only getting what they deserve, or that

God is helpless or indifferent in the face of innocent suffering? The
Book of Job suggests that the ways of God are not that simple:
righteousness is not necessarily rewarded; man cannot reason out what
lies behind those forces of the universe that affect his life; man must
accept whatever God sends—that is the *only* answer—and he must
continue to love God no matter what happens to him. In "The
Emancipator of Your God" from *A Masque of Reason,* Robert Frost
depicts God thanking Job for liberating Him from "mortal bondage to
the human race"; for Job has established "once and for all" that there
is "no connection man can reason out/Between his just deserts and
what he gets." Job had freed the God of Israel from playing the role of
the behavioral scientist who extorts obedience from his subjects by
doling out material rewards for desired behavior. Such conditioned
obedience would hardly serve as proof of mankind's devotion to God,
a point Satan made clear in his wager.

Finding meaning in a universe seemingly indifferent to human
suffering and injustice is no easy task. Several modern authors have
grappled with this issue, just as Job did. In "The Mysterious Stranger,"
Mark Twain depicts the gods of the universe as totally lacking in
moral purpose or concern for the consequences of their whimsical
behavior. The three boys of the story are entertained by a beautiful
stranger who gives his name as Satan. When questioned, the stranger
explains that many angels are named Satan, although only one, his
"uncle," fell from God's grace. He then shows his power by fashioning
little people from the dust of the earth and setting them to work. When
irritated by their behavior, he crushes them, turning a deaf ear to the
cries of those being ravaged by his destructive actions. The boys are
appalled by the lack of concern shown by the stranger for the welfare
of his creatures, but they are easily charmed by the "fatal music of
his voice." In similar fashion Robinson Jeffers, in his poem "Look, How
Beautiful," cries out that it is God's will to "make great things and
destroy them, and make great things, and destroy them again," yet he
too is charmed out of his indignation. Just as Job does after God speaks
to him out of the whirlwind, the poet considers the magnificence of
creation and concludes: "Look how beautiful are all the things
that he does."

Archibald MacLeish in his poetic drama *J.B.,* a modern adaptation
of the Job theme, comes to a conclusion similar to that of Robinson
Jeffers: a person cannot make sense out of the pattern of what happens
to him, especially in terms of mindless violence and destruction, but
he can always turn to the simple living beauty of God's creation
and to love to find meaning—for example, to the "green leaf on the
branch" which sparked in J.B.'s wife the rediscovery of her faith in life

after her children had all been violently killed. MacLeish makes of
J.B.'s salvation a human matter. Like Job, J.B. does not curse God for
all his undeserved suffering, but neither does he bow submissively
in the end to divine authority as Job did. J.B. finds all the answer he
needs as to the significance of his life in his love for his wife Sarah and
in the "first few leaves" and the "petals" growing from the ashes of
all that was left of his earthly possessions. God spoke to Job out of the
magnificence of the whirlwind. If we look for Him, He can be
found, each of these modern writers seems to suggest, in any of his
infinitely varied creations.

Suffering is not the only human condition that drives man to question
the meaning of his existence, as is shown by the example set by
the Preacher in Ecclesiastes. Unlike Job, the Preacher, traditionally
associated with King Solomon, has everything that Job lost and more:
riches, honor among family and friends, good health, and wisdom.
Yet he finds all of these to be "vanity and vexation of spirit."
With unrelenting honesty, the Preacher examines all that life has to
offer and finds it ultimately of little worth, for "there is nothing new
under the sun." All men must face the final absurdity, death, which
comes to the rich as well as the poor, the mighty as well as the weak,
the righteous as well as the wicked. No matter what a person
accomplishes in this life, it must all be left to another afterwards:
"And who knoweth whether he shall be a wise man or a fool?"

Had it not been for the traditional ascribing of the authorship of
the work to Solomon, Ecclesiastes might never have won a place in the
accepted canon of the Old Testament, inasmuch as some rabbis
earlier wished not to publicize the book because of its pessimistic,
almost heretical tone. The Preacher is not completely despairing in his
outlook, however. He seems to accept the daily joys God gives the
righteous man. "Go thy way, eat thy bread with joy, and drink
thy wine with a merry heart," he advises, "for God hath already
accepted thy works." In this respect his philosophy is an early
pronouncement of the existential concept of what Sartre calls
"engagement" in the face of ultimate absurdity. "Whatsoever thy hand
findeth to do, do it with thy might; for there is no work, nor device,
nor knowledge, nor wisdom, in the grave, whither thou goest."
Meaning comes also from a commitment to your fellow man: "Two are
better than one," the Preacher observes. "For if they fall, the one
will lift up his fellow: but woe to him that is alone when he falleth,
and hath not another to lift him up." Finally, he advises, "Remember
also thy creator in the days of thy youth." For it is the "whole duty of
man" to "fear God and keep his commandments."

Edmond Fleg in "Solomon the King," a portion of his novel entitled *The Life of Solomon,* elaborates upon the traditional association between the Preacher of Ecclesiastes and Solomon and, in so doing, captures the spirit of futility—of "vanity and vexation of spirit"— that underlies much of Ecclesiastes. Fleg depicts Solomon as a lonely king desperately searching for some means of dissipating his world weariness. He invites the Queen of Sheba to his palace in hope that she can help him find happiness, but nothing in her simplicity can quench his deep undefined longing. A final orgy of self-indulgence only leaves him further in despair. His wisdom did not show him the futility of attempting to find meaning and happiness through the pursuit of worldly possessions and the pleasures of the flesh: the Solomon of Fleg's story can purchase everything imaginable—except the love he so sadly lacked.

Far from the despairing pessimism of Ecclesiastes is the soaring lyricism and hope expressed in the Song of Songs, also traditionally associated with Solomon. Although the Song of Songs has been subjected to a variety of religious interpretations, some of which will be discussed later, its emphasis is primarily on the physical manifestations of love between a man and a woman. The Song is believed by many biblical scholars to be a pastoral ode or fragmentary idyll written originally for some notable wedding. The language it is written in is highly lyrical throughout. "Behold, thou art fair, my love," the poet sings. "Thou hast ravished my heart, my sister, my bride." The imagery is highly evocative, with nature serving as the primary source. The Shulamite maiden is "the rose of Sharon, and the lily of the valleys"; her hair is likened to "a flock of goats," and her breasts to "two roes that are twins, which feed among the lilies." "Let my beloved come into his garden," the Shulamite invites, "and eat his pleasant fruits."

In "The Sharing," taken from the novel *Earth Abides,* George Stewart echoes the sensuous imagery of the Song of Songs to heighten the intensity and emphasize the almost religious quality of the intimacy shared by a man and a woman who, only moments before, had felt that they might be forced to endure life alone, without companionship in a world made desolate by a plague that has ravaged the earth's population. Readers will also find this selection provocative for the way in which Isherwood Williams, the main character, responds to various books of the Bible—particularly Ecclesiastes, the Song of Songs, and the Gospels—in light of the tragic social transformation that has occurred.

Whether or not the Song of Songs should even be included in the

accepted canon of the Old Testament was vigorously debated by
rabbis critical of the attention it paid to the physical manifestations of
love. Nevertheless, like Ecclesiastes, the fact that the Song was
traditionally associated with Solomon was instrumental in securing its
place in the Jewish canon. Also influential in its being accepted was
a second-century rabbi's argument that the lyrics should be interpreted
as an allegory referring to the love between God and His chosen
people, a view in keeping with the literary tradition employed by
several prophets who had described the relationship between Israel
and its God in terms of a bride and groom. Christian readers have
similarly seen the work as an allegorical expression of Christ's love for
the church. It is this interpretation that Christina Rossetti depends
upon in her poem "Passing Away," in which the poetess's Ecclesiastes-
like despair over her "chances, beauty, and youth [being] sapped
day by day" is compensated for by her joy at the coming of the
"Bridegroom"—actually Jesus Christ—who beckons her as his faithful
bride to "Arise, come away . . . My love, My sister, My spouse."

Love and devotion are at the center of an earlier Old Testament
work as well, the Book of Ruth, often considered the most beautiful
short story in the Bible. Here the lyrical outpouring of romantic
love expressed in the Song of Songs is muted and transformed into the
quieter devotion of a young widow to her mother-in-law, Naomi, for
whom she left her people to live as a stranger in an alien land, and
her love for an older man, Boaz, who had shown her great kindness
despite her non-Jewish background.

The gentleness and beauty with which the story of Ruth is rendered,
however, has too often resulted in an overlooking of an even more
important theme, that of racial tolerance. Ruth was a Moabite, a
people so generally detested for their idolatry and child sacrifice that
they were refused entry into the congregation of the Lord. Although
the story is set in the period of the judges who ruled over Israel, it may
have been written around 450 B.C. as a protest against Ezra's rule
prohibiting interracial marriages. Underpinning this simple story of
tolerance and love is the message that the God of Abraham and
Moses is not merely the God of the Israelites, but the Lord of all
mankind; for, as is revealed at the end of the story, out of this union
of Hebrew and Moabite was to come David, the great-grandson of
Ruth and Boaz. Thus the family tree of David, king of Israel—and,
later, of Jesus—included the union of Jew and Gentile. It is this theme
of tolerance that threads its way through "In the Fields of Boaz,"
Irving Fineman's retelling of the story of Ruth.

The Book of Jonah, like that of Ruth, is a work of protest, a biblical short story focusing on a prophet whose intolerance is contrasted with God's love and concern for all mankind. This work has too often been considered little more than the story of a prophet who, because of his disobedience to God's will, was swallowed by a whale (literally, a "great fish"). While controversy still rages over whether or not a man could survive "in the belly of a fish three days and three nights," the real lesson of religious tolerance is frequently lost. The purpose of this allegorical tale is to show that God extends His mercy and grace even to the enemies of Israel. Among all forms of love, God's love for all mankind reigns supreme. The short story of Jonah, like that of Ruth, demonstrates that all nations are within God's concern, and that we therefore must show a similar tolerance towards all mankind.

This concern of God for all mankind is also the focus of Robert Nathan's novel *Jonah,* from which the selection "The Testing of Jonah" is taken. The young prophet is depicted as so convinced that his God is "God of Israel alone" that he fails to see that "beauty belongs to the world. It is the portion of all mankind in its God." In Nathan's rendering, the reader is made to see that Jonah's narrow parochialism is inconsistent with God's intent for the world. God should not be viewed merely as a vindictive avenger marching side by side with His chosen people, but as a merciful and gracious God of all mankind. William Blake also addresses himself to this idea in his poem "The Divine Image," in which he equates "God, our father dear" with "Mercy, Pity, Peace, and Love." But, as Blake observes, these qualities cannot be made operative on earth except through the agency of man, God's "child and care." Unless we all show mercy, pity, peace, and love in our dealings with our fellow man, then we all must suffer the consequences of vindictiveness, indifference, war, and hatred. The message of Ruth and Jonah—that man love others as God has loved him—must be applied by each of us before God's will for a more tolerant and peaceful world can be achieved.

The biblical works of wisdom and protest are as relevant to today's concerns as they were to those of ancient times. We are still trying to find meaning in a world so often seemingly filled with injustice and indifference. The ways of God are not easy to decipher, but it is the way of man to continue to search for their meaning, and it is in this search that our lives gain significance.

MY SOUL IS WEARY OF MY LIFE
(The Book of Job)

There was a man in the land of Uz, whose name was Job; and that man was perfect and upright, and one that feared God, and eschewed evil. And there were born unto him seven sons and three daughters. His substance also was seven thousand sheep, and three thousand camels, and five hundred yoke of oxen, and five hundred she asses, and a very great household; so that this man was the greatest of all the children of the east.

And his sons went and feasted in their houses, every one his day, and sent and called for their three sisters to eat and to drink with them. And it was so, when the days of their feasting were gone about, that Job sent and sanctified them, and rose up early in the morning, and offered burnt offerings according to the number of them all: for Job said, "It may be that my sons have sinned, and cursed God in their hearts." Thus did Job continually.

Now there was a day when the sons of God came to present themselves before the Lord, and Satan came also among them. And the Lord said unto Satan, "Whence comest thou?"

Then Satan answered the Lord, and said, "From going to and fro in the earth, and from walking up and down in it."

And the Lord said unto Satan, "Hast thou considered my servant Job, that there is none like him in the earth, a perfect and an upright man, one that feareth God, and escheweth evil?"

Then Satan answered the Lord, and said, "Doth Job fear God for nought? Hast thou not made a hedge about him, and about his house, and about all that he hath on every side? Thou hast blessed the work of his hands, and his substance is increased in the land. But put forth thine hand now, and touch all that he hath, and he will curse thee to thy face."

And the Lord said unto Satan, "Behold, all that he hath is in thy power; only upon himself put not forth thine hand." So Satan went forth from the presence of the Lord.

And there was a day when his sons and his daughters were eating and drinking wine in their eldest brother's house: and there came a messenger unto Job, and said, "The oxen were plowing, and the asses feeding beside them: and the Sabeans fell upon them, and took them away; yea, they have slain the servants with the edge of the sword; and I only am escaped alone to tell thee."

While he was yet speaking, there came also another, and said, "The fire of God is fallen from heaven, and hath burned up the sheep, and the servants, and consumed them; and I only am escaped alone to tell thee."

While he was yet speaking, there came also another, and said, "The Chaldeans made out three bands, and fell upon the camels, and have carried them away, yea, and slain the servants with the edge of the sword; and I only am escaped alone to tell thee."

While he was yet speaking, there came also another, and said, "Thy sons and thy daughters were eating and drinking wine in their eldest brother's house: and, behold, there came a great wind from the wilderness, and smote the four corners of the house, and it fell upon the young men, and they are dead; and I only am escaped alone to tell thee."

Then Job arose, and rent his mantle, and shaved his head, and fell down upon the ground, and worshipped, and said, "Naked came I out of my mother's womb, and naked shall I return thither: the Lord gave, and the Lord hath taken away; blessed be the name of the Lord."

In all this Job sinned not, nor charged God foolishly.

Again there was a day when the sons of God came to present themselves before the Lord, and Satan came also among them to present himself before the Lord. And the Lord said unto Satan, "From whence comest thou?"

And Satan answered the Lord, and said, "From going to and fro in the earth, and from walking up and down in it."

And the Lord said unto Satan, "Hast thou considered my servant Job, that there is none like him in the earth, a perfect and an upright man, one that fearest God and escheweth evil? And still he holdeth fast his integrity, although thou movedst me against him, to destroy him without cause."

And Satan answered the Lord, and said, "Skin for skin, yea, all that a man hath will he give for his life. But put forth thine hand now, and touch his bone and flesh, and he will curse thee to thy face."

And the Lord said unto Satan, "Behold, he is in thine hand; but save his life."

So went Satan forth from the presence of the Lord, and smote Job with sore boils from the sole of his foot unto his crown. And he took him a potsherd to scrape himself withal; and he sat among the ashes.

Then said his wife unto him, "Dost thou still retain thine integrity? Curse God, and die."

But he said unto her, "Thou speakest as one of the foolish women speaketh. What? Shall we receive good at the hand of God, and shall we not receive evil?"

In all this did not Job sin with his lips.

[Job: 1:1–2:10]

Job and His Comforters

Now when Job's three friends heard of all this evil that was come upon him, they came every one from his own place: Eliphaz the Temanite, and Bildad the Shuhite, and Zophar the Naamathite: for they had made an appointment together to come and mourn with him, and to comfort him. And when they lifted up their eyes afar off, and knew him not, they lifted up their voice, and wept; and they rent every one his mantle, and sprinkled dust upon their heads toward heaven. So they sat down with him upon the ground seven days and seven nights, and none spake a word unto him: for they saw that his grief was very great.

After this opened Job his mouth and cursed his day. And Job spake, and said,

> "Let the day perish wherein I was born,
> And the night in which it was said, 'There is a man child
>   conceived.'
> Let that day be darkness;
> Let not God regard it from above,
> Neither let the light shine upon it.
> Let darkness and the shadow of death stain it;
> Let a cloud dwell upon it;
> Let the blackness of the day terrify it.
> As for that night, let darkness seize upon it;
> Let it not be joined unto the days of the year;
> Let it not come into the number of the months.
> Lo, let that night be solitary;

Let no joyful voice come therein.
Let them curse it that curse the day,
Who are ready to raise up their mourning.
Let the stars of the twilight thereof be dark:
Let it look for light, but have none;
Neither let it see the dawning of the day:
Because it shut not up the doors of my mother's womb,
Nor hid sorrow from mine eyes.
Why died I not from the womb?
Why did I not give up the ghost when I came out of the belly?"

[Job 2:11–3:11]

Then Eliphaz the Temanite answered, and said,

"If we assay to commune with thee, wilt thou be grieved?
But who can withhold himself from speaking?

"Remember, I pray thee, who ever perished, being innocent?
Or where were the righteous cut off?
Even as I have seen, they that plow iniquity,
And sow wickedness, reap the same.
By the blast of God they perish,
And by the breath of his nostrils are they consumed.

"Behold, happy is the man whom God correcteth:
Therefore despise not thou the chastening of the Almighty.
For he maketh sore, and bindeth up;
He woundeth, and his hands make whole."

[Job 4:1–2, 7–9; 5:17–18]

But Job answered and said,

"Teach me and I will hold my tongue:
And cause me to understand wherein I have erred.
How forcible are right words!
But what doth your arguing reprove?
Do ye imagine to reprove words,
When the speeches of a desperate man are as wind?

"When I lie down, I say,
'When shall I arise and the night be gone?'
And I am full of tossings to and fro unto the dawning of the day.
My flesh is clothed with worms and clods of dust;
My skin is broken and become loathsome.
My days are swifter than a weaver's shuttle,
And are spent without hope.
Oh remember that my life is wind:
Mine eye shall no more see good.
The eye of him that hath seen me shall see me no more:
Thine eyes are upon me, but I am not.
As the cloud is consumed and vanisheth away,
So he that goeth down to the grave shall come up no more.
He shall return no more to his house,
Neither shall his place know him any more.
Therefore I will not refrain my mouth;
I will speak in the anguish of my spirit;
I will complain in the bitterness of my soul.

"I loathe my life; I would not live for ever
Let me alone; for my days are vanity.
What is man, that thou shouldest magnify him?
And that thou shouldest set thine heart upon him?
And that thou shouldest visit him every morning,
And try him every moment?
How long wilt thou not depart from me,
Nor let me alone till I swallow down my spittle?
I have sinned; what shall I do unto thee, O thou preserver of men?
Why hast thou set me as a mark against thee,
So that I am a burden to myself?
And why dost thou not pardon my transgression,
And take away mine iniquity?
For now shall I sleep in the dust;
And thou shalt seek me in the morning, but I shall not be."

[*Job 6:1, 24–26; 7:4-6, 7–11, 16–21*]

Then answered Bildad the Shuhite, and said,

"How long wilt thou speak these things?
And how long shall the words of thy mouth be like a strong wind?

Doth God pervert judgment?
If thy children have sinned against him,
And he have cast them away for their transgression;
If thou wouldest seek unto God betimes
And make thy supplication to the Almighty;
If thou wert pure and upright;
Surely now he would awake for thee,
And make the habitation of thy righteousness prosperous.
Though thy beginning was small,
Yet thy latter end should greatly increase.

"Behold God will not cast away a perfect man,
Neither will he help the evildoers:
Till he fill thy mouth with laughing,
And thy lips with rejoicing.
They that hate thee shall be clothed with shame;
And the dwelling place of the wicked shall come to nought."

[*Job 8:1–7, 20–22*]

Then Job answered and said,

"I know it is so of a truth:
But how should man be just with God?
If he will contend with him,
He cannot answer him one of a thousand.
He is wise in heart, and mighty in strength:
Who hath hardened himself against him, and hath prospered?
Which removeth the mountains, and they know it not,
Which overturneth them in his anger;
Which shaketh the earth out of her place,
And the pillars thereof tremble;
Which commandeth the sun, and it riseth not;
And sealeth up the stars;
Which alone spreadeth out the heavens,
And treadeth upon the waves of the sea.

"My soul is weary of my life;
I will leave my complaint upon myself;
I will speak in the bitterness of my soul.
I will say unto God, 'Do not condemn me;

Show me wherefore thou contendest with me.
Is it good unto thee that thou shouldest oppress,
That thou shouldest despise the work of thine hands,
And shine upon the counsel of the wicked?
Hast thou eyes of flesh?
Or seest thou as man seeth?
Are thy days as the days of man?
Are thy years as man's days,
That thou inquirest after mine iniquity,
And searchest after my sin?
Thou knowest that I am not wicked;
And there is none that can deliver out of thine hand.
Thine hands have made me and fashioned me together round
    about;
Yet thou dost destroy me.
Remember, I beseech thee, that thou hast made me as the clay;
And wilt thou bring me into dust again?' "

[Job 9:1–8; 10:1–9]

Then answered Zophar the Naamathite, and said,

"Should not the multitude of words be answered?
And should a man full of talk be justified?
Should thy lies make men hold their peace?
And when thou mockest, shall no man make thee ashamed?
For thou hast said, 'My doctrine is pure, and I am clean in thy
    eyes.'
But oh that God would speak, and open his lips against thee;
And that he would show thee the secrets of wisdom,
That they are double to that which is!
Know therefore that God exacteth of thee less than thine iniquity
    deserveth.
Canst thou by searching find out God?
Canst thou find out the Almighty unto perfection?
It is as high as heaven; what canst thou do?
Deeper than hell; what canst thou know?
The measure thereof is longer than the earth,
And broader than the sea.
If he cut off, and shut up, or gather together,
Then who can hinder him?"

[Job 11:1–10]

And Job answered and said,

"No doubt but ye are the people,
And wisdom shall die with you.
But I have understanding as well as you;
I am not inferior to you:
Yea, who knoweth not such things as these?
I am as one mocked of his neighbor,
Who calleth upon God, and he answereth him:
The just upright man is laughed to scorn.

"Man that is born of a woman
Is of few days, and full of trouble.
He cometh forth like a flower, and is cut down:
He fleeth also as a shadow, and continueth not.

"For there is hope of a tree, if it be cut down, that it will sprout
    again,
And that the tender branch thereof will not cease.
Though the root thereof wax old in the earth,
And the stock thereof die in the ground;
Yet through the scent of water it will bud,
And bring forth boughs like a plant.
But man dieth, and wasteth away:
Yea, man giveth up the ghost, and where is he?
As the waters fail from the sea,
And the river decayeth and drieth up;
So man lieth down and riseth not:
Till the heavens be no more, they shall not awake,
Nor be raised out of their sleep.

"Oh that thou wouldest hide me in the grave,
That thou wouldest keep me secret, until thy wrath be past,
That thou wouldest appoint me a set time, and remember me!
If a man die, shall he live again?
All the days of my appointed time will I wait,
Till my change come.

"Though I speak, my grief is not assuaged:
And though I forbear, what am I eased?
But now he hath made me weary:
Thou hast made desolate all my company."

[Job 12:1–4; 14:1–2, 7–14; 16:6–7]

Then answered Bildad the Shuhite, and said,

"How long will it be ere ye make an end of words?
Mark, and afterward we will speak.
Wherefore are we counted as beasts,
And reputed vile in your sight?
He teareth himself in his anger:
Shall the earth be forsaken for thee?
And shall the rock be removed out of his place?"

[Job 18:1–4]

Then answered Job and said,

"How long will ye vex my soul,
And break me in pieces with words?
These ten times have ye reproached me:
Ye are not ashamed that ye make yourselves strange to me.

"They that dwell in mine house, and my maids, count me for a
stranger:
I am an alien in their sight.
I called my servant, and he gave me no answer,
Though I entreated him with my mouth.
My breath is strange to my wife,
Loathsome to the sons of my own mother.
Yea, young children despised me;
I arose, and they spake against me.
All my inward friends abhorred me:
And they whom I loved are turned against me.
My bone cleaveth to my skin and to my flesh,
And I am escaped with the skin of my teeth.
Have pity upon me, have pity upon me, O ye my friends;
For the hand of God hath touched me.
Why do ye persecute me as God,
And are not satisfied with my flesh?
Oh that my words were now written!
Oh that they were printed in a book!
That they were graven with an iron pen and lead in the rock
for ever!
For I know that my Redeemer liveth,
And that he shall stand at the latter day upon the earth:

And though after my skin worms destroy this body,
Yet in my flesh shall I see God:
Whom I shall see for myself,
And mine eyes shall behold, and not another."

[*Job 19:2–3, 15–27*]

Then answered Zophar the Naamathite, and said,

"Knowest thou not this of old,
Since man was placed upon earth,
That the triumphing of the wicked is short,
And the joy of the hypocrite but for a moment?
Though his excellency mount up to the heavens,
And his head reach unto the clouds;
Yet he shall perish for ever like his own dung:
They which have seen him shall say, 'Where is he?'
He shall fly away as a dream, and shall not be found:
Yeah, he shall be chased away as a vision of the night.

"This is the portion of a wicked man from God,
And the heritage appointed unto him by God."

[*Job 20:1, 4–8, 29*]

But Job answered and said,

"Hear diligently my speech;
And let this be your consolations.
Suffer me that I also may speak;
And after that I have spoken, mock on.
As for me, is my complaint to man?
And if it were so, why should not my spirit be troubled?
Mark me, and be astonished,
And lay your hand upon your mouth.
Even when I remember I am afraid,
And trembling taketh hold on my flesh.
Wherefore do the wicked live,
Become old, yea, are mighty in power?
Their seed is established in their sight with them,
And their offspring before their eyes.
Their houses are safe from fear,

Neither is the rod of God upon them.
Their bull gendereth, and faileth not;
Their cow calveth, and casteth not her calf.
They send forth their little ones like a flock,
And their children dance.
They take the timbrel and harp,
And rejoice at the sound of the organ.
They spend their days in wealth,
And in a moment go down to the grave.
Therefore they say unto God, 'Depart from us;
For we desire not the knowledge of thy ways.
What is the Almighty, that we should serve him?
And what profit should we have, if we pray unto him?'

"Behold, I know your thoughts,
And the devices which ye wrongfully imagine against me.

"How then comfort ye me in vain,
Seeing in your answers there remaineth falsehood?

Oh that one would hear me!
(Here is my signature! Let the Almighty answer me!);
Oh, that I had the indictment written by mine adversary.
Surely I would take it upon my shoulder;
And bind it as a crown to me.
I would declare unto him the number of my steps;
As a prince would I go near unto him.
If my land cry against me,
Or that the furrows likewise thereof complain;
If I have eaten the fruits thereof without money,
Or have caused the owners thereof to lose their life:
Let thistles grow instead of wheat,
And cockle instead of barley."

The words of Job are ended.

[*Job 21:1–15, 27, 34; 31:35–40*]

The Voice Out of the Whirlwind

Then the Lord answered Job out of the whirlwind, and said,

"Who is this that darkeneth counsel by words without knowledge?
Gird up now thy loins like a man;

For I will demand of thee, and answer thou me.
Where wast thou when I laid the foundations of the earth?
Declare, if thou hast understanding.
Who hath laid the measures thereof, if thou knowest?
Or who hath stretched the line upon it?
Whereupon are the foundations thereof fastened?
Or who laid the corner stone thereof,
When the morning stars sang together,
And all the sons of God shouted for joy?
Or who shut up the sea with doors,
When it brake forth, as if it had issued out of the womb;
When I made the cloud the garment thereof,
And thick darkness a swaddlingband for it,
And brake up for it my decreed place,
And set bars and doors,
And said, 'Hitherto shalt thou come, but no further;
And here shall thy proud waves be stayed'?
Hast thou commanded the morning since thy days,
And caused the dayspring to know its place,
That it might take hold of the ends of the earth,
That the wicked might be shaken out of it?

"Hast thou entered into the springs of the sea?
Or hast thou walked in the search of the deep?
Have the gates of death been opened unto thee?
Or hast thou seen the doors of the shadow of death?
Hast thou perceived the breadth of the earth?
Declare if thou knowest it all.
Where is the way where light dwelleth,
And as for darkness, where is the place thereof,
That thou shouldest take it to the bound thereof,
And that thou shouldest know the paths to the house thereof?
Knowest thou it, because thou wast then born?
Or because the number of thy days is great?
Hast thou entered into the treasures of the snow,
Or hast thou seen the treasures of the hail,
Which I have reserved against the time of trouble,
Against the day of battle and war?

"Hath the rain a father?
Or who hath begotten the drops of dew?
Out of whose womb came the ice?
And the hoary frost of heaven, who hath gendered it?

The waters are hid as with a stone,
And the face of the deep is frozen.
Canst thou bind the sweet influences of the Pleiades,
Or loose the bands of Orion?
Canst thou bring forth Mazzaroth in his season?
Or canst thou guide Arcturus with his sons?
Knowest thou the ordinances of heaven?
Canst thou set the dominion thereof in the earth?
Canst thou lift up thy voice to the clouds,
That abundance of waters may cover thee?
Canst thou send lightnings, that they may go,
And say unto thee, 'Here we are'?
Who hath put wisdom in the inward parts?
Or who hath given understanding to the heart?
Who can number the clouds in wisdom?
Or who can stay the bottles of heaven,
When the dust groweth into hardness,
And the clods cleave fast together?
Wilt thou hunt the prey for the lion?
Or fill the appetite of the young lions,
When they couch in their dens,
And abide in the covert to lie in wait?
Who provideth for the raven his food,
When his young ones cry unto God,
And wander for lack of meat?

"Doth the hawk fly by thy wisdom,
And stretch her wings toward the south?
Doth the eagle mount up at thy command,
And make her nest on high?

"Shall he that contendeth with the Almighty instruct him?
He that reproveth God, let him answer it."

[Job 38:1–13, 16–23, 28–40; 39:26–27; 40:2]

Then Job answered the Lord, and said,

"Behold, I am vile; what shall I answer thee?
I will lay mine hand upon my mouth.
Once have I spoken, but I will not answer;
Yea, twice; but I will proceed no further."

[Job 40:3–5]

Then answered the Lord unto Job out of the whirlwind, and said,

"Gird up thy loins now like a man:
I will demand of thee, and declare thou unto me.
Wilt thou also disannul my judgment?
Wilt thou condemn me, that thou mayest be righteous?
Hast thou an arm like God?
Or canst thou thunder with a voice like him?
Deck thyself now with majesty and excellency,
And array thyself with glory and beauty.
Cast abroad the rage of thy wrath;
And behold every one that is proud, and abase him.
Look on every one that is proud, and bring him low;
And tread down the wicked in their place.
Hide them in the dust together, and bind their faces in secret.
Then will I also confess unto thee
That thine own right hand can save thee.

Canst thou draw out Leviathan with a fishhook?
Or his tongue with a cord which thou lettest down?
Canst thou put a hook into his nose?
Or bore his jaw through with a thorn?
Will he make many supplications unto thee?
Or will he speak soft words unto thee?
Will he make a covenant with thee?
Wilt thou take him for a servant for ever?
Wilt thou play with him as with a bird?
Or wilt thou bind him for thy maidens?

"Upon earth there is not his like, who is made without fear.
He beholdeth all high things:
He is a king over all the children of pride."

[*Job 40:6–14; 41:1–5, 33–34*]

Then Job answered the Lord, and said,

"I know that thou canst do every thing,
And that no thought can be withholden from thee.
'Who is he that hideth counsel without knowledge?'
Therefore have I uttered that I understood not,
Things too wonderful for me, which I knew not.
'Hear, I beseech thee, and I will speak;

I will demand of thee, and declare thou unto me.'
I have heard of thee by the hearing of the ear;
But now mine eye seeth thee:
Wherefore I abhor myself,
And repent in dust and ashes."

[Job 42:1–6]

Job's Prosperity Restored

And it was so, that after the Lord had spoken these words unto Job, the Lord said to Eliphaz the Temanite, "My wrath is kindled against thee, and against thy two friends: for ye have not spoken of me the thing that is right, as my servant Job hath. Therefore take unto you now seven bullocks and seven rams, and go to my servant Job, and offer up for yourselves a burnt offering; and my servant Job shall pray for you: for him will I accept: lest I deal with you after your folly, in that ye have not spoken of me the thing that is right, like my servant Job."

So Eliphaz the Temanite and Bildad the Shuhite and Zophar the Naamathite went, and did according as the Lord commanded them: and the Lord accepted Job's prayer.

And the Lord turned the captivity of Job, when he prayed for his friends: also the Lord gave Job twice as much as he had before. Then came there unto him all his brethren, and all his sisters, and all they that had been of his acquaintance before, and did eat bread with him in his house: and they bemoaned him, and comforted him over all the evil that the Lord had brought upon him: every man also gave him a piece of money, and every one an earring of gold.

So the Lord blessed the latter end of Job more than his beginning: for he had fourteen thousand sheep, and six thousand camels, and a thousand yoke of oxen, and a thousand she asses. He had also seven sons and three daughters. And he called the name of the first, Jemima; and the name of the second, Kezia, and the name of the third, Keren-happuch. And in all the land were no women found so fair as the daughters of Job: and their father gave them inheritance among their brethren.

After this lived Job a hundred and forty years, and saw his sons, and his sons' sons, even four generations. So Job died, being old and full of days.

[Job 42:7–17]

From Satan's point of view, why is Job so faithful? How does Job react to his losses? What makes it especially difficult for Job to understand what is happening to him? What reasons do the "comforters" give to account for Job's suffering? With what arguments does Job defend himself?

What is the point of the lengthy series of questions set forth by the Voice out of the whirlwind? Do you detect any hints of irony or sarcasm in these magnificent lines? Consider especially the lines beginning "Deck thyself now with excellence and dignity," which are probably among the lines most easily misunderstood. What must Job do before the Lord restores his prosperity, giving him twice as much as he had before?

Explain what you think the overall theme or message of the Book of Job is. In what respects (other than in terms of material possessions) is Job a better person as a result of his experiences? How might this lesson be applied today?

JOB

Elizabeth Sewell

They did not know this face
Where the chin rested on the sunken breastbone,
 So changed it was, emptied, rinsed out and dried,
 And for some future purpose put aside.
Expecting torment, they were much perplexed.

His world had gone
And he sat isolated, foul and flyblown,
 Without a world, with nothing but a mind
 Staggered to silence since it could not find
Language to utter its amazing text.

For where was Job?
In some strange state, unknown and yet well-known,
   A mask that stared hollowly in God's breath,
   Mind that perceived the irrelevance of death,
And the astonished heart unmoved, unvexed.

    They did not see his soul
Perched like a bird upon the broken hearthstone,
   Piping incessantly above the ashes
What next what next what next what next what next

THE EMANCIPATOR OF YOUR GOD

(*from* A Masque of Reason)

Robert Frost

GOD (speaking to JOB):
I've had you on my mind a thousand years
To thank you someday for the way you helped me
Establish once for all the principle
There's no connection man can reason out
Between his just deserts and what he gets.
Virtue may fail and wickedness succeed.
'Twas a great demonstration we put on.
I should have spoken sooner had I found
The word I wanted. You would have supposed
One who in the beginning *was* the Word
Would be in a position to command it.
I have to wait for words like anyone.
Too long I've owed you this apology
For the apparently unmeaning sorrow
You were afflicted with in those old days.
But it was of the essence of the trial
You shouldn't understand it at the time.

It had to seem unmeaning to have meaning.
And it came out all right. I have no doubt
You realize by now the part you played
To stultify the Deuteronomist
And change the tenor of religious thought.
My thanks are to you for releasing me
From moral bondage to the human race.
The only free will there at first was man's,
Who could do good or evil as he chose.
I had no choice but I must follow him
With forfeits and rewards he understood—
Unless I liked to suffer loss of worship.
I had to prosper good and punish evil.
You changed all that. You set me free to reign.
You are the Emancipator of your God.
And as such I promote you to a saint.

In what way has Job set God free? In the original version, the next-to-last line read: "You are the Emancipator of God." What reason might Frost have had for changing the line to "*your* God"?

THE MYSTERIOUS STRANGER

Mark Twain

Three of us boys were always together, and had been so from the cradle, being fond of each other from the beginning, and this affection deepening as the years went on—Nikolaus Baumann, son of the principal judge of the local court; Seppi Wohlmeyer, son of the keeper of the principal inn, The Golden Stag, which had a nice garden, with shade trees, reaching down to the riverside, and pleasure boats for hire; and I was the third—Theodor Fischer, son of the church organist, who was also leader of the village band, teacher of the violin, composer, tax collector of the commune, sexton, and in other ways a useful citizen and respected by all. We knew the hills and the woods as well as the birds knew them; for we were always roaming them when we had leisure—at least when we were not swimming or boating or fishing, or playing on the ice or sliding down hill.

And we had the run of the castle park, and very few had that. It was because we were pets of the oldest serving man in the castle— Felix Brandt; and often we went there, nights, to hear him talk about old times and strange things, and smoke with him (he taught us that), and drink coffee; for he had served in the wars, and was at the siege of Vienna; and there, when the Turks were defeated and driven away, among the captured things were bags of coffee, and the Turkish prisoners explained the character of it and how to make a pleasant drink out of it, and now he always kept coffee by him, to drink himself, and also to astonish the ignorant with. When it stormed he kept us all night; and while it thundered and lightened outside he told about ghosts and horrors of every kind, and of battles and murders and mutilations, and such things, and made it pleasant and cosy inside; and he told these things from his own experience largely. He had seen many ghosts in his time, and witches and enchanters, and once he was lost in a fierce storm at midnight in the mountains, and by the glare of the lightning had seen the Wild Huntsman rage by on the blast with his specter dogs chasing after him through the driving cloud-rack. Also he had seen an incubus once, and several times he had seen the great bat that sucks the blood from the necks of people while they are asleep, fanning them softly with its wings and so keeping them drowsy till they die. He encouraged us not to fear supernatural things, such as ghosts, and said they did no harm, but only wandered about because they were lonely and distressed and wanted kindly notice and compassion; and in time we learned to not be afraid, and even went down with him in the night to the haunted chamber of the dungeons of the castle. The ghost appeared only once, and it went by very dim to the sight and floating noiseless through the air, and then disappeared; and we scarcely trembled, he had taught us so well. He said it came up sometimes in the night and woke him up by passing its clammy hand over his face, but it did him no hurt, it only wanted sympathy and notice. But the strangest thing was that he had seen angels; actual angels out of heaven, and had talked with them. They had no wings, and wore clothes, and talked and looked and acted just like any natural person, and you would never know them for angels, except for the wonderful things they did which a mortal could not do, and the way they suddenly disappeared while you were talking with them, which was also a thing which no mortal could do. And he said they were pleasant and cheerful, not gloomy and melancholy, like ghosts.

It was after that kind of a talk, one May night, that we got up next morning and had a good breakfast with him and then went down and crossed the bridge and went away up into the hills on the left to a woody hilltop which was a favorite place of ours, and there we stretched out on the grass in the shade to rest and smoke and talk over those strange things, for they were in our minds yet, and impressing us. But we couldn't smoke, because we had been heedless and left our flint and steel behind.

Soon there came a youth strolling toward us through the trees, and he sat down and began to talk in a friendly way, just as if he knew us. But we did not answer him, for he was a stranger and we were not used to strangers and were shy of them. He had new and good clothes on, and was handsome and had a winning face and a pleasant voice, and was easy and graceful and unembarrassed, not slouchy and awkward and diffident like other boys. We wanted to be friendly with him, but didn't know how to begin. Then I thought of the pipe, and wondered if it would be taken as kindly meant if I offered it to him. But I remembered that we had no fire; so I was sorry and disappointed. But he looked up bright and pleased, and said—

"Fire? Oh, that is easy—I will furnish it."

I was so astonished I couldn't speak, for I had not said anything. He took the pipe and blew his breath on it, and the tobacco glowed red and spirals of blue smoke rose up. We jumped up and were going to run, for that was natural; and we did run a few steps, although he was yearningly pleading for us to stay, and giving us his word that he would not do us any harm, but only wanted to be friends with us and have company. So we stopped and stood, and wanted to go back, being full of curiosity and wonder, but afraid to venture. He went on coaxing, in his soft persuasive way; and when we saw that the pipe did not blow up and nothing happened, our confidence returned by little and little, and presently our curiosity got to be stronger than our fear, and we ventured back—but slowly, and ready to fly, at any alarm.

He was bent on putting us at ease, and he had the right art; one could not remain timorous and doubtful where a person was so earnest and simple and gentle and talked so alluringly as he did; no, he won us over, and it was not long before we were content and comfortable and chatty, and glad we had found this new friend. When the feeling of constraint was all gone, we asked him how he had learned to do that strange thing, and he said he hadn't learned it at all, it came natural to him—like other things—other curious things.

"What ones?"

"Oh, a number; I don't know how many."

"Will you let us see you do them?"

"Do—please!" the others said.

"You won't run away again?"

"No—indeed we won't. Please do, won't you?"

"Yes, with pleasure; but you mustn't forget your promise, you know."

We said we wouldn't, and he went to a puddle and came back with water in a cup which he had made out of a leaf, and blew upon it and threw it out, and it was a lump of ice, the shape of the cup. We were astonished and charmed, but not afraid any more; we were very glad to be there, and asked him to go on and do some more things. And he did. He said he would give us any kind of fruit we liked, whether it was in season or not. We all spoke at once—

"Orange!"

"Apple!"

"Grapes!"

"They are in your pockets," he said, and it was true. And they were of the best, too, and we ate them and wished we had more, though none of us said so.

"You will find them where those came from," he said, "and everything else your appetites call for; and you need not name the thing you wish; as long as I am with you, you have only to wish and find."

And he said true. There was never anything so wonderful and so interesting. Bread, cakes, sweets, nuts—whatever one wanted, it was there. He ate nothing himself, but sat and chatted, and did one curious thing after another to amuse us. He made a toy squirrel out of clay, and it ran up a tree and sat on a limb overhead and barked down at us. Then he made a dog that was not much larger than a mouse, and it treed the squirrel and danced about the tree, excited and barking, and was as alive as any dog could be. It frightened the squirrel from tree to tree and followed it up until both were out of sight in the forest. He made birds out of clay and set them free and they flew away singing.

At last I made bold to ask him to tell us who he was.

"An angel," he said, quite simply, and set another clay bird free and clapped his hands and made it fly away.

A kind of awe fell upon us when we heard him say that, and we were afraid again, but he said we need not be troubled, there was no occasion for us to be afraid of an angel, and he liked us anyway. He went on chatting as simply and unaffectedly as ever; and while he talked he made a crowd of little men and women the size of your finger, and they went diligently to work and cleared and leveled off a space a couple of yards square in the grass and began to build a cunning little castle in it, the women mixing the mortar and carrying it up the scaffoldings in pails on their heads, just as our workwomen have always done, and the men laying the courses of masonry—five hundred of those toy people swarming briskly about and working diligently and wiping the sweat off their faces as natural as life. In the absorbing interest of watching those five hundred little people make the castle grow step by step and course by course and take shape and symmetry, that feeling of awe soon passed away, and we were quite comfortable and at home again. We asked if we might make some people, and he said yes, and told Seppi to make some cannon for the walls, and told Nikolaus to make some halberdiers with breastplates and greaves and helmets, and I was to make some cavalry, with horses; and in alloting these tasks he called us by our names, but did not say how he knew them. Then Seppi asked him what his own name was, and he said tranquilly—

"*Satan*," and held out a chip and caught a little woman on it who was falling from the scaffolding and put her back where she belonged, and said, "She is an idiot to step backward like that and not notice what she is about."

It caught us suddenly, that name did, and our work dropped out of our hands and broke to pieces—a cannon, a halberdier, and a horse. Satan laughed, and asked what was the matter. It was a natural laugh, and pleasant and sociable, not boisterous, and had a reassuring influence upon us; so I said there was nothing much the matter, only it seemed a strange name for an angel. He asked why.

"Because it's—it's—well, it's *his* name, you know."

"Yes—he is my uncle."

He said it placidly, but it took our breath, for a moment, and made our hearts beat hard. He did not seem to notice that, but partly mended our halberdiers and things with a touch, handed them to us to finish, and said—

"Don't you remember?—he was an angel himself once."

"Yes—it's true," said Seppi, "I didn't think of that."

"Before the Fall he was blameless."

"Yes," said Nikolaus, "he was without sin."

"It is a good family—ours," said Satan; "there is not a better. He is the only member of it that has ever sinned."

I should not be able to make any one understand how exciting it all was. You know that kind of quiver that trembles around through you when you are seeing something that is so strange and enchanting and wonderful that it is just a fearful joy to be alive and look at it; and you know how you gaze, and your lips turn dry and your breath comes short, but you wouldn't be anywhere but there, not for the world. I was bursting to ask one question—I had it on my tongue's end and could hardly hold it back—but I was ashamed to ask it, it might be a rudeness. Satan set an ox down that he had been making, and smiled up at me and said—

"It wouldn't be a rudeness; and I should forgive it if it was. Have I *seen* him? Millions of times. From the time that I was a little child a thousand years old I was his second-best favorite among the nursery-angels of our blood and lineage—to use a human phrase—yes, from that time till the Fall; eight thousand years, measured as you count time."

"Eight—*thousand?*"

"Yes." He turned to Seppi, and went on as if answering something that was in Seppi's mind, "Why, naturally I look like a boy, for that is what I am. With us, what you call time is a spacious thing; it takes a long stretch of it to grow an angel to full age." There was a question in my mind, and he turned to me and answered it: "I am sixteen thousand years old—counting as you count." Then he turned to Nikolaus and said, "No, the Fall did not affect me nor the rest of the relationship. It was only he that I was named for who ate of the fruit of the tree and then beguiled the man and the woman with it. We others are still ignorant of sin; we are not able to commit it; we are without blemish, and shall abide in that estate always. We—" Two of the little workmen were quarreling, and in buzzing little bumble-bee voices they were cursing and swearing at each other; now came blows and blood, then they locked themselves together in a life-and-death struggle. Satan reached out his hand and crushed the life out of them with his fingers, threw them away, wiped the red from his fingers on his handkerchief and went on talking where he had left off: "We cannot do wrong; neither have we any disposition to do it, for we do not know what it is."

It seemed a strange speech, in the circumstances, but we barely noticed that, we were so shocked and grieved at the wanton murder he had committed—for murder it was, it was its true name, and it was without palliation or excuse, for the men had not wronged him in any way. It made us miserable; for we loved him, and had thought him so noble and beautiful and gracious, and had honestly *believed* he was an angel; and to have him do this cruel thing—ah, it lowered him so, and we had had such pride in him. He went right on talking, just as if nothing had happened: telling about his travels, and the interesting things he had seen in the big worlds of our solar system and of other solar systems far away in the remotenesses of space, and about the customs of the immortals that inhabit them, somehow fascinating us, enchanting us, charming us in spite of the pitiful scene that was now under our eyes: for the wives of the little dead men had found the crushed and shapeless bodies and were crying over them and sobbing and lamenting, and a priest was kneeling there with his hands crossed upon his breast praying, and crowds and crowds of pitying friends were massed about them, reverently uncovered, with their bare heads bowed, and many with the tears running down—a scene which Satan paid no attention to until the small noise of the weeping and praying began to annoy him, then he reached out and took the heavy board seat out of our swing and brought it down and mashed all those people into the earth just as if they had been flies, and went on talking just the same.

An angel, and kill a priest! An angel who did not know how to do wrong, and yet destroys in cold blood a hundred helpless poor men and women who had never done him any harm! It made us sick to see that awful deed, and to think that none of those poor creatures was prepared except the priest, for none of them had ever heard a mass or seen a church. And we were witnesses; we could not get away from that thought; we had seen these murders done and it was our duty to tell, and let the law take its course.

But he went talking right along, and worked his enchantments upon us again with that fatal music of his voice. He *made* us forget everything; we could only listen to him, and love him and be his slaves, to do with as he would. He made us drunk with the joy of being with him, and of looking into the heaven of his eyes, and of feeling the ecstasy that thrilled along our veins from the touch of his hand.

He had seen everything, he had been everywhere, he knew every-thing, and he forgot nothing. What another must study, he learned at a glance; there were no difficulties for him. And he made things live before you when he told about them. He saw the world made; he saw Adam created; he saw Samson surge against the pillars and bring the temple down in ruins about him; he saw Caesar's death; he told of the daily life in heaven, he had seen the damned writhing in the red waves of hell; and he made us see all these things, and it was as if we were on the spot and looking at them with our own eyes. And we *felt* them, too, but there was no sign that they were anything to him, beyond being mere entertainments. Those visions of hell, those poor babes and women and girls and lads and men shrieking and supplicat-ing in anguish—why, we could hardly bear it, but he was as bland about it as if it had been so many imitation rats in an artificial fire.

And always when he was talking about men and women here in the earth and their doings—even their grandest and sublimest—we were secretly ashamed, for his manner showed that to him they and their doings were of paltry poor consequence; often you would think he was talking about flies, if you didn't know. Once he even said, in so many words, that our people down here were quite interesting to him, notwithstanding they were so dull and ignorant and trivial and conceited, and so diseased and rickety, and such a shabby poor worthless lot all around. He said it in a quite matter-of-course way and without any bitterness, just as a person might talk about bricks or manure or any other thing that was of no consequence and hadn't feelings. I could see he meant no offence, but in my thoughts I set it down as not very good manners.

"Manners!" he said, "why it is merely the truth, and truth is good manners; manners are a fiction. The castle is done! Do you like it?"

Anyone would have been obliged to like it. It was lovely to look at, it was so shapely and fine, and so cunningly perfect in all its particulars, even to the little flags waving from the turrets. Satan said we must put the artillery in place, now, and station the halberdiers and deploy the cavalry. Our men and horses were a spectacle to see, they were so little like what they were intended for; for of course we had no art in making such things. Satan said they were the worst he had seen; and when he touched them and made them alive, it was just ridiculous the way they acted, on account of their legs not being of uniform lengths. They reeled and sprawled around as if they were drunk, and endangered everybody's lives around them, and finally fell over and lay helpless and kicking. It made us all laugh, though it was a shameful thing to see. The guns were charged with dirt, to fire a salute; but they were so crooked and so badly made that they all burst when they went off, and killed some of the gunners and crippled the others. Satan said we would have a storm, now, and an earthquake, if we liked, but we must stand off a piece, out of danger. We wanted to call the people away, too, but he said never mind them, they were of no consequence and we could make more, some time or other if we needed them.

A small storm cloud began to settle down black over the castle, and the miniature lightning and thunder began to play and the ground to quiver and the wind to pipe and wheeze and the rain to fall, and all the people flocked into the castle for shelter. The cloud settled down blacker and blacker and one could see the castle only dimly through it; the lightnings blazed out flash upon flash and they pierced the castle and set it on fire and the flames shone out red and fierce through the cloud, and the people came flying out, shrieking, but Satan brushed them back, paying no attention to our begging and crying and imploring; and in the midst of the howling of the wind and volleying of the thunder the magazine blew up, the earthquake rent the ground wide and the castle's wreck and ruin tumbled into the chasm, which swallowed it from sight and closed upon it, with all that innocent life, not one of the five hundred poor creatures escaping.

Our hearts were broken, we could not keep from crying.

"Don't cry," Satan said, "they were of no value."

"But they are gone to hell!"

"Oh, it is no matter, we can make more."

It was of no use to try to move him; evidently he was wholly without feeling, and could not understand. He was full of bubbling spirits, and as gay as if this were a wedding instead of a fiendish massacre. And he was bent on making us feel as he did, and of course his magic accomplished his desire. It was no trouble to him, he did whatever he pleased with us. In a little while we were dancing on that grave, and he was playing to us on a strange sweet instrument which he took out of his pocket; and the music—there is no music like that, unless perhaps in heaven, and that was where he brought it from, he said. It made one mad, for pleasure; and we could not take our eyes from him, and the looks that went out of our eyes came from our hearts, and their dumb speech was worship. He brought the dance from heaven, too, and the bliss of paradise was in it.

Do you see any connection between the angel's activities and Felix Brandt's "talk about old times and strange things," particularly the old man's fascination with war? How does Satan explain his name? Explain Satan's insistence that he and the other angels are "ignorant of sin" and hence "not able to commit it"? Does it help to think of such angels as forces of nature or of the universe? Of what consequence are the cries and pleadings of Satan's unfortunate "creatures"? What point is Mark Twain making here?

What manages to charm the boys out of their horror at such "wanton murder"? To what is this related in the Book of Job? What other parallels can you find between Job's experiences and those of the boys? What are both stories saying about the gods who control the universe? In what respects do you suspect that Mark Twain differs from the writer of the Book of Job in his attitude toward such gods?

THE GOD OF GALAXIES

Mark Van Doren

The god of galaxies had more to govern
Than the first men imagined, when one mountain
Trumpeted his anger, and one rainbow,
Red in the east, restored them to his love.
One earth it was, with big and lesser torches,
And stars by night for candles. And he spoke
To single persons, sitting in their tents.

Now streams of worlds, now powdery great whirlwinds
Of universes far enough away
To seem but fog-wisps in a bank of night
So measureless the mind can sicken, trying—
Now seas of darkness, shoreless, on and on
Encircled by themselves, yet washing farther
Than the last triple sun, revolving, shows.

The god of galaxies—how shall we praise him?
For so we must, or wither. Yet what word
Of words? And where to send it, on which night
Of winter stars, of summer, or by autumn
In the first evening of the Pleiades?
The god of galaxies, of burning gases,
May have forgotten Leo and the Bull.

But God remembers, and is everywhere.
He even is the void, where nothing shines.
He is the absence of his own reflection
In the deep gulf; he is the dusky cinder
Of pure fire in its prime; he is the place
Prepared for hugest planets: black idea,
Brooding between fierce poles he keeps apart.

These attitudes and oceans, though, with islands
Drifting, blown immense as by a wind,

And yet no wind; and not one blazing coast
Where thought could live, could listen—oh, what word
Of words? Let us consider it in terror,
And say it without voice. Praise universes
Numberless. Praise all of them. Praise Him.

How has man's conception of the universe changed since the god
of galaxies first spoke to man? What problem does this present for man
today? What is the significance of the shift in the fourth stanza
from the god of galaxies to God? How is this reflected in the final
lines? In what respects is this poem related to the Book of Job?

J.B.

(Selections)

Archibald MacLeish

*J.B. is more than a mere dramatization of the story of Job—it is very
definitely a "modernization." In this verse play the setting has
moved from the ancient land of Uz to a traveling circus. The
counterparts of God and Satan are two vendors, Mr. Zuss and Nickles
respectively, who decide to reenact the Job story, only to find that the
Godmask and Satanmask which they don begin to speak seemingly
beyond their volition. The question becomes: Is it they who are
playing God and Satan, or is it God and Satan who are playing them?*
 *The man chosen to play Job is J.B., a successful businessman, whose
family is outwardly religious. As in the biblical story tragedy soon
strikes. J.B.'s oldest son, who has been serving overseas in the military,
is killed by a careless officer's mistake after the war was declared over.
Two more of his children are killed in an automobile accident, his
youngest daughter savagely raped and killed by a psychopath,
and his bank destroyed by a bombing in which his last child dies.*

Finally, his wife forsakes him, leaving him "sitting on an earth reduced to ash-heap picking in agony at the cinders of a bomb-scorched skin."

Like his biblical counterpart, J.B. is visited by three friends. The "comfort" they offer him differs significantly from that offered Job, however, for they try to persuade him that he is not guilty—that, for psychological reasons, and because of the economic necessity of historical determinism, and because man is born in sin, individual guilt can be dispensed with. J.B. rejects their comfort, however, preferring to hold himself up as a man rather than to wash his hands in that "defiling innocence" which makes "an irresponsible ignorance responsible for everything."

Finally, J.B. does find a solution to his suffering. He finds it in human love and in "the green leaf on the branch," which to him and his wife represents affirmation that life goes on. Since "the candles in the churches are out" and "the lights have gone out in the sky," all that is left for man is to "blow on the coal of the heart," to risk everything once again in order to find his own meaning: "In love. To live."

In the final pages of his "Foreword" to the play, which is reprinted here along with two other selections from the drama, MacLeish attempts to show how "the God of Job seems closer to this generation than he has to any other in centuries." The first scene from J.B. *centers on Nickles' cynical examination of a God who is called "good," but who also allows so much suffering in the world. The second selection is from the conclusion of the play, in which Sarah returns clutching "a small green branch like a child," and J.B.—much to Mr. Zuss's surprise—declares his refusal to bow to the thundering voice of God, preferring instead to find his meaning in love, and in life itself.*

from the "Foreword"

My hero, called J.B. after the current fashion in business address, bears little relation, perhaps, to that ancient owner of camels and oxen and sheep. He is not a particularly devout man. But he is, at the beginning of the play, prosperous, powerful, possessed of a lovely wife, fine children—everything the heart of man can desire—and he is aware, as he could hardly help being, that God has made "an hedge about him and about his house and about all that he hath on every side." Not that the name of God is often in his mouth. He is one of those vastly successful American businessmen—not as numerous now as they were before the Great Depression—who, *having* everything, believe as a matter of course that they have a *right* to have everything. They do

not believe this out of vulgarity. They are not Babbitts: on the contrary, they are most often men of exuberance, of high animal spirits,
of force and warmth. They believe it because they possess in large
measure that characteristically American courage, which has so often
entertained Asian and European visitors, the courage to believe in
themselves. Which means to believe in their lives. Which means, if
their tongues can shape the words, to believe in God's goodness to
them. They are not hypocritical. They do not think that they *deserve*
more at God's hands than others. They merely think that they *have*
more—and that they have a right to have it.

Such a man is no better prepared than Job was for the sudden and
inexplicable loss of everything. And such a man must ask, as our time
does ask, Job's repeated question. Job wants *justice* of the universe. He
needs to know the reason for his wretchedness. And it is in those
repeated cries of his that we hear most clearly our own voices. For
our age is an age haunted and driven by the need to know. Not only
is our science full of it but our arts also. And it is here, or so it seems
to me, that our story and the story of Job come closest to each other.
Job is not *answered* in the Bible by the voice out of the whirlwind.
He is *silenced* by it—silenced by some thirty or forty of the greatest
lines in all literature—silenced by the might and majesty and magnificence of the creation. He is brought, not to *know*, but to *see*. As we
also have been brought.

And what follows that *seeing* which cannot *know?* What follows is
a chapter of the Book of Job which the theologians have tried again
and again to explain away. Job is given all he had before twice over
—all but his children who are the same in number but more beautiful. And that is not all. Not only is Job *given* his life again: Job *accepts*
his life again. The man who was once highest and happiest and has
now been brought lowest and made most miserable; the man who has
suffered every loss, every agony, and for no reason, moral or intelligible, the mind can grasp; the man who has cried out to God for death,
begged over and over to die, regretted the womb that bore him,
yearned never to have been, never to have breathed the air or seen the
light—*this* man accepts his life again, accepts to live his life again,
take back his wife again, beget new children mortal as those others,
risk himself upon the very hazard on which, before, his hopes were
wrecked. And why? Because his sufferings have been justified? They
have not been justified. God has merely lifted into the blazing fire of
the imagination his own power and Job's impotence; his own immeasurable knowledge and Job's poor, trembling, ridiculous ignorance.
Job accepts to live his life again in spite of all he knows of life, in

spite of all he knows now of himself, because he loves life still in spite of life—*can* love it still.

Our own demand for justice and for reasons comes to the same unanswering answer. A few days before he died, the greatest of modern poets, and the most modern of great poets, William Butler Yeats, wrote to a friend that he found what, all his life, he had been looking for. But when, in that letter, he went on to spell his answer out in words, it was not an answer made of words: it was an answer made of life: "When I try to put it all into a phrase I say, 'Man can embody truth but he cannot know it.'" Which means, to me at least, that man can *live* his truth, his deepest truth, but cannot speak it. It is for this reason that love becomes the ultimate human answer to the ultimate human question. Love, in *reason's* terms, answers nothing. We say that *Amor vincit omnia* but in truth love conquers nothing—certainly not death—certainly not chance. What love does is to affirm. It affirms the worth of life in spite of life. It affirms the wonder and the beauty of the human creature, mortal and insignificant and ignorant though he be: Even the mortal creature we ourselves have seen sitting on an earth reduced to ash-heap picking in agony at the cinders of a bomb-scorched skin. It answers life with life and so justifies that bravely tolling line of Shakespeare's which declares that love "bears it out even to the edge of doom." Love does: and for us no less than for that ancient man who took his life back after all that wretchedness.

J.B., like Job, covers his mouth with his hand; acquiesces in the vast indifference of the universe as all men must who truly face it; takes back his life again. In love. To live.

from Act I

MR. ZUSS.

    God never laughs! In the whole Bible!

NICKLES.

    How *could* He laugh? He made it—

                        the toy

    Top—the world—the dirty whirler!

MR. ZUSS.

    What's so wrong with the world?

NICKLES.

                  Wrong with it!

    Try to spin one on a dung-heap.

I heard upon his dry dung-heap
That man cry out who cannot sleep:
"If God is God He is not good,
If God is good He is not God;
Take the even, take the odd,
I would not sleep here if I could
Except for the little green leaves in the wood
And the wind on the water."

MR. ZUSS.

You are a bitter boy.

NICKLES.

     I taste of the world.
I've licked the stick that beat my brains out—
Stock that broke my father's bones.

MR. ZUSS.

I know. You've been around, you children!
Our modern hero! Our Odysseus
Sailing sidewalks toward the turd of
Truth and touching it at last . . . in triumph!
The honest, disillusioned—child!
You sicken me!

NICKLES.

     All right. I sicken you.
No need to be offensive, is there?
If you would rather someone else . . .

MR. ZUSS.

Did what?

NICKLES.

    Played Job.

MR. ZUSS.

     Played Job?

NICKLES.

      Nat-*u*-rally!
Who else could play the part like me?
God has killed his sons . . . his daughters . . .
Taken his camels, oxen, sheep,
Everything he has . . . and left him
Sick and stricken on a dung-heap—
Not even the consciousness of crime to comfort him.

MR. ZUSS.

Not Job. Not you. I wouldn't think of it.

NICKLES.
  You wouldn't think of me for Job?
  What would you think of?
MR. ZUSS.
                    Oh, there's always
  Someone playing Job.
NICKLES.
                There must be
  Thousands! What's that got to do with it?
  Millions and millions of mankind
  Burned, crushed, broken, mutilated,
  Slaughtered, and for what? For thinking!
  For walking round the world in the wrong
  Skin, the wrong-shaped noses, eyelids:
  Living at the wrong address—
  London, Berlin, Hiroshima—
  Wrong night—wrong city.
  There never could have been so many
  Suffered more for less. But where do
  I come in? . . . Play the dung-heap?
MR. ZUSS.
  All we have to do is start.
  Job will join us. Job will be there.

from Act II

(MR. ZUSS *flings off his robe in a gesture of triumph and strides down the stair, his face shining. He enters the ring where* J.B. *and* SARAH *stand opposite each other, she looking up at him, half tender, half afraid; he, his mouth grim, turned away.*)

MR. ZUSS.
  Job! You've answered him!
J.B.
  Let me alone. I am alone.
  I'll sweat it out alone.
MR. ZUSS.
                  You've found
  The answer at the end! You've answered him!
  We take what God has sent—the Godsend.
  There is no resolution of the mystery

Of unintelligible suffering but the dumb
Bowed head that makes injustice just
By yielding to the Will that willed it—
Yielding to the Will that willed
A world where there can be injustice.
You've learned that now. You've bowed your head.
The end is the acceptance of the end.
We take what God has willed.

J.B. (*to* MR. ZUSS. *Savagely.*)

                    I will not
Duck my head again to thunder—
That bullwhip crackling at my ears!—although
He kill me with it. I must know.

(NICKLES *has risen and is making his way slowly down the stair.*)

MR. ZUSS. (*Astonished. He could not have heard what he has heard.*)
We have no *peace* but in obedience.
Our peace is acquiescence in the Will of God.

J.B.
I'll find a foothold somewhere *knowing.*
(*To* NICKLES.)
Life is a filthy farce, you say,
And nothing but a bloody stage
Can bring the curtain down and men
Must have ironic hearts and perish
Laughing. . . .

            Well, *I* will not laugh!
(*He swings on* MR. ZUSS.)
And neither will I weep among
The obedient who lie down to die
In meek relinquishment protesting
Nothing, questioning nothing, asking
Nothing but to rise again and
                     bow!
Neither the bowing nor the blood
Will make an end for me now!
                  Neither the
Yes in ignorance . . .
               the No in spite. . . .
Neither of them!
(MR. ZUSS *exits.*)

     Neither of them!

(NICKLES *exits.*)

Sarah!

    Why have you come back again?

SARAH. (*Confused, holding out the small green branch like a child.*)

 Look, Job.

    The first few leaves . . .

          Not leaves though—

Petals. I found it in the ashes growing

Green as though it did not know . . .

All that's left there now is ashes. . . .

Mountains of ashes, shattered glass,

Glittering cliffs of glass all shattered

Steeper than a cat could climb

If there were cats still. . . .

J.B.

     Why?

SARAH.

       I broke the

Branch to strip the leaves off.

      Petals

(*Fastens branch to pole under perch.*)

Again!

    But they so clung to it!

J.B.

      Curse

God and die! You said that to me.

SARAH.

 Yes. You wanted justice, didn't you?

J.B.

 Cry for justice and the stars

Will stare until your eyes sting! Weep,

Enormous winds will thrash the water!

SARAH.

 Cry in sleep for your lost children,

Snow will fall . . .

     snow will fall.

J.B.

 You left me, Sarah.

SARAH.

    Yes, I left you.

I thought there was a way away.

Out of the world. Out of the world.
Water under bridges opens
Closing and the companion stars
Still float there afterwards. I thought the door
Opened into closing water.

J.B.

Sarah!

SARAH.

       Oh, I never could.
I never could. Even this—
Even the green leaf on the branch—could stop me.

J.B.

Why have you come back again?

SARAH. *(Kneels. She has found a stub of candle in her pocket.)*

Because I love you.

J.B.

             Because you love me!
The one thing certain in this hurtful world
Is love's inevitable heartbreak.
What's the future but the past to come
Over and over, love and loss,
What's loved most lost most.

(SARAH *has moved into the rubble of the ring. She kneels, setting things to rights. Her mind is on her task, not on* J.B.*'s words.*)

SARAH.

       I know that, Job.

J.B.

Nothing is certain but the loss of love.
And yet . . . you say you love me!

SARAH.

       Yes.

J.B.

The stones in those dead streets would crack
With terrible indecent laughter
Hearing *you* and *me* say love!

SARAH.

I have no light to light the candle.

J.B. *(Violently.)*

You have our love to light it with!
Blow on the coal of the heart, poor Sarah.

SARAH.

Blow on the coal of the heart . . .?

J.B.

The candles in churches are out.
The lights have gone out in the sky!

SARAH.

The candles in churches are out.
The lights have gone out in the sky.
Blow on the coal of the heart
And we'll see by and by. . . .

we'll see where we are.
We'll know. We'll know.

J.B. (*Slowly, with difficulty, the hard words said at last.*)

We can never *know.*
He answered me like the stillness of a star
That silences us asking.

No, Sarah, no:
(*Kneels beside her.*)
We *are* and that is all our answer.
We are and what we are can suffer.
But . . .

what suffers loves.

And love
Will live its suffering again,
Risk its own defeat again,
Endure the loss of everything again
And yet again and yet again
In doubt, in dread, in ignorance, unanswered,
Over and over, with the dark before,
The dark behind it . . . and still live . . . still love.

(J.B. *strikes match, touches* SARAH's *cheek with his hand.*)

(GAUZE CURTAIN DROPS. *MUSIC. LIGHTS FADE OUT.*)

THE PLAY IS ENDED

What connection do you see between the limerick beginning "If God is God He is not good" and the conclusion of the play? In answering, consider the "green leaf on the branch" that Sarah says could "stop" her. Why does Job "take back his life"? J.B. differs significantly from the biblical Job in what he has learned from his experiences. Describe this difference.

The original version of the play ended with Sarah's final words, "We'll know." How do you explain the playwright's dramatic reversal in the lines he later added? What does J.B. say is more important than *knowing?* Do you agree?

LOOK, HOW BEAUTIFUL

Robinson Jeffers

There is this infinite energy, the power of God forever working—
    toward what purpose?—toward none.
This is God's will; he works, he grows and changes, he has no
    object.
No more than a great sculptor who has found a ledge of fine
    marble, and lives beside it, and carves great images,
And casts them down. That is God's will: to make great things
    and destroy them, and make great things
And destroy them again. With war and plague and horror, and
    the diseases of trees and the corruption of stone
He destroys all that stands. But look how beautiful—
Look how beautiful are all the things that he does. His signature
Is the beauty of things.

Towards what purpose does the poet feel that God works? What is his reasoning? What makes up for all this, however? How does this relate to the conclusion of *J.B.?*

ALL IS VANITY
(Selections from Ecclesiastes)

There Is Nothing New Under the Sun

The words of the Preacher, the son of David, king in Jerusalem.

Vanity of vanities, saith the Preacher, vanity of vanities; all is vanity. What profit hath a man of all his labor which he taketh under the sun? One generation passeth away, and another generation cometh: but the earth abideth for ever. The sun also ariseth, and the sun goeth down, and hasteth to his place where he arose. The wind goeth toward the south, and turneth about unto the north; it whirleth about continually, and the wind returneth again according to his circuits. All the rivers run into the sea; yet the sea is not full: unto the place from whence the rivers come, thither they return again.

All things are full of labor; man cannot utter it: the eye is not satisfied with seeing, nor the ear filled with hearing. The thing that hath been, it is that which shall be; and that which is done is that which shall be done: and there is no new thing under the sun. Is there any thing whereof it may be said, "See, this is new"? It hath been already of old time, which was before us. There is no remembrance of former things; neither shall there be any remembrance of things that are to come with those that shall come after.

I the Preacher was king over Israel in Jerusalem. And I gave my heart to seek and search out by wisdom concerning all things that are done under heaven: this sore travail hath God given to the sons of man to be exercised therewith. I have seen all the works that are done under the sun; and, behold, all is vanity and vexation of spirit. That which is crooked cannot be made straight: and that which is wanting cannot be numbered.

I communed with my own heart, saying, "Lo, I am come to great estate, and have gotten more wisdom than all they that have been before me in Jerusalem: yea, my heart had great experience of wisdom and knowledge." And I gave my heart to know wisdom, and to know madness and folly: I perceived that this also is vexation of spirit. For in much wisdom is much grief: and he that increaseth knowledge increaseth sorrow.

[*Ecclesiastes 1:1–18*]

I Hated All My Labor

I said in my heart, "Go to now, I will prove thee with mirth; therefore enjoy pleasure: and, behold, this also is vanity. I said of laughter, "It is mad": and of mirth, "What doeth it?" I sought in mine heart to give myself unto wine, yet acquainting mine heart with wisdom; and to lay hold on folly, till I might see what was that good for the sons of men, which they should do under the heaven all the days of their life.

I made me great works; I builded me houses; I planted me vineyards: I made me gardens and orchards, and I planted trees in them of all kind of fruits: I made me pools of water, to water therewith the wood that bringeth forth trees: I got me servants and maidens, and had servants born in my house; also I had great possessions of great and small cattle above all that were in Jerusalem before me: I gathered me also silver and gold, and the peculiar treasures of kings and of the provinces: I got me men singers and women singers, and the delights of the sons of men, as musical instruments, and that of all sorts.

So I was great, and increased more than all that were before me in Jerusalem: also my wisdom remained with me. And whatsoever mine eyes desired I kept not from them, I withheld not my heart from any joy; for my heart rejoiced in all my labor: and this was my portion of all my labor. Then I looked on all the works that my hands had wrought, and on the labor that I had labored to do: and, behold, all was vanity and vexation of spirit, and there was no profit under the sun.

And I turned myself to behold wisdom, and madness, and folly: for what can the man do that cometh after the king? Only that which hath already been done. Then I saw that wisdom excelleth folly, as far as light excelleth darkness. The wise man's eyes are in his head; but the fool walketh in darkness: and I myself perceived also that one event happeneth to them all.

Then said I in my heart, "As it happeneth to the fool, so it happeneth even to me"; and why was I then more wise? Then I said in my heart, that this also is vanity. For there is no more remembrance of the wise more than of the fool for ever, seeing that which now is in the days to come shall all be forgotten. And how dieth the wise man? As the fool. Therefore I hated life; because the work that is wrought under the sun is grievous unto me: for all is vanity and vexation of spirit.

Yea, I hated all my labor which I had taken under the sun: because I should leave it unto the man that shall be after me. And who knoweth whether he shall be a wise man or a fool? Yet shall he have rule over all my labor wherein I have labored, and wherein I have showed myself wise under the sun. This also is vanity. Therefore I went about to cause my heart to despair of all the labor which I took under the sun.

There is nothing better for a man, than that he should eat and drink, and that he should make his soul enjoy good in his labor. This also I saw, that it was from the hand of God. For who can eat, or who else can hasten hereunto, more than I? For God giveth to a man that is good in his sight, wisdom, and knowledge, and joy: but to the sinner he giveth travail, to gather and to heap up, that he may give to him that is good before God. This also is vanity and vexation of spirit.

[*Ecclesiastes 2:1–20, 24–26*]

To Every Thing There is a Season

To every thing there is a season, and a time to every purpose under the heaven:

> A time to be born, and a time to die;
> A time to plant, and a time to pluck up that which is planted;
> A time to kill, and a time to heal;
> A time to break down, and a time to build up;
> A time to weep, and a time to laugh;
> A time to mourn, and a time to dance;
> A time to cast away stones, and a time to gather stones together;
> A time to embrace, and a time to refrain from embracing;
> A time to get, and a time to lose;
> A time to keep, and a time to cast away;
> A time to rend, and a time to sew;
> A time to keep silence, and a time to speak;
> A time to love, and a time to hate;
> A time of war, and a time of peace.

What profit hath he that worketh in that wherein he laboreth? I have seen the travail which God hath given to the sons of men to be exercised in it. He hath made every thing beautiful in its time: also he hath set the world in their heart, so that no man can find out the work that God maketh from the beginning to the end.

[*Ecclesiastes 3:1–11*]

The Heart of the Wise

Two are better than one; because they have a good reward for their labor. For if they fall, the one will lift up his fellow: but woe to him that is alone when he falleth, for he hath not another to help him up. Again, if two lie together, then they have heat: but how can one be warm alone? And if one prevail against him, two shall withstand him; and a threefold cord is not quickly broken.

A good name is better than precious ointment; and the day of death than the day of one's birth. It is better to go to the house of mourning, than to go to the house of feasting: for that is the end of all men; and the living will lay it to his heart. Sorrow is better than laughter: for by the sadness of the countenance the heart is made better. The heart of the wise is in the house of mourning; but the heart of fools is in the house of mirth. It is better to hear the rebuke of the wise, than for a man to hear the song of fools. For as the crackling of thorns under a pot, so is the laughter of the fool: this also is vanity.

[*Ecclesiastes 4:9–12; 7:1–6*]

All Things Come Alike to All

All things come alike to all: there is one event to the righteous, and to the wicked; to the good and to the clean, and to the unclean; to him that sacrificeth and to him that sacrificeth not: as is the good, so is the sinner; and he that sweareth, as he that feareth an oath. This is an evil among all things that are done under the sun, that there is one event unto all: yea, also the heart of the sons of men is full of evil, and madness is in their heart while they live, and after that they go to the dead.

For to him that is joined to all the living there is hope: for a living dog is better than a dead lion. For the living know that they shall die: but the dead know not any thing, neither have they any more a reward; for the memory of them is forgotten. Also their love, and their hatred and their envy, is now perished; neither have they any more a portion for ever in any thing that is done under the sun.

Go thy way, eat thy bread with joy, and drink thy wine with a merry heart; for God now accepteth thy works. Let thy garments be always white; and let thy head lack no ointment. Live joyfully with the wife whom thou lovest all the days of the life of thy vanity, which he hath given thee under the sun, all the days of thy vanity; for that is thy portion in this life and in thy labor which thou takest under the sun. Whatsoever thy hand findeth to do, do it with thy might; for there is no work, nor device, nor knowledge, nor wisdom, in the grave, whither thou goest.

I returned, and saw under the sun that the race is not to the swift, nor the battle to the strong, neither yet bread to the wise, nor yet riches to men of understanding, nor yet favor to men of skill; but time and chance happeneth to them all. For man also knoweth not his time: as the fishes that are taken in an evil net, and as the birds that are caught in the snare, so are the sons of men snared in an evil time, when it falleth suddenly upon them.

This wisdom have I seen also under the sun, and it seemed great unto me: there was a little city, and a few men within it; and there came a great king against it, and besieged it, and built great bulwarks against it. Now there was found in it a poor wise man, and he by his wisdom delivered the city; yet no man remembered that same poor man. Then said I, "Wisdom is better than strength: nevertheless the poor man's wisdom is despised, and his words are not heard." The words of the wise men are heard in quiet more than the cry of him that ruleth among fools. Wisdom is better than weapons of war: but one sinner destroyeth much good.

[*Ecclesiastes 9:2–18*]

Remember Now Thy Creator

Truly the light is sweet, and a pleasant thing it is for the eyes to behold the sun. But if a man live many years, and rejoice in them all, yet let him remember the days of darkness; for they shall be many. All that cometh is vanity.

Rejoice, O young man, in thy youth; and let thy heart cheer thee in the days of thy youth, and walk in the ways of thine heart, and in the sight of thine eyes: but know thou, that for all these things God will bring thee into judgment. Therefore remove sorrow from thy heart, and put away evil from thy flesh: for childhood and youth are vanity.

Remember now thy Creator in the days of thy youth,
While the evil days come not,
Nor the years draw nigh, when thou shalt say,
"I have no pleasure in them";
While the sun, or the light,
Or the moon, or the stars, be not darkened,
Nor the clouds return after the rain:
In the day when the keepers of the house shall tremble,
And the strong men shall bow themselves,
And the grinders cease because they are few,
And those that look out of the windows be darkened,
And the doors shall be shut in the streets,
When the sound of the grinding is low,
And he shall rise up at the voice of the bird,
And all the daughters of music shall be brought low;
Also when they shall be afraid of that which is high,
And fears shall be in the way,
And the almond tree shall flourish,
And the grasshopper shall be a burden,
And desire shall fail:
Because man goeth to his long home,
And the mourners go about the streets:
Or ever the silver cord be loosed,
Or the golden bowl be broken,
Or the pitcher be broken at the fountain,
Or the wheel broken at the cistern;
Then shall the dust return to the earth as it was:
And the spirit shall return unto God who gave it.

Vanity of vanites, saith the Preacher; all is vanity. And moreover, because the Preacher was wise, he still taught the people knowledge; yea, he gave good heed, and sought out, and set in order many proverbs. The Preacher sought to find out acceptable words: and that which was written was upright, even words of truth.

The words of the wise are as goads, and as nails fastened by the masters of assemblies, which are given from one shepherd. And further, by these, my son, be admonished: of making many books there is no end; and much study is a weariness of the flesh.

Let us hear the conclusion of the whole matter; Fear God, and keep his commandments: for this is the whole duty of man. For God shall bring every work into judgment, with every secret thing, whether it be good, or whether it be evil.

[*Ecclesiastes 11:7–10; 12:1–14*]

Why does the Preacher say that "all is vanity"? In what ways can it be said that "he that increaseth knowledge increaseth sorrow"? Does this mean that it is better to remain ignorant? What is it that makes all the Preacher's labors in the end so "grievous" to him?

The passage beginning "To everything there is a season" is extremely well known. Pete Seeger used it nearly intact in his song "Turn! Turn! Turn!," which the Byrds, a rock group, made into a "hit" in the late 1960s. What particular twist is given to this passage by the title of the song and the concluding words, "I swear it's not too late"? Why were lines like "A time to build up and a time to break down" and "A time for war and a time for peace" particularly relevant in the late 60s? Discuss the passage in light of the world situation today.

Why are two "better than one"? Why is sorrow "better than laughter"? What "one event" comes both "to the righteous and to the wicked"? How does this fact reinforce the overall observation of the Preacher that "all is vanity"? How should one approach his or her life nonetheless? What does it mean that "time and chance happeneth to them all"?

What do the extended metaphors represent which make up the poetic sequence beginning "Remember the days of thy youth"? Can you interpret each figure of speech? What is the Preacher's final admonition? Is it consistent with what has preceded it?

SOLOMON THE KING

Edmond Fleg

Solomon is traditionally associated with both the Preacher of Ecclesiastes and the bridegroom of the Song of Songs. He was the first living son born to David and Bathsheba. When asked by God what he most wanted, Solomon chose wisdom. For this, God granted him both wisdom and incredible riches, with which he built a splendid temple for God, palatial homes, and a navy of ships to fetch him gold.

*According to the First Book of Kings, Solomon "loved many strange
women." It was his seven hundred wives and three hundred
concubines that "turned away his heart after other gods," leading
to a division of the Hebrew nation. One of the most famous women
in Solomon's life was the Queen of Sheba, whose visit is the
focus of the next story, taken from Edmond Fleg's novel* The Life
of Solomon.

Now, from the time when he visited the Palace of Dust, King Solomon
knew sadness.

Each day, in the shadow of the winged vault that the birds of the
air arched above his throne, he pondered and meditated. And each day
he groaned in his heart:

"Of what use, King of the World, was it to grant me power, since
I may only wield the power of a man? Of what use was it to grant
me wisdom, since I may not know the wisdom of God?"

Now, one evening, a burning ray of light penetrated through two
ill-joined wings in the feathery canopy. And it struck the eyes of King
Solomon.

"Who hath quitted his post?" he cried, in his annoyance.

The eagle called one bird after the other, according to their names,
until he had numbered all the birds. And it turned out that the hoopoe
was absent.

"Go and seek her," ordered the king. "If her excuse avail not, let her
be dragged in sand for punishment, and eaten by vermin."

The eagle sought throughout the spaces of the air, and returned at
length with the hoopoe, who trembled for fear in all her feathers.

"Where wert thou?" demanded the angry king.

"Let my lord the king," answered the hoopoe, "deign to pardon his
handmaid. I have sinned but in loving thy glory. For I wished to sing
thy glory to all the world. And accordingly I sought a region which
had never heard of it. And, behold, after flying for three months with
neither food nor drink, I came upon a kingdom which knoweth not
thee, King Solomon, and which thou knowest not . . ."

"Have a care," growled the king. "Beware of lies."

"I do not lie, my lord," answered the hoopoe. "I have seen this kingdom among the countries of the East, as plain as I see thee. Sheba is
its name, and it hath for capital Chitor. The trees that grow there
were planted on the third day in the innocence of the Creation. The

streams that water those lawns flow out from Eden. The men who
inhabit there know not the point of arrow nor the blade of sword. And
Balkis, their queen, who holdeth regiment over them, is the mightiest
and the wisest of all mortal beings."

Then Solomon thought:

"If this queen laveth her limbs in the waters of Paradise: if she be
nourished by the fruit of trees planted before the Fall, her power is
perchance mightier than mine, and wiser than mine her wisdom."

And he had this letter written by his scribes:

"To the Queen Balkis, from Solomon the King. Peace and good
health. I am king over all the earth, and all the kings of the earth
bow themselves in homage to my power and my wisdom. If thou wilt
not come, as they have come, to prostrate thyself before me, and do
me homage, I will dispatch mine armies against thee. And in the ranks
of these armies are all the birds of the air, and the beasts of the earth
and of the waters, and all the spirits, both they that dwell in the deeps
and they that dwell on high."

And he tied the parchment, sealed with his seal, to the wing of the
hoopoe, and said to her:

"Carry this letter to Balkis."

And the hoopoe flew, and cried her cry as she went. And all the
birds of the air flew after her.

Now, they came unto Chitor in the hour of the morning, when the
queen, with arms outstretched toward the light, addressed her prayer
unto the sun. As she prayed, suddenly the light thickened, the sun was
extinguished, and, from the cloud of wings that darkened the sky,
Solomon's letter fell into the breast of Balkis. She took and read it.
And she trembled. Then, having assembled her Ministers, she asked
their counsel. And they answered:

"We hold as naught King Solomon; and his kingdom also we hold
as naught."

But in her wisdom she did not listen to them. Calling all her ship-
men about her, she loaded their vessels with gems and pearls. And she
sent into the ships six thousand youths clothed in purple. And all these
were born in the same day. And she sent them to Solomon with this
letter in answer:

"From the city of Chitor to the land of Israel is a journey of seven
years' length. But, since thou desirest to see me, in three years thou
shalt have thy will."

Now, along the road which should conduct Queen Balkis to him,

Solomon builded two mighty walls. And they began at the frontier of the land of Israel, and ended at the gate of Jerusalem.

From Thamar to Masada the two walls were of silver. From Masada to Enghedi they were of gold. From Enghedi to Hebron, of the pearl; and from Hebron to Jerusalem they were of diamond. And the same distances of the road he paved with silver, gold, pearls, and diamonds, in like degree.

Then he devised a lake of crystal. And in the middle of this lake a palace of crystal. In the crystal of the lake the whole world was mirrored. And in the crystal of the palace he set his throne. And there he awaited Balkis.

Now, on a day when he was enthroned in his palace of crystal, behold, Balkis appeared. And she was wrapped in purples, and she was crowned with purple also. Behind her purple fans wafted the scent of nard upon the air. And clouds of purple incense went up from her purple-clad escort. And Solomon longed in his heart:

"May she teach me a power greater than my power, and a wisdom mightier than my wisdom!"

But, when Balkis saw the lake of crystal where the world lay mirrored, her feet trembled. And in order to pass through it she raised her veils of purple even to her knee. Then Solomon thought in his heart:

"For me the world is no more than an image, and, lo! this queen trembleth at the image of the world."

Now, when Balkis had bowed herself before him, she spoke, saying:

"King Solomon, I brought thee my treasures to do thee honor. But when I beheld thy walls of silver I threw away my silver basins; when I beheld thy walls of gold I threw away my golden basins. And I have flung away my crowns of pearl and my crowns of diamond. For I beheld thy pavements of pearl and diamond. For all wealth is poverty beside thy wealth. And all riches are poor beside thy riches."

And he made answer:

"What will it profit a man to be rich in his riches, to be wealthy amid his own wealth, if the day whereon he must leave these things is already appointed? I have satisfied my mouth and I have filled mine eyes by my labor. And, behold, nothing is left me that I may desire. And I possess nothing that I may keep. For another shall be master in my place, who knoweth how to acquire these things, but without

King Solomon (c. 1860) by Gustave Doré. PHOTOGRAPH ARCHIVES OF THE JEW-ISH THEOLOGICAL SEMINARY OF AMERICA, NEW YORK. FRANK DARMSTAEDTER.

labor: who shall know how to deserve them, yet hath not understanding. Moreover, mine heart abominateth the ill that I have done myself under the sun, that I leave the fruit of my labors to the man who cometh after me. For my toil was vanity and my wealth is vanity."

But Balkis answered:

"The universe lauds the might of thy power, King Solomon. Is it the peer of mine? In my palace I have a throne adorned with twelve fountains, whence flow rare perfumes. Now, before quitting my palace I hid this throne in a certain room. To reach the room thou must first pass through six other rooms. And I have entrusted the seven keys to the most faithful among my servants. Art thou able, from this distance, to discover the keys, open the rooms, and bring the throne hither, that I may sit upon it before thee?"

Then Solomon said to Ornias:

"Go thou, and seek me this throne."

"I will bring it thee this evening," replied the demon.

"Shall I still live this evening?" demanded Solomon.

And the king turned towards Asmodeus, and said:

"Go thou, and seek me this throne."

"In one hour I will bring it thee," replied the Satan.

"Shall I still live in an hour's time?" demanded Solomon.

And the king turned towards Balkis:

"Look up," he said, "and then look down. And thou shalt see thy throne."

She looked up. And she looked down. And, lo! the earth opened before her. And the throne with the twelve fountains rose up from the earth.

"And now be seated," Solomon commanded Balkis.

"How shall I be enthroned in the place where thou art enthroned?" answered the queen. "My power is but weakness beside thy power."

But he groaned aloud, saying:

"What doth it profit a man to be powerful in the midst of his power, if the hour is already appointed when he shall be despoiled? A live dog availeth more than a dead lion. I gave commandment to the kings of all kingdoms, to all the spirits of the waters, of the earth, and of the sky. But my heart curseth the zeal with which it ran to command them. For all my toil was vanity, and my power also is vanity."

Then Balkis answered:

"Even the angels glorify thy knowledge, King Solomon. Is it the peer of mine?"

And she opened a casket that contained an emerald, two nosegays, and a cup.

"This emerald," she said, "is pierced twelve times by twelve spiral holes. Canst thou pass thereby a single thread?"

Solomon took from the mulberry tree close by a silkworm, and placed it upon the emerald.

And the worm wound his thread twelve times in and out of the twelve spirals, and at length reappeared under the emerald at the end of the thread.

"Of these nosegays," pursued the queen, "one is made of mock flowers and the other of real flowers. Naught distinguisheth one from another to the eye, to the hand, or to the nose. Canst thou distinguish the false flowers from the true?"

Solomon took a bee from the hive, and set him upon the nosegays. And the bee, scorning the false, plundered the true flowers.

"This cup," the queen said at last, "hath never been filled. Canst thou fill it with water that cometh neither from earth nor from heaven?"

And Solomon made his liveliest steed gallop twelve times about the plain. And when the animal returned to him, bathed in sweat, he filled the cup from the foam which covered him.

Then Balkis cried aloud:

"It is indeed truth, King Solomon, that which they sing of thy knowledge. I had heard tell of it, but I was not able to believe."

And Solomon sighed:

"Queen Balkis, thou settest me riddles that a horse, a bee, and a worm can decipher—and thou marvellest at my wisdom! For I gave my heart to seek and search out by wisdom concerning all things that are done under the sun. And I have gotten more knowledge than all they that have been before me in Jerusalem: this sore travail hath God given to the sons of men to be exercised therewith. For in much wisdom is much grief. And he that increaseth knowledge, increaseth sorrow. A man hath done well who addeth deed to deed, but, for all that, to what end doth he tend? He taketh account only of those things that escape him. All that exists is distant, and very deep. He knoweth not in what way the spirit goeth, nor how it animateth the seed that is in its mother's womb. And he knoweth not how to embrace the work of the six days. Moreover, my soul hateth the question that she hath made of them, and the answers that she hath been given. For all my search was vanity, and all vanity my knowledge."

Now, even as he spoke, a poor widow came before them and implored justice:

"What is thy complaint?" the king asked her.

"Having compassion because I went hungry," answered the woman, "my lord and the king bestowed a sack of flour upon his handmaid yesterday. Now when I opened the sack before the door of my dwelling, behold the wind blew, and carried away my flour."

"Let three sacks be given to her," ordered Solomon.

And the sacks were brought in and given to her. But the widow would by no means depart.

"What claim hast thou still to make?" asked the king.

"I claim thy justice, King Solomon. The wind robbed me. Let the wind be punished."

"The wind hath not deserved punishment," proclaimed the king.

But Balkis said: "This woman is in the right of it. The wind hath committed theft. Let the wind be punished."

Then Solomon summoned the east wind, and questioned him, saying: "Wherefore didst thou blow upon the flour that I gave this widow?"

"I did not so," answered the east wind.

Then he had the west wind and the south wind summoned, and they gave the same answer. And at last he summoned the north wind, and questioned him, saying:

"Wherefore didst thou blow upon the flour that I gave this widow?"

"I was constrained to do so, in fulfilling my service to the glory of the Most High," answered the wind. "A ship, whereon many of the faithful were passengers, was sailing thither that they might worship the Eternal in his Temple, and it was about to founder upon a rock in the Red Sea. To save the ship, I was forced to blow upon it, and in blowing upon it, behold, I blew also upon the flour of thy charity."

"Doth he deserve punishment?" Solomon asked Balkis.

And the queen cried aloud:

"Happy are thy race, and happy are thy people, who surround thee ceaselessly and who rejoice in thy word. And praise be to thy God, who hath set thee upon thy throne, who hath set justice upon thy lips and in thy mouth wisdom."

But he sighed:

"What profit hath a just man over the unrighteous? And how is the wise man exalted above the fool? Is not the same end reserved for them, doth not the same oblivion devour their names after their death? What availeth it that a man be chaste or lewd, that he sin or that he sin not, that prudence counsel him or folly lead him, that he walk open-eyed or like a blind man? All go alike toward darkness where the eye may not see at all. Queen Balkis, Queen Balkis, thou reignest over a country watered by the rivers of Eden, and trees born of the fruit of Paradise lend thee their shade. Behold, I had hoped of thee riches and might, science and wisdom surpassing all that I have. But thou hast given me naught that I do not possess. Thou hast taught me nothing that I did not already know. In every place under the sun, before the face of death, men and beast are equal. Vanity of vanities, all is but vanity."

And the queen answered:

"Wherefore dost thou hold life in hatred because death existeth? My power is mightier than thine if I esteem it. My wisdom is wiser than thine, if I honor it. There is a time to weep and a time to laugh, a time to love and a time to hate, a time to curse and a time to bless. There is a time to live, King Solomon, and a time to die."

And, when she had spoken thus, she drew her purples about her, and, beneath her purple crown, Balkis returned and went her way into the land of Sheba.

Now Solomon pondered the lesson of Balkis. And he thought:

"Wherefore have I said in my heart that man is no better than a beast? The bird is caught in the snare; the fish is taken in an evil net. But they know not the time when they must die. And, behold, man knoweth it. Before the light of thine eyes is extinguished, it is a pleasant thing to play in the sun. For truly the light is sweet. It is not good to be too wise. Nor is it not wise to be too holy. The better part is to make merry the hours and to chase away the careful days."

But, since he had not the simpleness of heart, nor the innocence of those gardens where Balkis dwelt, he added:

"Refuse thy hand nothing that it may take; refuse thine eyes nothing that they may desire, refuse thy lips nothing that they may lay hold on. Since there is neither wisdom nor folly, nor debaucheries, nor holiness, under the earth, eat, drink, and be merry. Escape thy nothingness by the awakening of thy flesh. Multiply thy life, whilst again thou enjoyest thy pleasures."

Then he had builded for himself new dwellings. And he planted new gardens. But to the end that his joy in them should not grow weary, he destroyed his palaces that he might erect them again, and he took up his gardens that he might lay them out again.

And, since he wished to taste the delights of the whole world, he quarried stones for his palaces from the rocks of all mountains; in the soil of his gardens he rooted trees from every forest; and he wove for his raiment, in the fabrics of his mantles, the diverse aspects of every land. For his jewels he distilled metals fallen from the stars. And, in their making, he made use of all the rays of dawn and of sunset, adding their colors to those of the sparkling gems. And their luster was more various than fine gold.

Since his horses no longer sufficed him, he increased their number tenfold. And as his tables no longer satisfied him, he enlarged their size and refined their delicacy an hundredfold. And the flesh of every kind of beast was dressed and served to him there, according to the tastes of all nations. And rivers of wine were poured out there, flowing from all the vines of the earth.

But, above all, it was in women that he sought to renew his pleasures. The seventy daughters of the kings, whom he had wedded to bring about the peace of the world, had held in their arms nothing but a soul distracted with thought. Therefore he took three hundred concubines wise in the caresses of the north and of the south, of the west, and of the east. And every night he took to wife a virgin princess. And he instructed her in the embraces of the courtesans.

Often he made festival for himself, and his wives were indistinguishable, for their number and their nakedness. And, full of meat and drunken with wine, amid the cry of every music known that might minister to the passions, he sank himself deeper and deeper into his lusts.

And in these days, at the foot of his empty throne, crowds were wont to await his justice. And his mother, Bathsheba, rousing herself at noon from her slumber, went in to him, and looking down upon his couch, she cried aloud:

"Solomon, Solomon, what doest thou with thy wisdom?"

How does King Solomon reveal his wisdom in this story? Why is this not satisfying to him? How does he try to make up for this feeling of emptiness? In what ways does the story make effective use of passages from the Book of Ecclesiastes? What do you feel is the overall theme?

THE SONG OF SONGS

(Selections)

O Thou Whom My Soul Loveth

The song of songs,
 which is Solomon's.
Let him kiss me with the kisses of his mouth:
 for thy love is better than wine.
Because of the savor of thy good ointments
 thy name is as ointment poured forth,
 therefore do the virgins love thee.
Draw me, we will run after thee:
 the king hath brought me into his chambers:
We will be glad and rejoice in thee,
 we will remember thy love more than wine:
 the upright love thee.

I am black but comely,
 O ye daughters of Jerusalem,
As the tents of Kedar,
 as the curtains of Solomon.
Look not upon me, because I am black,
 because the sun hath looked upon me:
My mother's children were angry with me;
 they made me keeper of the vineyards;
 but mine own vineyard have I not kept.

Tell me, O thou whom my soul loveth,
 where thou feedest,
 where thou makest thy flock to rest at noon:
For why should I be as one that turneth aside
 by the flocks of thy companions?

[*Song of Songs 1:1–7*]

I Am the Rose of Sharon

I am the rose of Sharon,
   and the lily of the valleys.
As the lily among thorns,
   so is my love among the daughters.
As the apple tree among the trees of the wood,
   so is my beloved among the sons.
I sat down under his shadow with great delight,
   and his fruit was sweet to my taste.
He brought me to the banqueting house,
   and his banner over me was love.
Stay me with flagons, comfort me with apples:
   for I am sick with love.

His left hand is under my head,
   and his right hand doth embrace me.
I charge you, O ye daughters of Jerusalem,
   by the roes, and by the hinds of the field,
That ye stir not up, nor awake my love,
   till he please.

The voice of my beloved! Behold, he cometh
   leaping upon the mountains, skipping upon the hills.
My beloved is like a roe or a young hart:
   behold, he standeth behind our wall,
He looketh forth at the windows,
   showing himself through the lattice.

My beloved spake, and said unto me,
   "Rise up, my love, my fair one, and come away.
For, lo, the winter is past, the rain is over and gone;
   the flowers appear on the earth;
The time of the singing of birds is come,
   and the voice of the turtle is heard in our land;
The fig tree putteth forth her green figs,
   and the vines with the tender grapes give a good smell.
Arise, my love, my fair one,
   and come away."

[Song of Songs 2:1–13]

Song of the Bridegroom

Behold, thou art fair, my love:
  behold, thou art fair;
Thou hast doves' eyes within thy locks:
    thy hair is as a flock of goats,
    that appear from mount Gilead.
Thy teeth are like a flock of sheep that are even shorn,
    which came up from the washing;
    whereof every one bear twins,
    and none is barren among them.
Thy lips are like a thread of scarlet,
    and thy speech is comely.
Thy temples are like a piece of a pomegranate
    within thy locks.
Thy neck is like the tower of David builded for an armory,
    whereon there hang a thousand bucklers,
    all shields of mighty men.
Thy two breasts are like two young roes that are twins,
    which feed among the lilies.
Until the day break, and the shadows flee away,
    I will get me to the mountain of myrrh,
    and to the hill of frankincense.
Thou art all fair, my love:
    there is no spot in thee.

Thou hast ravished my heart, my sister, my spouse;
    thou hast ravished my heart with one of thine eyes,
    with one chain of thy neck.
How fair is thy love, my sister, my spouse!
    How much better is thy love than wine!
    and the smell of thine ointments than all spices!
Thy lips, O my spouse, drop as the honeycomb:
    honey and milk are under thy tongue;
    and the smell of thy garments is like the smell of Lebanon.

A garden enclosed is my sister, my spouse:
    a spring shut up, a fountain sealed.
Thy plants are an orchard of pomegranates, with pleasant fruits:
    camphire, with spikenard, spikenard and saffron;
    calamus and cinnamon, with all trees of frankincense;
    myrrh and aloes, with all the chief spices:

A fountain of gardens, a well of living waters,
  and streams from Lebanon.

[Song of Songs 4:1–7, 9–15]

Song of the Bride

My beloved is white and ruddy,
  the chiefest among ten thousand.
His head is as the most fine gold;
  his locks are bushy, and black as a raven:
His eyes are as the eyes of doves by the rivers of waters,
  washed with milk, and fitly set:
His cheeks are as a bed of spices, as sweet flowers:
  his lips like lilies, dropping sweet smelling myrrh:
His hands are as gold rings set with the beryl:
  his belly is as bright ivory overlaid with sapphires:
His legs are as pillars of marble, set upon sockets of fine gold:
  his countenance is as Lebanon, excellent as the cedars:
His mouth is most sweet: yea, he is altogether lovely.
This is my beloved, and this is my friend,
  O daughters of Jerusalem.

[Song of Songs 5:10–16]

An Affirmation

Set me as a seal upon thine heart,
  as a seal upon thine arm;
For love is strong as death;
  jealousy is cruel as the grave:
The coals thereof are coals of fire,
  which hath a most vehement flame.
Many waters cannot quench love,
  neither can the floods drown it:
If a man would give all the substance of his house for love,
  it would utterly be contemned.

Thou that dwellest in the gardens,
  the companions hearken to thy voice:
  cause me to hear it.

Make haste, my beloved,
  and be thou like to a roe or to a young hart
  upon the mountains of spices.

[*Song of Songs 8:6–7, 13–14*]

THE SHARING

George Stewart

George Stewart's novel Earth Abides, *from which "The Sharing" is
taken, opens on an America whose population has been almost totally
devastated by a lethal virus that has ravaged the entire world. The
young geographer Isherwood Williams, alone in the mountains
recovering from the effects of a rattlesnake bite when the calamity
struck, returns to find that civilization as he knew it no longer existed.
Cities, highways, and homes were deserted. The few survivors Ish did
encounter were ill-suited for survival in a drastically altered world,
most of them either drinking themselves to death or living off
the remains of the old civilization, oblivious to the consequences of
what had happened. Before Ish lay the superhuman task of
rebuilding a ravaged America. But first he must find another with
whom he could share . . .*

The fading out of the lights had a strangely severe effect upon Ish.
Even in the full daylight, he seemed to feel those shadows creeping in
from the edges toward him. The Dark Ages were closing in.

He found himself hoarding matches and flashlights and candles,
piling them up in spite of himself, as a psychological protection.

Yet actually, in a little while, he discovered that the absence of electric light was not really as important to him as the absence of electric
power, particularly of refrigeration. The ice-box was dead now, and his
food spoiled. In the deep-freeze units the fresh meat, and butter, and
heads of lettuce soon relapsed into mere smelling masses of corruption.

Now came the change of the season. He was completely lost as to
the passage of the weeks and months, but with the geographer's eye

he could still tell something about the time of year from the look of things. Now he guessed it must be October, and the first rain came to confirm him; from the way it settled down, it seemed likely to last longer than one expected of the first storm.

He stayed at home, managing to amuse himself fairly well. He played his accordion. He browsed through several books—ones he had always meant to read and now was undoubtedly going to have time to do so. Now and then he looked out at the fine drifting rain and the clouds low over the tops of the houses.

During this time, when the rain kept him mostly indoors, his thoughts turned a little toward religion, as they had when he walked through the Cathedral. This time he found a large annotated Bible on his father's bookshelves, and tried browsing here and there in it.

The Gospels seemed strangely unsatisfying, probably because they dealt mostly with the problems of a man involved in the social group. "Render unto Caesar . . ." was a strangely unprofitable text when there was no more Caesar, and not even a Collector of Internal Revenue.

"Sell whatever thou hast, and give to the poor. . . . As ye would that men should do unto you . . . Love thy neighbor as thyself"—all these presupposed a functioning society of many people. As the world now was, a Pharisee or Sadducee might perhaps still follow the set rites of formalized religion, but the very humanity of the teachings of Jesus rendered them obsolete.

Turning back to the Old Testament, he began *Ecclesiastes,* and found himself suddenly more at home. The old fellow "The Preacher" —Koheleth, as the notes called him, whoever he might have been—had a curious way of striking the naturalistic note, of sensing the problem of the individual against the universe. Sometimes it was almost as if he had imagined what Ish was now experiencing: "And if the tree fall toward the south, or toward the north, in the place where the tree falleth, there it shall be." Ish thought of that tree in Oklahoma which had fallen to block Highway 66. And again he read, "Two are better than one . . . for if they fall, the one will lift up his fellow, but woe unto him that is alone when he falleth." And Ish thought of the great fear that had been upon him when he was left alone, and he had felt all too vividly that there would be none to help him up, if he fell. He read through, marveling at the clear-eyed naturalistic acceptance of the universe. There was even a line, "Surely the serpent will bite without enchantment."

He came to the end of the last chapter, and his eyes fell to the lines which began on the lower part of the page. "The song of songs, which is Solomon's." He read, "Let him kiss me with the kisses of his mouth: for thy love is better than wine."

Ish stirred uneasily. In all these long months he had rarely had such feelings. Now again he realized that, more than he thought from day to day, the shock of the whole catastrophe had affected him. It was all like some old story of enchantment in which a king sat and watched life pass by, unable to mingle with it. Other men had done differently. Even those who had drunk themselves to death had, in a sense, been partaking of life. But he himself, in observing what happened, had merely been rejecting life.

What made life anyway? Many people had asked that question— even Koheleth, the preacher, was far from the first. And each had come up with a different answer, except those who admitted that no answer could be found.

Here was he, Isherwood Williams, a strange mingling of realities and fantasies and pressures and reactions, and there all outside was the vast empty city with misty rain falling upon the long empty streets, and the twilight now beginning to deepen. Between the two, him and everything outside him, there lay some kind of strange bond; as one changed, so the other changed also.

It was as if there were a vast equation with many terms on each side, and yet only two great unknowns. He was on one side; x, perhaps, you could call him; and on the other side was y—everything which was called the world. And two sides of the equation always were trying to keep more or less in balance and never quite managed it. Perhaps the real balance only came with death. (Perhaps that was what Koheleth in his fine disillusioned mind was thinking when he wrote "The living know that they shall die; but the dead know not anything.") But, this side of death, the two halves of the equation tried always to be in balance. If the x side changed and he Ish felt within him the pressure of some gland or if he suffered shock or if there was even something so simple as that he grew bored, then he did something, and that changed the other side of the equation, if only a little, and then there was again a temporary balance. But if on the other hand, the world outside changed, if there was a catastrophe wiping out the human race, or if merely it should stop raining, then the x side, being Ish, would also have to change, and that would mean more action, and then there would be again a temporary balance. And who could say whether in the long run one side or the other side of the equation began more of the actions?

Then, before he really thought what he was doing, he had risen to his feet, and on second thought he knew that he had done so because again a feeling of desire had stirred within him. The equation had got out of balance, and he had risen restlessly to set it right again, and already he was affecting the world because Princess had leaped up at his rising and was wandering about the room. Yet at the same time he heard the rain beat a little harder against the window. Then he looked up at it to see what was happening. And so the world had also pressed in upon him and caused him to do something. And after that he set out to get himself some supper.

The almost complete removal of man, though in some ways an unprecedented earthly catastrophe, had not in the slightest affected the earth's relation to the sun, or the sizes and locations of the oceans and continents, or any other factor influencing the weather. Therefore, the first autumn storm which swept down from the Aleutians upon the coast of California was ordinary and conventional. Its moisture extinguished the forest-fires; its raindrops washed from the atmosphere the particles of smoke and dust. Behind it a brisk wind swept down cool and crystal-clear air from the northwest. The temperature dropped sharply.

Ish stirred in his sleep, and gradually came to consciousness. He was cold. "The other side has changed," he thought, and pulled up another blanket. He grew warm. "O prince's daughter!" he thought dreamily. "Thy breasts are like two . . ." And he drifted to sleep.

In the morning the house was chilly. He wore a sweater as he got himself his breakfast. He considered building a fire in the fireplace, but the cooler weather had also made him feel more active, and so he thought that he would not stay indoors much that day.

After breakfast he stood on the front porch to drink in the view. As always after one of these storms, the air was clear. The wind had died down. The red towers of the Golden Gate Bridge, miles away, stood against the blue sky, as if close enough to touch. He turned a little toward the north to look at the peak of Tamalpais, and suddenly started. Between him and the mountain, on this side of the Bay, a thin column of smoke rose straight up through the calm air, a slight wisp, the kind of smoke-column that should come from a small fire, particularly from one burning in a fireplace and ascending through a chimney. It might, he realized, have been rising there a hundred times before when he had looked out, but in the smoky and misty atmosphere he would not have noticed it. Now it was like a signpost.

Of course it might be a fire burning from some natural cause without any human being in its vicinity. He had investigated many smokes like that with no results. But that was not so likely now, because the rain would have smothered such fires.

In any case it could not be more than a couple of miles off, and his first thought was to jump into the station-wagon and investigate. That would cause no more harm than the loss of a few minutes for which he had no particular use anyway. But something stopped him. His attempts to establish human contact had not been rewarding. That old shyness rose up within him, as it had sometimes in the old days when the thought of attending a dance would put him into a sweat. He began to temporize, just as he used to do when he said that he had a great deal of work to do and so buried himself in a book instead of going to the dance.

Did Crusoe really want to be rescued from his desert island where he was lord of all that he surveyed? That was a question that people had asked. But even if Crusoe had been the kind of man who wanted to escape, to renew contacts with other people, that would not mean that he himself, Ish, was such a person. Perhaps he would cherish his island. Basically, perhaps, he feared human entanglements.

Almost in panic, as if fleeing from a temptress, he called Princess, got into the car, and drove off in the opposite direction.

He spent most of the day wandering restlessly through the hills. At times he observed what the rain had done to the roads. By now there was no longer that hard and fast line between road and what was not road. Leaves had dropped from the cold of the autumn and the high winds. Little dead branches had blown off, and fallen on the pavement. Here and there a washing stream of water had left a delta-like deposit of dirt and gravel. Once, very far off, he heard—or thought he heard—the bay of a pack of dogs. But he did not see them, and before the end of the afternoon he was back home again.

When he looked out toward the mountain, he could see no smoke against the sky. He had a certain sense of relief, and yet an even stronger sense of disappointment, now that he had a chance to think it over.

That was the way. When the opportunity was at your hand, you did not dare to seize it. When the opportunity was lost, it became precious. The other side of the equation had changed, and he had adjusted by running away. Of course, he might see the smoke again the next morning, but then again he might not. Perhaps that human being, whoever it was, had merely been passing through that way, and could never be found again.

He felt a quick rebound of excitement, at opporunity regranted, when he looked out in the early darkness after supper, and suddenly saw a faint but unmistakable light. He hesitated no longer. Now, instead of temporizing, he called Princess, got into the car, and drove in that direction.

It was a slow process. His seeing the light must mean merely that the windows of that house happened to face his porch; probably he could not have seen it at all before the storm had blown down most of the leaves. As soon as he left the house, he could no longer see the light. He drove back and forth along the streets for half an hour, finally relocated it, drove slowly down the right street and past the proper house. The shades had been pulled, but there was light shining through, even illuminating the street a little. It was bright, probably from a gasoline lamp.

He brought the car to a stop on the opposite side of the street, and waited a moment. Apparently, whoever was inside the house had not heard the motor. For a moment still he hesitated, almost ready now to put the car into gear again and slide off undiscovered. Yet, from some deeper drive within him, he leaned forward, and half opened the car door as if to get out. Suddenly Princess leaped by him, and ran toward the house with a fury of barking. She must have scented whoever was there. With a sudden curse, he got out, and started to walk after her. She had tipped his hand, this time, for certain. He hesitated again, suddenly realizing he was unarmed. Yet to advance against the house carrying a gun was not a good opening. Without much thought he reached back into the car, and grabbed his old hammer. Holding it in his hand, he advanced after the dog. In the window of the house he saw a shadow move.

When he had gained the sidewalk, the house-door opened a few inches, and suddenly the beam of a flashlight caught him. He could see nothing beyond it. He stopped, waiting for what the other person would have to say. Princess scuttled back, suddenly silent. Ish had the uncomfortable feeling that whoever was keeping him covered with the flashlight had him covered also with a gun held in the other hand. With the light in his eyes, he was blinded. This had been a crazy thing to do, he thought; an approach under cover of darkness always looked suspicious, and made people nervous. At least he was glad that he had shaved that morning, and that his clothes looked moderately clean.

There was a long pause. He stood waiting for the sharply barked question—the inevitable, if slightly ridiculous, "Who are you?" or else for that curt order, "Put up your hands!" That was why he had a sudden gasp of surprise when a woman's voice came with an affirmation: "That's a beautiful dog!"

There was a momentary silence, the memory of the voice in his ears was gentle and low, with a touch of some soft accent in it. At the sound he felt warm feelings rising up within him.

Now the light fell from his eyes, illuminating a path ahead of him, and Princess bounded up through the beam of light, her tail wagging in joy. The door of the house moved open wide, and against the dim light behind her he saw a woman on her knees patting the dog. He walked up toward her, still with the hammer dangling ridiculously but comfortably from his hand.

Then Princess, in a sudden flurry of excitement, burst away and went tearing into the house. The woman leaped up with an exclamation, half-screamed, half-laughed, and also dashed in. "My God, she must have a cat!" thought Ish, and rushed after her.

But when he arrived in the living-room, Princess was merely dashing around the table and smelling at the chairs, and the woman was standing erect beside a gasoline lamp sheltering it against being overthrown by the excited dog.

She was above middle height, brunette, not very young—no mere girl, certainly, but a fully developed woman.

She glanced at the antics of the scampering dog and laughed, and the sound of laughter was like something remembered from Paradise long ago. She turned to him, and he saw the flash of white teeth in the dark face. Then suddenly a barrier burst within him, and he laughed joyously.

After a moment she spoke again, neither questioning nor demanding. "It's good to see someone." This time Ish replied, but he could think of nothing better than an apology for the ridiculous hammer which still dangled from his hand. "Pardon me for bringing this thing in," he said, and he set it down on the floor upon its head with the handle sticking stiffly into the air.

"Don't worry," she said, "I understand. I went through it too—having to have something around to make you feel comfortable. Like a pocket-piece or a rabbit-foot, you remember. We're still about the same as we used to be, all of us."

After the sudden release of the laughter, he was trembling. All his body seemed growing weak. He felt, almost physically, more barriers breaking—those necessary barriers of defense, built up through the months of loneliness and desperation. He must touch another human being, and he put forward his hand in the old conventional gesture of the handshake. She took it, and doubtless as she noticed his trembling, she drew him toward a chair and almost pushed him into it. As he sat down, she patted his shoulder lightly.

She spoke again, once more neither questioning nor commanding: "I'll get you something to eat."

He did not protest, though he had just eaten heartily. But he knew that behind her quiet affirmation lay something more than any call of the body for food. There was need now for the symbolic eating together, that first common bond of human beings—the sitting at the same table, the sharing of the bread and salt.

Now they were sitting opposite each other. They ate a little, more in symbol than in reality. There was fresh bread. "I made it myself," she said, "but it's getting hard to find flour now that's got no weevils in it." There was no butter, but honey and jam for the bread, and a bottle of red wine.

And now, like a child, he began to talk. This was nothing like that time when he had sat with Milt and Ann on Riverside Drive. Then the barriers had still been up. Now, for the first time, he talked of all those days. He showed even the little scar of the fangs on his hand and the larger scars where he had slashed himself to apply the suction-pump. He told of his fear and of his flight and of the Great Loneliness that he had never quite dared face or imagine. And as he talked, she often said, "Yes, I know. Yes, I remember that, too. Tell me more."

As for her, she had seen the catastrophe itself. She had faced more than he had, and yet he could see that she had come through better than he. She talked little, seeming to have no need, but she drew him on.

As he talked with her, he knew now at last that this, at least as far as he was concerned, was no mere casual meeting—or passing moment. In this lay all the future. Since the disaster he had seen men and women here and there, and no one before had ever held him. Perhaps time had healed him. More likely, she herself was different.

Yet she was a woman. As the minutes slipped by, he sensed that basic reality more and more, with an intensity that made him tremble. As between man and man the breaking of bread was the reality; the shared table, all the symbol needed. But as between man and woman there must be still more, in reality and in symbol, a further sharing.

They realized suddenly that neither knew the other's name although each had been calling the dog Princess.

"Isherwood," he said. "That was my mother's maiden name and so she stuck it on me. Bad, wasn't it? Everybody called me 'Ish'."

"I'm Em!" she said. "Emma, that is, of course. Ish and Em! We won't get very far writing poetry about that combination!" And she laughed. And they laughed together.

Laughter—that was another sharing! And yet it was not the final one. There were ways these things were done. He had known men who could do them, had seen them at work. But he, Ish, was not the right kind. All those qualities which had permitted him to be by himself and survive through the bad days, alone—all those qualities now came up to work against him. And he sensed too, very deeply, that they would be wrong. The old methods had worked in the days when there were girls in every cocktail-bar, looking for adventure. But now such methods were not right, he knew, and knew deeply—at this time, when the vast city stretched away empty in all directions outside of the windows and all the ways of the world had vanished and this woman had lived through all the catastrophe and the fear and the loneliness and now had come out on the other side, still with courage in her eyes, and affirmation, and laughter.

For a wild moment he had an idea that they might say some kind of marriage vows. Quakers could marry themselves. Why couldn't others? They could stand up together, and face toward the east where the morning sun would rise. And then he sensed that the mere babbling of words was in itself much more dishonest even than a straightforward feeling for the knee under the table. He realized that he had been silent for what might have been a full minute. She was looking across at him with level calm eyes, and he knew that she read his thoughts.

In his embarrassment he rose suddenly to his feet, upsetting the chair as he got up. Then the table between them had ceased to be a symbol joining them together and now held them apart. He stepped from behind it, and across toward her as she rose up too. And then there was the softness of her body against his.

O Song of Songs! Thine eyes, my love, are gentle, and the fullness of thy lips is soft and firm. Thy neck is ivory, and the smoothness of thy shoulders like warm ivory. The softness of thy breasts against me is like fine wool. Thy thighs are firm and strong like the cedars. O Song of Songs!

She had gone now, into the inner room. He sat, still with breath and heart quick, tense and waiting. He had only one fear now. In a world where there were no doctors and even no other women, how could anyone risk the chance? But she had gone. He realized that she, too, in her great affirmation, would consider this also and care for it.

O Song of Songs. My love, thy bed is fragrant as boughs of the pine tree, and thy body is warm. Thou art Ashtoreth. Thou art Aphrodite, that keepest the gate of Love. Now my strength is upon me. Now the rivers are pent up. Now is my hour. Oh, receive me in thine infinitude.

Why did the Gospels seem "strangely unsatisfying" to Ish in his present situation? Why did Ecclesiastes and the Song of Songs suddenly seem more relevant to him? Discuss the notion of "sharing" that runs through Ish's head during his first meeting with Em. What does Stewart achieve through his use of italicized passages echoing the Song of Songs?

===

PASSING AWAY

Christina Rossetti

Passing away, saith the World, passing away:
Chances, beauty, and youth, sapped day by day:
Thy life never continueth in one stay.
Is the eye waxen dim, is the dark hair changing to grey
That hath won neither laurel nor bay?
I shall clothe myself in Spring and bud in May:
Thou, root-stricken, shalt not rebuild thy decay
On my bosom for aye.
Then I answered: Yea.

Passing away, saith my Soul, passing away:
With its burden of fear and hope, of labour and play,
Hearken what the past doth witness and say:

Rust in thy gold, a moth is in thine array,
A canker is in thy bud, thy leaf must decay.
At midnight, at cockcrow, at morning, one certain day
Lo, the Bridegroom shall come and shall not delay;
Watch thou and pray.
Then I answered: Yea.

Passing away, saith my God, passing away:
Winter passeth after the long delay:
New grapes on the vine, new figs on the tender spray,
Turtle calleth turtle in Heaven's May.
Though I tarry, wait for Me, trust Me, watch and pray:
Arise, come away, night is past and lo it is day,
My love, My sister, My spouse, thou shalt hear Me say—
Then I answered: Yea.

In what way do many of these lines reflect the attitudes you found in Ecclesiastes? What traces of the Song of Songs do you find? In answering this question, consider why "My" is capitalized in referring to the "Bridegroom." Who is this "Bridegroom"? In what way is the Christian interpretation of the Song of Songs used to mitigate the cynicism of these passages?

WHITHER THOU GOEST

(The Book of Ruth)

Now it came to pass in the days when the judges ruled, that there was a famine in the land. And a certain man of Bethlehem-judah went to sojourn in the country of Moab, he, and his wife, and his two sons. And the name of the man was Elimelech, and the name of his wife Naomi, and the name of his two sons Mahlon and Chilion, Ephrathites of Bethlehem-judah. And they came into the country of Moab, and continued there. And Elimelech Naomi's husband died; and she was left, and her two sons. And they took them wives of the women of Moab; the name of the one was Orpah, and the name of the other Ruth: and they dwelt there about ten years. And Mahlon and Chilion died also both of them; and the woman was left of her two sons and her husband.

Then she arose with her daughters-in-law, that she might return from the country of Moab: for she had heard in the country of Moab how that the Lord had visited his people in giving them bread. Wherefore she went forth out of the place where she was, and her two daughters-in-law with her; and they went on the way to return unto the land of Judah.

And Naomi said unto her two daughters-in-law, "Go, return each to her mother's house: the Lord deal kindly with you, as ye have dealt with the dead, and with me. The Lord grant you that ye may find rest, each of you in the house of her husband."

Then she kissed them; and they lifted up their voice, and wept. And they said unto her, "Surely we will return with thee unto thy people."

And Naomi said, "Turn again, my daughters: why will ye go with me? Are there yet any more sons in my womb, that they may be your husbands? Turn again, my daughters, go your way; for I am too old to have a husband. If I should say, I have hope, if I should have a husband also tonight, and should also bear sons, would ye tarry for them till they were grown? Would ye stay for them from having husbands? Nay, my daughters; for it grieveth me much for your sakes that the hand of the Lord is gone out against me."

And they lifted up their voice, and wept again: and Orpah kissed her mother-in-law; but Ruth clave unto her. And she said, "Behold, thy sister-in-law is gone back unto her people, and unto her gods: return thou after thy sister-in-law."

And Ruth said, "Entreat me not to leave thee, or to return from following after thee: for whither thou goest, I will go; and where thou lodgest, I will lodge: thy people shall be my people, and thy God my God: where thou diest, will I die, and there will I be buried: the Lord do so to me, and more also, if aught but death part thee and me."

When she saw that she was steadfastly minded to go with her, then she left speaking unto her.

So they two went until they came to Bethlehem. And it came to pass, when they were come to Bethlehem, that all the city was moved about them, and they said, "Is this Naomi?"

And she said unto them, "Call me not Naomi, call me Mara: for the Almighty hath dealt very bitterly with me. I went out full, and the Lord hath brought me home again empty: why then call ye me Naomi, seeing the Lord hath testified against me, and the Almighty hath afflicted me?"

So Naomi returned, and Ruth the Moabitess, her daughter-in-law, with her, which returned out of the country of Moab: and they came to Bethlehem in the beginning of barley harvest.

And Naomi had a kinsman of her husband's, a mighty man of wealth, of the family of Elimelech; and his name was Boaz. And Ruth the Moabitess said unto Naomi, "Let me now go to the field, and glean ears of corn after him in whose sight I shall find grace."

And she said unto her, "Go, my daughter."

And she went, and came, and gleaned in the field after the reapers: and her hap was to light on a part of the field belonging unto Boaz, who was of the kindred of Elimelech.

And, behold, Boaz came from Bethlehem, and said unto the reapers, "The Lord be with you." And they answered him, "The Lord bless thee."

Then said Boaz unto his servant that was set over the reapers, "Whose damsel is this?"

And the servant that was set over the reapers answered and said, "It is the Moabitish damsel that came back with Naomi out of the country of Moab: and she said, 'I pray you, let me glean and gather after the reapers among the sheaves': so she came, and hath continued even from the morning until now, that she tarried a little in the house."

Then said Boaz unto Ruth, "Hearest thou not, my daughter? Go not to glean in another field, neither go from hence, but abide here fast by my maidens: let thine eyes be on the field that they do reap, and go thou after them: have I not charged the young men that they shall not touch thee? And when thou art athirst, go unto the vessels, and drink of that which the young men have drawn."

Then she fell on her face, and bowed herself to the ground, and said unto him, "Why have I found grace in thine eyes, that thou shouldest take knowledge of me, seeing I am a stranger?"

And Boaz answered and said unto her, "It hath fully been showed me all that thou hast done unto thy mother-in-law since the death of thine husband; and how thou hast left thy father and thy mother, and the land of thy nativity, and art come unto a people which thou knewest not heretofore. The Lord recompense thy work, and a full reward be given thee of the Lord God of Israel, under whose wings thou art come to trust."

Then she said, "Let me find favour in thy sight, my lord; for that thou hast comforted me, and for that thou hast spoken friendly unto thine handmaid, though I be not like unto one of thine handmaidens."

And Boaz said unto her, "At mealtime come thou hither, and eat of the bread, and dip thy morsel in the vinegar."

And she sat beside the reapers: and he reached her parched corn, and she did eat, and was sufficed, and left.

And when she was risen up to glean, Boaz commanded his young men, saying, "Let her glean even among the sheaves, and reproach her not: and let fall also some of the handfuls of purpose for her, and leave them, that she may glean them, and rebuke her not."

So she gleaned in the field until even, and beat out that she had gleaned: and it was about an ephah of barley. And she took it up, and she went into the city; and her mother-in-law saw what she had gleaned: and she brought forth, and gave to her that she had reserved after she was sufficed.

And her mother-in-law said unto her, "Where hast thou gleaned today? And where wroughtest thou? Blessed be he that did take knowledge of thee."

And she showed her mother-in-law with whom she had wrought, and said, "The man's name with whom I wrought today is Boaz."

And Naomi said unto her daughter-in-law, "Blessed be he of the Lord, who hath not left off his kindness to the living and to the dead." And Naomi said unto her, "The man is near of kin unto us, one of our next kinsmen."

And Ruth the Moabitess said, "He said unto me also, 'Thou shalt keep fast by my young men, until they have ended all my harvest.'"

And Naomi said unto Ruth her daughter-in-law, "It is good, my daughter, that thou go out with his maidens, that they meet thee not in any other field."

So she kept fast by the maidens of Boaz to glean unto the end of barley harvest and of wheat harvest, and dwelt with her mother-in-law.

Then Naomi her mother-in-law said unto her, "My daughter, shall I not seek rest for thee, that it may be well with thee? And now is not Boaz of our kindred, with whose maidens thou wast? Behold, he winnoweth barley tonight in the threshingfloor. Wash thyself therefore, and anoint thee, and put thy raiment upon thee, and get thee down to the floor: but make not thyself known unto the man, until he shall have done eating and drinking. And it shall be, when he lieth down, that thou shalt mark the place where he shall lie, and thou shalt go in, and uncover his feet, and lay thee down; and he will tell thee what thou shalt do."

And she said unto her, "All that thou sayest unto me I will do." And she went down unto the floor, and did according to all that her mother-in-law bade her.

And when Boaz had eaten and drunk, and his heart was merry, he went to lie down at the end of the heap of corn: and she came softly, and uncovered his feet, and laid her down.

And it came to pass at midnight, that the man was afraid, and turned himself: and, behold, a woman lay at his feet. And he said, "Who art thou?"

And she answered, "I am Ruth thine handmaid: spread therefore thy skirt over thine handmaid; for thou art a near kinsman."

And he said, "Blessed be thou of the Lord, my daughter: for thou hast showed more kindness in the latter end than at the beginning inasmuch as thou followedst not young men, whether poor or rich. And now, my daughter, fear not; I will do to thee all that thou requirest: for all the city of my people doth know that thou art a virtuous woman. And now it is true that I am thy near kinsman: howbeit there is a kinsman nearer than I. Tarry this night, and it shall be in the morning, that if he will perform unto thee the part of a kinsman, well, let him do the kinsman's part: but if he will not do the part of a kinsman to thee, then will I do the part of a kinsman to thee, as the Lord liveth: lie down until the morning."

And she lay at his feet until the morning: and she rose up before one could know another.

And he said, "Let it not be known that a woman came into the floor." Also he said, "Bring the veil that thou hast upon thee, and hold it." And when she held it, he measured six measures of barley, and laid it on her: and she went into the city.

And when she came to her mother-in-law, she said, "Who art thou, my daughter?"

And she told her all that the man had done to her. And she said, "These six measures of barley gave he me; for he said to me, 'Go not empty unto thy mother-in-law.' "

Then she said, "Sit still, my daughter, until thou know how the matter will fall: for the man will not be in rest, until he have finished the thing this day."

Then went Boaz up to the gate, and sat him down there: and, behold, the kinsman of whom Boaz spoke came by, unto whom he said, "Ho, such a one! Turn aside, sit down here." And he turned aside, and sat down.

And he took ten men of the elders of the city, and said, "Sit ye down here." And they sat down.

And he said unto the kinsman, "Naomi, that is come again out of the country of Moab, selleth a parcel of land, which was our brother Elimelech's: and I thought to advertise thee, saying, 'Buy it before the inhabitants, and before the elders of my people. If thou wilt redeem it, redeem it': but if thou wilt not redeem it, then tell me, that I may know: for there is none to redeem it besides thee; and I am after thee."

And he said, "I will redeem it."

Then said Boaz, "What day thou buyest the field of the hand of Naomi, thou must buy it also of Ruth the Moabitess, the wife of the dead, to raise up the name of the dead upon his inheritance."

And the kinsman said, "I cannot redeem it for myself, lest I mar mine own inheritance: redeem thou my right to thyself; for I cannot redeem it."

Now this was the manner in former time in Israel concerning redeeming and concerning changing, for to confirm all things: a man plucked off his shoe, and gave it to his neighbor, and this was a testimony in Israel.

Therefore the kinsman said unto Boaz, "Buy it for thee." So he drew off his shoe.

And Boaz said unto the elders, and unto all the people, "Ye are witnesses this day, that I have bought all that was Elimelech's, and all that was Chilion's and Mahlon's, of the hand of Naomi. Moreover Ruth the Moabitess, the wife of Mahlon, have I purchased to be my wife, to raise up the name of the dead upon his inheritance, that the name of the dead be not cut off from among his brethren, and from the gate of his place: ye are witnesses this day."

And all the people that were in the gate, and the elders, said, "We are witnesses. The Lord make the woman that is come into thine house like Rachel and like Leah, which two did build the house of Israel: and do thou worthily in Ephratah, and be famous in Bethlehem: and let thy house be like the house of Pharez, whom Tamar bare unto Judah, of the seed which the Lord shall give thee of this young woman."

So Boaz took Ruth, and she was his wife: and when he went in unto her, the Lord gave her conception, and she bare a son.

And the women said unto Naomi, "Blessed be the Lord, which hath not left thee this day without a kinsman, that his name may be famous in Israel. And he shall be unto thee a restorer of thy life, and a nourisher of thine old age: for thy daughter-in-law which loveth thee, which is better to see than seven sons, hath borne him."

And Naomi took the child, and laid it in her bosom, and became nurse unto it. And the women her neighbors gave it a name, saying, "There is a son born to Naomi." And they called him Obed: he is the father of Jesse, the father of David."

[*Ruth 1–4:17*]

IN THE FIELDS OF BOAZ

Irving Fineman

They rode their donkeys, the dove-gray and the milk-white one, through the dark narrow streets of Bethlehem, quiet and empty in the festival night, past the windows of houses all cheerfully lighted for the Passover. And they crossed the market place, lying deserted now between the two city gates with their tall, massive towers, one round and one square, where sentinels stood watch on the heaps of round stones piled up for missiles in case of attack and for the execution of judgment upon evildoers condemned to stoning.

And they rode out through the right hand gate, the square stone

Gate of the Judges before which stood the bench of the judges; and, after following a stony path that ran close outside the city wall, the two women came to the lightless ruin of a house on a hill. The late-rising moon sent beams through its broken walls; the stars shone down through holes in its sagging roof. A jackal howled, leaped out through a window and trotted away as they approached. When Naomi unlocked and opened the door a flock of bats flew out. And the rotted door which had come away from its hinges could not be closed again.

Then Ruth had to plead with frightened Naomi to enter after her. And in the moonlit darkness it was Ruth who made the bed on which the two weary women lay down. And she stayed awake, though her heart and her eyelids were heavy with sadness, talking bravely of what they would do on the morrow, until the old woman ceased her trembling. Then as they lay there in the darkness they heard the distant voices of men calling to each other, and Ruth asked, "What is that?"

And Naomi said: "They are gathering the omer, the first fruits of the harvest, which are set aside for an offering to the Lord God of Israel. For the men of Israel though they no longer sacrifice their first-born sons yet give up to their God the first fruits of their fields."

Then Ruth rose up from her bed and went to the broken door and looked out; and she saw in the valley below the men moving about in the moonlit fields, swinging sickles and scythes; and some were calling, and others answered the callers' questions, their strong voices rising up in the night to the moonlit heavens:

"Is the sun set?"
"Yea!"
"Is this a sickle?"
"Yea!"
"Is this a basket?"
"Yea!"
"Shall we reap?"
"Reap!"
"Let us reap for the Lord!"
And once again from a further field:
"Is the sun set?"
"Yea!"

Over and over they called and answered as they gathered. And there was a comfort in the manly strength of their peaceful voices. And Ruth lay down again beside Naomi who had fallen asleep; and she lay listening a long time to those strange reapers. She lay looking out through the open door at the strange moonlit land, its hills so different from the wide wild plains of Moab, her dark eyes filled with wonder before her destiny . . . until she, too, slept.

The two women rose up at dawn. The day was bright and they set to work with a will, cleansing the long-neglected house and making such repairs as they could. They took two water jars and brought water up from the well at the foot of the hill. They washed the dust-covered pottery and utensils in the kitchen; they heated the oven for baking, ground grain in Naomi's stone quern, and baked their own unleavened bread.

Naomi found her old loom and instructed Ruth in its use; and Ruth said she would weave woolen curtains for the door and the windows through which the chill night wind had blown in upon them unhindered. And as they worked Naomi sang for Ruth that old Israelite song she had promised to teach her:

> *A woman of valor who can find?*
> *Her worth is far above rubies.*
> *The heart of her husband trusteth in her,*
> *And he shall lack for nothing.*
> *She doeth him good and not evil*
> *All the days of her life.*
> *She seeketh out wool and flax*
> *And worketh well with her hands.*
> *She is like the fine ships*
> *Bringing food from afar. . . .*

And hearing their singing, the neighboring women on their way down to the well stopped to greet Naomi, and they spread the news of her coming at the well so that many others came up to welcome Naomi back to Bethlehem, and they brought her gifts of food; but all stared with suspicion upon the strange woman—the Moabitess whom Naomi had brought in among them, to become one of them.

And on that first day and in the days that followed, when Ruth took a tall jar and, carrying it gracefully upon her head in the manner of the women of Moab, went down to the well for water, she was looked upon curiously by the women gathered and gossiping there and by the children playing there with the fountain of water; but none spoke to her. And when she spoke to them none answered her, and some even mocked amongst themselves at her strange way of speaking.

One day Reba the daughter of Tobias was there, and she began speaking of Ruth to the others, saying: "Can it be that there are no men remaining in Moab, that their women must come with their golden charms to capture the men of Israel? . . ." until Ruth silenced her with a glance from her dark eyes that boded no good for Reba if she continued. Then Ruth spoke forthrightly: "Rest assured that I have no designs on the men of Israel, having left the husband I loved in a grave in Moab. It is for his memory alone, because they once pleased him, that I wear these charms. Surely you who live here under the wing of the Almighty God of Israel need have no fear of Ashtar, a goddess of Moab. And I came into the land of Israel because Mahlon weaned me away from the ways of Moab and taught me to love the ways of Israel, which he had kept in his heart. And you who are Israelites merely because you were born so have no cause to scorn one who has chosen to be an Israelite." Then she took up her water jar and left the chastened women at the well.

But it was more difficult to deal with the children playing about the well, who had been told by young Joel of the evil things he heard spoken about the Moabitess in the house of his grandfather, Tobias.

Led by Joel the children would follow after Ruth up the hill, whispering and pointing and mimicking her speech, until once she stopped and called them to her saying softly: "Come and speak to me, children, for I, too, am now one of the children of Israel, and I dearly wish I had children of my own like you, especially a lad like thee, Joel, whom I would teach to become a good Israelite, to learn the words of Moses and to obey the laws of the Lord God of Israel which tell thee to be good to the stranger among you."

"And would you teach him," asked Joel, "to sling stones as you did at the wild beasts on the way from Moab?"

"Indeed I would," answered Ruth, "and I will teach thee, too, if thou wishest." And Joel watched with delight as she took some tufts of wool left by passing sheep on the nearby thorn bushes and twisted them into cords and braided the cords into a stout strand flat and wide in the middle from which she made him a sling. And she showed him how to loop the ends over a finger and how she could hit a tree with a smooth round stone, which Joel promptly did also, to his own great wonder and satisfaction and the awe of the other children.

"Now let the Philistine giants come!" Joel cried, letting another stone fly at the tree with a resounding crash. And picking up still another stone he said: "And this is how I shall fight any raiding Jebusites or Ammonites or Moabites——" Whereupon he stopped and looked in confusion at Ruth.

And she said: "To be sure, whoever they are, if they come not with peace in their hearts but to molest thee, then sling it with all thy might!"

But, alas, on this try Joel's stone went wild and flew down to the well where it smashed the great jar of water which his aunt Reba had filled, and it deluged her dress. And then there was a great outcry from Reba and all the women with her at the well, calling the children away from the woman of Moab.

Yet thereafter, the innocent eyes of the children, having looked into the dark eyes of Ruth and seen there the truth and the goodness of her love for them and her longing for their love, they trooped after her up the hill, no longer whispering and pointing, but holding to her skirts and laughing and talking to her as if she were their mother. And she made them strange little Moabite cakes, crescents of crushed barley; and for the girls she shaped and baked and painted cunning clay dolls, and rattles of clay for the little ones. But their mothers, the neighboring women, took from the children the cakes and the toys for fear of some Moabite magic in the figures she made, thinking they might be figures of evil Ashtar.

And the heart of Naomi was saddened when she saw this; she was sorely troubled for the plight of Ruth in the face of that ancient fear and hatred of all Moab in the heart of Israel. And she was angered at the women, her neighbors, who chided her for bringing a Moabitess in to live among them; and because of her anger the women left off coming to Naomi and bringing her gifts of food. Then Naomi became sorely troubled about her own plight; and one day when Ruth gave to the hungry children, who despite their mothers still came running after her, some cakes she had made out of their scanty store of grain Naomi admonished Ruth, saying: "Where are we now to get our own livelihood?"

But Ruth was undismayed. And she said: "Is not the sun shining bright on the land of Israel, and is not the Lord God of Israel a good and bountiful God? Perhaps if we prayed to him or made some sacrifice—"

They were sitting on the step before the broken door in the pleasant spring sunshine, grinding the last of their corn, Naomi feeding the grains into the quern while Ruth worked the heavy grindstone with her young arms.

"Have I not taught you," said Naomi impatiently, "that the Lord God of Israel, unlike the gods other men have made, is not to be moved by wishful prayers or even sacrifices, which he accepts as his due; he is good and bountiful to those who know his laws and keep them faithfully. But unfortunately it is sometimes very difficult to know what his laws are. Especially for a woman," she added bitterly. "And when a woman is married it would seem that she suffers alike for her husband's transgressions. Though I did not want my Elimelech to leave Israel yet here am I still suffering for his wrongdoing."

And Naomi was certain that the Lord had forsaken them forever. But Ruth would not be downcast and, having finished the grinding, she stood and looked down from the neglected land of Elimelech upon the rich fertile farms in the valley below, where the morning breeze stirred the shimmering green and yellow fields of young corn and wheat and ripe barley. And there rose up to them the crowing of cocks from the barnyards, the lowing of cattle, the bark of dogs, the braying of donkeys, and the shouts of men reaping the barley harvest, swinging their sickles of flint and gathering the grain into sheaves. And Ruth observed how women went after the harvesters, gleaning the fallen grain and reaping the corners of the fields which the men left uncut. "Are those the bondwomen of the master of the field?" she asked of Naomi.

"No," said Naomi. "It is a law among us, which Moses brought down from Mount Sinai, that the owner of the harvest may not take the gleanings thereof for himself. The law says: *And when ye reap the harvest of your land, thou shalt not wholly reap the corners of thy field, neither shalt thou gather the gleaning of thy harvest; thou shalt leave them for the poor, and for the stranger.*

Ruth said: "It is indeed a good and bountiful God whose law it is that men must provide for those among them who have not."

And Naomi said: "Indeed our law says further: *When thou reapest thine harvest in thy field, and hast forgot a sheaf in the field, thou shalt not go again to fetch it: it shall be for the stranger, for the fatherless, and for the widow: that the Lord Thy God may bless thee in all the work of thine hands. And when thou beatest thine olive tree, thou shalt not go over the boughs again: it shall be for the stranger, for the fatherless, and for the widow. And when thou gatherest the grapes of thy vineyard, thou shalt not glean it after thee: it shall be for the stranger, the fatherless, and the widow.*"

"And am I not all of these," said Ruth, "a stranger, fatherless, and a widow? So shall I go gleaning and shall bring barley that we may eat and thrive here, Naomi."

"But it is not seemly," said Naomi sharply, "for a woman of the family of Elimelech to go gleaning in the fields, else would I myself have gone down. And the men in the field may molest you."

Ruth said: "But didst thou not tell me that they think better of women than do the men of Moab?"

And Naomi said: "Perhaps I should have told you also that the difference between men lies less in what they do than in what they think.

And besides, did you not hear what Tobias said? The women of Bethlehem will speak ill of you."

"Let them speak," said Ruth, her dark eyes flashing. "They can say no worse of me than they now think." And Ruth said: "Let me now go down to the fields and glean after him in whose sight I shall find favor."

Naomi smiled then and said: "Sometimes it seems to me that you are not my daughter-in-law but the true daughter of my flesh and my spirit." And she kissed Ruth and said: "Go, my daughter," and gave her a large apron in which to gather the barley and pointed out to her the richest of the fields in the valley below. "Go there, my daughter," she said.

So Ruth got up on her milk-white donkey and rode down to the valley and went to that field which Naomi had shown her. And it happened to be one of the fields of Boaz; for cool-eyed Elias, who watched over his men, was standing within the entrance to the field, wearing the ram's horn at his belt with which he summoned the men. And Ruth got down from her donkey and went over to Elias and was relieved to see in his austere face that this was the kind of man who would not molest a woman. And she said to him: "Let me glean, I pray thee, and gather after the reapers among thy sheaves."

But his look upon her was not friendly, and Elias said sternly: "You are a Moabitess, are you not?"

Ruth nodded her head, being too fearful to speak.

And he said: "Our law requires of us that we do not forbid the stranger to glean. This is not a matter of kindness but of justice. I must let you in. But I counsel you not to divert the men in the field. And you had best take off those Moabite amulets; and you had best veil your face."

So Ruth, seeing that otherwise he would not let her in, removed the golden amulets from her forehead and put them in the pocket of her dress; and she veiled her face with the end of her black headcloth and entered quickly into the field and took her place with the women gleaning after the harvesters.

And among the harvesters who went stripped to the waist and sweating in the sun she saw Gibbor the Benjamite, the mighty young man who had come to sit beside her at the Passover feast in the house of Tobias; and his powerful chest was as hairy as his hands, a red fell covered his flesh. But Gibbor did not see Ruth, for he was hard at work at the head of the men, reaping faster than all the rest though he laughed and made light of the labor. He led them in the singing of songs as they worked:

Rise up, my love, my fair one,
And come away.

The men sang together as they moved forward upon the standing grain, swinging their scythes:

For, lo, the winter is past,
The rain is over and gone;
The flowers appear on the earth;
The time of the singing of birds is come,
And the voice of the turtle is heard in our land;
The fig tree ripeneth her green figs,
And the vines are in blossom
They give forth their fragrance,
Arise my love
And come away.

And Ruth worked hard and steadily, bending in the hot sun to gather the fallen grain, and moving forward with the women after the

Ruth Gleaning the Fields (c. 1950) by Ben Zion. PHOTOGRAPH ARCHIVES OF THE JEWISH THEOLOGICAL SEMINARY OF AMERICA, NEW YORK. FRANK DARMSTAEDTER.

men; and though the heat and the unaccustomed labor wearied her, though her arms and back ached, and the sun burnt her hands and the stubble cut her feet, she was happy and content as she saw the good barley heaped in her apron, for she persevered and gathered as much as the other, more practiced women.

They, for the most part, were older than Ruth, inured by time to the labor, burnt brown by the sun, and hardened by their unfortunate lot. Yet they spoke cheerfully to each other and chaffed the men whom they followed; and they too broke into song:

> *My beloved is white and ruddy,*
> > *Towering above ten thousand*
> *His head is as the most fine gold,*
> > *His locks are curled and black as the raven.*

And the men answered them singing:

> *Thou hast ravished my heart, my sister, my bride;*
> *Thou hast ravished my heart with one look of thine eyes.*

And again the women sang:

> *His eyes are like doves beside water brooks*
> > *Washed with milk and most fitly set,*
> *His cheeks are as beds of spices, as banks of sweet herbs*
> > *His lips are like lilies flowing with myrrh.*

And again the men answered:

> *How fair is thy love, my sister, my bride*
> > *How much better is thy love than wine,*
> *Thy lips, O my bride, are as honeycomb*
> > *Honey and milk are under thy tongue.*

Then one of the women working near by to Ruth and seeing that she was a newcomer and had not joined in the song, called to her saying: "You are a stranger here, are you not?" And Ruth saw that the woman lacked one hand, which had been hacked off at the wrist, though she gleaned very dexterously nonetheless.

"I have just lately come up into Judah," said Ruth.

"But why do you veil your face?" asked the woman. "Where are you from?"

And Ruth said hastily: "It is to keep my too tender skin from the sun."

Then the other laughed harshly and said: "When you have gleaned in the fields so long as I have you will cease caring for your skin, and no part of you will be tender. This is no place for the tender. You see this?" And she raised up the stump of her arm. "My husband was fighting another man harvesting in his field and my poor husband was getting the worst of it so I went to his aid and took hold of his adversary by the secret parts, which is against our law. So they cut off my hand; though my husband died of his wounds. Men put great store by their manhood. You'd think it was something holy—the way they safeguard it, and they give the Lord God a tiny bit of it at birth—when they are circumcised. It is their most precious sacrifice." And she laughed aloud. "Anyway I am no longer tender, I can tell you."

And it happened that Gibbor had stopped near by them to bind up a sheaf of grain and he heard the woman's laughter and the last of her talk. And Gibbor called out to the woman and said: "Do you not know, my little flower, why it is that you are no longer tender? It is because having no husband you lack for love, without which no woman remains tender."

And the woman answered him harshly: "I am no little flower; but you are a hairy bumble bee lighting wherever you can."

And Gibbor said: "It is because the sons of Benjamin are the sons of Rachel whom Jacob loved dearly that we are great lovers."

The woman said: "You are all alike whether sons of a son of Rachel whom Jacob loved or of Leah whom he did not love yet gave to her many sons. You are all alike wanting forever to display your precious manhood."

And Gibbor answered her, singing:

> *Thou hast ravished my heart, my sister, my bride;*
> *Thou hast ravished my heart with one look of thine eyes....*

And the woman answered him: "Sing rather of what *you* have ravished, O wolf of Benjamin!"

And Gibbor sang:

> *How fair and pleasant art thou, O love, for delights!*

And having finished binding the sheaf he approached the woman, still singing:

> *Come, my beloved, let us go forth into the field.*

But the woman rose up from her gleaning and said: "I want none of your idle song of love when I am gathering good barley. Go back to your reaping, Gibbor." And the other women working nearby laughed and pointed at him and cried: "Go back to your reaping, you left-handed son of Benjamin, you shall reap no women today."

And Gibbor was about to turn away from the one-handed woman when his eyes lighted upon the bent figure nearby her. And he saw that this woman was young and new to the field. So he came close to her and went around to look upon her face, but it was darkly veiled.

And it happened that Elias, the foreman, was going across the field and he saw Gibbor among the women, so he blew a blast on his ram's horn and called to Gibbor to return to his work and Gibbor returned to his place at the head of the reapers. But he looked back again and again at the young figure of that silent veiled stranger until, seeing that she was gleaning alone between two of the sheaves and that Elias was gone to meet Boaz, who had come to the entrance to the field, Gibbor went over to her and stood before her and said: "Who are you?"

She looked up at him and said nothing; but he saw above the black veil those dark eyes which had drawn him to her at the table of Tobias. And Gibbor put out his hairy left hand and lifted the veil from her face. "You are the Moabite woman who came with Naomi," he said, his avid eyes lighting. "And I have heard of your springtime revelry in Moab, of how the women there go up to the high place and give themselves freely to the men."

Ruth stood up before him.

"Surely," said Gibbor, "you will not deny me a kiss or two." And he put his two red-haired hands upon her.

And Ruth let fall the grain she had gathered and retreated from before him until she came up against one of the sheaves; but Gibbor pressed close upon her there, holding her to his hairy chest in his powerful arms while she struggled against him.

And Gibbor was intent upon having his way with Ruth so that he did not perceive that Boaz had come into the field to look upon the work of his young men. Boaz was riding his roan stallion, Yohfe, and he greeted the men as he came, saying: "The Lord be with you!" and they answered him, saying: "The Lord bless you!" And Elias was walking beside his horse.

And Boaz as he approached heard the struggling of Ruth with Gibbor and came upon them between the sheaves. And Boaz reached down from his horse and took Gibbor by the scruff of the neck and flung him away from Ruth, who turned and bowed her head and stood weeping against the sheaf so that Boaz could not see her face.

And Boaz was very angry, saying: "You know well, Gibbor, that I will have no one forced in my fields."

And Gibbor was angry, too, saying: "There is no king in Israel, and every man does what is right in his own eyes."

And Boaz answered: "But none are slaves here; neither women nor men."

And they might have come to blows had not cool-eyed Elias put a restraining hand upon the arm of Gibbor and said: "Go back to your labor," and Gibbor turned away and went among the reapers. Then Elias took the head of Yohfe, the horse of Boaz, and drew him away, saying: "Come, Boaz, there are still the flocks in the pasture to be seen."

And Boaz went on with Elias a little way, leaving Ruth by the sheaf of grain; but his eyes were drawn back to that forlorn figure as he listened to Elias, who asked: "Shall I send Gibbor away? With women in the field he behaves like an ox."

Then Boaz, smiling, said: "There is an old saying: '*Where there are no oxen the crib is clean; but much is got from the vigor of the ox.*'" And still looking back at that strange woman bending now to gather up the grain she had dropped, Boaz said: "It is not for me who am not lacking in lust to chastise Gibbor, who is not pleasing in the eyes of women and lacks a wife because of the curse our fathers put upon the sons of Benjamin."

Elias said: "Regardless of what Moses said, if I had my way women would not be let into the fields to glean, at least not while the men are working there. . . ." And he went on complaining of the trouble women made between men when they came in among them.

But Boaz was not listening to Elias. He reined in his horse, saying, "Wait, Yohfe; wait, my beauty." And he said to Elias, still looking backward: "Tell me, who is that young woman? Do I not know her?"

And Elias was loath to tell him: "It is Ruth, the strange woman that came with Naomi out of the country of Moab. She came down to the field and asked me to let her glean and she had been gleaning diligently since morning. It is time for the midday meal." And he raised the ram's horn to his lips and sounded a loud cheerful call, summoning the reapers to their food. And Elias said: "Let us go and eat, Boaz."

But Boaz gave no heed. "Ruth," he had heard, and was recalling how she had stood in the dark doorway of Tobias' house; and he wheeled his horse and left Elias and rode after Ruth who was walking away with her burden of grain. He called after her and she stood waiting until Yohfe came and halted nearby her. And Boaz said gently: "Do not go away to glean in another field. Stay here among the women and I shall see to it that no man molests you. And when you are thirsty go to the jars they have filled, and fear not."

Ruth dropped her dark veil as he spoke and she turned her tear-stained face up to Boaz, searching to see what had moved him toward her, but her eyelids fell before the strength of his manly gaze. "Why have I found grace in thy sight," she said softly, her words flowing slowly, "that thou shouldst take knowledge of me, seeing that I am a stranger?"

And Boaz said: "You did not observe me when you first arrived at the house of Tobias, my kinsman, but I observed you. And I heard what Naomi told of your loyalty to her, and how you left the land of your birth and came to live among us—a people strange to you." He looked upon her in silence, and then spoke again: "You are—" and he was about to put out his hand to touch her, but Boaz restrained himself and said: "You will be rewardèd by the Lord God of Israel, under whose wing you have come to take refuge."

Then Ruth said, "Let me find grace in thy sight, Boaz, for thou hast comforted me, thou hast spoken kindly to me though I am not a woman of thy people."

And Elias sounded his horn again, summoning Boaz to the midday meal. But Boaz was loath now to leave Ruth. "Come, eat with us," he said; and he got down off his horse and led Yohfe after him, and Ruth went with him, followed by the envious eyes and knowing glances of the others, the less favored women who were eating there in the field.

"A well-matched pair," said the one-handed woman.

"A Moabitess!" said another and spat on the ground beside her.

"A woman for all that," said the one-handed one.

But Ruth was content to be going beside the tall and well-favored man whose bearing was at once gentle and strong, whose look was at once proud and kindly, whose speech was at once warm and wise. And then, looking up at Boaz and observing his grave gray eyes and the raven-black hair glinting red where it curled on his brow and beard, it seemed to Ruth that indeed Naomi was right about the men of Israel, for never had Ruth seen his like in Moab.

And as they walked together Boaz spoke of the goodness of God who had made the richness of his burgeoning fields. And when they came to the pasture where his flocks were grazing, he stopped to look upon the woolly sheep with their gamboling lambs and the long-haired goats with their skipping kids, and he recited the sage advice of his old father Salmon who had left him this land:

> Be thou diligent to know the state of thy flocks,
>   and look well to thy herds;
> When the hay is mown, and the tender grass showeth itself,

> *and the herbs of the mountains are gathered in;*
> *The lambs will be for thy clothing,*
> *and the goats the price for a field;*
> *And there will be goats' milk enough for thy food,*
> *for the food of thy household,*
> *And maintenance for thy maidens. . . .*

And Ruth saw that Naomi had spoken truly: There were men in Israel who were indeed unlike the men of Moab. And Ruth felt for the first time that she was safe and secure in this strange land as she went beside Boaz toward the place where his men were gathered about the plentiful food which he had provided for them.

———————

Contrast the children's attitude toward Ruth with that of the women. How do you account for this difference in treatment? Why does Ruth feel that Naomi's God is so "good and beautiful"? How is other biblical material woven into the story? How does Boaz justify his interfering with Gibbor's "rights"? Explain Ruth's observation that there were "men in Israel who were indeed unlike the men of Moab." What aspect of the biblical story does Fineman emphasize in his account?

THOU ART A GRACIOUS GOD

(The Book of Jonah)

Now the word of the Lord came unto Jonah the son of Amittai, saying, "Arise, go to Nineveh, that great city, and cry against it; for their wickedness is come up before me."

But Jonah rose up to flee unto Tarshish from the presence of the Lord, and went down to Joppa; and he found a ship going to Tarshish: so he paid the fare thereof, and went down into it, to go with them unto Tarshish from the presence of the Lord.

But the Lord sent out a great wind into the sea, and there was a mighty tempest in the sea, so that the ship was like to be broken. Then the mariners were afraid, and cried every man unto his god, and cast forth the wares that were in the ship into the sea, to lighten it of them. But Jonah was gone down into the sides of the ship; and he lay, and was fast asleep.

So the shipmaster came to him, and said unto him, "What meanest thou, O sleeper? Arise, call upon thy God, if so be that God will think upon us, that we perish not."

And they said every one to his fellow, "Come, and let us cast lots, that we may know for whose cause this evil is upon us." So they cast lots, and the lot fell upon Jonah.

Then said they unto him, "Tell us, we pray thee, for whose cause this evil is upon us? What is thine occupation? And whence comest thou? What is thy country? And of what people art thou?"

And he said unto them, "I am a Hebrew; and I fear the Lord, the God of heaven, which hath made the sea and the dry land."

Then were the men exceedingly afraid, and said unto him, "Why hast thou done this?" For the men knew that he fled from the presence of the Lord, because he had told them.

Then said they unto him, "What shall we do unto thee, that the sea may be calm unto us?" for the sea wrought, and was tempestuous.

And he said unto them, "Take me up, and cast me forth into the sea; so shall the sea be calm unto you: for I know that for my sake this great tempest is upon you."

Nevertheless the men rowed hard to bring it to the land; but they could not: for the sea wrought, and was tempestuous against them. Wherefore they cried unto the Lord, and said, "We beseech thee, O Lord, we beseech thee, let us not perish for this man's life, and lay not upon us innocent blood: for thou, O Lord, hast done as it pleased thee."

So they took up Jonah, and cast him forth into the sea: and the sea ceased from her raging. Then the men feared the Lord exceedingly, and offered a sacrifice unto the Lord, and made vows.

Now the Lord had prepared a great fish to swallow up Jonah. And Jonah was in the belly of the fish three days and three nights.

Then Jonah prayed unto the Lord his God out of the fish's belly, and said,

> "I cried by reason of mine affliction unto the Lord, and he heard me;
> Out of the belly of hell cried I, and thou heardest my voice.
> For thou hadst cast me into the deep, in the midst of the seas;
> And the floods compassed me about:
> All thy billows and thy waves passed over me.
> Then I said, 'I am cast out of thy sight;
> Yet I will look again toward thy holy temple.'
> The waters compassed me about, even to the soul:
> The depth closed me round about,
> The weeds were wrapped about my head.
> I went down to the bottoms of the mountains;
> The earth with her bars was about me for ever:
> Yet hast thou brought up my life from corruption, O Lord my God.
> When my soul fainted within me I remembered the Lord:
> And my prayer came in unto thee, into thine holy temple.
> They that observe lying vanities forsake their own mercy.
> But I will sacrifice unto thee with the voice of thanksgiving;
> I will pay that that I have vowed.
> Salvation is of the Lord."

And the Lord spake unto the fish, and it vomited out Jonah upon the dry land.

And the word of the Lord came unto Jonah the second time, saying, "Arise, go unto Nineveh, that great city, and preach unto it the preaching that I bid thee."

So Jonah arose, and went unto Nineveh, according to the word of the Lord. Now Nineveh was an exceeding great city of three days' journey. And Jonah began to enter into the city a day's journey, and he cried, and said, "Yet forty days, and Nineveh shall be overthrown."

So the people of Nineveh believed God, and proclaimed a fast, and put on sackcloth, from the greatest of them even to the least of them. For word came unto the king of Nineveh, and he arose from his throne, and he laid his robe from him, and covered him with sackcloth, and sat in ashes. And he caused it to be proclaimed and published through Nineveh by the decree of the king and his nobles, saying, "Let neither man nor beast, herd nor flock, taste any thing: let them not feed, nor drink water: but let man and beast be covered with sackcloth, and cry mightily unto God: yea, let them turn every one from his evil way, and from the violence that is in their hands. Who can tell if God will turn and repent, and turn away from his fierce anger, that we perish not?"

And God saw their works, that they turned from their evil way; and God repented of the evil that he had said that he would do unto them; and he did it not.

But it displeased Jonah exceedingly, and he was very angry. And he prayed unto the Lord, and said, "I pray thee, O Lord, was not this my saying, when I was yet in my country? Therefore I fled before unto Tarshish: for I knew that thou art a gracious God, and merciful, slow to anger, and of great kindness, and repentest thee of the evil. Therefore now, O Lord, take, I beseech thee, my life from me; for it is better for me to die than to live."

Then said the Lord, "Doest thou well to be angry?"

So Jonah went out of the city, and sat on the east side of the city, and there made him a booth, and sat under it in the shadow, till he might see what would become of the city.

And the Lord God prepared a gourd, and made it to come up over Jonah, that it might be a shadow over his head, to deliver him from his grief. So Jonah was exceeding glad of the gourd.

But God prepared a worm when the morning rose the next day, and it smote the gourd that it withered.

And it came to pass, when the sun did arise, that God prepared a vehement east wind; and the sun beat upon the head of Jonah, that he fainted, and wished in himself to die, and said, "It is better for me to die than to live."

And God said to Jonah, "Doest thou well to be angry for the gourd?"

And he said, "I do well to be angry, even unto death."

Then said the Lord, "Thou hast had pity on the gourd, for the which thou hast not labored, neither madest it grow, which came up in a night, and perished in a night: and should not I spare Nineveh, that great city, wherein are more than sixscore thousand persons that cannot discern between their right hand and their left hand; and also much cattle?"

[Jonah 1–4, complete]

THE TESTING OF JONAH

Robert Nathan

Jonah stood leaning upon his staff in the darkness. A few lights gleamed among the trees, whose branches bent above him as though to envelope him in their quiet embrace. The odors of night crept around him; he remembered his youth, spent in this village, and he felt in his heart a longing for that lonely boy whose only friends had been an old man and his own dreams. So much of life had gone by, yet here he was again, wearier, wiser, still led by hopes, of what he did not know, hurt by memories, but why he could not tell. He heard the voices of Aaron and his friends fading in the distance; he knew that in the shadows young lovers whispered together, although he could not see them. All about him trembled the happy laughter of youth, the peace of age, the quietness of rest after labor. The sky of heaven, shining with stars, bent upon his home a regard of kindness; and the wind, moving through the sycamores, spoke to him in the accents of the past.

Bowing his head upon his breast, he thought, "Jonah, Jonah, what have you done with your youth?"

God was worried about Jonah. Watched by reverent cherubim, whose wings fanned the air all about Him, the Lord of Hosts walked up and down in the sky, and said to Moses, who was accompanying Him,

"I must find something for this young man to do."

Moses looked down at Jonah with an expression of contempt. "He is hardly worth the effort," he declared gloomily. "He seems to me to lack character."

"You are right," said God. "Still, he expects something from Me."

And He added, smiling gently, "Perhaps that is why I am fond of him. He has not your strong and resourceful mind, Moses, nor Noah's faithful heart; but he has suffered. He is simply a man, like anybody."

"What?" cried Noah, hurrying up, "are you talking about me?"

God replied: "I was saying that Jonah did not trust Me as you did, My friend."

"No," said Noah; "but then, what do you expect? There are so many different ideas now in the world. I do not recognize my posterity in these warring nations. Let us have another flood, Lord."

Moses looked sadly down at Jerusalem, where golden idols were being sold in the streets. "You are right, Noah," he said, "but I do not like the idea of a flood. A flood does not teach people how to live. Sometimes I wonder if anything can teach people what they are unwilling to learn."

"Nonsense," said Noah. "A flood is the most sanitary thing. Wait and see; even you could learn something about sewers from a good flood."

God checked the old patriarch with a kindly hand. "Things are not the same as they used to be in the early days," He said. "I cannot drown the world today without drowning My wife, Israel. She is young, and a nuisance, but she has yet to bear Me a son. I foresee that He will give His mother a great deal of pain, but that cannot be helped.

"Let us not think of Israel now, but of the prophet Jonah. Moses is of the opinion that he is not a first-class prophet, and I am inclined to agree with him. He is a poet; and for that reason I feel warmly inclined toward him. After all, you, Noah, and you, Moses, see only one side of My nature. You try to look upon the Greater Countenance, but what you see is the Lesser Countenance. It is different with a poet. He does not see Hod, or Chesed, the thrones of Glory and Mercy. He looks through Beauty to the Crown itself. Whereas you, Moses, have never seen beyond Knowledge; and you, my good Noah, have seen My face only in Severity."

Moses and Noah bowed their heads. "It is true, Lord," said Noah humbly.

God continued:

"At this moment Jonah does not see Me at all. In the first place, he is unhappy, and he no longer looks toward beauty. He believes that there is no more beauty in the world because his heart is broken. He is mistaken; and after a while his sorrow will sharpen his eyes. Then he will see more than before."

"In that case," said Moses, "why do You bother Yourself?"

The Lord considered a moment before replying. It was obvious that He wished to express Himself in terms intelligible to His hearers.

"The trouble, My friends," He said at last, "is this: our young prophet is a patriot. He is convinced that I am God of Israel alone. I do not mind that point of view in a prophet, but it will not do in a poet. Severity, glory, knowledge, belong to the nations, if you like. But beauty belongs to the world. It is the portion of all mankind in its God.

"I have covered the heavens with beauty, the green spaces of the earth, the cloudy waters, the tall and snowy peaks. These are for all to see, these are for all to love. Shall any one take beauty from another, and say, 'This is mine'?"

"Now He is beginning to talk," said Moses in an undertone to Noah; "this is like old times."

But God grew silent again. Presently he continued wearily,

"It is your fault, Moses, that the Jews believe I belong to them entirely. Well, I do not blame you, for you could not have brought them safely through the desert otherwise. But you did not tell them that I was a bull. I foresee that for a long time yet men will be irresistibly led to worship Me in the form of an animal."

"Well, then," said Noah, "if You foresee so much . . ."

"Be silent," said God, in a voice of thunder which made the wings of angels tremble. He continued more gently, "Actually, at the moment, I am not interested in theology. I am thinking of Jonah."

And He walked quietly up and down in the sky, thinking. The cherubim, moving all about Him, beat with their snowy wings the air perfumed with frankincense; and the clouds rolled under His feet.

Left to themselves, Moses and Noah regarded each other in an unfriendly manner. At last Moses shrugged his shoulders. He was vexed to think that he did not know everything.

"Well, old man," he said to Noah, "have you nothing to talk about except the flood? You do not understand conditions in the world today."

"I understand this much," replied Noah calmly, "that faith is more important than knowledge. Where would you be, with all your wisdom, if it had not been for me and my ark? You would be a fish, swimming in the sea."

"Do you take credit for saving your own skin?" cried Moses. "Wonderful. I, on the other hand, was very comfortable in Egypt. What I did was from the highest motives. I am not even sure that I am a Jew."

"I believed in God," said Noah stoutly, "and I did as He told me."

"So did I," said Moses angrily, "but I also used my wits a little. Faith is nothing; any animal can have faith. You and your faith had to get inside a wooden ark, in order to keep dry. But when I wished to take an entire nation across the sea, I simply parted the waters. I shall not tell you how I did it, because it would be lost on you. It takes a first-rate intelligence to understand such a thing."

Noah replied excitedly, "Please remember that I am your ancestor, and treat me with more respect."

"You are an old drunkard," said Moses.

But at this point God joined them again, and they were silent, to hear what the Holy One had to say.

"This young man," said God, "does not believe in Me any more. How then shall I convince him of Myself?"

Desirous of showing his knowledge, Moses began to quote from the Book of Wisdom: "Infidelity, violence, envy, deceit, extreme avariciousness, a total want of qualities, with impurity, are the innate faults of womankind."

"Nevertheless," said God, "they are also My creations. In My larger aspects I am as impure as I am pure; otherwise there would not be a balance. However, as I have said, we are not concerned with My larger aspects."

Noah broke in at this point. "Send him to sea, Lord," he begged. "There is nothing like a long trip at sea to quiet the mind. It is very peaceful on the water. One forgets one's disappointments."

"You are right," said God; "we need the sea; it will give him peace. But as a matter of fact, I do not care whether he finds peace or not. As I have told you, I simply wish this poet to understand that I am God, and not Baal of Canaan. The attempt to confuse Me with a sun-myth, with the fertility of earth as symbolized by the figure of a bull, or a dove, vexes Me. Increase is man's affair, not God's. Besides, where will all this increase end? I regret the days of Adam and Eve and the Garden of Eden. Already there are more people on earth than I have any use for, socially speaking. Now I could wish there were more beauty in the world. I should like some poet to speak of Me in words other than those of a patriot. Yet if I try to explain Myself, who will understand Me? Not even you, Moses, with all your wisdom. And so I, in turn, must forget My wisdom, in order to explain Myself. I must act as the not-too-wise God of an ignorant people. That this is possible is due to the fact that along with infinite wisdom, I include within Myself an equal amount of ignorance."

He sighed deeply. "I shall send Jonah to Nineveh," he concluded.

"The subjects of King Shalmaneser the Third are honest, hard-working men and women. I enjoy, in some of My aspects, their vigorous and spectacular festivals. Nevertheless, repentance will not do them any harm, since for one thing they will not know exactly what it is they are asked to repent of, and for another, they will soon go back to their old ways again.

"Thus I shall convince Jonah of Myself where he least expects to find Me. He shall hear from Me at sea, and again within the walls of Nineveh. It will surprise him. And perhaps the rude beauty of that city will speak to his heart, dreamy with woe."

"I do not doubt that it will surprise him," said Moses, "but will he be convinced?"

God did not answer. Already He was on His way to earth. And Noah, looking after Him, shook his hoary head with regret.

"A flood would have been the better way," he said.

God went down to the water. He stood on the shores of the sea and called; like the voice of the storm a name rolled forth from those august lips across the deep. And the deeps trembled. Presently a commotion took place in the waters; wet and black the huge form of Leviathan rose gleaming from the sea, and floated obediently before its God.

The Lord spoke, and the whale listened. After He had explained the situation, God said:

"I foresee that Jonah will not go to Nineveh as I command. He will attempt to flee from Me, and he will choose the sea as the best means of escape. It will not help him. I shall raise a storm upon the waters, and the ignorant sailors will cast him overboard as a sacrifice to the gods of the storm. That is where you can be of assistance to Me, My old friend. As he sinks through the water, I wish you to advance upon him, and swallow him."

"Ak," said the whale; "O my."

"Well," said God impatiently, "what is the matter?"

The great fish blew a misty spray of water into the air. "It is impossible," he declared; "in the first place, I should choke to death."

"You are an ignorant creature," said God; "you have neither faith, nor science. Let Me tell you a few things about yourself in the light of future exegesis. Know then, that you are a cetacean, or whalebone type of whale. Such animals obtain their food by swimming on or near the surface of the water, with their jaws open."

"That is true," said the whale, reverent and amazed.

"The screen of whalebone," continued the Lord, "opens inward, and admits solid objects to the animal's mouth. This screen does not allow

Jonah Cast Up by the Whale (c. 1400). Persian illuminated manuscript. THE METROPOLITAN MUSEUM OF ART, BEQUEST OF JOSEPH PULITZER, 1933.

the egress of any solid matter, only of water. As the gullet is very small, only the smallest objects can pass down it.

"Jonah will therefore be imprisoned in your mouth. You cannot swallow him; and he cannot get out, because of the screen of whale-bone."

"Then he will suffocate," said the whale.

"Nonsense," said God. "Remember that you are an air-breathing, warm-blooded animal, and can only dive because of the reservoir of air in your mouth. When this air becomes unfit to breathe, you must rise to the surface for a fresh supply.

"While you have air to breathe, Jonah will have it also.

"So do not hesitate any longer, but do as you are told."

The whale heaved a deep sigh; his breath groaned through the ocean, causing many smaller fish, terrified, to flee with trembling fins.

"How horrid for me," he exclaimed.

God replied soothingly, "It will assure you a place in history."

So saying, the Lord blessed Leviathan, who sank sadly back to the depths of the sea; and, turning from the shore, the Light of Israel rolled like thunder across the valleys toward Golan.

The night came to meet Him from the east, pouring down over the hills like smoke. In the cold night air God went to look for Jonah.

Poor Jonah, he had not found peace after all. The lonely desert, so calm and quiet in the past, had given no rest to his thoughts. His mind went back over and over again to those days at home; he felt the wonder of the lovenight, his heart shrank again with sickness for what followed. And he asked himself for the thousandth time how such things could be. Then he cried out against Judith for her cruelty; yet the next moment he forgave her.

And these thoughts, climbing and falling wearily up and down through his head, kept him awake until long after the desert was asleep. In the morning, when he awoke, it was with regret; he tried to sleep a little longer, to keep his eyes closed, to keep from thinking again . . . why wake at all? he wondered. There was nothing to wake to. Only the hot sun over the desert, only his heavy heart, which grew no lighter as the days went by.

Why wake at all?

God found him sitting wearily upon a rock, his head bowed between his hands. The Lord spoke, and the desert was silent.

"Jonah," said God in a voice like a great wave breaking, slowly, and with the peace of the sea, "Jonah, you have wept enough."

Jonah replied simply, "I have been waiting for You a long while, and I am very tired."

"I had not forgotten you," said God; "I have been thinking."

And He added, "Now I have something for you to do."

Jonah remained seated without looking up. He seemed no longer to care what God had for him to do.

"Arise, Jonah," said God, "and go to Nineveh. Cry out against that great city for its sins."

But Jonah looked more dejected than ever. "What have I to do with Nineveh?" he asked. "Am I prophet to the Assyrians? I am a Jew. Do not mock me, Lord."

"I do not mock you," said God gravely. "Go, then, and do My bidding."

And as Jonah did not reply, He added sadly, "Do you still doubt Me?"

Jonah rose slowly to his feet. His eyes blazed, and his hands were tightly clenched. "Oh," he cried bitterly, all the passion in his heart storming out at last in a torrent of despair, "You . . . what are You God of? Were You God of Israel when a Tyrian stole my love? Was I Your Prophet then? Have You Power over Tyre, that You let Your servant suffer such anguish? Or are You God of the desert, where the demons mock me night and day, where the very stones cry out against

me, and the whole night is noisy with laughter? Nineveh . . . Nineveh
. . . in whose name shall I cry out against Nineveh? Do the gods of
Assur visit their wrath upon Jerusalem? What power have you in
Nineveh? For my youth which I gave You, what have You given me?
How have You returned my love, with what sorrow? What have You
done to me, Lord? I stand in the darkness, weary, and with a heavy
heart. What are You God of? Answer: what are You God of?

And God answered gently, "I am your God, Jonah, and where you
go, there you will find Me."

Jonah sank down upon the rock again. His passion had exhausted
him; but he was not convinced. "Well," he said in a whisper, "You are
not God in Nineveh, and I will not go."

Then the wrath of the Lord, slow to start, flamed for a moment
over the desert, and Jonah cowered to earth while the heavens groaned
and the ground shook with fright. And in his hole by the pool in the
Land of Tob, the little fox said to himself, "Jonah is talking to God."

But God's anger passed, leaving Him sad and holy.

"Peace unto you, Jonah," He said in tones of divine sweetness; "take
up your task, and doubt Me no more."

And He returned to heaven in a cloud. Overcome with weariness,
empty of passion, Jonah fell asleep upon the ground.

No jackals laughed that night. Silence brooded over the desert. The
stars kept watch without a sound, and Jonah slept with a quiet heart. . . .

Jonah was let out of the whale in the North, near Arvad, and not
far from Kadesh as the crow might fly, which is to say, over the coastal
hills and then in a straight line across the jungles and the desert. This
was the route he took as being the shortest way to Nineveh. He was
in a hurry; he was impatient to begin his mission. He was filled with
enthusiasm.

How different from his flight to sea, this vigorous return across the
land dry with the sun of midsummer. Now he marched with a firm
and hurried step, his face darkly radiant with divine purpose, with
pious anger. Yes, he would speak; Nineveh would hear him. Let them
stone him if they liked, God would amply repay them for it. What
glory.

And this was all his, not hers, not for her sake; let her be proud
of him if she liked; what did it matter any more? She would hear
enough of it in Tyre; Jonah here, and Jonah there . . .

Yes, they would speak of it in Tyre.

As he passed the wayside altars of the baalim with their pillars sur-
mounted by horns of sacrifices, he smiled at them in derision.

"You," he said scornfully, "you . . . what are you gods of, anyway?"

At Kadesh he saw statues of the river deities, Chrysonhoa and Pegai. He spat in the dust before them; fortunately, no one was looking. In the sun of late afternoon their shadows pointed like great spears toward Nineveh.

"Israel will hear my name again," he thought proudly.

The evergreen oaks of the hills gave way to the tamarisks of the Syrian jungles, and the palms and scrub of the desert. He slept the first night in the wilderness between Kadesh and Rehoboth. The jackals were silent, awed by the presence of lions among the rocks. Padding to and fro, the great beasts watched Jonah from afar, with eyes like flames. . . .

In the fresh light of early morning a mother goat divided her milk between the prophet and her ewe. "These are stirring times, Jonah," she said; "angels are abroad in great numbers." Recognizing a minor deity, Jonah blessed her and resumed his journey.

At the end of the second day he began to pass the boundary stones of Assyria, set up to warn trespassers upon private property. Thinking them altars, Jonah cursed each one as he went by. The next day he passed kilns in which colored bricks were being baked. As far as he could see, the blue, green, and yellow bricks stood in rows on the red earth.

That night he slept outside the gates of Nineveh. The city rose above him in the dark; he heard the sentries challenge on the walls.

In the morning he entered the city with some farmers on their way to the markets. The sun was rising, gleaming upon the great winged bulls before the temples, the green and yellow lions upon the walls. Under the clear upland sky the city shone with color like a fair. The markets opened; the streets filled with men and women in their colored shawls and clashing ornaments. And Jonah, looking and looking, was astonished. "Why," he thought, "this is strange; there is something bright and bold about all this. This is fine, after all." And he felt a gayety of heart take hold of him. How vigorous these mountain people looked with their insolent faces and their swaggering air. There was nothing old or sad in Nineveh. He forgot why he had come; he was excited, and happy. It was not at all what he had expected; and he forgot himself.

But not for long. As the hours passed, he grew weary; and as the brightness wore off, and he began to think of his own life again, he began to hate Nineveh, to hate the bold colors all around him, the youth that carried itself so proudly and carelessly in the streets. "Yes," he thought, "that is all very well for you; but you know nothing about life." And, lifting his arms, he cried aloud with gloomy satisfaction, "Yet forty days, and Nineveh shall be overthrown."

The success of this remark astonished him. Without waiting to find out any more about it, the Assyrians hurried home and put ashes on their heads. Nineveh repented like a child of its sins; in an orgy of humility the city gave up its business, and dressed itself in sackcloth. The king, even, left his throne, and sat down in some ashes.

Jonah was vexed. This, also, was not what he had expected. He had looked for a wind of fury, for stones, and curses, and a final effect of glory. And when he learned that because of its repentance Nineveh was to be spared, his courage gave way in a flood of disappointment.

"I knew it," he said bitterly to God; "I knew You'd never do it."

And with an angry countenance he retired to an open field on the east side of the city, to see what would happen. His heart was very sore.

"Where is my glory now?" he thought.

Then God, who was anxiously watching, spoke to Jonah from the sky. "Why are you angry?" said the Holy One. "Have I done you a wrong?"

Jonah replied, sighing, "Who will ever believe me now, Lord?"

And for the rest of the day he maintained a silence, full of reproach.

Then because the sun was very hot, and because where Jonah was sitting there was no shade of any sort, God made a vine grow up, overnight, to shelter Jonah.

"There," said God, "there is a vine for you. Rest awhile and see."

That day Jonah sat in comfort beneath his shelter. The wind was in the west, full of agreeable odors; at noon a farmer brought him meal, salt, and oil; he ate, was refreshed, and dozed beneath his vine. The sun went down over the desert; and the evening star grew brighter in the sky, which shone with a peaceful light. The dews descended; and Jonah, wrapped in his cloak, dreamed of home.

But in the morning worms had eaten the leaves of the vine; gorged and comfortable, they regarded Jonah from the ground with pious looks. As the day progressed, the sun beat down upon him without pity, a strong wind blew up from the east, out of the desert, and the prophet grew faint with misery. Too hot even to sweat, he nevertheless refused to move.

"No," he said, "I shall sit here."

An obstinate rage kept him out in the sun, although he half expected to die of it. "Well," he said to himself, "what if I do?"

It seemed to him that he had nothing more to live for.

Then God said to Jonah, "Do you do well to be angry, My son?"

Jonah did not wish to reply. But he was sure of one thing: that he had every right to be angry. "Why did You wither my vine, Lord?" he asked bitterly. "Was that also necessary?"

God, looking down on His prophet, smiled sadly. "What is a vine?" He said gently. "Was it your vine, Jonah? You neither planted it nor cared for it. It came up in a night, and it perished in a night. And now you think I should have spared the vine for your sake. Yes . . . but what of Nineveh, that great city, where there are so many people who cannot discern between their right hand and their left hand? Shall I not spare them, too, for My sake, Jonah?"

Jonah rose wearily to his feet. "Well," he said, "I may as well go home again."

And with bowed head he passed through the city, and out of the western gate. In the streets the citizens made way for him with pious murmurs and anxious looks, but Jonah did not notice them. All his courage was gone, his pride, his hope of glory, all gone down in the dust of God's mercy to others, to all but him. To him alone God had been merciless and exacting. One by one the warm hopes of the youth, the ardors of the man, had been denied him; peace, love, pride, everything had been taken from him. What was there left? Only the desert, stony as life itself . . . only the empty heart, the deliberate mind, the bare and patient spirit. Well, Jonah . . . what a fool to think of anything else. Glory . . . yes, but the glory is God's, not yours.

But he had not learned even that. He was not a good prophet. The flowers of his hope, the bitter blossoms of his grief, sprang up everywhere, where there should have been only waste brown earth. No, he was not a prophet; he was a man, like anybody else, whose love had been false, whose God had been unkind.

And as he trudged dejectedly along, his heart, bare now of pride, filled with loneliness and longing. He thought of Judith, of the happiness that would never be his, and he wept.

High among the clouds, God turned sadly to Moses. "You Jews," He said wearily, "you do not understand beauty. With you it is either glory or despair."

And with a sigh He looked westward to the blue Aegean. Warm and gold the sunlight lay over Greece.

Why is Jonah so discontented at the beginning of the story? Explain the distinction God makes between those things that belong to nations and that which belongs to the world. Why does Jonah flee Nineveh? What does his experience in the belly of a whale teach him? What has he still not learned? What lesson is God trying to teach Jonah with the gourd? Why is he still unhappy? How is this incident used to comment on the Jews (and probably on nations in general)?

To what end is each of the other biblical characters employed?
What does God mean when he tells Noah, "I cannot drown the whole
world today without drowning my wife, Israel?" What birth is God
referring to in the subsequent lines?

THE DIVINE IMAGE

William Blake

To Mercy, Pity, Peace, and Love
All pray in their distress;
And to these virtues of delight
Return their thankfulness.

For Mercy, Pity, Peace, and Love
Is God, our father dear,
And Mercy, Pity, Peace, and Love
Is Man, his child and care.

For Mercy has a human heart,
Pity a human face,
And Love, the human form divine,
And Peace, the human dress.

Then every man, of every clime,
That prays in his distress,
Prays to the human form divine,
Love, Mercy, Pity, Peace.

And all must love the human form,
In heathen, turk, or jew;
Where Mercy, Love, and Pity dwell
There God is dwelling too.

In what ways is this lyric a fitting summation to the themes
presented in this unit?

UNIT 4

GREATER LOVE

Agony in the Garden of Gethsemane (c. 1585) by El Greco. NATIONAL GALLERY, LONDON.

With the beginning of the New Testament, the direction and purpose of biblical writing changes. The books of the Bible from this point forward no longer represent a repository of Jewish belief, doctrine, and history; instead they reflect the emerging development of a Christian theology that builds upon but irrevocably separates itself from that which has come before. Christians view Jesus as the fulfillment of Old Testament prophecies, such as those of Isaiah and Jeremiah, that predict the coming of a Messiah who would be "wounded for our transgressions" [Isaiah 53:5] before assuming the throne of David and instituting universal peace; Jews deny Jesus this role and still await the promised savior. This does not mean, however, that the New Testament represents a radical departure from the Old. The Latin word *testament* means "covenant," and, to be fully understood, the New Testament must be seen in the context of God's covenant with the Israelites as recorded in the Hebrew Bible. Christ was understood to be the bearer of a "new" covenant based on love, forgiveness, and understanding, a covenant which was

> written not with ink, but with the spirit of the living God, not on tablets of stone but on tablets of the human heart . . . a new covenant, not in a written code but in the Spirit, for the written code kills, but the Spirit gives life. [2 Corinthians 3:3, 6]

In a sense, the message Christ carried was seen explicitly to be a redefinition of the spirit of the original covenant between God and His chosen people as it was embodied in the code of laws that Moses brought down from Mount Sinai. Indeed, throughout the New Testament, Christian doctrine can be seen as being grounded in and branching out from Hebrew thought. It is natural for this to have been so, for the early Christians were, after all, Jews—as was Jesus himself.

The New Testament, like the Old, is a library of books, twenty-seven in all, which relate the life, death, and Resurrection of Jesus Christ; the experiences of his early disciples; the founding of the Christian

church; and finally a prophecy of the Second Coming of Christ.
The first four books—the Gospels (from the Anglo-Saxon word meaning
"good tidings") According to Matthew, Mark, Luke, and John—set
forth accounts of Jesus' life and ministry, each from a different point of
view. These are followed by The Acts of the Apostles, which traces
the spread of Christ's teachings from Jerusalem to Rome through the
ministry of Peter and Paul over a period of about thirty years. The
rest of the New Testament consists largely of a series of letters to,
the early Christians, the majority of them written by Paul. The
last book, the Revelation of St. John the Divine, is a prophecy of the
apocalyptic events of Christ's Second Coming, including the Last
Judgment and the permament establishment of God's heavenly
kingdom on the "new" earth.

Of all the books in the New Testament, the four Gospels are
undoubtedly the most familiar to us by virtue of the stirring composite
portrait of the life of Jesus that they set forth. Even those who have
never read the Gospels have some knowledge of the life of Jesus;
for just as the Old Testament stories of figures like Adam and Eve,
Noah, Abraham, and Moses (to name just a few) have endured and
through constant retelling have become a part of our everyday
knowledge, so too the story of Jesus has assumed a life of its own
beyond the printed word of the Gospels.

Our almost innate familiarity with the details of Jesus' life causes
us to think of the Gospels as a unified account and therefore to skim
over the subtle distinctions in style, content, and intent that exists
among them. Three of the four accounts—Matthew, Mark, and Luke
—are synoptic in nature; that is, they present a common view and
follow the same general arrangement, so that if they were placed
together in parallel columns they could be "seen together," as the word
synoptic suggests. Nevertheless the synoptic Gospels differ in
significant respects. The Gospel According to Mark, generally agreed
to be the earliest of the Gospels upon which the other accounts are
based (though it is usually placed second, between Matthew and
Luke), emphasizes Jesus' role as a great revolutionary humanitarian;
the narrative repeatedly calls attention to his being "the Son of man."
Matthew's account reflects his concern for proving to the Jews that
Jesus was the Messiah whom they had been anticipating. He depicts
the life of Jesus as the fulfillment of the Old Testament prophecies
and traces his lineage back to David to stress Jesus' right to the throne
of David. This placed Jesus within the scope of the covenant between
God and the Hebrews: as "seed of Abraham," Jesus was able to
extend God's blessings to all nations; he provided the essential link

between the promises God made to Israel and their fulfillment through the Christian church. Luke, Gentile convert and companion of Paul, seems to have had the non-Jewish reader more in mind, particularly the Greeks and Romans. In his depiction of Jesus as a man of love and compassion, serving, forgiving, and healing others, he stresses that Jesus was a savior to *all* men, his ministry knowing no racial barriers. This particular emphasis makes the Gospel According to Luke the most universal in its appeal. The fourth Gospel, John, is less biographical and more openly theological than the synoptic Gospels. It was written so "that you may openly believe that Jesus is the Christ, the Son of God, and that believing you may have life in his name" [John 20:31]. John saw Jesus as "the Word"—that is, as God's verbal expression of himself, his message to mankind, who existed with God before Creation and who "became flesh and dwelt among us, full of grace and truth" [John 1:14]. His focus throughout is the love of God for man and of man for God.

A study of the subtle distinctions among the four Gospels is a fascinating endeavor, one which has held the attention of students and scholars for many years. Ultimately, however, we must return to the fact that it is the composite picture of Christ emerging from the four Gospels, rather than any one of the four depictions, that has been the greatest source of religious, artistic, and literary inspiration stemming from the New Testament since the time of its writing. For this reason (and for more practical reasons of space limitations), the biblical selections in this unit focus solely on the life of Christ; the selections attempt to pinpoint some of the highlights of Jesus' life as they are revealed in whichever of the Gospel narratives presents them most vividly. The material has been divided to reflect the various stages of Christ's career: his birth and early childhood; his initiation, including his baptism by John the Baptist and the temptation in the wilderness; highlights of his ministry, such as the marriage at Cana and the raising of Lazarus; his final days in Jerusalem; and finally, the Crucifixion and Resurrection.

No single man has had a more profound influence on the shaping of our history and our culture than Jesus of Nazareth. It is an influence that is still widely attested to in the literature and art of our own times. Among the aspects of Jesus' life that have appealed to modern writers are the message of love and freedom that he bore with him and his willingness to dedicate, even sacrifice, his life to spreading this message aimed at bringing new hope to the common man. W. H. Auden celebrates the significance of Jesus' birth for the common man in "The Vision of the Shepherds," wherein a chorus of angels heralds the birth of the Christ child as the "ingression of Love" and beckons the shepherds to run to Bethlehem to see the child, "the new-born Word" who

> Declares that the old
> Authoritarian
> Constraint is replaced
> By His Covenant,
> And a city based
> On love and consent
> Suggested to men,
> *All, all, all of them.*
>
> > (Italics added)

Auden seems to suggest throughout the piece that a time has come when *all* men, not only the rich, would receive the benefits of the universe. Ewan MacColl in "The Ballad of the Carpenter," recounting the final moments of Christ's career, also turns to Jesus' relation to the common man. He depicts "the Carpenter" as a radical labor leader rallying the workers to revolution: "If you only will organize, the world belongs to you." Maxwell Anderson has seized upon Christ as a symbol of "that individual dignity upon which individual freedom is established." In *Journey to Jerusalem*, a dramatic adaptation of Luke's description of the 12-year-old Christ teaching the rabbis in the Temple, Anderson seems to be holding a mirror up to Christ's thoughts and actions in hope that individuals in the twentieth century would benefit by his example of dedication and sacrifice and be better equipped to fight the injustice and tyranny still rampant in the modern world. Anderson's young Messiah comes to feel himself as chosen "to be tortured for the others"; he is "willing to die rather than accept injustice." As John so eloquently and simply states in his Gospel,

> Greater love hath no man than this: that a man lay down his life for his friends. [John 15:13]

Other writers have made allusions to the Gospel narratives in order to comment on the continuing presence of violence in the world, especially as it is revealed in time of war. Robert Lowell in his poem "The Holy Innocents," commenting on the innocent victims slaughtered in World War II, remarks that in the year 1945 "the world out-Herods Herod." The deathlike calm that is evoked in the concluding line —"Lamb of the shepherds, Child, how still you lie"—poignantly suggests that the brutalities of war have somehow triumphed over the promise of peace and love traditionally associated with the infant Jesus lying in the manger. Edwin Arlington Robinson achieves a similar effect by recalling the Crucifixion in his poem "Calvary," in which he asks, "how long/Are we to keep Christ writhing on the cross?" For World War I poet Wilfred Owen in his poem "At a Calvary Near the Ancre," the Crucifixion has also continued into modern times. Striking a blow against the horrors of war and the blind nationalism it inspires, he depicts national leaders in terms of the "priests" and "scribes" responsible for putting Christ to death. These latter—as they "brawl allegiance to the state," enlisting the sympathies of the people and rousing their prejudices and need for revenge— are placed in striking contrast to those who would follow in Christ's footsteps:

> They who love the greater love
> Lay down their life; they do not hate.

Many writers have focused on the humanity of Jesus, his humility and compassion, his patience, and his strength to endure. For black slaves, Jesus stood as a symbol of infinite patience and inner strength, a model for those who had to bear up under the burdens of slavery: despite the agony of his Crucifixion, Jesus "never said a mumblin' word," as the title of the spiritual included in this unit acknowledges. Geoffrey Household in his short story "The Eye of a Soldier" describes Jesus as a young prophet who, despite his obvious "power to command," went to his death willingly as his "duty to civilization." The compassionate, gentle Jesus is paid tribute in Paul Engle's "An Old Palestinian Donkey," in which Jesus is seen through the eyes of the now-aged donkey upon whose back he had made his triumphant entry into Jerusalem. As the donkey recalls years afterwards, Jesus was the only gentle man it had ever known, a man whose "hand was soft on my mouth" and who "rode lightly."

All of these writers have viewed Jesus as a man of love, a man who had the faith to endure incredible hardships and ultimately death in order to bring mankind his message of love, freedom, individual dignity, and the promise of a new and better life. As the promised Messiah, Jesus had a mission to accomplish. But as a man, he first had to face the fears, uncertainties, and temptations to which the flesh falls prey. It is this image of Jesus confronting and conquering his human weaknesses that makes him such an appealing figure, a person who can touch our hearts and engage our sympathies, whatever our religious orientation. Boris Pasternak in his poem "Evil Days" depicts Christ riding triumphantly into Jerusalem, all too humanly aware of the ominous forces at work to destroy him. Jesus recalls the earlier days when he had escaped Herod's Massacre of the Innocents, when he had withstood the temptation in the wilderness, performed his first miracle, and walked on the sea of Galilee. Also vivid in his mind, however, was the very human, haunting, and frightening image of the risen Lazarus, dead so many days, "trying to get to his feet," an image with which he could not help but identify as he rode knowingly toward his own death and Resurrection. Jesus' struggle to endure and transcend the savage conflict between the flesh and spirit—his yearning "to attain to God" while attempting at the same time to escape his divinity—receives epic treatment in Nikos Kazantzakis' novel *The Last Temptation of Christ*. Kazantzakis views Jesus, in his continual battle to overcome his human fears and weaknesses, as a "supreme model to the man who struggles." The author's unique vision of the ramifications of Jesus' dilemma of mortality is provocatively displayed in "Voices in the Wilderness," the portion of the novel in which Christ's temptation in the wilderness is retold. Kazantzakis' "Prologue" to the novel, included as the finale to this unit, is a moving statement of his reasons for emphasizing the humanness of Christ. As he says therein, it is "that part of Christ's nature which was profoundly human [which] helps us to understand him and love him and to pursue his Passion as though it were our own."

In a sense, the life of Jesus as it is revealed and alluded to through the words of the Gospel writers and the modern poets, dramatists, and novelists included in this unit represents a synthesis of the major themes set forth in all four units of THE ENDURING LEGACY. For both the Gospel writers and the writers of our own time, Jesus and the message he carried with him signify a new beginning. They have celebrated him as a man of supreme courage and vision, capable of providing us with new insights into the ways of God and men; and, as such, they have held a mirror up to his actions, hoping that the image of "greater love" by which he governed his life will serve as a profound inspiration to free and would-be free men everywhere.

THE STAR IN THE EAST
(Luke and Matthew)

The Annunciation

And in the sixth month the angel Gabriel was sent from God unto a city of Galilee, named Nazareth, to a virgin espoused to a man whose name was Joseph, of the house of David; and the virgin's name was Mary. And the angel came in unto her, and said, "Hail, thou that art highly favored, the Lord is with thee: blessed art thou among women."

And when she saw him, she was troubled at his saying, and cast in her mind what manner of salutation this should be.

And the angel said unto her, "Fear not, Mary: for thou hast found favor with God. And, behold, thou shalt conceive in thy womb, and bring forth a son, and shalt call his name JESUS. He shall be great, and shall be called the Son of the Highest: and the Lord God shall give unto him the throne of his father David: and he shall reign over the house of Jacob for ever; and of his kingdom there shall be no end."

Then said Mary unto the angel, "How shall this be, seeing I know not a man?"

And the angel answered and said unto her, "The Holy Ghost shall come upon thee, and the power of the Highest shall overshadow thee: therefore also that holy thing which shall be born of thee shall be called the Son of God. And, behold, thy cousin Elisabeth, she hath also conceived a son in her old age: and this is the sixth month with her, who was called barren. For with God nothing shall be impossible."

And Mary said, "Behold the handmaid of the Lord; be it unto me according to thy word."

And the angel departed from her.

[*Luke 1:26—38*]

The Birth of Jesus

Now the birth of Jesus Christ was on this wise: when as his mother Mary was espoused to Joseph, before they came together, she was found with child of the Holy Ghost. Then Joseph her husband, being a just man, and not willing to make her a public example, was minded to put her away privily.

But while he thought on these things, behold, the angel of the Lord appeared unto him in a dream, saying, "Joseph, thou son of David, fear not to take unto thee Mary thy wife: for that which is conceived in her is of the Holy Ghost. And she shall bring forth a son, and thou shalt call his name JESUS: for he shall save his people from their sins."

Now all this was done, that it might be fulfilled which was spoken of the Lord by the prophet, saying, "Behold, a virgin shall be with child, and shall bring forth a son, and they shall call his name Emmanuel, which being interpreted is 'God with us.'"

Then Joseph being raised from sleep did as the angel of the Lord had bidden him, and took unto him his wife: and knew her not till she had brought forth her first born son: and he called his name JESUS.

[*Matthew 1:18–25*]

Shepherds Abiding in the Field

And there were in the same country shepherds abiding in the field, keeping watch over their flock by night. And, lo, the angel of the Lord came upon them, and the glory of the Lord shone round about them: and they were sore afraid.

And the angel said unto them, "Fear not: for, behold, I bring you good tidings of great joy, which shall be to all people. For unto you is born this day in the city of David a Savior, which is Christ the Lord. And this shall be a sign unto you: ye shall find the babe wrapped in swaddling clothes, lying in a manger."

And suddenly there was with the angel a multitude of the heavenly host praising God, and saying, "Glory to God in the highest, and on earth peace, good will toward men."

And it came to pass, as the angels were gone away from them into heaven, the shepherds said one to another, "Let us now go even unto Bethlehem, and see this thing which is come to pass, which the Lord hath made known unto us."

And they came with haste, and found Mary, and Joseph, and the babe lying in a manger. And when they had seen it, they made known abroad the saying which was told them concerning this child. And all they that heard it wondered at those things which were told them by the shepherds. But Mary kept all these things, and pondered them in her heart. And the shepherds returned, glorifying and praising God for all the things that they had heard and seen, as it was told unto them.

[*Luke 2:8–20*]

The Three Wise Men

Now when Jesus was born in Bethlehem of Judea in the days of Herod the king, behold, there came wise men from the east to Jerusalem, saying, "Where is he that is born King of the Jews? For we have seen his star in the east, and are come to worship him."

When Herod the king had heard these things, he was troubled, and all Jerusalem with him. And when he had gathered all the chief priests and scribes of the people together, he demanded of them where Christ should be born. And they said unto him, "In Bethlehem of Judea: for thus it is written by the prophet, 'And thou Bethlehem, in the land of Juda, art not the least among the princes of Juda: for out of thee shall come a Governor, that shall rule my people Israel.' "

Then Herod, when he had privily called the wise men, inquired of them diligently what time the star appeared. And he sent them to Bethlehem, and said, "Go and search diligently for the young child; and when ye have found him, bring me word again, that I may come and worship him also."

When they had heard the king, they departed; and, lo, the star, which they saw in the east, went before them, till it came and stood over where the young child was. When they saw the star, they rejoiced with exceeding great joy. And when they were come into the house, they saw the young child with Mary his mother, and fell down, and worshipped him; and when they had opened their treasures, they presented unto him gifts: gold, and frankincense, and myrrh. And being warned of God in a dream that they should not return to Herod, they departed into their own country another way.

[*Matthew 2:1–12*]

Herod's Wrath: The Flight into Egypt and the Massacre of the Innocents

And when they were departed, behold, the angel of the Lord appeareth to Joseph in a dream, saying, "Arise, and take the young child and his mother, and flee into Egypt, and be thou there until I bring thee word: for Herod will seek the young child to destroy him."

When he arose, he took the young child and his mother by night, and departed into Egypt: and was there until the death of Herod: that it might be fulfilled which was spoken of the Lord by the prophet, saying, "Out of Egypt have I called my son."

Then Herod, when he saw that he was mocked of the wise men, was exceedingly wroth, and set forth, and slew all the children that were in Bethlehem, and in all the coasts thereof, from two years old and under, according to the time which he had diligently inquired of the wise men. Then was fulfilled that which was spoken by Jeremiah the prophet, saying, "In Rama was there a voice heard, lamentation, and weeping, and great mourning, Rachel weeping for her children, and would not be comforted, because they are not."

But when Herod was dead, behold, an angel of the Lord appeareth in a dream to Joseph in Egypt, saying, "Arise, and take the young child and his mother, and go into the land of Israel: for they are dead which sought the young child's life."

And he arose, and took the young child and his mother, and came into the land of Israel. But when he heard that Archelaus did reign in Judea in the room of his father Herod, he was afraid to go thither: notwithstanding, being warned of God in a dream, he turned aside into the parts of Galilee. And he came and dwelt in a city called Nazareth: that it might be fulfilled which was spoken by the prophets, "He shall be called a Nazarene."

[*Matthew 2:13–23*]

THE VISION OF THE SHEPHERDS

W. H. Auden

I

THE FIRST SHEPHERD:
  The winter night requires our constant attention,
    Watching that water and good-will,
  Warmth and well-being, may still be there in the morning.
THE SECOND SHEPHERD:
  For behind the spontaneous joy of life
  There is always a mechanism to keep going,
THE THIRD SHEPHERD:
  And someone like us is always there.

THE FIRST SHEPHERD:

    We observe that those who assure us their education
        And money would do us such harm,
    How real we are just as we are, and how they envy us,
        For it is the centreless tree
    And the uncivilised robin who are truly happy,
        Have done pretty well for themselves:

THE SECOND SHEPHERD:

    Nor can we help noticing how those who insist that
        We ought to stand up for our rights,
    And how important we are, keep insisting also
        That it doesn't matter a bit
    If one of us gets arrested or injured, for
        It is only our numbers that count.

THE THIRD SHEPHERD:

    In a way they are right,

THE FIRST SHEPHERD:

                    But to behave like a cogwheel
    When one knows one is no such thing,

THE SECOND SHEPHERD:

    Merely to add to a crowd with one's passionate body,
        Is not a virtue.

THE THIRD SHEPHERD:

             What is real
    About us all is that each of us is waiting.

THE FIRST SHEPHERD:

    That is why we are able to bear
    Ready-made clothes, second-hand art and opinions
        And being washed and ordered about;

THE SECOND SHEPHERD:

    That is why you should not take our conversation
        Too seriously, nor read too much
    Into our songs;

THE THIRD SHEPHERD:

             Their purpose is mainly to keep us
    From watching the clock all the time.

THE FIRST SHEPHERD:

    For, though we cannot say why, we know that something
        Will happen:

THE SECOND SHEPHERD:

             What we cannot say,

THE THIRD SHEPHERD:
   Except that it will not be a reporter's item
     Of unusual human interest;
THE FIRST SHEPHERD:
   That always means something unpleasant.
THE SECOND SHEPHERD:
                      But one day or
   The next we shall hear the Good News.

II

THE THREE SHEPHERDS:
   Levers nudge the aching wrist;
     "You are free
     Not to be,
     Why exist?"
   Wheels a thousand times a minute
     Mutter, stutter,
   "End the self you cannot mend,
   Did you, friend, begin it?"
     And the streets
     Sniff at our defeats.
   Then who is the Unknown
   Who answers for our fear
   As if it were His own,
   So that we reply
   Till the day we die;
   "No, I don't know why,
   But I'm glad I'm here"?

III

CHORUS OF ANGELS:
   Unto you a Child,
   A Son is given.
   Praising, proclaiming
   The ingression of Love,
   Earth's darkness invents
   The blaze of Heaven,
   And frigid silence

Meditates a song;
For great joy has filled
The narrow and the sad,
While the emphasis
Of the rough and big,
The abiding crag
And wandering wave,
Is on forgiveness:
Sing Glory to God
And good-will to men,
All, all, all of them.
Run to Bethlehem.

SHEPHERDS:

Let us run to learn
How to love and run;
Let us run to Love.

CHORUS:

Now all things living,
Domestic or wild,
With whom you must share
Light, water, and air,
And suffer and shake
In physical need,
The sullen limpet,
The exuberant weed,
The mischievous cat,
And the timid bird,
Are glad for your sake
As the new-born Word
Declares that the old
Authoritarian
Constraint is replaced
By His Covenant,
And a city based
On love and consent
Suggested to men,
All, all, all of them.
Run to Bethlehem.

SHEPHERDS:

Let us run to learn
How to love and run;
Let us run to Love.

CHORUS:

    The primitive dead
    Progress in your blood,
    And generations
    Of the unborn, all
    Are leaping for joy
    In your veins today
    When the Many shall,
    Once in your common
    Certainty of this
    Child's lovableness,
    Resemble the One,
    That after today
    The children of men
    May be certain that
    The Father Abyss
    Is affectionate
    To all Its creatures,
    All, all, all of them.
    Run to Bethlehem.

What is the "mechanism" that must be kept going "behind the spontaneous joy of life"? Cite other examples of "machine" images in the poem and discuss how these are related to the shepherds' view of themselves and the passage of time. Who are those that envy the shepherds? Why do they envy the shepherds? Why do they think their money and education would do the shepherds harm? Do the shepherds find anything suspect in the attitude of those who urge them "to stand up for their rights"? What are the shepherds waiting for? Do they know precisely? What message do the shepherds hear in the "mutter" and "stutter" of the wheels? Why do they resist this message?

What event has occurred that prompts the chorus of angels to urge all to "Run to Bethlehem"? What do they say has replaced the "old Authoritarian Constraint"? What does Auden suggest is the significance of the birth of the Child for the shepherds and the unborn generations that now "leap for joy in their veins"?

JOURNEY OF THE MAGI

T. S. Eliot

'A cold coming we had of it,
Just the worst time of the year
For a journey, and such a long journey:
The ways deep and the weather sharp,
The very dead of winter.'
And the camels galled, sore-footed, refractory,
Lying down in the melting snow.
There were times we regretted
The summer palaces on slopes, the terraces,
And the silken girls bringing sherbet.
Then the camel men cursing and grumbling
And running away, and wanting their liquor and women,
And the night-fires going out, and the lack of shelters,
And the cities hostile and the towns unfriendly
And the villages dirty and charging high prices:
A hard time we had of it.
At the end we preferred to travel all night,
Sleeping in snatches,
With the voices singing in our ears, saying
That this was all folly.

Then at dawn we came down to a temperate valley,
Wet, below the snow line, smelling of vegetation;
With a running stream and a water-mill beating the darkness,
And three trees on the low sky,
And an old white horse galloped away in the meadow.
Then we came to a tavern with vine-leaves over the lintel,
Six hands at an open door dicing for pieces of silver,
And feet kicking the empty wine-skins.
But there was no information, and so we continued
And arrived at evening, not a moment too soon
Finding the place; it was (you may say) satisfactory.

Adoration of the Magi (16th c.) by Joos van Cleve. COURTESY OF THE DETROIT INSTITUTE OF ARTS.

All this was a long time ago, I remember,
And I would do it again, but set down
This set down
This: were we led all that way for
Birth or Death? There was a Birth, certainly,
We had evidence and no doubt. I had seen birth and death,
But had thought they were different; this Birth was
Hard and bitter agony for us, like Death, our death.
We returned to our places, these Kingdoms,
But no longer at ease here, in the old dispensation,
With an alien people clutching their gods.
I should be glad of another death.

———————

From what vantage point in time does the narrator (one of the Magi) recall the journey? How does this affect the telling of his story?

Why were there times the Magi regretted their journey as they
were making it? What do you make of the reference to the "three
trees"? Why does the speaker say, "This Birth was/. . . like Death, our
death"? Discuss the use of "Birth" and "birth," "Death" and
"death" in the poem. What other images and statements reinforce
the speaker's focus on death? What other "death" would he
"be glad of"?

    Describe some of the traditional, religious artistic representations
of the Three Magi you have seen. In what ways is the mental
picture you get from Eliot's rendition significantly different from
these traditional portrayals? Do the details of the journey, as cited
by Eliot's Magi, change or add to your impression of the event?

THE HOLY INNOCENTS

Robert Lowell

Listen, the hay-bells tinkle as the cart
Wavers on rubber tires along the tar
And cindered ice below the burlap mill
And ale-wife run. The oxen drool and start
In wonder at the fenders of a car,
And blunder hugely up St. Peter's hill.
These are the undefiled by woman—their
Sorrow is not the sorrow of this world:
King Herod shrieking vengeance at the curled
Up knees of Jesus choking in the air,

A king of speechless clods and infants. Still
The world out-Herods Herod; and the year,
The nineteen-hundred forty-fifth of grace,
Lumbers with losses up the clinkered hill
Of our purgation; and the oxen near
The worn foundations of their resting-place,

The holy manger where their bed is corn
And holly torn for Christmas. If they die,
As Jesus, in the harness, who will mourn?
Lamb of the shepherds, Child, how still you lie.

What effect does the poet wish to achieve by juxtaposing "oxen" and "car" in the fourth and fifth lines. Why is Jesus described as "choking in the air"? Briefly summarize what Herod did to the "innocents" in the Bible. What does Lowell mean in observing that "The world out-Herods Herod"? (In answering, consider the year reference.) What is achieved by the poet's remarking in the final line, "Lamb of the shepherds, Child, how still you lie"?

Discuss the overall message of the poem. You might wish to compare the theme and technique of the poem to Edward Arlington Robinson's "Calvary" and William Owen's "At a Calvary Near the Ancre," which appear later in this unit.

CHRIST IN THE TEMPLE
(Luke)

Now his parents went to Jerusalem every year at the feast of the passover. And when he was twelve years old, they went up to Jerusalem after the custom of the feast. And when they had fulfilled the days, as they returned, the child Jesus tarried behind in Jerusalem; and Joseph and his mother knew not of it. But they, supposing him to have been in the company, went a day's journey; and they sought him among their kinsfolk and acquaintance.

And when they found him not, they turned back again to Jerusalem, seeking him. And it came to pass that after three days they found him in the temple, sitting in the midst of the doctors, both hearing them, and asking them questions. And all that heard him were astonished at his understanding and answers.

And when they saw him, they were amazed: and his mother said unto him, "Son, why hast thou thus dealt with us? Behold, thy father and I have sought thee sorrowing."

And he said unto them, "How is it that ye sought me? Wist ye not that I must be about my Father's business?"

And they understood not the saying which he spake unto them. And he went down with them, and came to Nazareth, and was subject unto them: but his mother kept all these sayings in her heart. And Jesus increased in wisdom and stature, and in favor with God and man.

[*Luke 2:41–52*]

JOURNEY TO JERUSALEM
(from Act III, Scene 2)

Maxwell Anderson

Although Maxwell Anderson was not, as he says in the Preface to Journey to Jerusalem, *a "professing Christian," he recognized in Christianity a source of "human dignity and respect," capable of "teaching men faith in themselves and in their destinies." As he observes elsewhere in the Preface, "Weakened though it has been of late years, Christianity is still the strongest influence among us toward that individual dignity upon which individual freedom is established." Desirous of presenting Jesus as a figure of supreme human dignity, who was able to rise above the despair, faithlessness, and surrender of an entire historical era and in turn find meaning in his existence, Anderson seized upon the idea of adapting Luke's description of the twelve-year-old Jesus' visit to the Temple to make his point:*

> *This story of a Child of God in the court of Sanhedrin finding His way to the meaning of the universe as He walks alone among the columns—this appeared to me the perfect symbol of the soul of man searching for its own meaning.*

In the following scene, taken from near the conclusion of the play, the youthful visionary Jeshua reveals to Miriam, his mother, the full significance of the dreams and premonitions he has had of his adult life. (Anderson has chosen to call his characters by their Hebrew names: Jeshua is, of course, Jesus; and Miriam is Mary.)

MIRIAM:
You should take your eyes
from your book sometimes, my Jeshua. You read
as if there were great haste.
JESHUA:
Do I, Mother?

MIRIAM:

Yes.

As if you were fevered, and only more and more reading
would quench your thirst.

JESHUA:

It is like that.

MIRIAM:

What water
is it you seek, my son, reading your eyes out
early in the morning, and then into the night,
till the last light's gone?

(He is silent.)

What was it happened
the night you were late at the Temple?

JESHUA:

Oh, Mother, tell me—
is it true—or did I imagine it—
that I stayed all night with the prophet before he died
in the court of the Temple—and you found me there
in the early morning?

MIRIAM:

We came in the early morning
and found you there.

JESHUA:

Then it may all be true—
it may be true—even in this bright daylight!
Oh, Mother,
is it so sure—is it certain, Mother, that I—
am this one—who is chosen?

MIRIAM:

Your father's not sure.

JESHUA:

But you—you, Mother—or was it my father alone
who dreamed? Did nothing come to you?

MIRIAM:

No dream.

JESHUA:

Then was it all his wishing, as he had feared,
his own desire?

MIRIAM:

Could you believe so, Jeshua?

JESHUA:

I could wish to believe so.

MIRIAM:

When you are older
you shall know all my heart in all these things,
when you're only a little older.

JESHUA:

Tell me your heart.
Say it now.

MIRIAM:

Why, Jeshua?

JESHUA:

Because it's part of my fever—
that I must hear it. Because I must know what I am
and what will come to me. In all this I read
in the holy books it's as if I set my lips
to Dead Sea water, so that I'm thirstier still—
and must know more!

MIRIAM:

What do you read?

JESHUA:

The prophecies.

MIRIAM:

Concerning the Messiah?

JESHUA:

Yes.

MIRIAM:

If I
could tell you now—

(She puts out her hand to JESHUA. JESHUA *sits on floor at her feet.)*

Mine was no dream, but a vision.
I've never said this—
perhaps I can't say it now. When a mother speaks
to a son who is twelve years old, there's a veil woven
between what she may know and he may hear—
it's as it was when you tried to tell your dream—
do you remember?

JESHUA:

Yes.

MIRIAM:

And now I find
that I cannot speak. Only an angel came

to me in a vision, saying when you were born
your name was to be called Jeshua, and of your kingdom
there was to be no end.
This you may keep in your heart, as I have kept it
till now in mine. You are indeed—you are He.
Whatever has been prophesied for Him
will be yours, will come to us—and we shall see it
when you are grown a man.

JESHUA:

Oh, Mother, I know
you wouldn't hurt me—

MIRIAM:

Hurt you, Jeshua?
But it was you who said in the outer court
of the Temple, that this was not a burden—that it
could mean only happiness.

JESHUA:

Yes, I said it then.
When you spoke with the angel did you learn from him
how the Messiah must die?

MIRIAM:

I have never heard
that he will die. There is to be no end
to the Messiah's kingdom.

JESHUA:

But he must die.
This is what I heard from the robber prophet,
from Ishmael, when he lay dying in the court,
and I held his hand. The Messiah will not live
to see his kingdom. He will be arraigned and tortured,
and die under torture. He will find a teaching
which can save men, but they will not follow it.
They will despise him, will send soldiers to find him
and set him before the judges. He will die
to save others. This was said to me by the robber,
and I couldn't believe him. But now I read the rolls
day and night—read all the passages
that have to do with his coming. And it's true
if I'm chosen the Messiah then what it means
is that I'm chosen out of all the children
to be tortured for the others when the time comes
for us to be men together. It's not a kingship—

not to lead armies, not to die old, or in battle,
but to be hurried to a sacrifice
and die young, a criminal's death!

MIRIAM:

He was evil, evil—
this man from the desert!

JESHUA:

I said he was evil! Yes,
it seemed like madness to me! But all the books
say what he said—it's there to be read by all
who wish to read it!

MIRIAM:

But it has no meaning!

JESHUA:

Yes,
Mother, it has a meaning. Its meaning is
that the death of the innocent will work in the hearts
of those who murder them, till the murderers
are sorry, and have changed, and never again
take life unjustly! It may mean more, may mean even
that our race is chosen, our poor race of Israel,
to suffer for other races, as the Messiah
must suffer for our own.

MIRIAM:

Where have you read this?

JESHUA:

In all of them. That's why I've lain awake
to read when light came into the sky at morning,
and at night till my lamp went out. And they do say this.
How we could all have missed it, and hoped so long
for angels out of Heaven, I don't know—
for it's plain there in the prophecies; there's to be
no help come down from God. Our help must come
from within, from our hearts, from those who are willing to die
rather than accept injustice. And now you tell me
your vision. And I know. I must somehow find
the truth, according to my soul, and speak it,
and die for it—hoping somehow it will prevail
long after I'm dead.

MIRIAM:

I will not believe this, Jeshua—

JESHUA:

But I wish you would.
Then I wouldn't be alone. In all the world
there was only Ishmael knew this; and he died
for saying it to me. And now I must carry it.
Will you read the books?

MIRIAM:

I'll read them if you like.
If it will help.

JESHUA:

And then we can talk about them.

MIRIAM:

Yes.

Why does Jeshua come to the conclusion he must die? How does
Miriam react to this knowledge? What meaning will his death have?

INITIATION: BAPTISM AND TEMPTATION
(John and Matthew)

And the Word Was Made Flesh

In the beginning was the Word, and the Word was with God, and the Word was God. The same was in the beginning with God. All things were made by him; and without him was not any thing made that was made. In him was life; and the life was the light of men. And the light shineth in darkness; and the darkness comprehended it not.

There was a man sent from God, whose name was John. The same came for a witness, to bear witness of the Light, that all men through him might believe. He was not that Light, but was sent to bear witness of that Light. That was the true Light, which lighteth every man that cometh into the world. He was in the world, and the world was made by him, and the world knew him not. He came unto his own, and his own received him not. But as many as received him, to them gave he power to become the sons of God, even to them that believe on his name: which were born, not of blood, nor of the will of the flesh, nor of the will of man, but of God. And the Word was made flesh, and dwelt among us (and we beheld his glory, the glory as of the only begotten of the Father), full of grace and truth.

John bare witness of him, and cried, saying, "This was he of whom I spake, 'He that cometh after me is preferred before me: for he was before me.'" And of his fulness have all we received, and grace for grace. For the law was given by Moses, but grace and truth came by Jesus Christ.

[John 1:1–17]

Jesus Baptized by John

In those days came John the Baptist, preaching in the wilderness of Judea, and saying, "Repent ye: for the kingdom of heaven is at hand." For this is he that was spoken of by the prophet Isaiah, saying, "The voice of one crying in the wilderness, 'Prepare ye the way of the Lord, make his paths straight.'" And the same John had his raiment of camel's hair, and a leathern girdle about his loins; and his meat was locusts and wild honey.

322

Then went out to him Jerusalem, and all Judea, and all the region round about Jordan, and were baptized of him in Jordan, confessing their sins. But when he saw many of the Pharisees and Sadducees come to his baptism, he said unto them, "O generation of vipers, who hath warned you to flee from the wrath to come? Bring forth therefore fruits meet for repentance: and think not to say within yourselves, 'We have Abraham to our father': for I say unto you, that God is able of these stones to raise up children unto Abraham. And now also the axe is laid unto the root of the trees: therefore every tree which bringeth not forth good fruit is hewn down, and cast into the fire.

"I indeed baptize you with water unto repentance: but he that cometh after me is mightier than I, whose shoes I am not worthy to bear: he shall baptize you with the Holy Ghost, and with fire: whose fan is in his hand, and he will thoroughly purge his floor, and gather his wheat into the garner; but he will burn up the chaff with unquenchable fire."

Then cometh Jesus from Galilee to Jordan unto John, to be baptized of him. But John forbade him, saying, "I have need to be baptized of thee, and comest thou to me?"

And Jesus answering said unto him, "Suffer it to be so now: for thus it becometh us to fulfill all righteousness." Then he suffered him.

And Jesus, when he was baptized, went up straightway out of the water: and, lo, the heavens were opened unto him, and he saw the Spirit of God descending like a dove, and lighting upon him: and lo, a voice from heaven, saying, "This is my beloved Son, in whom I am well pleased."

[*Matthew 3:1–17*]

Temptation in the Desert

Then was Jesus led up of the spirit into the wilderness to be tempted of the devil. And when he had fasted forty days and forty nights, he was afterward ahungered.

And when the tempter came to him, he said, "If thou be the Son of God, command that these stones be made bread."

But he answered and said, "It is written, 'Man shall not live by bread alone, but by every word that proceedeth out of the mouth of God.'"

Then the devil taketh him up into the holy city, and setteth him on a pinnacle of the temple, and saith unto him, "If thou be the Son of God, cast thyself down: for it is written, 'He shall give his angels charge concerning thee: and in their hands they shall bear thee up, lest at any time thou dash thy foot against a stone.'"

Jesus said unto him, "It is written again, 'Thou shalt not tempt the Lord thy God.'"

Again, the devil taketh him up into an exceeding high mountain, and showeth him all the kingdoms of the world, and the glory of them, and saith unto him, "All these things will I give thee, if thou wilt fall down and worship me."

Then saith Jesus unto him, "Get thee hence, Satan: for it is written, 'Thou shalt worship the Lord thy God, and him only shalt thou serve.'"

Then the devil leaveth him, and behold, angels came and ministered unto him.

[*Matthew 4:1–11*]

Of what importance is the "Word" to Jews and Christians? In answering, consider the role "hearing" played in the lives of such Old Testament figures as Abraham, Moses, and Job. Explain in what sense "the Word was made flesh."

What role does John the Baptist play in the mission of Jesus? Why is he so hesitant to baptize Jesus? What does the "dove" symbolize in this scene?

What is the significance of Jesus' temptation? By what authority does he answer the devil's taunts?

In what ways has Jesus undergone an *initiation* in these pages?

VOICES IN THE WILDERNESS

Nikos Kazantzakis

"Every moment of Christ's life is a conflict and a victory," says Kazantzakis in the "Prologue" * to The Last Temptation of Christ, *his uniquely imaginative novel based on the life and death of Jesus. "He conquered the invincible enchantment of simple human pleasures; he conquered temptations, continually transubstantiated*

---

* The "Prologue" is reprinted in its entirety as the concluding section in this unit, beginning on p. 373.

flesh into spirit, and ascended." In the selection that follows,
Kazantzakis reinterprets Christ's encounter with Satan in the
wilderness in light of these themes, presenting the reader with a highly
unorthodox, yet provocative, recreation of the familiar event.

Jesus opened his eyes. The river Jordan, the Baptist and the baptized, the camels and the lamentations of the people—all flared up in the air and were snuffed out. The desert now stretched before him. The sun had risen high and was burning: the stones steamed like loaves of bread. He felt his insides being mowed down by hunger. "I'm hungry," he murmured, looking at the stones, "I'm hungry!" He remembered the bread which the Old Samaritan woman had presented them. How delicious it had been, sweet like honey! He remembered the honey, split olives and dates he was treated to whenever he passed through a village; and the holy supper they had when, kneeling on the shore of Lake Gennesaret, they removed the grill, with its row of sweet-smelling fish, from the andirons. And afterward, the figs, grapes and pomegranates came to his mind, agitating him still further.

His throat was dry and parched from thirst. How many rivers flowed in the world! All these waters which bounded from rock to rock, rolled from one end of the land of Israel to the other, ran into the Dead Sea and disappeared—and he had not even a drop to drink! He thought of these waters and his thirst increased. He felt dizzy; his eyes fluttered. Two cunning devils in the shape of young rabbits emerged from the burning sand, stood up on their hind legs and danced. They turned, saw the eremite, screamed happily and began to hop toward him. They climbed onto his knees and jumped to his shoulders. One was cool, like water, the other warm and fragrant, like bread; but as he longingly put out his hands to grasp them, with a single bound they vanished into the air.

He closed his eyes and recollected the thoughts which hunger and thirst had dispersed. God came to his mind: he was neither hungry nor thirsty any more. He reflected on the salvation of the world. Ah, if the day of the Lord could only come with love! Was not God omnipotent? Why couldn't he perform a miracle and by touching men's hearts make them blossom? Look how each year at the Passover bare stems, meadows and thorns opened up at his touch. If only one day men could awake to find their deepest selves in bloom!

He smiled. In his thoughts the world had flowered. The incestuous king was baptized, his soul cleansed. He had sent away his sister-in-law Herodias and she had returned to her husband. The high priests and noblemen had opened their larders and coffers, distributed their goods to the poor; and the poor in their turn breathed freely once more and banished hate, jealousy and fear from their hearts. . . . Jesus looked at his hands. The ax which the Forerunner had surrendered to him had blossomed: a flowering almond branch was now in his palm.

The day concluded with this feeling of relief. He lay down on the rock and fell asleep. All night long in his sleep he heard water running, small rabbits dancing, a strange rustling, and two damp nostrils examining him. It seemed to him that toward midnight a hungry jackal came up and smelled him. Was this a carcass, or wasn't it? The beast stood for a moment unable to make up its mind. And Jesus, in his sleep, pitied it. He wanted to open his breast and give it food, but restrained himself. He was keeping his flesh for men.

He woke up before dawn. A network of large stars covered the sky; the air was fluffy and blue. At this hour, he reflected, the cocks awake, the villages are roused, men open their eyes and look through the skylight at the radiance which has come once more. The infants awake in their turn, the bawling begins and the mothers approach, holding forth their full breasts. . . . For an instant the world undulated over the desert with its men and houses and cocks and infants and mothers —all made from the morning frost and breeze. But the sun would now rise to swallow them up! The eremite's heart skipped a beat. If only I could make this frost everlasting! he thought. But God's mind is an abyss, his love a terrifying precipice. He plants a world, destroys it just as it is about to give fruit, and then plants another. He recalled the Baptist's words: "Who knows, perhaps love carries an ax . . ." and shuddered. He looked at the desert. Ferociously red, it swayed under the sun, which had risen angrily, zoned by a storm. The wind blew; the smell of pitch and sulphur came to his nostrils. He thought of Sodom and Gomorrah—palaces, theaters, taverns, prostitutes—plunged in the tar. Abraham had shouted, "Have mercy, Lord; do not burn them. Are you not good? Take pity, therefore, on your creatures." And God had answered him, "I am just, I shall burn them all!"

Was this, then, God's way? If so, it was a great impudence for the heart—that clod of soft mud—to stand up and shout, Stop! . . . What is our duty? he asked himself. It is to look down, to find God's tracks in the soil and follow them. I look down; I clearly see God's imprint on Sodom and Gomorrah. The entire Dead Sea is God's imprint. He trod, and palaces, theaters, taverns, brothels—the whole of Sodom and Gomorrah—were engulfed! He will tread once more, and once more the earth—kings, high priests, Pharisees, Sadducees—all will sink to the bottom.

Without realizing it, he had begun to shout. His mind was wild with fury. Forgetting that his knees were unable to support him, he tried to rise, to set out on God's trail, but he collapsed supine onto the ground, out of breath. "I am unable; don't you see me?" he cried, lifting his eyes toward the burning heavens. "I am unable; why do you choose me? I cannot endure!" And as he cried out, he saw a black mass on the sand before him: the goat, disemboweled, its legs in the air. He remembered how he had leaned over and seen his own face in the leaden eyes. "I am the goat," he murmured. "God placed him along my path to show me who I am and where I am heading. . . ." Suddenly he began to weep. "I don't want . . . I don't want . . ." he murmured, "I don't want to be alone. Help me!"

And then, while he was bowed over and weeping, a pleasant breeze blew, the stench of the tar and the carcass disappeared and a sweet perfume pervaded the world. The eremite heard water, bracelets and laughter jingling in the distance and approaching. His eyelids, armpits and throat felt refreshed. He lifted his eyes. On a stone in front of him a snake with the eyes and breasts of a woman was licking its lips and regarding him. The eremite stepped back, terrified. Was this a snake, a woman, or a cunning demon of the desert? Such a serpent had wrapped itself around the forbidden tree of Paradise and seduced the first man and woman to unite and give birth to sin. . . . He heard laughter and the sweet, wheedling voice of a woman: "I felt sorry for you, son of Mary. You cried, 'I don't want to be alone. Help me!' I pitied you and came. What can I do for you?"

"I don't want you. I didn't call you. Who are you?"

"Your soul."

"My soul!" Jesus exclaimed, and he closed his eyes, horrified.

"Yes, your soul. You are afraid of being alone. Your great-grandfather Adam had the same fear. He too shouted for help. His flesh and soul united, and woman emerged from his rib to keep him company."

"I don't want you, don't want you! I remember the apple you fed to Adam. I remember the angel with the scimitar!"

"You remember, and that's why you're in pain and you cry out and cannot find your way. I shall show it to you. Give me your hand. Don't look back; don't recall anything. See how my breasts take the lead. Follow them, my spouse. They know the way perfectly."

"You are going to lead me also to sweet sin and the Inferno. I'm not coming. Mine is another road."

The serpent giggled derisively and showed her sharp, poisonous teeth. "Do you wish to follow God's tracks, the tracks of the eagle—you worm! You, son of the Carpenter, wish to bear the sins of an entire race! Aren't your own sins enough for you? What impudence to think that it's your duty to save the world!"

She's right . . . she's right . . . the eremite thought, trembling. What impudence to wish to save the world!

"I have a secret to tell you, dear son of Mary," said the snake in a sweet voice, her eyes sparkling. She slid down from the rock like water and began, richly decorated, to roll toward him. She arrived at his feet, climbed onto his knees, curled herself up and with a spring reached his thighs, loins, breast and finally leaned against his shoulder. The eremite, despite himself, inclined his head to hear her. The snake licked Jesus' ear with her tongue. Her voice was seductive and far away: it seemed to be coming from Galilee, from the edge of Lake Gennesaret.

"It's Magdalene . . . it's Magdalene . . . it's Magdalene . . ."

"What?" said Jesus, shuddering. "What about Magdalene?"

". . . it's Magdalene you must save!" the snake hissed imperatively. "Not the Earth—forget about the Earth. It's her, Magdalene, you must save!"

Jesus tried to shake the serpent away from his head, but she thrust herself forward and vibrated her tongue in his ear. "Her body is beautiful, cool and accomplished. All nations have passed over her, but it has been written in God's hand since your childhood that she is for you. Take her! God created man and woman to match, like the key and the lock. Open her. Your children sit huddled together and numb inside her, waiting for you to blow away their numbness so that they may rise and come out to walk in the sun. . . . Do you hear what I'm telling you? Lift your eyes, give me some sign. Just nod your head, my darling, and this very hour I shall bring you, on a fresh bed—your wife."

"My wife?"

"Your wife. Look how God married the whore Jerusalem. The nations passed over her, but he married her to save her. Look how the prophet Hosea married the whore Gomer, daughter of Debelaim. In the same way, God commands you to sleep with Mary Magdalene, your wife, to have children, and save her."

The serpent had now pressed its hard, cool, round breast against Jesus' own and was sliding slowly, tortuously, wrapping itself around him. Jesus grew pale, closed his eyes, saw Magdalene's firm, high-rumped body wriggling along the shores of Lake Gennesaret, saw her gaze toward the river Jordan and sigh. She extended her hand—she was seeking him; and her bosom was filled with children: his own. He had only to twitch the corner of his eye, to give a sign, and all at once: what happiness! How his life would change, sweeten, become more human! This was the way, this! He would return to Nazareth, to his mother's house, would become reconciled with his brothers. It was nothing but youthful folly—madness—to want to save the world and die for mankind. But thanks to Magdalene, God bless her, he would be cured; he would return to his workshop, take up once more his old beloved craft, once more make plows, cradles and troughs; he would have children and become a human being, the master of a household. The peasants would respect him and stand up when he passed. He would work the whole week long and on Saturday go to the synagogue in the clean garments woven for him of linen and silk by his wife Magdalene, with his expensive kerchief over his head, his golden wedding ring on his finger; and he would have his stall with the elders, would sit and listen peacefully and indifferently while the seething, half-insane Scribes and Pharisees sweated and shivered to interpret the Holy Scriptures. He would snigger and look at them with sympathy. Where would they ever end up, these theologians! He was interpreting Holy Scripture quietly and surely by taking a wife, having children, by constructing plows, cradles, and troughs. . . .

He opened his eyes and saw the desert. Where had the day gone! The sun was once more inclining toward the horizon. The serpent, her breast glued to his own, was waiting. She hissed tranquilly, seductively, and a tender, plaintive lullaby flowed into the evening air. The entire desert rocked and lullabied like a mother.

"I'm waiting . . . I'm waiting . . ." the snake hissed salaciously. "Night has overtaken us. I'm cold. Decide. Nod to me, and the doors of Paradise will be opened to you. Decide, my darling. Magdalene is waiting. . . ."

The eremite felt paralyzed with fear. As he was about to open his mouth to say Yes, he felt someone above looking down on him. Terrified, he lifted his head and saw two eyes in the air, two eyes only, as black as night, and two white eyebrows which were moving and signaling to him: No! No! No! Jesus' heart contracted. He looked up again beseechingly, as if he wished to scream: Leave me alone, give me permission, do not be angry! But the eyes had grown ferocious and the eyebrows vibrated threateningly.

"No! No! No!" Jesus then shouted, and two large tears rolled from his eyes.

All at once the serpent writhed, unglued herself from him and with a muffled roar exploded. The air was glutted with the stench.

Jesus fell on his face. His mouth, nostrils and eyes filled with sand. His mind was blank. Forgetting his hunger and thirst, he wept—wept as though his wife and all his children had died, as though his whole life had been ruined.

"Lord, Lord," he murmured, biting the sand, "Father, have you no mercy? Your will be done: how many times have I said this to you until now, how many times shall I say it in the future? All my life I shall quiver, resist and say it: Your will be done!"

In this way, murmuring and swallowing the sand, he fell asleep; and as the eyes of his body closed, those of his soul opened and he saw the specter of a serpent as thick as the body of a man and extending in length from one end of the night to the other. She was stretched out on the sand with her wide, bright-red mouth opened at his side. Opposite this mouth hopped an ornate, trembling partridge struggling in vain to open its wings and escape. It staggered forward uttering small, weak cries, its feathers raised out of fear. The motionless serpent kept her eyes glued on it, her mouth opened. She was in no hurry, for she was sure of her prey. The partridge advanced little by little directly toward the opened mouth, stumbling on its crooked legs. Jesus stood still and watched, trembling like the partridge. At daybreak the bird had at last reached the gaping mouth. It quivered for a moment, glanced quickly around as though seeking aid; then suddenly stretched forth its neck and entered head first, feet together. The mouth closed. Jesus was able to see the partridge, a ball of feathers and meat and ruby-colored feet, descend little by little toward the dragon's belly.

He jumped up, terrified. The desert was a mass of swelling rose-colored waves.

The sun was rising. "It is God," he murmured, trembling. "And the partridge is . . ."

His voice broke. He did not have the strength to complete his reflection. But inside himself he thought: . . . man's soul. The partridge is man's soul!

He remained plunged in this reflection for hours. The sun came up, set the sand on fire; it pierced Jesus' scalp, went inside him and parched his mind, throat and breast. His entrails were suspended like bunches of left-over grapes after the autumn vintage. His tongue had stuck to his palate, his skin was peeling off, his bones emerging; and his fingertips had turned completely blue.

Time, within him, had become as small as a heartbeat, as large as death. He was no longer hungry or thirsty; he no longer desired children and a wife. His whole soul had squeezed into his eyes. He saw —that was all: he saw. But at precisely noon his sight grew dim; the world vanished and a gigantic mouth gaped somewhere in front of him, its lower jaw the earth, its upper jaw the skies. Trembling, he dragged himself slowly forward toward the opened mouth, his neck stretched forward. . . .

The days and nights went by like flashes of white and black lightning. One midnight a lion came and stood in front of him, proudly shaking its mane. Its voice was like a man's: "Welcome to my lair, victorious ascetic. I salute the man who conquered the minor virtues, the small joys, and happiness! We don't like what's easy and sure; our sights are on difficult things. Magdalene isn't a big enough wife for us: we wish to marry the entire Earth. Bridegroom, the bride has sighed, the lamps of the heavens are lighted, the guests have arrived: let us go."

"Who are you?"

"Yourself—the hungry lion inside your heart and loins that at night prowls around the sheepfolds, the kingdoms of this world, and weighs whether or not to jump in and eat. I rush from Babylon to Jerusalem, from Jerusalem to Alexandria, from Alexandria to Rome, shouting: I am hungry; everything is mine! At daybreak I re-enter your breast and shrink; the terrifying lion becomes a lamb. I play at being the humble ascetic who desires nothing, who seems able to live on a grain of wheat, a sip of water, and on a naïve, accommodating God whom he tries to flatter with the name of Father. But secretly, in my heart, I am ashamed; I grow fierce and yearn for nightfall when I can throw off my sheepskin and begin once more to roar, roam the night and stamp my four feet down on Babylon, Jerusalem, Alexandria and Rome."

"I don't know who you are. I never desired the kingdom of this world. The kingdom of heaven is sufficient for me."

"It is not. You deceive yourself, friend. It is not sufficient for you, You don't dare gaze within yourself, deep within your loins and heart —to find me. . . . Why do you look askance and think ill of me? Do you believe I am Temptation, an emissary of the Sly One, come to mislead you? You brainless hermit, what strength can external temptation have? The fortress is taken only from within. I am the deepest voice of your deepest self; I am the lion within you. You have wrapped yourself in the skin of a lamb to encourage men to approach you, so that you can devour them. Remember, when you were a small child a Chaldean sorceress looked at your palm. 'I see many stars,' she said, 'many crosses. You shall become king.' Why do you pretend to forget? You re-member it day and night. Rise, son of David, and enter your kingdom!"

Jesus listened with bowed head. Little by little he recognized the voice, little by little he recalled having heard it sometimes in his dreams and once when he was a child and Judas had thrashed him, and one other time when he had left his house and roamed the fields for days and nights pinched by hunger, then returned shamefully home, to be greeted with hoots by his brothers, lame Simon and pious Jacob, who were standing in the doorway. Then, truly, he had heard the lion roar inside him. . . . And only the other day, when he carried the cross to the Zealot's crucifixion and passed before the stormy crowd, everyone looking at him with disgust and moving out of his path, the lion had again jumped up within him, and with such force that he was thrown down.

And now, in this forsaken midnight—look! The bellowing lion inside him had come out and stood before him. It rubbed itself against him, vanished and reappeared, as though going in and out of him, and playfully tapped him with its tail. . . . Jesus felt his heart grow more and more ferocious. The lion is really right, he thought. I've had enough of all this. I'm fed up with being hungry, with wanting to play at humility, with offering the other cheek only to get it slapped. I'm tired of flattering this man-eating God with the name of Father in order to cajole him to be more gentle; tired of hearing my brothers curse me, my mother weep, men laugh when I go by; sick of going barefooted, of not being able to buy the honey, wine and women I see when I pass by the market, and of finding courage only in my sleep to have God bring them to me, so that I can taste and embrace the empty air! I'm sick of it all! I shall rise, gird myself with the ancestral sword—am I not the son of David?—and enter my kingdom! The lion is right. Enough of ideas and clouds and kingdoms of heaven. Stones and soil and flesh—that is my kingdom!

He rose. Somewhere he found the strength to jump up and gird himself, gird himself interminably with an invisible sword, bellowing like a lion. He was ready. "Forward!" he cried. He turned, but the lion had disappeared. He heard pulsating laughter above him and a voice: "Look!" A flash of lightning knifed through the night and stood fixed, motionless. Under it were cities with walls and towers, houses, roads, squares, people; and all around, plains, mountains, sea. Babylon was to the right, Jerusalem and Alexandria to the left, and across the sea was Rome. Once more he heard the voice: "Look!"

Jesus raised his eyes. A yellow-winged angel dropped headfirst from the sky. Lamentations were heard: in the four kingdoms the people lifted their arms to heaven, but their hands fell off, gnawed away by leprosy. They parted their lips to cry *Help!* and their lips fell, devoured by leprosy. The streets filled with hands and noses and mouths.

And while Jesus cried with upraised arms, "Mercy, Lord, have pity on mankind!" a second angel, dapple-winged, with bells around his feet and neck, fell headfirst from heaven. All at once laughter and guffawing broke out over the entire earth: struck down by madness, the lepers were running helter-skelter. Whatever remained of their bodies had burst into peals of laughter.

Trembling, Jesus blocked his ears so that he would not hear. And then a third angel, red-winged, fell like a meteor from the sky. Four

The Temptation of Christ on the Mountain (c. 1308–11) by Duccio. COPYRIGHT
THE FRICK COLLECTION.

fountains of fire rose up, four columns of smoke, and the stars were
extinguished for want of air. A light breeze blew, scattering the fumes.
Jesus looked. The four kingdoms had become four handfuls of ashes.

The voice sounded once more: "These, wretch, are the kingdoms of
this world which you are setting out to possess; and those are my three
beloved angels: Leprosy, Madness and Fire. The day of the Lord has
come—my day, mine!" With this last clap of thunder the lightning
disappeared.

The dawn found Jesus with his face plunged in the sand. During
the night he must have rolled off his stone and wept and wept, for his
eyes were swollen and smarting. He looked around him. Could this
endless sand be his soul? The desert was shifting, coming to life. He
heard shrill cries, mocking laughter, weeping. Small animals resembling

rabbits, squirrels and weasels, all with ruby-red eyes, were hopping toward him. It is Madness, he thought, Madness, come to devour me. He cried out, and the animals disappeared; an archangel with the half moon suspended from his neck and a joyous star between his eyebrows towered up before him and unfurled his green wings.

Jesus shaded his eyes against the dazzling light. "Archangel," he whispered.

The archangel closed his wings and smiled. "Don't you recognize me?" he said. "Don't you remember me?"

"No, no! Who are you? Go farther away, Archangel. You're blinding me."

"Do you remember when you were a small child still unable to walk, you clung to the door of your house and to your mother's clothes so that you would not fall, and shouted within yourself, shouted loudly, 'God, make me God! God, make me God! God, make me God!' "

"Don't remind me of that shameless blasphemy. I remember it!"

"I am that inner voice. I shouted then; I shout still, but you're afraid and pretend not to hear. Now, however, you are going to listen to me, like it or not. The hour has come. I chose you before you were born —you, out of the whole of mankind. I work and gleam within you, prevent you from falling into the minor virtues, the small pleasures, into happiness. Behold how just now when Woman came into the desert where I brought you, I banished her. The kingdoms came, and I banished them. I did, I, not you. I am reserving you for a destiny much more important, much more difficult."

"More important . . . more difficult . . . ?"

"What did you long for when you were a child? To become God. That is what you shall become!"

"I? I?"

"Don't shrink back; don't moan. That is what you shall become, what you have already become. What words do you think the wild dove threw over you at the Jordan?"

"Tell me! Tell me!"

" 'You are my son, my only son!' That was the message brought you by the wild dove. But it was not a wild dove; it was the archangel Gabriel. I salute you, therefore: Son, only son of God!"

Two wings beat within Jesus' breast. He felt a large rebellious morning star burning between his eyebrows. A cry rose up within him: I am not a man, not an angel, not your slave, Adonai—I am your son. I shall sit on your throne to judge the living and the dead. In my right hand I shall hold a sphere—the world—and play with it. Make room for me to sit down!

He heard peals of laughter in the air. Jesus gave a start. The angel had vanished. He uttered a piercing cry, "Lucifer!" and fell prone onto the sand.

"I shall see you again," said a mocking voice. "We shall meet again one day—soon!"

"Never, never, Satan!" Jesus bellowed, with his face buried in the sand.

"Soon!" the voice repeated. "At this Passover, miserable wretch!"

Jesus began to wail. His tears fell in warm drops on the sand, washing, rinsing, purifying his soul. Toward evening a cool breeze blew; the sun became gentle and colored the distant mountains pink. And then Jesus heard a merciful command, and an invisible hand touched his shoulder.

"Stand up, the day of the Lord is here. Run and carry the message to men: I am coming!"

Kazantzakis' recreation of the temptation in the wilderness is radically different from the New Testament versions of it. Discuss and analyze each of the three temptations in Kazantzakis' version and then compare them to those recounted by Matthew in the previous selection. In what ways is Kazantzakis' version a depiction of Christ's victory over himself as well as over Satan? Do you find any hints of such a victory in Matthew's account? Discuss why Kazantzakis might have chosen to depict the scene in this way. (For added insight into Kazantzakis' conception of Christ's struggle and its significance, you may wish at this time to read the "Prologue" to *The Last Temptation of Christ*, the final selection of this unit.)

AND ALL THE PEOPLE WERE AMAZED
(John and Luke)

Little is known of Jesus' life between the age of twelve, when he visited the Temple, and the age of thirty, when he was baptized by John and then tempted in the wilderness. During the next three years, beginning with the choosing of his disciples, his teaching in Capernaum, the performance of his first miracle at a wedding in Cana, and the deliverance of the memorable Sermon on the Mount in Galilee, Jesus entered into public life and began to preach in the manner of the Messiah prophesied in the Old Testament. Wherever he went, thousands flocked to hear the young man of Nazareth who promised a new life to those bound in despair. His miracles, defying rational explanation, convinced many to repent and "seek the kingdom of God." Often he would speak in parables, stories which were based on experiences familiar to his listeners but which communicated profound spiritual truths to those who could penetrate their seemingly simple surfaces. The passages that follow represent only a few of the highlights from those three known years of Jesus' public life as a teacher and worker of miracles.

The Marriage at Cana

And the third day there was a marriage in Cana of Galilee; and the mother of Jesus was there: and both Jesus was called, and his disciples, to the marriage. And when they wanted wine, the mother of Jesus saith unto him, "They have no wine."

Jesus saith unto her, "Woman, what have I to do with thee? Mine hour is not yet come."

His mother saith unto the servants, "Whatsoever he saith unto you, do it." And there were set there six waterpots of stone, after the manner of the purifying of the Jews, containing two or three firkins apiece.

Jesus saith unto them, "Fill the waterpots with water." And they filled them up to the brim.

And he saith unto them, "Draw out now, and bear unto the governor of the feast." And they bare it.

When the ruler of the feast had tasted the water that was made wine, and knew not whence it was (but the servants which drew the water knew), the governor of the feast called the bridegroom, and saith unto him, "Every man at the beginning doth set forth good wine; and when men have well drunk, then that which is worse: but thou hast kept the good wine until now."

This beginning of miracles did Jesus in Cana of Galilee, and manifested forth his glory; and his disciples believed on him.

[*John 2:1–11*]

Jesus Walks on the Sea

And when even was now come, his disciples went down unto the sea, and entered into a ship, and went over the sea toward Capernaum. And it was now dark, and Jesus was not come to them. And the sea arose by reason of a great wind that blew. So when they had rowed about five and twenty or thirty furlongs, they see Jesus walking on the sea, and drawing nigh unto the ship: and they were afraid.

But he saith unto them, "It is I; be not afraid."

Christ at the Sea of Galilee (c. 1575–80) by Tintoretto. NATIONAL GALLERY OF ART, WASHINGTON, D.C.: SAMUEL H. KRESS COLLECTION.

Then they willingly received him into the ship: and immediately the ship was at the land whither they went.

[John 6:16–21]

The Centurion and His Servant

Now when he had ended all his sayings in the audience of the people, he entered into Capernaum.

And a certain centurion's servant, who was dear unto him, was sick, and ready to die. And when he heard of Jesus, he sent unto him the elders of the Jews, beseeching him that he would come and heal his servant. And when they came to Jesus, they besought him instantly, saying that he was worthy for whom he should do this: for he loveth our nation, and he hath built us a synagogue. Then Jesus went with them.

And when he was now not far from the house, the centurion sent friends to him, saying unto him, "Lord, trouble not thyself: for I am not worthy that thou shouldest enter under my roof: wherefore neither thought I myself worthy to come unto thee: but say in a word, and my servant shall be healed. For I also am a man set under authority, having under me soldiers, and I say unto one, 'Go,' and he goeth; and to another, 'Come,' and he cometh; and to my servant, 'Do this,' and he doeth it."

When Jesus heard these things, he marveled at him, and turned him about, and said unto the people that followed him, "I say unto you, I have not found so great faith, no, not in Israel."

And they that were sent, returning to the house, found the servant whole that had been sick.

[Luke 7:1–10]

Lazarus Raised from the Dead

Now a certain man was sick, named Lazarus, of Bethany, the town of Mary and her sister Martha. (It was that Mary which anointed the Lord with ointment, and wiped his feet with her hair, whose brother Lazarus was sick.) Therefore his sisters sent unto him, saying, "Lord, behold, he whom thou lovest is sick."

When Jesus heard that, he said, "This sickness is not unto death, but for the glory of God, that the Son of God might be glorified thereby."

Now Jesus loved Martha, and her sister, and Lazarus. When he had heard therefore that he was sick, he abode two days still in the same place where he was. Then after that saith he to his disciples, "Let us go into Judea again."

His disciples said unto him, "Master, the Jews of late sought to stone thee; and goest thou thither again?"

Jesus answered, "Are there not twelve hours in the day? If any man walk in the day, he stumbleth not, because he seeth the light of this world. But if a man walk in the night, he stumbleth, because there is no light in him." These things said he: and after that he saith unto them, "Our friend Lazarus sleepeth; but I go, that I may awake him out of sleep."

Then said his disciples, "Lord, if he sleep, he shall do well."

Howbeit Jesus spake of his death: but they thought that he had spoken of taking of rest in sleep. Then said Jesus unto them plainly, "Lazarus is dead."

Then when Jesus came, he found that he had lain in the grave four days already. Now Bethany was nigh unto Jerusalem, about fifteen furlongs off: and many of the Jews came to Martha and Mary, to comfort them concerning their brother. Then Martha, as soon as she heard that Jesus was coming, went and met him: but Mary sat still in the house.

Then said Martha unto Jesus, "Lord, if thou hadst been here, my brother had not died. But I know that even now, whatsoever thou wilt ask of God, God will give it thee."

Jesus saith unto her, "Thy brother shall rise again."

Martha saith unto him, "I know that he shall rise again in the resurrection at the last day."

Jesus said unto her, "I am the resurrection, and the life: he that believeth in me, though he were dead, yet shall he live: and whosoever liveth and believeth in me shall never die. Believest thou this?"

She saith unto him, "Yea, Lord: I believe that thou art the Christ, the Son of God, which should come into the world."

And when she had so said, she went her way, and called Mary her sister secretly, saying, "The Master is come, and calleth for thee." As soon as she heard that, she arose quickly, and came unto him.

Now Jesus was not yet come into the town, but was in that place where Martha met him. The Jews then which were with her in the house, and comforted her, when they saw Mary, that she rose up hastily and went out, followed her, saying, "She goeth unto the grave to weep there."

Then when Mary was come where Jesus was, and saw him, she fell down at his feet, saying unto him, "Lord, if thou hadst been here, my brother had not died."

When Jesus therefore saw her weeping, and the Jews also weeping which came with her, he groaned in the spirit, and was troubled, and said, "Where have ye laid him?"

They said unto him, "Lord, come and see." Jesus wept. Then said the Jews, "Behold how he loved him!" And some of them said, "Could not this man, which opened the eyes of the blind, have caused that even this man should not have died?"

Jesus therefore again groaning in himself cometh to the grave. It was a cave, and a stone lay upon it. Jesus said, "Take ye away the stone."

Martha, the sister of him that was dead, saith unto him, "Lord, by this time he stinketh: for he hath been dead four days."

Jesus saith unto her, "Said I not unto thee, that, if thou wouldest believe, thou shouldest see the glory of God?"

Then they took away the stone from the place where the dead was laid. And Jesus lifted up his eyes, and said, "Father, I thank thee that thou hast heard me. And I knew that thou hearest me always: but because of the people which stand by I said it, that they may believe that thou hast sent me."

And when he thus had spoken, he cried with a loud voice, "Lazarus, come forth."

And he that was dead came forth, bound hand and foot with grave-clothes: and his face was bound about with a napkin. Jesus saith unto them, "Loose him, and let him go."

Then many of the Jews which came to Mary, and had seen the things which Jesus did, believed on him. But some of them went their ways to the Pharisees, and told them what things Jesus had done.

[John 11:1–14, 17–46]

The Triumphant Entry into Jerusalem

And when they drew nigh unto Jerusalem, and were come to Bethphage, unto the mount of Olives, then sent Jesus two disciples, saying unto them, "Go into the village over against you, and straightway ye shall find an ass tied, and a colt with her: loose them, and bring them unto me. And if any man say aught unto you, ye shall say, 'The Lord hath need of them'; and straightway he will send them."

All this was done, that it might be fulfilled which was spoken by the prophet, saying, "Tell ye the daughter of Zion, 'Behold, thy King cometh unto thee, meek, and sitting upon an ass, and a colt the foal of an ass.' "

And the disciples went, and did as Jesus commanded them, and brought the ass, and the colt, and put on them their clothes, and they set him thereon.

And a very great multitude spread their garments in the way; others cut down branches from the trees, and strewed them in the way. And the multitudes that went before, and that followed, cried, saying "Hosanna to the Son of David: Blessed is he that cometh in the name of the Lord; Hosanna in the highest."

And when he was come into Jerusalem, all the city was moved, saying, "Who is this?"

And the multitude said, "This is Jesus the prophet of Nazareth of Galilee."

[*Matthew 21:1–11*]

Parable of the Vineyard

Then began he to speak to the people this parable: "A certain man planted a vineyard, and let it forth to husbandmen, and went into a far country for a long time. And at the season he sent a servant to the husbandmen, that they should give him of the fruit of the vineyard: but the husbandmen beat him, and sent him away empty. And again he sent another servant: and they beat him also, and entreated him shamefully, and sent him away empty. And again he sent a third: and they wounded him also, and cast him out. Then said the lord of the vineyard, 'What shall I do? I will send my beloved son: it may be they will reverence him when they see him.' But when the husbandmen saw him, they reasoned among themselves, saying, 'This is the heir: come, let us kill him, that the inheritance may be ours.' So they cast him out of the vineyard, and killed him. What therefore shall the lord of the vineyard do unto them? He shall come and destroy these husbandmen, and shall give the vineyard to others."

And when they heard it, they said, "God forbid."

And he beheld them, and said, "What is this then that is written,

'The stone which the builders rejected,
The same is become the head of the corner'?

Whosoever shall fall upon that stone shall be broken; but on whomsoever it shall fall, it will grind him to powder."

And the chief priests and the scribes the same hour sought to lay hands on him; and they feared the people: for they perceived that he had spoken this parable against them. And they watched him, and sent forth spies, which should feign themselves just men, that they might take hold of his words, so that they might deliver him unto the power and authority of the governor.

And they asked him, saying, "Master, we know that thou sayest and teachest rightly, neither acceptest thou the person of any, but teachest the way of God truly: Is it lawful for us to give tribute to Caesar, or no?"

But he perceived their craftiness, and said unto them, "Why tempt ye me? Show me a penny. Whose image and superscription hath it?"

They answered and said, "Caesar's."

And he said unto them, "Render therefore unto Caesar the things which be Caesar's, and unto God the things which be God's."

And they could not take hold of his words before the people: and they marveled at his answer, and held their peace.

[*Luke 20:9–26*]

In light of what you know about the Old Testament and the life of Christ, try to decipher the "Parable of the Vineyard." Your analysis should attempt to unravel and explain each of the following details: the "certain man," the "vineyard" he planted, the "husbandmen" placed in charge of it, the treatment of his "messengers," the reception his "son" received and at whose hands, what became of the son, and lastly the "stone" which the builders rejected. Why do you think the chief priests and scribes believed that Christ "had spoken this parable against them"?

THE EYE OF A SOLDIER

Geoffrey Household

The older I get, the more I see that it is trust between man and man which keeps civilization together. You wondered just now how I stand the strain of commanding on the Syrian frontier. And I must admit that Caesar has graciously given me more responsibility than troops.

Tell him we are alert, but not alarmed. I have the confidence of the Parthian governor across the border, and between the pair of us we settle any frontier incidents. A much more able general than I am, he can do what he likes with his home government. As soon as I realized that, I set myself to win his friendship.

If the fates send you a man worthy of trust, then trust him—that has always been my principle! I will give you a very odd instance. It happened twenty years ago. Do you remember Silvanus? Yes, that one— a possible for color sergeant if only he had been tall enough. Now there's a man who has left a beloved memory behind him!

You were at Caesarea then with the legion, and I was commanding the detachment of instructors which we had lent to Herod Antipas to train his local levies. A delicate job for any centurion, even of my seniority! But it was no use sending Herod a battalion commander. Except for the very few who have come up the hard way, like ourselves, they never know anything about drill.

We made a handy little force of the levies, too—just as fast as the Arab raiders and twice as efficient. Lack of discipline always means so much unnecessary bloodshed.

I often wonder how much it was all due to Silvanus. I should never have persuaded him to come with me if he hadn't been feeling mutinous because the pay was cut. He was just a loyal, sturdy Italian peasant who might have gone far if only he could have bothered to learn to read and write. As it was, a proper old soldier, wise as an owl and not above feathering his nest! The gods know he needed it! But a man on whom his centurion could utterly rely. You know how fond of them one gets.

Of course my handful of instructors thought themselves Romans among barbarians when they first arrived, and I saw that Silvanus sweated the wine out of them on an early parade in our own barracks before turning them loose on recruits. Meanwhile I made it my business to learn Aramaic in order to keep the lot of them out of trouble.

They looked for it sometimes. At Capernaum there was a beautiful little grove with its own stream, set just where the blue spearhead of Lake Tiberias would join the shaft, which they insisted was the perfect site for a temple to Jupiter.

I quite agreed with them. But it could not possibly be allowed. Jews are absurdly sensitive about what they call graven images. You remember all the excitement when Pilate carried the Eagles into Jerusalem —a first-class revolt on his hands in twenty-four hours! Myself, I used to warn the villagers whenever there was a color party marching up the Damascus road from Caesarea, so that they could look the other way. And they did—all but the small boys, of course.

Well, the main point was that there should be some sort of worship on a site which was made for it, and my fellows were not fussy about the various aspects of Jove. So I asked the headman of Capernaum if they would take over the services of a temple themselves and dedicate it to their own Jupiter. Rather like Plato's God, if I understood it—who must exist, but a simple soul like mine needs an intermediary. They were delighted, and so were my instructors. We had a couple of army surveyors with us, training road foremen, and it was child's play for them to run up a temple from the priest's drawings, though it looked a bit bare to me when it was finished.

After that we were as popular as a foreign military mission can ever hope to be. The local population used to talk to me about their history and religion—which seemed one and the same thing—and take me to visit their schools of wisdom. I made very little of it all, but I did learn to feel the mystery behind the words.

One summer evening several of my friends rowed me over to the east shore of the lake to listen to a philosopher who was making a considerable stir by his healing and his curious doctrines. They were doubtful about his politics, and I think they may have wanted me to question him. He was sitting by the side of a goat track and talking to some fishermen. I listened for half an hour, or more. Once our eyes met, and he smiled at me. But I had no right to speak.

I cannot describe him to you at all. You know what every intelligent man thinks when he worships Caesar as a god—that he could never have been such a master of his own luck unless he were as much above plain mortals as the gods are. So was this philosopher compared to ordinary men. He was divine. But his gold was the dust haze of the road, and his purple the bare hills in the last of the sun. He made me believe that law and the sword are only a beginning, and that the true virtue in making order is to prepare the way for gentleness and pity. I tell you he was young and lovely as Apollo in the stories of the Golden Age.

Soon after that Silvanus got his last attack of marsh fever. A shocking place for it, the Jordan Valley! I saw that he obeyed the doctor's orders to stay off the low ground, but it made no difference. The disease kept on coming back. And when hemorrhage set in, the doctor said Silvanus had had it. A clever Greek he was, true to his Hippocratic oath and excellent on wounds. Provided you could crawl off the field at all, you had a good chance of recovery.

If Silvanus had just been indispensable, I do not think I could have done what I did. But I loved the man; and that, I felt, gave me the right to call in the Galilean philosopher. When you appealed to him for the right reason he would heal. Never for show, or for money.

Of course I asked our Greek first. He called the cures harmless witch-craft which was efficacious when a man felt ill and wasn't, and of no use at all in a case of acute marsh fever.

Sound medical theory, no doubt. Yet I believe that if you feel ill you are, and healing is just as mysterious whether it is marsh fever or a Parthian spear in your liver or thinking you are Cincinnatus at the full moon. Somewhere is a divine law which we do not understand.

I did not like to ask the Galilean to come to my quarters, where Silvanus was lying. I had a bust of Grandfather up, and a *Roma Dea* and my delightful little bronze Aphrodite from Alexandria. Not that I thought he would have objected. But I hate putting people in a false position.

So I wrote him one of those flowery Oriental letters which all Syrians understand, saying that I was not worthy to receive him but that I should much appreciate a word from him about Silvanus.

And just to be on the safe side, I asked a delegation of my Caper-naum friends to carry the letter, as I knew they would tell him all about the temple, and that for a Roman centurion I was a reasonable com-panion. Myself, I doubted if any of this ceremoniousness was necessary. Apollo would not expect you to carry on like the court jeweler trying to get something on account out of Herod Antipas.

Having made all the proper gestures, I walked down the valley to see him myself. I left my uniform at home. I knew he would not be impressed by it. As a matter of fact, I do not think his own followers had any clear idea who I was. They were not interested in Rome.

And then a second time I looked into his eyes. It was as one soldier to another, as if I were saluting Caesar. You know the feeling. There you are, a very small part of the world and yet in contact with all of it. But, as I have tried to tell you, he had an utterly different kind of greatness. We were not in Caesar's world.

I told him about Silvanus, and how I loved the man.

"You need not go out of your way, sir," I said. "Just—do it."

"What makes you think I can?" he asked.

I am very bad at explaining myself. But I had a sense that what I said would, in some strange way, matter—matter more, I mean, than even words of mine which could now compel life or death on the frontier.

"Because there is a law in life as in the legion," I answered, "and you, sir, know what it is. I give an order. I say to a man Go, and he goes; or Come, and he comes. I do not have to be present to see that the order is carried out. Nor do you."

"Go back," he said. "Your servant is healed."

And then he turned to the crowd which had collected, and told them he had not seen such faith in all the Jews.

I do not understand what he meant to this day. I have no faith at all. I am a professional soldier, not a priest. But I know the power to command when I see it, and who was I to impose any limit upon his?

I shall never forget him. I cannot help recognizing that he must have gone to his death as willingly as you would or I, provided we knew it our duty to civilization—though, speaking for myself, if I foresaw that pain was going to be as cruel as upon the cross I should think twice about it. Yes, he was crucified by Pilate.

———————

What is it about the "young philosopher" that impressed the centurion? Why did he not ask him to come to his quarters? What insights into the mind of the centurion has Geoffrey Household provided us with that make his "act of faith," as we know it from the New Testament, so remarkable? What reason does the centurion give to explain the Galilean's willingness to go to his death?

Has reading this story changed your perception of the biblical account in any way? Is there a message in this story for us today?

AN OLD PALESTINIAN DONKEY

Paul Engle

I'd rather carry loads of olive wood
Or jugs of wine, than a man, for they won't trick you.
They'll bend your back, you'll carry more than you should,
But a man will jerk your mouth, and swear and kick you.

But once I took a man down streets paved with palms,
And crowds of people yelling, packed in tightly.
Slowly I walked. He smiled as they sang psalms.
His hand was soft on my mouth. He rode lightly.

The Triumphal Entry into Jerusalem (12th c.). From *The Book of Psalms*, English illuminated manuscript written at St. Albans. CHURCH OF ST. GODEHARD, HILDE-SHEIM, WEST GERMANY.

He wasn't a governor; although that crowd
Screamed, it was honest praise and not plain fear.
He wasn't a general; although they bowed,
There wasn't a soldier to threaten with his spear.

Head up, ears straight, I carried that man well.
(A donkey has his stubborn little pride.)
Who was he? Where did he go? I cannot tell.
He never came back to *me* for another ride.

I suppose he's a shepherd now, counting sheep,
Or lost in the wars, a sword-scooped hole for a grave,
Or farmer scanning the sky before his sleep,
Or dragged to Imperial Rome, a galley slave.

I had a gray colt trotting by my side,
Nudging into my ribs, scared of the noise.
Maybe it's trudging somewhere now, its hide
Itching, overloaded, beaten by boys.

And look what's happened to me: my hoofs are chipped,
My ears (they were handsome once) are raw and torn.
My old bones ache, and yesterday I slipped
And gashed my shoulders in a patch of thorn.

I've carried children, pine roots, every load
In sand and stone, wherever donkeys go.
But still my back rides lightly where he rode,
The fur is cross-shaped and it seems to glow.

EVIL DAYS

Boris Pasternak

When He was entering Jerusalem
During that last week

He was hailed with thunderous hosannas;
The people ran in His wake, waving palm branches.

Yet the days were becoming ever more ominous, more grim.
There was no stirring the hearts of men through love:
Their eyebrows knit in disdain.
And now, the epilogue. Finis.

The heavens lay heavy over the houses,
Crushing with all of their leaden weight.
The Pharisees were seeking evidence against Him,
Yet cringed before Him like foxes.

Then the dark forces of the Temple
Gave Him up to be judged by the offscourings.
And, with the same fervor with which they once sang His praises,
Men now reviled Him.

The rabble from the vicinity
Was peering in at the gateway.
They kept jostling as they bided the outcome,
Surging, receding.

The neighborhood crawled with sly whispers
And rumors crept in from all sides.
He recalled the flight into Egypt and His childhood
But recalled them now as in a dream.

He remembered the majestic cliffside in the wilderness
And that exceeding high mountain
Whereon Satan had tempted Him,
Offering Him all the kingdoms of the world.

And the marriage feast at Cana
And the guests in great admiration over the miracle.
And the sea on which, in a mist,
He had walked to the boat as if over dry land.

And the gathering of the poor in a hovel
And His going down into a cellar by the light of a taper
Which had suddenly gone out in affright
When the man risen from the dead was trying to get to his feet.

What effect does the poet achieve by placing the reference to Lazarus in the final line? Why is the image of Lazarus "risen from the dead . . . *trying* to get to his feet" an appropriate way to end a poem that anticipates the last days of Christ's life and the Resurrection?

THE LAST DAYS OF CHRIST

(Luke and Matthew)

The Last Supper

Now the feast of unleavened bead drew nigh, which is called the passover. Then entered Satan into Judas surnamed Iscariot, being of the number of the twelve. And he went his way, and communed with the chief priests and captains, how he might betray him unto them. And they were glad, and covenanted to give him money. And he promised, and sought opportunity to betray him unto them in the absence of the multitude.

Then came the day of unleavened bread, when the passover must be killed. And Jesus sent Peter and John, saying, "Go and prepare us the passover, that we may eat."

And they said unto him, "Where wilt thou that we prepare?"

And he said unto them, "Behold, when ye are entered into the city, there shall a man meet you, bearing a pitcher of water; follow him into the house where he entereth in. And ye shall say unto the goodman of the house, 'The Master saith unto thee, "Where is the guest chamber, where I shall eat the passover with my disciples?"' And he shall show you a large upper room furnished: there make ready."

And they went, and found as he had said unto them: and they made ready the passover.

And when the hour was come, he sat down, and the twelve apostles with him. And he said unto them, "With desire I have desired to eat this passover with you before I suffer: for I say unto you, I will not any more eat thereof, until it be fulfilled in the kingdom of God."

And he took the cup, and gave thanks, and said, "Take this, and divide it among yourselves: for I say unto you, I will not drink of the fruit of the vine, until the kingdom of God shall come." And he took bread, and gave thanks, and brake it, and gave unto them, saying, "This is my body which is given for you: this do in remembrance of me."

Likewise also the cup after supper, saying, "This cup is the new testament in my blood, which is shed for you. But, behold, the hand of him that betrayeth me is with me on the table. And truly the Son of Man goeth, as it was determined: but woe unto that man by whom he is betrayed!" And they began to inquire among themselves, which of them it was that should do this thing.

And the Lord said, "Simon, Simon, behold, Satan hath desired to have you, that he may sift you as wheat: but I have prayed for thee, that thy faith fail not: and when thou art converted, strengthen thy brethren."

And he said unto him, "Lord, I am ready to go with thee, both into prison, and to death."

And he said, "I tell thee, Peter, the cock shall not crow this day, before that thou shalt thrice deny that thou knowest me."

[*Luke 22:1, 3–23, 31–34*]

Jesus Betrayed

And he came out, and went, as he was wont, to the mount of Olives; and his disciples also followed him. And when he was at the place, he said unto them, "Pray that ye enter not into temptation." And he was withdrawn from them about a stone's cast, and kneeled down, and prayed, saying, "Father, if thou be willing, remove this cup from me: nevertheless not my will, but thine, be done."

And there appeared an angel unto him from heaven, strengthening him. And being in an agony he prayed more earnestly: and his sweat was as it were great drops of blood falling down to the ground. And when he rose up from prayer, and was come to his disciples, he found them sleeping for sorrow, and said unto them, "Why sleep ye? Rise and pray, lest ye enter into temptation."

And while he yet spake, behold a multitude, and he that was called Judas, one of the twelve, went before them, and drew near unto Jesus to kiss him.

But Jesus said unto him, "Judas, betrayest thou the Son of man with a kiss?"

When they which were about him saw what would follow, they said unto him, "Lord, shall we smite with the sword?" And one of them smote the servant of the high priest, and cut off his right ear.

And Jesus answered and said, "Suffer ye thus far." And he touched his ear, and healed him.

Then Jesus said unto the chief priests, and captains of the temple, and the elders, which were come to him, "Be ye come out, as against a thief, with swords and staves? When I was daily with you in the temple, ye stretched forth no hands against me: but this is your hour, and the power of darkness."

Then took they him, and led him, and brought him into the high priest's house. And Peter followed afar off. And when they had kindled a fire in the midst of the hall, and were set down together, Peter sat down among them.

But a certain maid beheld him as he sat by the fire, and earnestly looked upon him, and said, "This man was also with him."

And he denied him, saying, "Woman, I know him not."

And after a little while another saw him, and said, "Thou art also of them."

And Peter said, "Man, I am not."

And about the space of one hour after another confidently affirmed, saying, "Of a truth this fellow also was with him: for he is a Galilean."

And Peter said, "Man, I know not what thou sayest."

And immediately, while he yet spake, the cock crew. And the Lord turned, and looked upon Peter. And Peter remembered the word of the Lord, how he had said unto him, "Before the cock crow, thou shalt deny me thrice." And Peter went out, and wept bitterly.

When the morning was come, all the chief priests and elders of the people took counsel against Jesus to put him to death: and when they had bound him, they led him away, and delivered him to Pontius Pilate the governor.

Then Judas, which had betrayed him, when he saw that he was condemned, repented himself, and brought again the thirty pieces of silver to the chief priests and elders, saying, "I have sinned in that I have betrayed the innocent blood."

And they said, "What is that to us? See thou to that."

And he cast down the pieces of silver in the temple, and departed, and went and hanged himself.

[*Luke 22:39–62; Matthew 27:1–5*]

THE LAST SUPPER

(as told by James the Brother of the Lord)

Kahlil Gibran

A thousand times I have been visited by the memory of that night. And I know now that I shall be visited a thousand times again.

The earth shall forget the furrows ploughed upon her breast, and a woman the pain and joy of childbirth, ere I shall forget that night.

In the afternoon we had been outside the walls of Jerusalem, and Jesus had said, "Let us go into the city now and take supper at the inn."

It was dark when we reached the inn, and we were hungry. The innkeeper greeted us and led us to an upper chamber.

And Jesus bade us sit around the board, but He Himself remained standing, and His eyes rested upon us.

And He spoke to the keeper of the inn and said, "Bring me a basin and a pitcher full of water, and a towel."

And He looked at us again and said gently, "Cast off your sandals."

We did not understand, but at His command we cast them off.

Then the keeper of the inn brought the basin and the pitcher; and Jesus said, "Now I will wash your feet. For I must needs free your feet from the dust of the ancient road, and give them the freedom of the new way."

And we were all abashed and shy.

Then Simon Peter stood up and said: "How shall I suffer my Master and my Lord to wash my feet?"

And Jesus answered, "I will wash your feet that you may remember that he who serves men shall be the greatest among men."

Then He looked at each one of us and He said: "The Son of Man who has chosen you for His brethren, He whose feet were anointed yesterday with myrrh of Arabia and dried with a woman's hair, desires now to wash your feet."

And He took the basin and the pitcher and kneeled down and washed our feet, beginning with Judas Iscariot.

Then He sat down with us at the board; and His face was like the dawn rising upon a battlefield after a night of strife and blood-shedding.

And the keeper of the inn came with his wife, bringing food and wine.

And though I had been hungry before Jesus knelt at my feet, now I had no stomach for food. And there was a flame in my throat which I would not quench with wine.

Then Jesus took a loaf of bread and gave to us, saying, "Perhaps we shall not break bread again. Let us eat this morsel in remembrance of our days in Galilee."

And He poured wine from the jug into a cup, and He drank, and gave to us, and He said, "Drink this in remembrance of a thirst we have known together. And drink it also in hope for the new vintage. When I am enfolded and am no more among you, and when you meet here or elsewhere, break the bread and pour the wine, and eat and drink even as you are doing now. Then look about you; and perchance you may see me sitting with you at the board."

The Last Supper (20th c.) by Mattheus Weigman. NETHERLANDS CONSULATE GENERAL, NEW YORK.

After saying this He began to distribute among us morsels of fish and pheasant, like a bird feeding its fledgings.

We ate little yet we were filled; and we drank but a drop, for we felt that the cup was like a space between this land and another land.

Then Jesus said, "Ere we leave this board let us rise and sing the joyous hymns of Galilee."

And we rose and sang together, and His voice was above our voices, and there was a ringing in every word of His words.

And He looked at our faces, each and every one, and He said, "Now I bid you farewell. Let us go beyond these walls. Let us go unto Gethsemane."

And John the son of Zebedee said, "Master, why do you say farewell to us this night?"

And Jesus said, "Let not your heart be troubled. I only leave you to prepare a place for you in my Father's house. But if you shall be in need of me, I will come back to you. Where you call me, there I shall hear you, and wherever your spirit shall seek me, there I will be.

"Forget not that thirst leads to the winepress, and hunger to the wedding feast.

"It is in your longing that you shall find the Son of Man. For longing is the fountainhead of ecstasy, and it is the path to the Father."

And John spoke again and said, "If you would indeed leave us, how shall we be of good cheer? And why speak you of separation?"

And Jesus said, "The hunted stag knows the arrow of the hunter before he feels it in his breast; and the river is aware of the sea ere it comes to her shore. And the Son of Man has traveled the ways of men.

"Before another almond tree renders her blossoms to the sun, my roots shall be reaching into the heart of another field."

Then Simon Peter said: "Master, leave us not now, and deny us not the joy of your presence. Where you go we too will go; and wherever you abide there we will be also."

And Jesus put His hand upon Simon Peter's shoulder, and smiled upon him, and He said, "Who knows but that you may deny me before this night is over, and leave me before I leave you?"

Then of a sudden He said, "Now let us go hence."

And He left the inn and we followed Him. But when we reached the gate of the city, Judas of Iscariot was no longer with us. And we crossed the Valley of Jahannam. Jesus walked far ahead of us, and we walked close to one another.

When He reached an olive grove He stopped and turned towards us saying, "Rest here for an hour."

The evening was cool, though it was full spring with the mulberries unfolding their shoots and the apple trees in bloom. And the gardens were sweet.

Each one of us sought the trunk of a tree, and we lay down. I myself gathered my cloak around me and lay under a pine tree.

But Jesus left us and walked by Himself in the olive grove. And I watched Him while the others slept.

He would suddenly stand still, and again He would walk up and down. This He did many times.

Then I saw Him lift His face towards the sky and outstretch His arms to east and west.

Once He had said, "Heaven and earth, and hell too, are of man." And now I remembered His saying, and I knew that He who was pacing the olive grove was heaven made man; and I bethought me that the womb of the earth is not a beginning nor an end, but rather a chariot, a pause; and a moment of wonder and surprise; and hell I saw also, in the valley called Jahannam, which lay between Him and the Holy City.

And as He stood there and I lay wrapped in my garment, I heard His voice speaking. But He was not speaking to us. Thrice I heard Him pronounce the word *Father*. And that was all I heard.

After a while His arms dropped down, and He stood still like a cypress tree between my eyes and the sky.

At last He came over among us again, and He said to us, "Wake and rise. My hour has come. The world is already upon us, armed for battle."

And then He said, "A moment ago I heard the voice of my Father. If I see you not again, remember that the conqueror shall not have peace until he is conquered."

And when we had risen and come close to Him, His face was like the starry heaven above the desert.

Then He kissed each one of us upon the cheek. And when His lips touched my cheek, they were hot, like the hand of a child in fever.

Suddenly we heard a great noise in the distance, as of numbers, and when it came near it was a company of men approaching with lanterns and staves. And they came in haste.

As they reached the hedge of the grove Jesus left us and went forth to meet them. And Judas of Iscariot was leading them.

There were Roman soldiers with swords and spears, and men of Jerusalem with clubs and pickaxes.

And Judas came up to Jesus and kissed Him. And then he said to the armed men, "This is the Man."

And Jesus said to Judas, "Judas, you were patient with me. This could have been yesterday."

Then He turned to the armed men and said: "Take me now. But see that your cage is large enough for these wings."

Then they fell upon Him and held Him, and they were all shouting.

But we in our fear ran away and sought to escape. I ran alone through the olive groves, nor had I power to be mindful, nor did any voice speak in me except my fear.

Through the two or three hours that remained of that night I was fleeing and hiding, and at dawn I found myself in a village near Jericho.

Why had I left Him? I do not know. But to my sorrow I did leave Him. I was a coward and I fled from the face of His enemies.

Then I was sick and ashamed at heart, and I returned to Jerusalem, but He was a prisoner, and no friend could have speech with Him.

He was crucified, and His blood has made new clay of the earth.

And I am living still; I am living upon the honeycomb of His sweet life.

PETER AND JOHN

Elinor Wylie

Twelve good friends
Walked under the leaves,
Binding the ends
Of the barley sheaves.

Peter and John
Lay down to sleep
Pillowed upon
A haymaker's heap.

John and Peter
Lay down to dream.

The air was sweeter
Than honey and cream.

Peter was bred
In the salty cold:
His hair was red
And his eyes were gold.

John had a mouth
Like a twig bent down:
His brow was smooth
And his eyes were brown.

Peter to slumber
Sank like a stone,
Of all their number
The bravest one.

John more slowly
Composed himself,
Young and holy
Among the twelve.

John as he slept
Cried out in grief,
Turned and wept
On the golden leaf:

"Peter, Peter,
Stretch me your hand
Across the glitter
Of the harvest land!

"Peter, Peter,
Give me a sign!
This was a bitter
Dream of mine—

"Bitter as aloes
It parched my tongue.
Upon the gallows
My life was hung.

"Sharp it seemed
As a bloody sword.

Peter, I dreamed
I was Christ the Lord!"

Peter turned
To holy Saint John:
His body burned
In the falling sun.

In the falling sun
He burned like flame:
"John, Saint John,
I have dreamed the same!

"My bones were hung
On an elder tree;
Bells were rung
Over Galilee.

"A silver penny
Sealed each of my eyes.
Many and many
A cock crew thrice."

When Peter's word
Was spoken and done,
"Were you Christ the Lord
In your dream?" said John.

"No," said the other,
"That I was not.
I was our brother
Iscariot."

INTO THY HANDS
(Luke and Matthew)

Jesus before Pilate and Herod

And the men that held Jesus mocked him, and smote him. And when they had blindfolded him, they struck him on the face, and asked him, saying, "Prophesy, who is it that smote thee?" And many other things blasphemously spake they against him.

And as soon as it was day, the elders of the people and the chief priests and the scribes came together, and led him into their council, saying, "Art thou the Christ? Tell us."

And he said unto them, "If I tell you, ye will not believe: and if I also ask you, ye will not answer me, nor let me go. Hereafter shall the Son of Man sit on the right hand of the power of God."

Then said they all, "Art thou then the Son of God?"

And he said unto them, "Ye say that I am."

And they said, "What need we any further witness? For we ourselves have heard of his own mouth."

And the whole multitude of them arose, and led him unto Pilate. And they began to accuse him, saying, "We found this fellow perverting the nation, and forbidding to give tribute to Caesar, saying that he himself is Christ a King."

And Pilate asked him, saying, "Art thou the King of the Jews?"

And he answered him and said, "Thou sayest it."

Then said Pilate to the chief priests and to the people, "I find no fault in this man."

And they were the more fierce, saying, "He stirreth up the people, teaching throughout all Jewry, beginning from Galilee to this place."

When Pilate heard of Galilee, he asked whether the man were a Galilean. And as soon as he knew that he belonged unto Herod's jurisdiction, he sent him to Herod, who himself also was at Jerusalem at that time. And when Herod saw Jesus, he was exceeding glad: for he was desirous to see him of a long season, because he had heard many things of him; and he hoped to have seen some miracle done by him. Then he questioned with him in many words; but he answered him nothing. And the chief priests and scribes stood and vehemently accused him. And Herod with his men of war set him at nought, and mocked him, and arrayed him in a gorgeous robe, and sent him again to Pilate. And the same day Pilate and Herod were made friends together: for before they were at enmity between themselves.

And Pilate, when he had called together the chief priests and the rulers and the people, said unto them, "Ye have brought this man unto me, as one that perverteth the people: and, behold, I, having examined him before you, have found no fault in this man touching those things whereof ye accused him: no, nor yet Herod: for I sent you to him; and, lo, nothing worthy of death is done unto him. I will therefore chastise him, and release him." (For of necessity he must release one unto them at the feast.)

And they cried out all at once, saying, "Away with this man, and release unto us Barabbas" (who for a certain sedition made in the city, and for murder, was cast into prison).

Pilate therefore, willing to release Jesus, spake again to them.

But they cried, saying, "Crucify him! Crucify him!"

And he said unto them the third time, "Why, what evil hath he done? I have found no cause of death in him: I will therefore chastise him, and let him go."

And they were instant with loud voices, requiring that he might be crucified.

When Pilate saw that he could prevail nothing, but that rather a tumult was made, he took water, and washed his hands before the multitude, saying, "I am innocent of the blood of this just person: see ye to it."

Then answered all the people, and said, "His blood be on us, and on our children."

Then released he Barabbas unto them: and when he had scourged Jesus, he delivered him to be crucified.

[*Luke 22:63–23.23a; Matthew 27:24–26*]

The Crucifixion

And as they led him away, they laid hold upon one Simon, a Cyrenian, coming out of the country, and on him they laid the cross, that he might bear it after Jesus. And there followed him a great company of people, and of women, which also bewailed and lamented him. But Jesus turning unto them said, "Daughters of Jerusalem, weep not for me, but weep for yourselves, and for your children. For, behold, the days are coming, in the which they shall say, 'Blessed are the barren, and the wombs that never bore, and the paps which never gave suck.' Then shall they begin to say to the mountains, 'Fall on us!' and to the hills, 'Cover us!' For if they do these things in a green tree, what shall be done in the dry?"

And there were also two others, malefactors, led with him to be put to death. And when they were come to the place, which is called Calvary, there they crucified him, and the malefactors, one on the right hand, and the other on the left.

Then said Jesus, "Father, forgive them; for they know not what they do."

And they parted his raiment, and cast lots. And the people stood beholding. And the rulers also with them derided him, saying, "He saved others; let him save himself, if he be Christ, the chosen of God."

And the soldiers also mocked him, coming to him, and offering him vinegar, and saying, "If thou be the King of the Jews, save thyself."

And a superscription also was written over him in letters of Greek, and Latin, and Hebrew: THIS IS THE KING OF THE JEWS.

And one of the malefactors which were hanged railed on him, saying, "If thou be Christ, save thyself and us." But the other answering rebuked him, saying, "Dost not thou fear God, seeing thou art in the same condemnation? And we indeed justly; for we receive the due reward of our deeds: but this man hath done nothing amiss."

And he said unto Jesus, "Lord, remember me when thou comest into thy kingdom."

And Jesus said unto him, "Verily I say unto thee, 'Today shalt thou be with me in paradise.' "

And it was about the sixth hour, and there was a darkness over all the earth until the ninth hour.

And about the ninth hour Jesus cried with a loud voice, saying, "Eli, Eli, lama sabachthani?" that is to say, "My God, my God, why hast thou forsaken me?"

Some of them that stood there, when they heard that, said, "This man calleth for Elias*." And straightway one of them ran, and took a sponge, and filled it with vinegar, and put it on a reed, and gave him to drink. The rest said, "Let be, let us see whether Elias will come to save him."

And when Jesus had cried with a loud voice, he said, "Father, into thy hands, I commend my spirit": and having said thus, he gave up the ghost.

* *Elias:* the Greek form of "Elijah."

And, behold, the veil of the temple was rent in twain from the top to the bottom; and the earth did quake, and the rocks rent; and the graves were opened; and many bodies of the saints which slept arose, and came out of the graves after his resurrection, and went into the holy city, and appeared unto many. Now when the centurion, and they that were with him, watching Jesus, saw the earthquake, and those things that were done, they feared greatly, saying, "Truly this was the Son of God."

And many women were there beholding afar off, which followed Jesus from Galilee, ministering unto him: among which was Mary Magdalene, and Mary the mother of James and Joses, and the mother of Zebedee's children.

When the even was come, there came a rich man of Arimathea, named Joseph, who also himself was Jesus' disciple. He went to Pilate, and begged the body of Jesus. Then Pilate commanded the body to be delivered. And when Joseph had taken the body, he wrapped it in a clean linen cloth, and laid it in his own new tomb, which he had hewn out in the rock: and he rolled a great stone to the door of the sepulcher, and departed. And there was Mary Magdalene, and the other Mary, sitting over against the sepulcher.

[*Luke 23:26–44; Matthew 27:46–49; Luke 23:46; Matthew 27:51–61*]

The Resurrection and Ascension

In the end of the sabbath, as it began to dawn toward the first day of the week, came Mary Magdalene and the other Mary to see the sepulcher.

And, behold, there was a great earthquake: for the angel of the Lord descended from heaven, and came and rolled back the stone from the door, and sat upon it. His countenance was like lightning, and his raiment white as snow: and for fear of him the keepers did shake, and became as dead men.

And the angel answered and said unto the women, "Fear not ye: for I know that ye seek Jesus, which was crucified. He is not here: for he is risen, as he said. Come, see the place where the Lord lay. And go quickly, and tell his disciples that he is risen from the dead; and, behold, he goeth before you into Galilee; there shall ye see him: lo, I have told you."

And they departed quickly from the sepulcher with fear and great joy; and did run to bring his disciples word.

And as they went to tell his disciples, behold, Jesus met them, saying, "All hail!" And they came and held him by the feet, and worshiped him. Then said Jesus unto them, "Be not afraid: go tell my brethren that they go into Galilee, and there shall they see me."

And he led them out as far as to Bethany, and he lifted up his hands, and blessed them. And it came to pass, while he blessed them, he was parted from them, and carried up into heaven. And they worshiped him, and returned to Jerusalem with great joy: and were continually in the temple, praising and blessing God. Amen.

[*Matthew 28:1–10; Luke 24:50–53*]

AND HE NEVER SAID A MUMBLIN WORD

(A Spiritual)

They crucified my Lord,
   An' He never said a mumblin' word.
They crucified my Lord,
   An' He never said a mumblin' word.
Not a word—not a word—not a word.

They nailed Him to the tree,
   An' He never said a mumblin' word.
They nailed Him to the tree,
   An' He never said a mumblin' word.
Not a word—not a word—not a word.

They pierced Him in the side,
   An' He never said a mumblin' word.
They pierced Him in the side,
   An' He never said a mumblin' word.
Not a word—not a word—not a word.

The blood came twinklin' down,
   An' He never said a mumblin' word.
The blood came twinklin' down,

An' He never said a mumblin' word.
Not a word—not a word—not a word.

He bowed His head an' died,
   An' He never said a mumblin' word.
He bowed His head an' died,
   An' He never said a mumblin' word.
Not a word—not a word—not a word.

CALVARY

Edwin Arlington Robinson

Friendless and faint, with martyred steps and slow,
Faint for the flesh, but for the spirit free,
Stung by the mob that came to see the show,
The Master toiled along to Calvary;
We gibed him, as he went, with houndish glee,
Till his dimmed eyes for us did overflow;
We cursed his vengeless hands thrice wretchedly—
And this was nineteen hundred years ago.

But after nineteen hundred years the shame
Still clings, and we have not made good the loss
That outraged faith has entered in his name.
Ah, when shall come love's courage to be strong!
Tell me, O Lord—tell me, O Lord, how long
Are we to keep Christ writhing on the cross!

Why does the poet say that we have continued to keep Christ "writhing on the cross"? Who are the "we" of the poem?

AT A CALVARY NEAR THE ANCRE

Wilfred Owen

One ever hangs where shelled roads part.
   In this war He too lost a limb,
But His disciples hide apart;
   And now the soldiers bear with Him.

Near Golgotha strolls many a priest,
   And in their faces there is pride
That they were flesh-marked by the Beast
   By whom the gentle Christ's denied.

The scribes on all the people shove
   And brawl allegiance to the state,
But they who love the greater love
   Lay down their life; they do not hate.

Wilfred Owen was killed in action during the World War I at the age of twenty-five. The Ancre, which he writes about here, is a river in northern France. It was the scene of several battles during the course of the war, most notably of a successful Allied advance against the Germans in November 1916 in which tanks were employed for the first time. Why does Owen make reference to "Calvary" and "Golgotha"? Why do you think the disciples "hide apart"? What is Owen's attitude toward the "priests" and "scribes"? What point is he making about "allegiance to the state"? Discuss the poet's vision of "the greater love." Do you think this an appropriate title for the unit? You may wish to compare the theme and technical devices of this poem with Owen's "The Parable of the Old Men and the Young" in Unit I, as well as with Robert Lowell's "The Holy Innocents" and Edwin Arlington Robinson's "Calvary" in this unit.

THE BALLAD OF THE CARPENTER*

Ewan MacColl

Jesus was a working man, a hero you shall hear,
Born in the slums of Bethlehem, at the turning of the year,
Yes, the turning of the year.

When Jesus was a little boy, the streets rang with his name,
For he argued with the aldermen and he put them all to shame,
Yes, he put them all to shame.

His father he apprenticed him a carpenter to be,
To plane and drill and work with skill in the town of Galilee,
Yes, the town of Galilee.

He become a roving journeyman and he wandered far and wide,
And he saw how wealth and poverty live always side by side,
Yes, always side by side.

He said, "Come all you working men, you farmers
    and weavers, too—
If you will only organize, the world belongs to you,
Yes, the world belongs to you."

So the fishermen sent two delegates and the farmers
    and weavers too,
And they formed a working committee of twelve to see
    the struggle through,
Yes, to see the struggle through.

When the rich men heard what the carpenter had done,
    to the Roman troops they ran,
Saying, "Put this rebel, Jesus, down, he's a menace to
    God and Man,
Yes, a menace to God and Man."

Modern Migration of the Spirit or *Christ Destroying the Cross* (1932–34) by José Clemente Orozco. HOPKINS CENTER ART GALLERIES, DARTMOUTH COLLEGE, HANOVER, N. H.

The commander of the occupying troops, he laughed and
    then he said,
"There's a cross to spare on Calvary Hill, by the weekend
    he'll be dead,
Yes, by the weekend he'll be dead."

Now, Jesus walked among the poor, for the poor
    were his own kind,
And they wouldn't let the cops get near enough to
    take him from behind,
Yes, to take him from behind.

So they hired a man of the traitor's trade, and a
    stool pigeon was he,
And he sold his brother to the butcher's men for a
    fistful of silver money,
Yes, a fistful of money.

When Jesus lay in the prison cell, they beat him and
    offered him bribes,
To desert the cause of his own poor folk and work for
    the rich man's tribe,
Yes, to work for the rich man's tribe.

The sweat stood out upon his brow, and the blood was in his eye,
And they nailed his body to the Roman Cross and they
    laughed as they watched him die,
Yes, they laughed as they watched him die.

Two thousand years have passed and gone, and many a hero, too,
And the dream of this poor carpenter, at last it's coming true,
Yes, at last it's coming true.

Ewan MacColl is a British folk singer and composer writing in the
tradition of Pete Seeger and Woody Guthrie, both of whom were often
associated with the labor movement of the 1930s and 1940s. How
is this association reflected in the lyrics of the ballad? Considering the
1960 date of composition, what "dream" does Ewan MacColl feel
is at last "coming true"? Do you feel we are any closer to realizing this
dream today?

THE RESURRECTION IS TO LIFE, NOT TO DEATH

D. H. Lawrence

The Rainbow by D. H. Lawrence traces the history of the Brangwens through three generations, as the members of the humble Midlands family confront the challenges, frustrations, hardships, and promises brought about by the rapid industrialization of English society in the nineteenth and early twentieth centuries. The age is one of dramatic social, moral, and intellectual change in which the Brangwens are forced to come to grips with themselves, their mates, and society as they struggle to discover new values and modes of being to replace the old forms of life that no longer apply in the radically altered world. Religion is among the major aspects of existence that are thrown into question in the course of the novel, as the following selection taken from the third generation of the family chronicle so dramatically illustrates.

Gradually there gathered the feeling of expectation. Christmas was coming. In the shed, at nights, a secret candle was burning, a sound of veiled voices was heard. The boys were learning the old mystery play of St. George and Beelzebub. Twice a week, by lamplight, there was choir practice in the church, for the learning of old carols Brangwen wanted to hear. The girls went to these practices. Everywhere was a sense of mystery and rousedness. Everybody was preparing for something.

The time came near, the girls were decorating the church, with cold fingers binding holly and fir and yew about the pillars, till a new spirit was in the church, the stone broke out into dark, rich leaf, the arches put forth their buds, and cold flowers rose to blossom in the dim, mystic atmosphere. Ursula must weave mistletoe over the door, and over the screen, and hang a silver dove from a sprig of yew, till dusk came down, and the church was like a grove.

In the cow-shed the boys were blacking their faces for a dress-rehearsal; the turkey hung dead, with opened, speckled wings, in the dairy. The time was come to make pies, in readiness.

The expectation grew more tense. The star was risen into the sky, the songs, the carols were ready to hail it. The star was the sign in the sky. Earth too should give a sign. As evening drew on, hearts beat fast with anticipation, hands were full of ready gifts. There were the tremulously expectant words of the church service, the night was past and the morning was come, the gifts were given and received, joy and peace made a flapping of wings in each heart, there was a great burst of carols, the Peace of the World had dawned, strife had passed away, every hand was linked in hand, every heart was singing.

It was bitter, though, that Christmas Day, as it drew on to evening, and night, became a sort of bank holiday, flat and stale. The morning was so wonderful, but in the afternoon and evening the ecstasy perished like a nipped thing, like a bud in a false spring. Alas, that Christmas was only a domestic feast, a feast of sweetmeats and toys! Why did not the grown-ups also change their everyday hearts, and give way to ecstasy? Where was the ecstasy?

How passionately the Brangwens craved for it, the ecstasy. The father was troubled, dark-faced and disconsolate, on Christmas night, because the passion was not there, because the day was become as every day, and hearts were not aflame. Upon the mother was a kind of absentness, as ever, as if she were exiled for all her life. Where was the fiery heart of joy, now the coming was fulfilled; where was the star, the Magi's transport, the thrill of new being that shook the earth?

Still it was there, even if it were faint and inadequate. The cycle of creation still wheeled in the Church year. After Christmas, the ecstasy slowly sank and changed. Sunday followed Sunday, trailing a fine movement, a finely developed transformation over the heart of the family. The heart that was big with joy, that had seen the star and had followed to the inner walls of the Nativity, that there had swooned in the great light, must now feel the light slowly withdrawing, a shadow falling, darkening. The chill crept in, silence came over the earth, and then all was darkness. The veil of the temple was rent, each heart gave up the ghost, and sank dead.

They moved quietly, a little wanness on the lips of the children, at Good Friday, feeling the shadow upon their hearts. Then, pale with a deathly scent, came the lilies of resurrection, that shone coldly till the Comforter was given.

But why the memory of the wounds and the death? Surely Christ rose with healed hands and feet, sound and strong and glad? Surely the passage of the cross and the tomb was forgotten? But no—always the memory of the wounds, always the smell of grave-clothes? A small thing was Resurrection, compared with the Cross and the death, in this cycle.

So the children lived the year of christianity, the epic of the soul of mankind. Year by year the inner, unknown drama went on in them, their hearts were born and came to fulness, suffered on the cross, gave up the ghost, and rose again to unnumbered days, untired, having at least this rhythm of eternity in a ragged, inconsequential life.

But it was becoming a mechanical action now, this drama: birth at Christmas for death at Good Friday. On Easter Sunday the life-drama was as good as finished. For the Resurrection was shadowy and over-come by the shadow of death, the Ascension was scarce noticed, a mere confirmation of death.

What was the hope and the fulfilment? Nay, was it all only a useless after-death, a wan, bodiless after-death? Alas, and alas for the passion of the human heart, that must die so long before the body was dead.

For from the grave, after the passion and the trial of anguish, the body rose torn and chill and colourless. Did not Christ say, "Mary!" and when she turned with outstretched hands to him, did he not hasten to add, "Touch me not; for I am not yet ascended to my father."

Then how could the hands rejoice, or the heart be glad, seeing them-selves repulsed. Alas, for the resurrection of the dead body! Alas, for the wavering, glimmering appearance of the risen Christ. Alas, for the Ascension into heaven, which is a shadow within death, a complete passing away.

Alas, that so soon the drama is over; that life is ended at thirty-three; that the half of the year of the soul is cold and historiless! Alas, that a risen Christ has no place with us! Alas, that the memory of the passion of Sorrow and Death and the Grave holds triumph over the pale fact of Resurrection!

But why? Why shall I not rise with my body whole and perfect, shining with strong life? Why, when Mary says: Rabboni, shall I not take her in my arms and kiss her and hold her to my breast? Why is the risen body deadly, and abhorrent with wounds?

The Resurrection is to life, not to death. Shall I not see those who have risen again walk here among men perfect in body and spirit, whole and glad in the flesh, living in the flesh, loving in the flesh, begetting children in the flesh, arrived at last to wholeness, perfect without scar or blemish, healthy without fear of ill health? Is this not the period of manhood and of joy and fulfilment, after the Resurrec-tion? Who shall be shadowed by Death and the Cross, being risen, and who shall fear the mystic, perfect flesh that belongs to heaven?

Can I not, then, walk this earth in gladness, being risen from sorrow? Can I not eat with my brother happily, and with joy kiss my beloved, after my resurrection, celebrate my marriage in the flesh with feastings, go about my business eagerly, in the joy of my fellows? Is heaven impatient for me, and bitter against this earth, that I should hurry off, or that I should linger pale and untouched? Is the flesh which was crucified become as poison to the crowds in the street, or is it as a strong gladness and hope to them, as the first flower blossoming out of the earth's humus?

———

What do the Brangwens' feel is missing from this Christmas? What is it about the "cycle of the Church year" that so oppresses the narrator? Why is the traditional concept of the Resurrection not enough to compensate for this? What is different about the Resurrection that the "I" in the latter part of the selection—presumably Jesus— envisions? Do you see any similarities between Lawrence's desire to celebrate the physical aspects of secular life and the spirit of the Song of Songs?

"PROLOGUE" to
THE LAST TEMPTATION OF CHRIST

Nikos Kazantzakis

The dual substance of Christ—the yearning, so human, so super-human, of man to attain to God or, more exactly, to return to God and identify himself with him—has always been a deep inscrutable mystery to me. This nostalgia for God, at once so mysterious and so real, has opened in me large wounds and also large flowing springs.

My principal anguish and the source of all my joys and sorrows from my youth onward has been the incessant, merciless battle between the spirit and the flesh.

Within me are the dark immemorial forces of the Evil One, human and pre-human; within me too are the luminous forces, human and pre-human, of God—and my soul is the arena where these two armies have clashed and met.

The anguish has been intense. I loved my body and did not want it to perish; I loved my soul and did not want it to decay. I have fought to reconcile these two primordial forces which are so contrary to each other, to make them realize that they are not enemies but, rather, fellow workers, so that they might rejoice in their harmony— and so that I might rejoice with them.

Every man partakes of the divine nature in both his spirit and his flesh. That is why the mystery of Christ is not simply a mystery for a particular creed: it is universal. The struggle between God and man breaks out in everyone, together with the longing for reconciliation. Most often this struggle is unconscious and short-lived. A weak soul does not have the endurance to resist the flesh for very long. It grows heavy, becomes flesh itself, and the contest ends. But among responsible men, men who keep their eyes riveted day and night upon the Supreme Duty, the conflict between flesh and spirit breaks out mercilessly and may last until death.

The stronger the soul and the flesh, the more fruitful the struggle and the richer the final harmony. God does not love weak souls and flabby flesh. The Spirit wants to have to wrestle with flesh which is strong and full of resistance. It is a carnivorous bird which is incessantly hungry; it eats flesh and, by assimilating it, makes it disappear.

Struggle between the flesh and the spirit, rebellion and resistance, reconciliation and submission, and finally—the supreme purpose of the struggle—union with God: this was the ascent taken by Christ, the ascent which he invites us to take as well, following in his bloody tracks.

This is the Supreme Duty of the man who struggles—to set out for the lofty peak which Christ, the first-born son of salvation, attained. How can we begin?

If we are to be able to follow him we must have a profound knowledge of his conflict, we must relive his anguish: his victory over the blossoming snares of the earth, his sacrifice of the great and small joys of men and his ascent from sacrifice to sacrifice, exploit to exploit, to martyrdom's summit, the Cross.

I never followed Christ's bloody journey to Golgotha with such terror, I never relived his Life and Passion with such intensity, such understanding and love, as during the days and nights when I wrote *The Last Temptation of Christ*. While setting down this confession of the anguish and the great hope of mankind I was so moved that my eyes filled with tears. I had never felt the blood of Christ fall drop by drop into my heart with so much sweetness, so much pain.

In order to mount to the Cross, the summit of sacrifice, and to God, the summit of immateriality, Christ passed through all the stages which the man who struggles passes through. That is why his suffering is so familiar to us; that is why we share it, and why his final victory seems to us so much our own future victory. That part of Christ's nature which was profoundly human helps us to understand him and love him and to pursue his Passion as though it were our own. If he had not within him this warm human element, he would never be able to touch our hearts with such assurance and tenderness; he would not be able to become a model for our lives. We struggle, we see him struggle also, and we find strength. We see that we are not all alone in the world: he is fighting at our side.

Every moment of Christ's life is a conflict and a victory. He conquered the invincible enchantment of simple human pleasures; he conquered temptations, continually transubstantiated flesh into spirit, and ascended. Reaching the summit of Golgotha, he mounted the Cross.

But even there his struggle did not end. Temptation—the Last Temptation—was waiting for him upon the Cross.* Before the fainted eyes of the Crucified the spirit of the Evil One, in an instantaneous flash, unfolded the deceptive vision of a calm and happy life. It seemed to Christ that he had taken the smooth, easy road of men. He had married and fathered children. People loved and respected him. Now, an old man, he sat on the threshold of his house and smiled with satisfaction as he recalled the longings of his youth. How splendidly, how sensibly he had acted in choosing the road of men! What insanity to have wanted to save the world! What joy to have escaped the privations, the tortures, and the Cross!

This was the Last Temptation which came in the space of a lightning flash to trouble the Saviour's final moments.

But all at once Christ shook his head violently, opened his eyes, and saw. No, he was not a traitor, glory be to God! He was not a deserter. He had accomplished the mission which the Lord had entrusted to him. He had not married, had not lived a happy life. He had reached the summit of sacrifice: he was nailed upon the Cross.

Content, he closed his eyes. And then there was a great triumphant cry: It is accomplished!

In other words: I have accomplished my duty, I am being crucified, I did not fall into temptation. . . .

* Kazantzakis is here summarizing the climax of his novel, his own imaginative projection of what was going through Christ's mind a few moments before his death.

This book was written because I wanted to offer a supreme model to the man who struggles; I wanted to show him that he must not fear pain, temptation or death—because all three can be conquered, all three have already been conquered. Christ suffered pain, and since then pain has been sanctified. Temptation fought until the very last moment to lead him astray, and Temptation was defeated. Christ died on the Cross, and at that instant death was vanquished forever.

Every obstacle in his journey became a milestone, an occasion for further triumph. We have a model in front of us now, a model who blazes our trail and gives us strength.

This book is not a biography; it is the confession of every man who struggles. In publishing it I have fulfilled my duty, the duty of a person who struggled much, was much embittered in his life,
and had many hopes. I am certain that
every free man who reads this book, so filled as it
is with love, will more than ever before,
better than ever before, love
Christ.

What does "the incessant, merciless battle between the spirit and the flesh" that Kazantzakis dwells on mean to you? How does this "battle" relate to Lawrence's belief in the previous selection that "The Resurrection is to life, not to death"? Explain the "Supreme Duty" of man as the author here discusses it. What was Christ's triumph? What has his victory done for "every free man" that should move him to love Christ "better than ever before"? In what sense is this "Prologue" a fitting conclusion to a collection of literature reflecting the contemporaneity of biblical themes?

Familiar Phrases and Sayings from the Bible

Old Testament

bone of my bones, flesh of my flesh	Genesis 2:23
the sweat of thy brow	Genesis 3:19
dust to dust	Genesis 3:19
Am I my brother's keeper?	Genesis 4:9
Sodom and Gommorah	Genesis 19:24
She became a pillar of salt.	Genesis 19:26
He sold his birthright for a mess of pottage.	Genesis 25:33
Jacob's ladder	Genesis 28:22
Behold, this dreamer cometh.	Genesis 37:19
his coat of many colors	Genesis 37:23
a stranger in a strange land	Exodus 2:22
a land flowing with milk and honey	Exodus 3:8
Let my people go!	Exodus 5:1
the fleshpots of Egypt	Exodus 16:37
An eye for an eye, a tooth for a tooth.	Exodus 21:24
Thou shalt love thy neighbor as thyself.	Leviticus 19:18
the apple of his eye	Deuteronomy 32:10
the everlasting arms	Deuteronomy 33:27
shibboleth	Judges 12:6
All the people arose as one man.	Judges 20:8
Whither thou goest, I will go.	Ruth 1:16
God save the king!	I Samuel 10:24
a man after his own heart	I Samuel 13:14
five smooth stones	I Samuel 17:40
How are the mighty fallen!	II Samuel 1:25
O my son Absalom! My son, my son Absalom!	II Samuel 18:33
The half was not told me.	I Kings 10:7
a still, small voice	I Kings 19:12
She painted her face.	II Kings 9:30
Set thine house in order.	II Kings 20:1
His ears shall tingle.	II Kings 21:12
the skin of my teeth	Job 19:20
the root of the matter	Job 19:28
in the land of the living	Job 28:13
out of the mouth of babes	Psalm 8:2
fire and brimstone	Psalm 11:6
All they that see me laugh me to scorn.	Psalm 22:7
My cup runneth over.	Psalm 23:5
Deep calleth unto deep.	Psalm 42:7

whiter than snow	Psalm 51:7
wings like a dove	Psalm 55:6
We went through fire and through water.	Psalm 66:12
His enemies shall lick the dust.	Psalm 72:9
We spend our years as a tale that is told.	Psalm 90:9
The days of our years are three score and ten.	Psalm 90:10
as far as the east is from the west	Psalm 103:12
down to the sea in ships	Psalm 107:23
at their wits end	Psalm 107:27
the issues of life	Proverbs 4:23
Go to the ant, thou sluggard.	Proverbs 6:6
The fear of the Lord is the beginning of wisdom.	Proverbs 9:10
He that spareth his rod hateth his son.	Proverbs 13:24
A soft answer turneth away wrath.	Proverbs 15:1
A merry heart maketh a cheerful countenance.	Proverbs 15:13
Pride goeth before destruction, and a haughty spirit before a fall.	Proverbs 16:18
heap coals of fire on his head	Proverbs 25:22
the way of a man with a maid	Proverbs 30:19
The sun also ariseth, and the sun goeth down.	Ecclesiastes 1:5
There is no new thing under the sun.	Ecclesiastes 1:9
He that increaseth knowledge increaseth sorrow.	Ecclesiastes 1:18
To everything there is a season.	Ecclesiastes 3:1
Two are better than one.	Ecclesiastes 4:9
A good name is better than precious ointment.	Ecclesiastes 7:1
A living dog is better than a dead lion.	Ecclesiastes 9:4
Time and chance happeneth to them all.	Ecclesiastes 9:11
Cast thy bread upon the waters.	Ecclesiastes 11:1
Much study is a weariness of the flesh.	Ecclesiastes 12:12
Let him kiss me with the kisses of his mouth.	Song of Songs 1:2
I am the rose of Sharon, and the lily of the valleys.	Song of Songs 2:1
The voice of the turtle is heard in our land.	Song of Songs 2:12
How beautiful are thy feet with shoes.	Song of Songs 7:1
Many waters cannot quench love.	Song of Songs 8:7
Come now, and let us reason together.	Isaiah 1:18
They shall beat their swords into plowshores, and their spears into pruning hooks: nation shall not lift sword against nation, neither shall they learn war any more.	Isaiah 2:4
A little child shall lead them.	Isaiah 11:6
Let us eat and drink; for tomorrow we shall die.	Isaiah 22:13
The desert shall rejoice, and blossom as the rose.	Isaiah 35:1
a drop in the bucket	Isaiah 40:15
see eye to eye	Isaiah 52:8
holier than thou	Isaiah 65:5
Can the Ethiopian change his skin, or the leopard his spots?	Jeremiah 13:23

with my whole heart and with my whole soul	Jeremiah 32:41
valley of bones	Ezekiel 27:1
the handwriting on the wall	Daniel 5:5
For they have sown the wind, and they shall reap the whirlwind.	Hosea 8:7
the valley of decision	Joel 3:14
They shall sit every man under his vine and under his fig tree.	Micah 4:4
like a refiner's fire	Malachi 3:2

New Testament

The heavens were opened unto him, and he saw the Spirit of God descending like a dove.	Matthew 3:16
Man shall not live by bread alone.	Matthew 4:4
Ye are the salt of the earth.	Matthew 5:13
Turn the other cheek.	Matthew 5:39
Go the second mile.	Matthew 5:41
Love your enemies.	Matthew 5:44
Let not thy left hand know what thy right hand doeth.	Matthew 6:3
Lead us not into temptation, but deliver us from evil.	Matthew 6:13
No man can serve two masters.	Matthew 6:24
Consider the lilies of the field.	Matthew 6:28
Judge not, that ye be not judged.	Matthew 7:1
pearls before swine	Matthew 7:6
Beware of false prophets.	Matthew 7:15
a wolf in sheep's clothing	Matthew 7:15
Let the dead bury their dead.	Matthew 8:22
wise as serpents, and harmless as doves	Matthew 10:16
The very hairs of your head are all numbered.	Matthew 10:30
Ye are of more value than many sparrows.	Matthew 10:31
I came not to send peace, but a sword.	Matthew 10:34
Every city or house divided against itself shall not stand.	Matthew 12:25
O generation of vipers!	Matthew 12:34
a pearl of great price	Matthew 13:46
A prophet is without honor in his own country.	Matthew 13:57
the signs of the times	Matthew 16:3
become as little children	Matthew 18:3
a millstone about his neck	Matthew 18:6
If thine eye offend thee, pluck it out.	Matthew 18:9
until seventy times seven	Matthew 18:22
a den of thieves	Matthew 21:13
For ye have the poor always with you.	Matthew 26:11
thirty pieces of silver	Matthew 26:15
He washed his hands of the matter.	Matthew 27:24

My God, my God, why hast thou forsaken me?	Matthew 27:46
the half of my kingdom	Mark 6:23
the head of John the Baptist	Mark 6:24
the widow's mite	Mark 12:42
Peace on earth, good will toward men.	Luke 2:14
Physician, heal thyself.	Luke 4:23
as lambs among wolves	Luke 10:3
The laborer is worthy of his hire.	Luke 10:7
the good Samaritan	Luke 10:30–37
the prodigal son	Luke 15:11–32
Father, forgive them; for they know not what they do.	Luke 23:34
In the beginning was the Word.	John 1:1
the voice of one crying in the wilderness	John 1:23
the bread of life	John 6:48
He that is without sin among you, let him first cast a stone at her.	John 8:7
The truth shall make you free.	John 8:32
In my father's house are many mansions.	John 14:2
God is no respecter of persons.	Acts 10:34
the quick and the dead	Acts 10:42
turned the world upside down	Acts 17:6
a law unto themselves	Romans 2:14
The wages of sin is death.	Romans 6:23
be of the same mind	Romans 12:16
all things to all men	I Corinthians 9:22
faith, hope, charity	I Corinthians 13:13
in the twinkling of an eye	I Corinthians 15:52
O death, where is thy sting? O grave, where is thy victory?	I Corinthians 15:55
a thorn in the flesh	II Corinthians 12:7
tossed to and fro	Ephesians 4:14
a labor of love	I Thessalonians 1:3
filthy lucre	I Timothy 3:3
old wives' tales	I Timothy 4:7
The love of money is the root of all evil.	I Timothy 6:10
Some have entertained angels unawares.	Hebrews 13:2
all of one mind	I Peter 3:8
God is love.	I John 4:8
the Alpha and the Omega	Revelation 1:8
open the seventh seal	Revelation 6:1
the four horsemen of the apocalypse	Revelation 6:2–8
the blood of the lamb	Revelation 7:1
Alas, alas, that great city Babylon!	Revelation 18:10
the bottomless pit	Revelation 20:3
a new heaven and a new earth	Revelation 21:1
clear as crystal	Revelation 22:1
the healing of the nations	Revelation 22:2

Selected Bibliography

The following lists of books, recordings, and films are highly selective in nature. Choices have been made on the basis of their relevance for students concerned with the Bible as literature and as a source book for the humanities, rather than for those concerned with the historical and theological aspects of the Bible. Availability was also a factor in selection. For the most part, books that are currently out of print have not been included. Titles available in inexpensive paperback editions are preceded by an asterisk (*). Those seeking further suggestions should consult the resource books listed, most of which contain excellent bibliographies which go far beyond the scope of these listings.

Bibles for Students

Abbot, Walter M. et. al. *The Bible Reader: An Interfaith Interpretation.* Beverly Hills, Calif.: Bruce, 1969.

Bates, Ernest Sutherland. *The Bible Designed to Be Read as Living Literature.* New York: Simon and Schuster, 1936, revised 1970. A King James Version, complete except for genealogies, repetitions, and other relatively unimportant passages. Presented in paragraphs rather than by chapter and verse. Useful, but contains no specific chapter and verse references. Contains a very helpful "Glossary of Biblical Terms."

————. *The Pocket Bible: The Bible Designed to Be Read as Living Literature,* abridged by Cyril C. Richardson. New York: Washington Square Press, 1951. An abridgment of the preceding entry. Contains selections from 34 books of the Old and New Testaments (King James Version). Literary value seems to have been the prime consideration in the choice of selections. Conveniently arranged and inexpensive.

Chamberlin, Roy and Feldman, Herman, eds. *The Dartmouth Bible,* rev. ed. Boston: Houghton Mifflin, 1950. The King James Version with helpful textual notes and historical commentary. An excellent reference Bible for students and teachers.

Harrison, G. B. *The Bible for Students of Literature and Art.* New York: Anchor Books, 1964.

Reference Works

Baly, Denis and Tushingham, A. D. *Atlas of the Biblical World.* New York: World Publishing Company, 1971. Physical geography and climate receive the major emphasis, but there is also considerable information con-

382 / Selected Bibliography

cerning the political and historical geography. 48 maps and 69 unique plates, many in full color.

Brownrigg, Ronald. *Who's Who in the New Testament*. New York: Holt, Rinehart and Winston, 1971. An encyclopedia focusing on the characters and major places in the New Testament. Also covers places linked with the life and growth of the early Christian church. Easy to read and heavily illustrated.

Comay, Joan. *Who's Who in the Old Testament*. New York: Holt, Rinehart and Winston, 1971. Companion volume to *Who's Who in the New Testament*. Encyclopedia covering the history and geography of Israel, supported with evidence drawn from archeological discoveries in the Holy Land.

Hastings, James, ed. *Dictionary of the Bible*, rev. Frederick C. Grant and Harold H. Rowley. New York: Scribners, 1963. Includes entries on all proper names, as well as biblical doctrines and theological concepts. 16 maps in full color.

Keller, Werner. *The Bible as History*. New York: William Morrow & Co., 1956. Provides archeological "confirmation" on various Old and New Testament events.

Resource Books

Ackerman, James S. *On Teaching the Bible as Literature*. Bloomington, Ind.: Indiana University Press, 1967. Old Testament background for the teacher of biblical literature. Discusses the development of Israel's literature from oral tradition to printed Bibles and gives guidelines for the study of selected Old Testament narratives (primeval and patriarchal legends, including Joseph, Moses, Samson, and David).

Asimov, Isaac. *Asimov's Guide to the Bible*. 2 vols. New York: Doubleday, 1968–69. The author discusses the Bible book by book, verse by verse, providing historical, geographical, and biographical information in a relaxed, down-to-earth style.

Chase, Mary Ellen. *The Bible and the Common Reader*, rev. ed. New York: Macmillan, 1952. A lively introduction to the Bible and the Hebrews, followed by a discussion of the literature of the Old and New Testaments.

———. *Life and Language in the Old Testament*. New York: Norton, 1955. A sequel to the above. Discusses "The Ancient Hebrew Mind," "Imagination in the Old Testament," and "Language in the Old Testament."

Leach, Maria. *The Beginning: Creation Myths Around the World*. New York; Funk & Wagnalls, 1956.

Nonfiction Books on Specific Subjects

Chute, Marchette G. *Jesus of Israel*. New York: Dutton, 1961.

Muggeridge, Malcolm and Vidler, Alec. *Paul, Envoy Extraordinary*. New York: Harper and Row, 1972. The writers underwent an arduous two-month trek, following Paul's journey between Jerusalem and Rome, in order to understand what the Apostle stood for and what he had achieved. Included are maps and reproductions of mosaics and other works of art.

Shippen, Katherine B. *Moses*. New York: Harper and Row, 1949. Moses' sense of dedication and his singleness of purpose emerge clearly in this exceptional biography.

Young, Mary. *Singing Windows*. Nashville, Tenn.: Abingdon Press, 1963. This illustrated book relates the stained-glass windows of famous cathedrals to the biblical stories and legends they depict.

Fiction (Old Testament)

Asch, Sholem. *Moses*. New York: Putnam, 1951. A sensitive recreation of the life and times of Moses, the first great biblical revolutionary leader.

Bradford, Roark. *Ol' Man Adam and His Chillun*. New York: Harper, 1928. Black folk retellings of some of the most popular Old Testament stories.

Bothwell, Jean. *Flame in the Sky: The Story of the Prophet Elijah*. New York: Vanguard Press, 1954.

DeWohl, Lewis. *David of Jerusalem*. Philadelphia: Lippincott, 1963.

Fast, Howard M. *My Glorious Brothers*. New York: Popular Library, 1948. The story of Judas Maccabaeus and his valiant brothers who carry on their father's campaign against incredible odds to win back Jerusalem from the Syrians and restore its independence nearly two hundred years before Christ. *Moses, Prince of Egypt*—currently out-of-print—may still be available in some libraries.

Garnett, David. *Two by Two*. New York: Norton, 1966. A humorous and imaginative account of what happened aboard Noah's ark, as told from the perspective of playful young stowaway twin girls.

Hogan, Bernice. *Deborah*. Nashville, Tenn.: Abingdon Press, 1964. The story of a teenage tent-dwelling Jewish girl who overcomes many obstacles to become the first woman judge of her people.

Lofts, Norah. *Esther*. New York: Bantam, 1970. Colorfully portrays ancient times as it recreates the fascinating story of Esther, the beautiful young Hebrew woman who risked her throne and her life to save her people.

Malvern, Gladys. *Behold Your Queen*. New York: McKay, 1951. The life and times of Esther in the Persian court.

———. *The Foreigner*. New York: McKay, 1954. Effective retelling of the story of Ruth's devotion to Naomi and her love for Boaz.

Selden, Ruth, ed. *The Ways of God and Men: Great Stories from the Bible in World Literature*. New York: Stephen Daye Press, 1950. An outstanding collection of fiction based on Old and New Testament themes by such authors as Sholem Asch, Anatole France, Soren Kierkegaard, Thomas Mann, and Mark Twain. Contains four of the stories included in THE

ENDURING LEGACY. "Solomon the King," "In the fields of Boaz," "The Testing of Jonah," and "The Last Supper: James the Brother of the Lord."

Fiction (New Testament)

Buckmaster, Henrietta. *And Walk in Love*. New York: Random House, 1956. Life in the early days of Christianity is effectively portrayed in this story of the Apostle Paul.

Caldwell, Taylor. *Dear and Glorious Physician*. New York: Doubleday, 1959. The travels of Lucanus, or Luke the physician, through such early cities as Antioch, Rome, and Judea.

Costain. Thomas B. *The Silver Chalice*. New York: Doubleday, 1954. Historical novel based on the legends which sprang up after the Crucifixion concerning the chalice used to hold the wine at the Last Supper and the artisan who fashioned it.

DeWohl, Louis. *The Spear*. New York: Popular Library, 1955. A young centurion reacts to the corruption around him by losing his faith in everything except gaining revenge on his enemies—that is, until he surrenders to the power of the compassionate love of the newly resurrected Christ.

Douglas, Lloyd C. *The Big Fisherman*. Boston: Houghton Mifflin, 1948. The life of Simon, the simple fisherman who later becomes the Apostle Peter, is interwoven with that of an Arabian princess whose life has been touched by Jesus.

———. *The Robe*. Boston: Houghton Mifflin, 1942. A young Roman nobleman helps carry out the Crucifixion and then wins Jesus' robe in a dice game. These events lead to his conversion to Christianity and ultimately to his martyrdom.

Holmes, Marjorie. *Two from Galilee*. New York: Bantam, 1972. A recreation of the story of Mary and Joseph and how their love deepened with the announcement of the advent of the birth of Christ.

Kazantzakis, Nikos. *The Last Temptation of Christ*. New York: Simon and Schuster, 1960.

Lagerkvist, Par. *Barabbas*. New York: Random House, 1951. An enigmatic and unforgettable novel depicting the tormented spiritual quest of the condemned thief in whose place Christ died.

Lofts, Norah. *How Far to Bethlehem*. New York: Doubleday, 1965. The engrossing drama behind Mary's vision, the birth of Jesus, and the events culminating in the visit of the Three Wise Men.

Selden, Ruth, ed. *The Ways of God and Men: Great Stories from the Bible in World Literature*. See listing under *Fiction (Old Testament)*.

Sienkiewicz, Henryk. *Quo Vadis*. Boston: Little, Brown, 1896. Famous love story in which the licentiousness of pagan Rome under Nero is contrasted with the purity of the early Christians.

Slaughter, Frank. *God's Warrior*. New York: Doubleday, 1967. Popularized account of the life and times of Saul of Tarsus, who became a convert to Christianity and spread the Gospel throughout Rome as Paul the Apostle. Other historical novels by Slaughter include: *The Curse of Jezebel*; *David: Warrior and King*; *Song of Ruth*; *Road to Bythiana* (Luke); and *Thorn of Arimathea* (early Christian period), all available in paperback from Popular Library.

Speare, Elizabeth G. *The Bronze Bow*. Boston: Houghton Mifflin, 1961. A young man, obsessed with hatred for the Romans and a desire for vengeance, and his sister, driven nearly mad with fear, find their lives changed when they meet a rabbi named Jesus.

Wallace, Lew. *Ben Hur*. New York: Harper, 1880. The enduring story of a Jewish nobleman who was made a galley slave during the time of Christ.

Wibberley, Leonard. *The Centurion*. New York: Doubleday, 1967. The bitterly ironic story of the centurion in charge of the Crucifixion who was tolerant of Jews and an admirer of Jesus.

Plays

Anderson, Maxwell. *Journey to Jerusalem*, from *Three Plays by Maxwell Anderson*. New York: Washington Square Press, 1962.

Connelly, Marc. *Green Pastures*. New York: Holt, Rinehart and Winston, 1930. Based on some of the most popular tales in Roark Bradford's *Ol' Man Adam and His Chillun*, black folk retellings of the lives of various Old Testament heroes.

Goodman, Kenneth Sawyer. *Dust of the Road*, from *15 American One-Act Plays*, ed. Paul Kozelka. New York: Washington Square Press, 1961. An old tramp confronts a man whose friend had entrusted 30 hundred-dollar bills in his care, to be held after his death for his son. But this tramp knows what happens when a man betrays a friend for money.

Halverson, Marvin, ed. *Religious Drama 1: Five Plays*. New York: World Publishing Company, 1957. Included are W. H. Auden's *For the Time Being*, Christopher Fry's *The Firstborn*, D. H. Lawrence's *David*, and two other dramas not directly based on the Bible.

MacLeish, Archibald. *J.B. (A Play in Verse)*. New York: Samuel French, Inc., 1958.

Obey, André. *Noah*, translated by Arthur Wilmurt. New York: Samuel French, Inc., 1935.

Shaw, George Bernard. *Back to Methusaleh*, adapted and abridged by Arnold Moss. New York: Samuel French, Inc., 1957. Adapted from a series of five plays designed by Shaw to reaffirm his faith in humanity and in the future of mankind. It explores the significance of original sin, death, and the first murder, focusing finally on what happens when a man finds he can live three hundred years.

Tyler, Royall. *Joseph and His Brethren* and *The Judgment of Solomon*, from *America's Lost Plays*, ed. Barrett H. Clark, vol. 15. Bloomington: Indiana University Press, 1964–69.

Records

Arroyo, Martina. "Little David Play on Your Harp," from *There's a Meeting Here Tonight*. Angel S–36072. Includes other spirituals as well, accompanied by massed choral voices.

Bradford, Roark. *Ol' Man Adam*. Caedmon 1174. Humorous retellings of biblical stories in black folktale style. The basis of Marc Connelly's musical, *Green Pastures*. Highlights include the retellings of the stories of Noah and of David's sin with "Miz Uriah."

Britten, Benjamin. *Noye's Fludde*. Argo ZNF–1. A modern musical version of the medieval morality play about Noah and the Flood.

The Byrds. "Turn! Turn! Turn!" from *The Byrds' Greatest Hits*. Columbia CS–9516. Popular rendition of Pete Seeger's folk treatment of the passage from Ecclesiastes which begins "To everything there is a season."

Bikel, Theodore. *Song of Songs and Other Bible Prophecies*. Legacy 118. Sensitive readings of the Song of Songs, the Creation and Fall, selected Psalms, and passages from the prophets. An original musical score adds to the appeal of the album.

Cohen, Leonard. "Story of Isaac," from *Songs from a Room*. Columbia CS–9767.

Collins, Judy. "Story of Isaac," from *Who Knows Where the Time Goes*. Elektra 74033. A modified version of the original by Leonard Cohen.

Copland, Aaron. *In the Beginning*. Lyrichord 7124. Original composition for chorus. (Randall Thompson's *Peaceable Kingdom* is on the flip side.)

Cosby, Bill. "Noah, Me and You, Lord," from *Bill Cosby Is a Very Funny Fellow, Right*. Warner Brothers Records 1518. A delightful series of dialogs between Noah and the Lord.

Dylan, Bob. "A Hard Rain's Gonna Fall," from *Freewheelin'*. Columbia KCS–8786. Also on *Greatest Hits*, vol. 2. Columbia KG–31120. Dylan's apocalyptic vision of a nuclear deluge.

Everyman. Caedmon 1031. Burgess Meredith plays the lead in this most famous of medieval morality plays, in which Everyman comes to the realization that neither Fellowship, Kinsman and Goods nor Beauty, Strength, Discretion, Five Wits and Knowledge will enable him to account for his life before God as he makes his final journey.

Godspell: A Musical Based on The Gospel According to St. Matthew. Bell 1102. Popular rock musical by Stephen Schwartz representing Jesus' ministry and the faith of his followers.

Haydn, Franz Joseph. *The Creation*. 2–Decca DXS–7191. An English version of Haydn's popular oratorio depicting the stages of Creation. Other oratorios dealing with biblical themes include Georg Friedrich Händel's *Israel in Egypt, Saul, Samson, Solomon*, and *The Messiah*.

Jesus Christ Superstar. Decca 71503. This rock opera by Anthony Lloyd Webber and Tim Rice focuses on the last days of Jesus and lends sympathetic treatment to Judas. The Messiah here is portrayed as a man swept up by forces he doesn't fully understand. Highly effective, especially when the script is followed while listening.

Joseph and the Amazing Technicolor Dreamcoat. MCA–399. The lyrics of this rock cantata by *Superstar* creators Andrew Lloyd Webber and Tim Rice follow the biblical story of Joseph and his brothers quite closely. The music encompasses a number of styles and is very entertaining.

Menotti, Gian Carlo. *Amahl and the Night Visitors.* RCA LSC–2762. This modern opera tells the story of a crippled shepherd boy who is visited by the Three Wise Men on their trip to Bethlehem.

Johnson, James Weldon. *God's Trombones.* Folkways 9788. A collection of black folk sermons, including "God's Trombones."

Marshall and cast. *Job.* Caedmon 1076. A dramatic reading of the Book of Job (abridged).

Mitchell, Joni. "Woodstock," from *Ladies of the Canyon.* Reprise S–6376. The original version of a song that has been widely recorded, most notably by Crosby, Stills, Nash, and Young on *Déjà Vu* (Atlantic 7200).

Robeson, Paul. "Go Down, Moses," from *At Carnegie Hall*, vol. 2. Vanguard 79193.

Shaw, George Bernard, *Back to Methusaleh.* CMS 565/2

Welles, Orson. *Begatting of the President.* United Artists 5521. Satirical review of the presidency in the 1960s which makes allusion to various biblical events.

Films

NOTE: Titles in this section which are preceded by an asterisk are also available from The University of Michigan Audio-Visual Education Center (416 Fourth Street, Ann Arbor, Michigan 48103), at very reasonable rates.

Barabbas. Dayton, Ohio: Twyman Films, 1962 (color, 144 minutes). Early Christian times come vividly to life as the Crucifixion of Jesus and the devotion of the early disciples are retold from the point of view of Barabbas, as he searches for the reality of God and the meaning of his singular, apocalyptic life.

The Bible: A Literary Heritage. New York: Learning Corporation of America, 1971 (color, 27 minutes). One of the series *Western Civilization: Majesty and Madness*, this film explores the variety of literary forms found in the Bible—the short story (Abraham and Isaac), drama (Job), poetry (Song of Songs), and social criticism (Ecclesiastes)—and examines the Bible's impact on Western art and culture.

Coming of Christ. Skokie, Ill.: Films, Inc., 1965 (color, 30 minutes). Beautiful art work, mainly from the Renaissance and Baroque eras, is used to complement passages from the Bible dealing with the life of Christ.

The Cornish Ordinalia. Berkeley, Calif.: The University of California, 1971 (color, 33 minutes). Highlights from the Cornish cycle of medieval miracle plays show how in the Middle Ages everything in the Old Testament was thought to prefigure some event in the life of Christ: Adam as the first Christ; Abel and Isaac as Christ-like martyrs; Moses as a redeemer, etc. Christianity is shown here as being the focus of all creative art in the Middle Ages.

Crucifixion: Theme and Variations. Mount Vernon, N.Y.: Macmillan Audio Brandon Films, 1951 (color, 15 minutes). Variations by three Flemish painters on the theme of Christ's passion (Christ carrying the cross, Christ on the cross, and a pieta) are accompanied by commentary from the King James Bible and piano arrangements from Verdi and Bach.

Green Pastures. New York: United Artists, 1936 (93 minutes). Marc Connelly's Broadway musical based on several of Roark Bradford's tales in *Ol' Man Adam and His Chillun.* Features an all-black cast and a soundtrack resplendent with beautiful choral arrangements of a number of spirituals.

°Holy Land: Background for History and Religion. Chicago, Ill.: Coronet Films, 1954 (color, 10 minutes). An exploration of the sites and scenes associated with the great events, men, and ideas of the Holy Land. Familiar biblical passages related to the various scenes form the narrative background.

It's About This Carpenter. New York: New York University Film Library, 1963 (10 minutes). A young man carries a cross through the streets of New York, eliciting a variety of unusual responses.

°Jerusalem: Center of Many Worlds. Thousand Oaks, Calif.: Atlantis Productions, Inc., 1969 (color, 29 minutes). The religious, economic, and educational aspects of the city. Much of the commentary is taken from scriptural references from the three great religions that claim the city. Includes a history of the Holy City from its inception to the present.

°Jerusalem—The Holy City. Chicago, Ill.: Encyclopedia Britannica Educational Corp., 1951 (color, 10 minutes). Shows important biblical sites as well as contemporary ceremonies involving the Christians, Jews, and Muslims who inhabit or make pilgrimages to the Holy City.

°Let My People Go. Rochester, N.Y.: Xerox Corp., 1965 (54 minutes). A brief history of the Jews up to the twentieth century precedes the telling of the story of their attempts to return to the land of their ancestors during the past fifty years. Documents the faith and determination of a people who have nurtured a dream for over two thousand years and have finally begun to realize their goal despite incredible hardships.

°The Life of Christ in Art. Chicago, Ill.: Coronet Films, 1956 (color, 23 minutes). Paintings representing the art of seven centuries accompany biblical narration dealing with the life of Christ.

°Parable. New York: The Protestant Council of Churches, 1964 (color, 22 minutes). In this allegorical story in which the world is represented as a circus, a white-faced clown takes upon himself the burdens and sufferings of others, impressing them with his deeds of kindness. The provocative conclusion makes this a film that should be viewed more than once for full effect.

°Powers of Ten. Venice, Calif.: Charles and Kay Eames, 1969 (color, 10 minutes). A filmic trip beyond the galaxies and then back into the atom,

providing a scientific counterpart to the Voice out of the Whirlwind in Job and Mark Van Doren's "The God of Galaxies."

Three Paintings by Hieronymus Bosch. Mount Vernon, N.Y.: Macmillan Audio Brandon Films, 1951 (color, 10 minutes). A film study of three works by the Flemish artist dealing with the life of Christ: "The Adoration of the Kings," "The Mocking of Christ," and "Ecce Homo."